D1363047

INTERNATIONAL BUSINESS:
A Competitiveness Approach

Frank L. Bartels
Christopher L. Pass

Prentice
Hall

Singapore London New York Toronto Sydney Tokyo Madrid
Mexico City Munich Paris Capetown Hong Kong Montreal

Published in 2000 by
Prentice Hall
Pearson Education Asia Pte Ltd
317 Alexandra Road
#04-01 IKEA Building
Singapore 159965

Pearson Education offices in Asia: *Bangkok, Beijing, Hong Kong, Jakarta, Kuala Lumpur, Manila, New Delhi, Seoul, Singapore, Taipei, Tokyo*

Printed in Singapore

5   4   3   2   1
04   03   02   01   00

ISBN 0-13-032146-X

Copyright © 2000 by Pearson Education Asia Pte Ltd. All rights reserved. This publication is protected by Copyright and permission should be obtained from the publisher prior to any prohibited reproduction, storage in a retrieval system, or transmission in any form or by any means, electronic, mechanical, photocopying, recording, or likewise. For information regarding permission(s), write to: Rights and Permissions Department.

CONTENTS

ABOUT THE AUTHORS

Dr Frank L. Bartels is Assistant Professor at Nanyang Business School, Nanyang Technological University, Singapore. Until 1993, he was manager for industrial and technical operations of major multinational energy companies, including Dow and Schlumberger, during which time he created four UK and European commercial engineering patents for industrial applications in energy services business. He has carried out institutional research at University of Bradford Management Centre, UK; Groupe HEC School of Management, Paris, France; and University of Deusto Comercial, Bilbao, Spain. His current research is on Foreign Direct Investment Dynamics in ASEAN. He has been consultant to UNESCO in management of capacity building for developing countries. His publications include "Strategic Management Interaction between French Multinational Enterprises and Subsidiaries in Sub-Saharan Africa" in *The Strategy and Organization of International Business*, and "Towards a Strategy for Enhancing ASEAN's Locational Advantages for Attracting Greater Foreign Direct Investment" in *Dynamics in Pacific Asia: Conflict, Competition and Cooperation*. He has published on international business, technology transfer issues, multinational enterprises and regionalisation issues in *Management International Review*, *Competitiveness Review*, *British Journal of Management* and *The Cornell Quarterly*.

Dr Christopher L. Pass is Reader in Comparative Industrial Economics at the University of Bradford Management Centre, having previously worked as an economist for Metal Box and Barclays Bank. His current major research area is international business; recent publications include *Servicing International Markets* (with P.J. Buckley and K. Prescott) and *Canada-UK Bilateral Trade and Investment Relations* (with P.J. Buckley and K. Prescott). Dr Pass has also produced a number of business textbooks, including *Business and Microeconomics* (with B. Lowes) and *Companies and Markets* (with B. Lowes and S. Sanderson), and he is a co-author of the Harper Collins *Dictionary of Business* and *Dictionary of Economics*.

PREFACE

We are delighted to present the first edition of *International Business: A Competitiveness Approach.*

Purpose and Scope of the Content

The text, and numerous illustrations, are written and crafted with the final year undergraduate and the Masters student in mind. The central place of different aspects of international business in business administration and management courses is widely acknowledged. Increasingly, world business and commerce is hallmarked by the significance of fierce competitiveness between international firms as they configure and reconfigure their operational architectures to extract maximum advantage from organisational capabilities and production capacities. Without a thorough grounding in the different dimensions of this competitiveness and the factors that drive multinational corporations (MNCs), the graduating student is likely to be handicapped in discussing managerial and competitive implications of international business.

International Business: A Competitiveness Approach attempts to capture the essence of late twentieth century international business dynamics evident in the interactions of multinational corporations as they manoeuvre within industrial sectors and between factor markets. The key unit of analysis is the multinational corporation – a uniquely late twentieth century organisation but by no means a new phenomenon (the history of global trade from the fifteenth century onwards is mainly the history of large firms organised to capture value and project commercial power). The rise of the multinational corporation is a story of competition and its management, in all its myriad guises, for profit and market gain. In this dynamic, the nature of international competition among firms has changed over the past 50 years or so from *laissez-faire* capitalist zero-sum competition to the positive-sum co-operation of alliance capitalism. Collaboration among businesses rather than the rugged individualism of standalone firms is used increasingly by firms to gain advantage. Within this inter-play competition and co-operation co-exist.

The contents of the book, descriptive of the dynamics of competition, are given contemporary contextual illustrations to reflect the actual behaviour of multinational corporations and other international firms. Each chapter provides an outline and the objectives of study as well as a summary and questions for discussion. Illustrating the chapter content are micro cases.

This book should be used as an integrated text for describing and illustrating the processes of competitiveness. The first four chapters permit the reader to appreciate and understand the competitive dynamics of international business in terms of the options available from which international firms select means to service their markets, create and maintain competitiveness. The multinational corporation, underlying strategic frameworks and formulation of competitive strategies are presented and inter-linked. The remaining chapters assist the reader in assimilating respective expressions of competitiveness in managing the process of being an international firm. They do so by bringing to the fore and inter-linking multinational corporations and their market development and managerial structures as well as their impact on national economies and the competitive implications of the Asian economic distress.

Finally, it is our anticipation that students, and teachers, of international business will gain from the approach taken in this book; and it is our expectation that students, as managers, will be better able to take competitive advantage of the changing circumstances in international business.

ACKNOWLEDGEMENTS

Many people have contributed in many ways, at various times, to the creation and production of this book. We extend our deep appreciation and gratitude to all. We would like to thank in particular those involved in the labour of the work: Christine Barkby at the University of Bradford Management Centre for typing the working manuscript and Ina Hon in Singapore for working on the word processing of the several versions of the manuscript; Ang Lee Ming, Editorial Manager and Chiang Yew Kee, Publishing Manager of Pearson Education Asia, whose tireless pursuit of excellence finally made this book practicable.

The single-minded quest of this goal would not have been possible without their dedication and willingness to engage with our project.

DEDICATION

This book is dedicated to our respective ancestors and families, without whom it would not have been possible.

FLB & CLP

July 2000

CHAPTER
1
International Business:
An Introduction

CHAPTER OUTLINE

- An introduction to international business
- The historical antecedents to competitiveness in international business
- International business operations
- The trade foundations of international business

CHAPTER OBJECTIVES

After studying this chapter you should be able to:

- Demonstrate an appreciation of the historical significance of international business.
- Identify aspects of competitiveness in international business.
- Describe the significance of international business.
- Discuss the importance of international business and its trade.

TWO FUNDAMENTAL FACTS have vastly altered the way in which international business is perceived and studied. The first is the proliferation of sovereign states in the post-World War II era. International business is increasingly conducted across the juridical, socio-cultural and physical borders of these sovereign states. There were 62 separate states in 1914, 74 in 1946, 149 in 1978 and 193 in 1999.[1] The critical concomitant of this proliferation is aptly expressed by Gary S. Becker, 1992 Economics Nobel Laureate, "as nations splinter, global markets are merging" (Becker, 1991: 8). Hence international business and its actors, international firms and multinational corporations (MNCs), have to manage the dynamics of global commerce, investment and trade within twin countervailing forces of increasing disintegration at the political level and increasing integration at the economic level. The second fact is the enormous growth, in absolute terms, of global wealth and trade. Up to and including the proto-capitalist era, that is AD 1500–1820, world gross domestic product (GDP) per capita is estimated to have increased by a minuscule 0.07% per annum. However, after 1820 – widely acknowledged as the onset of the capitalist epoch – world GDP per capita is calculated to have grown at a rate of 1.17% per annum. The result is that while world GDP per capita now stands at a modest US$5,188, GDP per capita for Western Europe, North America and Japan is US$19,990. In comparison it is a lowly US$2,971 for Other Europe, Latin America, China, Other Asia and Africa.[2] The major implication of these combined facts is that, in the majority, the economic functions of international business and its actors are confined necessarily to the geo-economic boundaries of Western Europe, North America and Japan and their immediate neighbours.

An introductory chapter permits the reader to look back as well as forward in the subject matter of international business and its inherent competitiveness. Neither international business nor MNCs and the economic competition they are engaged in are new phenomena (Moore and Lewis, 1999). Since pre-modern times, generally accepted as before AD 1500, commercial agents (individuals or groups) have been a central feature of the rational organisation of the economy of states and empires of the 'great civilisations'. However, it is not the purpose of this introductory chapter to chart lessons in economic history but rather to provide the reader with a certain perspective, not necessarily continuous, that informs the study of international business. The rise of the modern MNCs may be traced back

---

[1] "A Survey of the New Geopolitics", *The Economist*, 31 July 1999.

[2] All figures are in 1990 US dollars; see Angus Maddison, "Poor Until 1820", *The Asian Wall Street Journal*, 18 January 1999, p. 8.

to *circa* the fourteenth century. By the sixteenth and seventeenth centuries, the processes of colonisation and concomitant merchant capitalism had led to the emergence of intensely articulated organisations for international sourcing, production and marketing of a broad variety of goods and services. Incidentally, and interestingly, some of these early forms, that included trafficking in people and narcotics as components of goods and services, in part resonate with aspects of the international black economies in parts of collapsed and fragmented states of the late twentieth century.[3]

1.1 Pre-modern International Enterprise

Pre-modern forms of international business, including Assyrian international trade (Orlin, 1970; Veenhof, 1972; Larsen, 1976), characterising the first forms of organised international business are well documented. In the Middle Bronze Age period, Assyrian businesses from Ashur intermediated textiles and tin exports from Afghanistan to Kanesh. It is at Kanesh that evidence of large-scale multinational enterprise and its incorporation come to light (Adams and Nissen, 1972). The dynamics of competitiveness known to the student of modern international business – ownership, location and internalisation advantages – for example were evident in Ashur. These were in terms of monopolistic advantages in the importation of metals and smaller tariffs compared with other locations external to the its kingdom.[4] Veenhof (1972) and Larsen (1976) suggest that the organisation of international business at the time was highly sophisticated both in the arrangements for cross-border financial intermediation (typical of modern MNCs) and production technologies.

An example from another part of the world is provided by the 'merchant priesthood' of the Shona people based in the Zambezi River area (now Zimbabwe). This merchant class controlled, between AD 1100 and 1300, the regional and international trade in precious minerals and ivory, with exports to the entrepots of the Middle East and as far away as Persia and China (Cockroft, 1990).

For many, the MNC is par excellence an agent of globalisation. However, arguably the first practitioners of globalisation were the early thirteenth century

---

[3] David A. Andelman, 1994, "The Drug Money Maze", *Foreign Affairs*, Vol. 73, No. 4, July/August, pp. 94–108.

[4] Karl Moore and David Lewis, 1998, "The First Multinationals: Assyria *circa* 2000 BC", *Management International Review*, Vol. 38, Second Quarter, pp. 95–107 for the antecedents of the multinational enterprise.

Mongolian adventurers. With their Khanate system of organisation, their leadership exercised political and economic control over approximately 13 million square kilometres of territory from China in the east to European Russia in the west. Within this system, with paper currency and networks of postal stations, business intermediation and trade flourished between the East and West. The Silk Route, stretching across East Asia to the Mediterranean and famous for its fabulous cities as well as the opportunities, and uncertainties, of commerce throughout the period represents a good example of pre-modern forms of international business. As such, exchange and intermediation was in terms of sourcing on the one hand, and on the other hand advanced production techniques in paper manufacturing, chemistry, textiles and the technology of warfare.

As we move towards the dawn of the modern era, developments that reflect the origins of MNCs, competitiveness and foreign direct investment (FDI) begin to straddle the world in a manner that is critically and spatially different from earlier forms. In the fourteenth century, trading hierarchies of merchant capitalism began to shape economic modernity through forms of intermediation heavily dependent on sophisticated capital markets. The first and most significant at that time became known as the Hanseatic League – an international trading company owned by an association of Hanseatic merchants from Lubeck, Germany. The League, as a consortium, organised commerce between, and within, European and Levantine cities with a refinement that belies the age. The consortium demonstrated some, if not all, the ownership advantages of the modern MNC – the capacity to co-ordinate and the capability to manage spatially distributed sources of international capital and production. Another good example of consortia formed for international investment and trade was the Merchant Adventurers from Britain. This group, as a consortium of wool and textile barons, set up wholesale and retail outlets in the European region then known as the Low Countries for their production. The importance of the banking and financial services part of these organisations cannot be overemphasised. By 1531, the first stock exchange was set up in Antwerp, a major transshipment and trading centre, for brokers to trade commodities, shares and securities. By the late 1600s, stock exchanges and capital markets were available to international business in Hamburg, Amsterdam, London and Paris.

Another dimension of early forms of international business and commerce, especially that which links Asia with Europe on the one hand and international business with political behaviour on the other hand, is encapsulated by the history of the trade in spices – critical for the preservation of foodstuffs during harsh

European winters. Between AD 1000 and 1400, with the hegemony of Italian international financial acumen and banking systems, supporting multinational operations and funding international investments (Heaton, 1936), the merchants of Venice controlled Asian trade in spices and commanded monopoly prices. Competitiveness drove Spain and Portugal to finance international investments with the business objectives of capturing the supply and finding alternative supplies. Hence, over time, firstly the voyages of discovery by Vasco da Gama, Christopher Columbus, Ferdinand Magellan and Sebastian del Cano were mounted during the 1500s. Incidentally, the first marine insurance policies for international business were offered in Florence in 1523. Secondly, this competitiveness later drew in the British as well as the Dutch and led directly to the formation of the forerunners of the trading MNC. On 31 December in 1600 the British chartered a trading company known as the English East India Company which was to last until 1873 after permutation as The United Company. In opposition and competition, Holland formed, in 1602, the Vereenigde Oost-Indische Compagnie – VOC (United East India Company) – commonly known as the Dutch East India Company which was to survive until 1799. Companies such as these, and their durable descendants, were to play very significant roles not only in colonisation of large regions in the New World but also in maintaining unrivalled European hegemony from the 1600s until 1945 (Dunning, 1993).

The Industrial Revolution and industrial organisation gave rise, through the need to appropriate the returns from investments in invention and technological innovation, to the modern MNC. Previous forms of intermediation, characterised by merchant capitalism, gave way finally to industrial capitalism and its counterpart finance capitalists (Cantwell, 1989). The international business dimensions of the Industrial Revolution are well documented. The critical point is that, despite the sometimes symbiotic, sometimes antagonistic, relationship between the nation-state and agents of commerce, competition and competitiveness have driven the evolution of the MNC species. By 1850, European firms had set up subsidiaries in the Americas, and foreign firms were establishing subsidiaries in British manufacturing (Bostock and Jones, 1994). They were doing so in patterns of spatially distributed and managed sourcing of input factors, manufacturing and production, as well as marketing that are the recognised hallmarks of the modern late twentieth century MNC.[5]

---

[5] "The Making of Global Enterprise", Special Issue of *Business History*, Vol. 36, No. 1, January 1994.

1.2 MODERN INTERNATIONAL ENTERPRISE

The MNC came into its own as an efficient organisation from 1870 onwards. When coupled with paradigm breaking advances in science and technology from applications of new chemicals and materials, electro-magnetism, steam and the internal combustion engines as well as new managerial philosophies, this form of industrial organisation had few challengers. From this age onwards, international business became increasingly characterised by dynamic competition, intense investment and high rates of global trading both within and without the boundaries of the international firm. Until World War I in 1914–18, and for a short time after, MNCs operated across the commercial landscape in ways reflected to a notable extent by their present day competitive strategies. These comprised essentially powerful combinations of the advantages of hierarchies and the efficiencies of markets for delivering goods to customers and services to clients. These are described in the remaining chapters of this book. From the 1950s onwards these strategic combinations were to reach their most powerful such that the end of the nation-state was contemplated seriously.

The first kind of competition, investment and trade was operationalised by capturing and controlling the input factors for production. These input factors may have been either primary resources of materials, minerals and agricultural commodities or intermediate products like latex or semi-processed cocoa beans. This type of operation is referred to as *resource-seeking investments*. European cosmopolitan powers sourced their raw materials from their colonies through their international firms. American firms preferred Canada and Mexico while Japanese firms preferred Asian sources. The developments in international business cannot be divorced from competition between European nations epitomised by the phrase 'the scramble for Africa'. However, an important corollary was the emergence of mass standard product markets in Europe and America that required economies of scale for investments to provide handsome returns. Hence the pressure for owning and integrating all the stages of production from the raw materials to manufacture and marketing the final products. This ownership not only shut out competition from the process but more importantly secured supplies and eliminated the vagaries of the marketplace at a time when contract law was in its infancy. Some famous company brand names, representative of this type of MNCs from this epoch, still survive to this day: Dunlop and Firestone (latex and rubber); Cadbury and Unilever (agricultural commodities); DuPont (minerals and chemicals); Royal Dutch Shell (oil). The list goes on.

The second type of operation, typified by strategies to create foreign demand through a proliferation of new products and services based on competitive advantages of owning proprietary rights (Wilkins, 1970), is termed *market-seeking investments*. American and British firms demonstrated these traits to an extreme in oligopolistic market structures. The primary reason for this investment behaviour by MNCs was the existence of sovereign states which had the will and power to impose economic barriers such as import quotas, tariffs, etc. Thus in protecting their domestic markets and industries foreign governments forced outsiders to establish operational facilities in their countries. Along with these economic reasons, the high costs of the developing global transportation industry in the late nineteenth century forced early MNCs to locate manufactures in the country of consumption.

In the late nineteenth century a third type of operation that fitted neither in resource-seeking nor market-seeking investments was typified in two ways as follows:

1. By investments in the production of communications and public utility infrastructure – road, rail, telegraphy, and gas and electric power. The vast undertakings firstly across the American and European continents and secondly across the colonised continents are testament to their financial and syndicated organisational powers.

2. By investments in financial and transportation services (especially shipping). The international banks of the mid-1800s allowed international business to flourish in far-away places. Barclays Bank (UK) in Africa and Banque de l'Indochine (France) in Asia are two examples from the era; the former is still extant under its original name. European firms were not the only early examples of early MNCs in services. Japanese financial firms were also active overseas investors. The ancestor of the Bank of Tokyo (Yokohama Specie bank) is known to have opened branches in New York in 1880 and another in Bombay in 1894.[6]

The foregoing provides a rich field for exploration. Looking forward, during the decades from the 1960s to the 1990s a set of four highly significant changes, which lies at the heart of the competitiveness of international business, occurred in the organisational structure and spatial management of the MNC. These changes, in themselves responses to the changing environment, have been given the general term 'globalisation' lately and have given MNCs a significantly new

---

[6] M. Wilkins, 1986, "Japanese Multinational Enterprise Before 1914", *Business History Review*, Vol. 60, pp. 199–231 and "Japanese Multinationals in the United States: Continuity and Change 1879–1990", *Business History Review*, Vol. 64, pp. 585–629.

edge in competitiveness. Although the intensity of these changes may be arguable, the facts and direction of changes are beyond dispute.

The first set of changes involves the dynamics of what may be aptly termed 'global reach' – the encirclement of the world by the tentacular relations of MNCs. As indicated by Barnet and Muller (1974: 13, 15–16) today's "global corporations are the first in history with the organisation, technology, money and ideology to make a credible try at managing the world as an integrated economic unit.... What they are demanding in essence is the right to transcend the nation-state, and in the process, transform it". This demand is not a hollow one and makes MNCs the heart of the world economy. The global reach of MNCs means that thousands of components and sub-assemblies, of widely different shapes and sizes and volumes, from all over the world can be brought together in a co-ordinated and timely manner to create a single product. The multifaceted competitiveness that accrues to MNCs from this capability for integrated international sourcing, production and marketing (IISPM) is simply enormous. One result of this reach is the continued widespread international relocation of production and competitive 'clustering' of investments, which occurred only partly in response to regionalism and the trend towards trade blocs.

The second set of changes concerns finance capital, or money, and the dynamics of intermediation by global capital markets in international business, involving huge capital flows that are enabled by convergent and integrated computer, communications and information technologies. The fact of the matter regarding money is that "billions can flow in or out of an economy in seconds".[7] While different types of money have different 'top speeds' in capital flows, the direction and pace of private flows of direct equity investment confer competitiveness not only to the MNC in question but also the location of that investment. The steep rise in capital inflows to Asia in the latter part of the 1980s and throughout the 1990s until 1997/98,[8] in process and production implementation, increased the competitiveness of MNCs by turning regional locational specificities into company advantages. This in turn increased the global competitiveness of Asian host economies (especially the so-called Asian Tiger economies). The subsequent capital outflows in 1997 to 1999,[9] a consequence of the Asian economic crisis (see

---

[7] "Hot Money", *Business Week*, 20 March 1995, p. 46.

[8] UNCTAD, *World Investment Report 1998: Trends and Determinants*, UN, New York, Figure 1.3, p. 9.

[9] Institute of International Finance, *Capital Flows to Emerging Markets*, 30 April 1998, pp. 4–5 and 25 April 1999, pp. 2–3.

Chapter 8), had almost the opposite effect but with asymmetric vectors. Whereas the competitiveness of only some MNCs (those with market-seeking investment) was negatively affected, the competitiveness of Asian hosts as a whole was, at least temporarily, very seriously dented. The alliance capitalism, and intermediation abilities, of MNCs[10] provide a certain immunity for MNCs.

The third set of changes is described by the unflattering term 'corporate cannibalism' and is inherent in the frenzy of mergers and acquisitions activity that has characterised the late 1980s and 1990s. In 1998 mergers, acquisitions and other forms of corporate takeovers amounted to US$288 billion in the US (Dugger, 1989: x). This propensity for high stakes predatory competition in which big MNCs gobble up little MNCs (occasionally a little MNC eats up a bigger one) has increased from very little activity in 1980 to over 20,000 deals in 1997 valued at US$1,600 billion (UNCTAD, 1998: 20). Transnational mergers and acquisitions amounted to US$342 billion in 1997 and constituted 60% of FDI, an increase from about 30% at the start of the 1990s. The critical issue is that the 6,000 or so transnational mergers and acquisitions in 1997 show little sign of abating. In the first half of 1999, cross-border mergers and acquisitions for the UK and US totalled more than US$320 billion with continuing established trends in banking and finance, chemicals and pharmaceuticals, telecommunications and media industrial sectors. Other sectors such as aerospace and automotive, defence contractors and metallurgical, and retail are witnessing increasing levels of international mergers and acquisitions activity.[11] This drive by MNCs for access to economies of scale is largely in reaction to the pressures for efficiency that have come partly from the demanding and empowered shareholders of the 1990s. The other reason for this is the desire for market share. The result of this particular world-wide mergers and acquisitions activity is an increasingly spatially distributed array of IISPM networks internalised within and between MNCs particularly, but not exclusively, in automobile, aerospace, electronic component and silicon chip manufacturing.[12]

---

[10] Frank L. Bartels and Hafiz Mirza, "Multinational Corporations' Foreign Direct Investment in Asia's Emerging Markets: Before and After the Crisis – Any Changes?", *Management International Review*, Special Issue on Emerging Markets, 1999, Vol. 39, No. 4, pp. 13–26.

[11] See *The Economist*, "A Survey of the Global Defence Industry", 14 June 1997, p. 6 for the genealogy and merger activity of defence MNCs.

[12] See Peter Dicken, 1992, *Global Shift: The Internationalization of Economic Activity*, Second Edition, Paul Chapman, London, p. 292; and UNCTAD, *World Investment Report 1998: Trends and Determinants*, UN, New York, p. 22 for a view on the collaborative and merger and acquisition relationships among the automotive oligopoly.

Consequently, as a percentage of world trade in terms of exports of goods and non-factor services, intra-firm exports by MNCs (parent firms and subsidiaries) amount to about 34% of world trade. Inter-firm exports by MNCs (between different parent firms and different subsidiaries) total about 33% of world trade.[13] The concomitant of these figures is that an ever increasing portion of the world's productive assets are under the direct managerial control of MNCs and there is an overall trend towards oligopolistic structures in the major industries of the world.

The fourth set of changes revolves round the quest for efficiency related to the abilities, and motivations, of MNCs to relocate production globally. According to Rifkin (1995: xiv): "We are entering a new phase in human history – one in which fewer and fewer workers will be needed to produce the goods and services for the global population." The substitution of labour by capital within MNCs' industrial organisation has been accelerating since the 1990s following corporate restructuring in the 1980s. In response to increasing labour factor costs, MNCs have firstly increased capital investments, both domestically and internationally, moved production to lower labour cost locations and reduced 'their inventories of people' – they have 'downsized'. Secondly, they have applied the production efficient concept of 'just-in-time' to workers at all levels. The result is increased symbiotic competitiveness along two interrelated dimensions: increased competitiveness in the international business of MNCs and increased competition by host locations for the labour intensive stages of production within the IISPM networks of MNCs.

The responses of MNCs to these aggregate changes not only model their flexibility[14] but also permeate the contestability in, and set the scene for, *International Business: A Competitiveness Approach*. In broad terms the book deals with the subject matter as follows: an overview of international business with a focus on the main actor – the MNC; the strategic options in global production and marketing; competitiveness and internationalisation; foreign market entry and the developments for serving markets; the managerial dimensions of co-ordinating, commanding and controlling the multinational organisation for competitiveness; the impact of the MNC on national economies; and implications for international business competitiveness consequential to the Asian economic crisis.

---

[13] UNCTAD, *World Investment Report 1995: Transnational Corporations and Competitiveness*, "Overview", UN, New York, p. 23.

[14] Peter J. Buckley and Mark C. Casson, "Models of the Multinational Enterprise", *Journal of International Business Studies*, Vol. 29, No. 1, First Quarter, 1998, pp. 22–44.

1.3 THE CHAPTERS OUTLINED

This chapter brings a modern as well as a historical perspective to bear on the sweep of international business by way of introducing the reader to key concepts in the field. Statistical dimensions of international business are supplied to provide the reader with an appreciable measure of the boundaries of the subject. The chapter addresses some of the characteristics of pre-modern international business and links them not only with the first era of globalisation – the expansion of the metropolitan powers of the East and West, but also with the Industrial Revolution and the second era of globalisation in the 1800s. The chapter concludes by addressing four sets of changes that characterise international business today – the global reach of multinational enterprise; international finance capital; the corporate cannibalism of mergers and acquisitions; and the quest for efficiency.

Chapter 2 on International Business: An Overview introduces the reader to the underlying features, characteristics and themes of international business. It brings into relief firstly, the competitive and strategic dimensions of international business; secondly, it exposes the range of international business operations performed by MNCs; and thirdly, it unveils the overall trends in, and directions of, international investment and trade. Dynamic examples from real operations of MNCs are used to bring into focus applications of international business by firms.

Chapter 3 on Global Production and Marketing: The Strategic Options develops the theme of international location of sourcing and manufacturing operations from the strategic perspective. It does so in terms of the variety of unique and combined portfolio of competitive routines available to MNCs for engaging in foreign markets. Three generic strategic approaches – independent, co-operative and location bound – are examined in turn to expose the characteristic features that impart competitiveness to MNCs. Examples from North American and European MNCs are employed to bring out these elements.

Chapter 4 on Competitiveness and Internationalisation expands the theme of competition in terms of the dimensions of competitive advantage and the dynamics and structure of industry. It provides a perspective on how industry competitiveness translates into advantages for regions and countries. Once the fundamentals of industry structure and dynamics are appreciated, the chapter addresses the key issue of formulating strategy for attaining international competitiveness. Various examples for each of the formulated strategies are provided with cases illustrating the business application of competitive strategy. The chapter concludes by addressing the operationalisation of competitiveness by international firms, and indicates the range of advantages and disadvantages that emerge from the competitive choices of foreign market servicing.

Chapter 5 on Foreign Market Entry and Development addresses the considerations for servicing foreign markets in general and the organisational and strategic modalities in particular. Issues of timing of entry, and servicing mode switching, are illustrated with business examples showing the strategic advantages that modal forms confer. The point that international conditions, and the degree of ease or difficulty of entry, vary enormously over different markets is brought into relief by considering three different industries – plasterboard, scientific instruments and pharmaceuticals. Cases describing market entry in telecommunications, insurance, tobacco and retail are used to reinforce the competitive dimensions.

Chapter 6 on Aspects of Managing MNCs examines the variety of organisational structures, and relations therein, available to MNCs for articulating their international competitiveness and configuring their global reach. As previously indicated, the pace of mergers and acquisitions continues unabated. This brings to the fore the issue of how the management of MNCs orchestrates coherently the dispersed and different corporate assets that are the result of mergers and acquisitions. The challenge of communications, co-ordination, command and control of operations is addressed and illustrated through different organisational structures. The critical dimension of treasury management in MNCs – exchange rate exposure and international transfer pricing – that optimises their exposure to overall taxation and other fiscal disadvantages is dealt with in detail. The issues therein are illustrated by examples of MNCs that are adept at minimising tax exposure. The quality of intra-organisational decision-making in managing diversity of subsidiaries is addressed.

Chapter 7 on Multinational Corporations and Their Impact on National Economies initiates the conclusion of the book by indicating some of the economic outcomes of MNC competition and international business competitiveness. The dimensions of outward and inward FDI are traced in order to place in context the balance of payments and trade effects on the one hand and resource transfers, output and employment effects on the other hand. The importance of technology transfer is given close attention to emphasise the possible advantages and disadvantages that accrue from the presence of MNCs in host economies. The policy framework that cradles FDI is analysed to expose issues of economic sovereignty and development. These issues of advantage and disadvantage bring us to the threshold of Asia's remarkable economic development trajectory, and its temporary demise in the shape of the Asian economic crisis of 1997–99.

Chapter 8 on Asia's Economic Crisis, International Business and Competitiveness concludes a competitiveness approach to international business by encapsulating the unprecedented events of the Asian currency, banking, economic, social and political crisis of 1997–99. In the context of globalisation and international business, it addresses approaches to the management of economic development while tracing trajectories and raising issues for competitiveness. The impact of the crisis on Asian growth and international business and the strategic actions and counter-actions by competing MNCs to gain further advantages in Asia are explored within the various dimensions of the crisis. Differences in impact on different Asian economies are elicited and issues about the implications for international business are indicated. The chapter promotes the relevance of a long-term perspective and cautions the challenges to MNC FDI in Asia in general and Southeast Asia in particular. Cases delineating the implications for individual businesses and MNCs illustrate the dynamics involved in the crisis from the perspective of competition. Two possibilities, the uncertainties of a transformed 'economic space' and the unwillingness by Asia to accept the obligations of globalisation, are examined.

CHAPTER
2

International Business:
An Overview

CHAPTER OUTLINE

- What is international business?
- What are the competitive and strategic dimensions of international business?
- International business operations
- Foreign market servicing – dimensions of integrated international sourcing, production and marketing
- Options for foreign market entry and motives for foreign direct investment (FDI)
- Multinational corporations (MNCs) in international business
- The trade and FDI dimensions of international business

CHAPTER OBJECTIVES

After studying this chapter you should be able to:

- Demonstrate an understanding of the importance of international business.
- Identify the key dimensions of competitiveness in international business.
- Explain the competitive significance of international business.
- Discuss the strategic importance of international business.
- Describe the foreign market servicing options and relationships in international business.
- Discuss the selection of foreign market servicing strategies in international business.
- Characterise the trade and investment dimensions of international business.

14

INTERNATIONAL BUSINESS IS concerned with firms' overseas operations with respect to managerial activities involved in the sourcing of materials and intermediate products, the manufacture and supply of goods or services and the distribution and marketing of these products to international consumers and customers. The internationalisation of its operations provides a firm with an opportunity to expand its sales and profits and to establish and maintain competitive advantage. This is important when the domestic market is small, or where domestic sales have reached maturity, or are declining. Horizontal global expansion can be an alternative to domestic conglomerate expansion in sustaining firm growth, although some firms may wish to pursue, either sequentially or simultaneously, horizontal, vertical and conglomerate expansion in a global context because of the distribution of lower costs and progressive marketing advantages bestowed by international operations. The motives for going international, the particular forms and scope of a firm's overseas activities and the integrated management of overseas operations constitute the core subject matter of international business.

2.1 (INTERNATIONAL) BUSINESS STRATEGY

For many companies, even small companies, globalisation of their operations plays an important part in the formulation of their overall business strategy. It will be useful, therefore, at this point to introduce briefly two key elements of business strategy that impact on internationalisation imperatives.

Business strategy is concerned with the formulation of long-term plans by a company to achieve its corporate mission or business objectives. These plans have many functional dimensions: economic, organisational, behavioural, production, marketing and financial. Thus business strategy is inevitably holistic in approach and seeks to integrate functional activities in order to develop appropriate policies for dealing with the changing environment while preserving, and adding to, the company's advantages.

Within this framework there are two critical areas of corporate decision-making – the *strategic direction* of the company and the formulation of *competitive strategy* – that are fundamental to the achievement of corporate success. The strategic direction in essence consists of a bundle of 'internalised' resources under the direction of senior management that can, at its discretion, be deployed between a number of product markets or industries and geographic markets and, over time, be expanded and repositioned in accordance with actual and perceived opportunities for revenue enhancement and profit gain. The first key strategic decision for a company is therefore to decide on what products to supply (thus determining the industries in which it operates) and the geographical spread of its operations (for example, local or regional within a particular country, nationwide within that country, international or global). The second key issue is the formulation of competitive strategy, since no matter how few or many product and geographic markets the company chooses to be in, its corporate prosperity will depend fundamentally on how well it succeeds in the *individual* product and geographic markets making up its business.

Strategic direction

The product-market matrix shown in Figure 2.1 provides a framework for highlighting and analysing the various growth opportunities open to a company. The matrix depicts products on one axis and markets on the other. By way of example let us consider a company currently specialising in the production of rayon (a cellulosic fibre) in the UK which is currently sold to UK textile fabricators to be made into clothing. The matrix indicates that the company has four main strategic options (a fifth option, that of vertical integration is closely linked with strategy.

Figure 2.1   Product–market framework

		Market	
		Present	**New**
Product	*Present*	1 – Market penetration	2 – Market development
	New	3 – Product development	4 – Diversification

1. It can seek to achieve a greater penetration of its *existing* market, increasing its share of the UK textile fabrication market by various competitive means (low costs and prices, product differentiation). It can also undertake backward integration (into supply industries) and forward integration into textile fabrication to lower costs and secure supplies and outlets. However, if the firm is already a dominant supplier, or if the market itself is mature, further growth opportunities are strictly limited.

2. The company can aim to develop *new markets* for its existing products, capitalising on the company's production expertise. In our example, the company can adapt rayon for use as a geo-textile (for civil engineering applications) or packaging

material (cellophane film for products such as crisps and cigarettes), or *the company can globalise its operations by selling rayon in international markets.*

3. The company can seek to develop *new products* for its existing markets, exploiting the company's marketing strengths. The company can, for example, add other synthetic fibres to its product range or blend together rayon with natural wool to create 'hybrid' fabrics of various strengths and textures for use by clothiers. This strategy, however, in the case of maturing markets, suffers from the same general limitations as strategy (1).

4. The company can aim to diversify away from its existing activity by developing *new products* for *new markets.* The rayon company might decide that the clothing industry had too little long-term growth potential, or that the market had become too cut-throat to make decent profit returns. In this case, disinvestment of its rayon business or a gradual move away from rayon production into, say, the electronics industry may be considered. This is generally the highest risk strategy since it takes the company furthest away from its core expertise in production and expertise in marketing. All of these moves can be international in scope. As indicated under strategy (2), one obvious way for the firm to expand is by putting its existing products on foreign markets. This can be done by exporting from its UK production base, and employing the services of agents and distributors to handle its products in export markets. More particularly, the firm may decide to relocate production itself by establishing manufacturing plants in selected overseas markets. The company may decide to become vertically integrated on a global basis, sourcing some of its raw material requirements and intermediate products from overseas subsidiaries or suppliers, and establishing overseas sales subsidiaries in order to put its international marketing operations on a more dedicated footing. Likewise, the company may choose to diversify its business by acquiring suitable foreign companies.

Competitive strategy

Competitive strategy involves the formulation of strategic plans by a company aimed at ensuring that the firm is able to meet and beat its competitors in supplying a specific product or servicing a particular market. The main concerns of competitive strategy are to:

- Identify the competitive advantages and strengths of one's own company and of rival companies.
- Identify the characteristics and strength of the various forces driving competition in a market (Figure 2.2).

The keys to a successful competitive strategy are (1) to understand fully what product attributes are demanded by buyers (whether it be low prices or product

Figure 2.2   Forces driving competition in a market

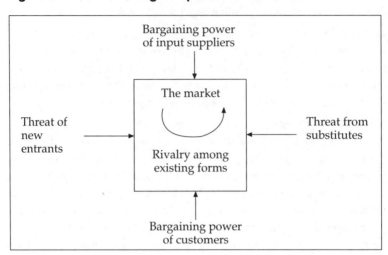

sophistication), with a view to (2) establishing operationally, a position of *competitive advantage*, which makes the company less vulnerable to attack either from established competitors and potential new entrants, or to erosion from the direction of buyers, suppliers and substitute products.

Competitive advantage refers to the possession by a firm of various assets and attributes (low-cost plants, innovative brands, ownership of key technologies, etc.) which give it a competitive edge over rival suppliers. To succeed against competitors in winning customers on a viable (profitable) and sustainable (long run) basis, a company must, depending on the nature of the market, be cost-effective and able to provide products offering attributes and features which customers regard as preferable to the products presented by rivals. The former enables a firm to meet and beat competitors on price, while the latter reflects the company's ability to establish product differentiation advantages over competitors. These are discussed further in Chapter 3.

Internationalisation can help create and sustain competitive advantages in a number of ways. For example, the cost or price advantages deriving from exporting from a centralised home production base may be negated by the imposition of tariffs or a currency appreciation. In this case, production in target markets may be more economical. Similarly, it may be advantageous to relocate production to a foreign country where labour and other input factor costs are lower than in the company's home country in order to reduce its supply costs and hence its prices. In the case of product differentiation, cultural differences between countries often require companies to 'customise' their marketing efforts and modify products to meet local buyer preferences. An 'in-market' presence through local manufacturing and sales subsidiaries may thus facilitate a more effective penetration of a target market by eliminating the channel intermediaries involved in arm's-length exporting. Similarly, for example, establishing a research and development (R&D) operation in an advanced industrial country may enable a company to tap into state-of-the-art developments and technologies in order to create innovative products.

Building on these competitive advantages, there are, according to Porter (1980, 1985), three main strategies for competitive success nationally and internationally: cost leadership, differentiation and focus (Figure 2.3). Low costs, particularly in commodity-type markets, help the company not only to survive a price war should one break out, but also to achieve above-average profitability in more stable market conditions. By adopting a product differentiation strategy, a company seeks to be unique within a market in a way that is valued by its customers, thus reducing the likelihood of defections to rival brands and often enabling the company to establish premium prices over competitors' offerings. General cost leadership and differentiation strategies seek to establish a competitive advantage over rival suppliers across the whole market or most of it. By contrast, focus strategies aim to build competitive advantages in narrow segments of a market, but again either in terms of cost or, more usually, differentiation characteristics, with niche suppliers catering for customised products or special demands.

Figure 2.3   Competitive strategy

Strategic target	Strategic advantage	
	Uniqueness as perceived by customers	*Low-cost position*
Industry-wide	Differentiation	Cost leadership
Particular segment only	Differentiation focus	Cost focus

International operations

Figure 2.4 provides a schematic summary of the foregoing discussion and how internationalisation fits into the picture. The figure highlights two key elements of business strategy, namely, strategic direction (what business activities to engage in and the location of these activities) and competitive strategy (the means of achieving competitive success in the chosen activities). For the international scope of its activities, the company has a number of strategic options open to it to enhance its competitiveness and sales and profit potential as shown in Figure 2.5. The company may choose *to service* a foreign market by exporting from a home production plant using channel intermediaries – local agents and distributors – to sell its products; it may establish a company-owned sales subsidiary; or it may establish a co-marketing alliance with a foreign partner. Alternatively, the firm may decide to appoint a licensee to undertake local production or the company may decide to establish its own production subsidiary in the target market. In the case of *sourcing* raw materials or components (and final products), the company may decide to buy from international suppliers or it may choose to self-supply from overseas based subsidiaries as part of a networking operation.

Figure 2.4   Firm, industry and location factors and competitive strategy

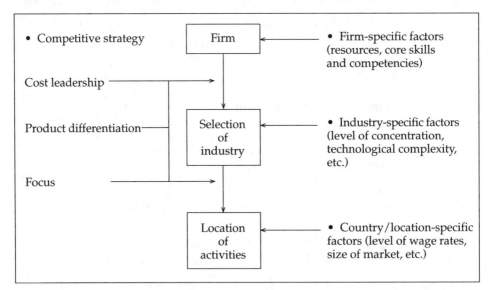

Figure 2.5 Foreign market servicing and sourcing

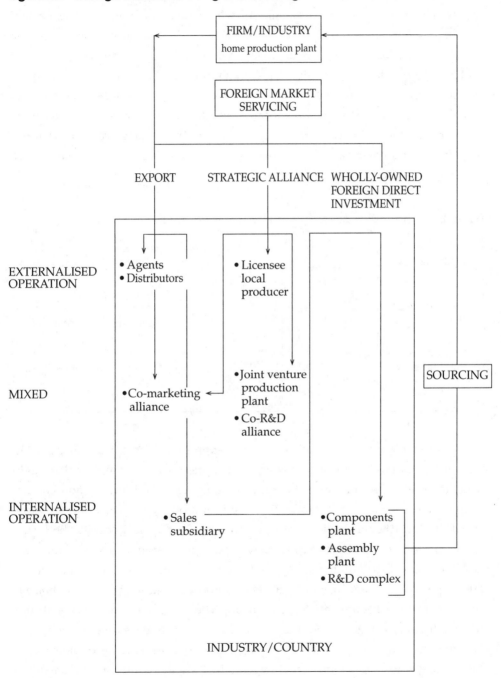

Which of the available foreign market servicing options a company will choose, either singly or in combination, will depend on not only the general advantages and disadvantages of each particular mode (see Chapter 3 for a detailed discussion) but also on an amalgam of firm-specific, industry-specific and country-specific factors, as illustrated in Figure 2.6. There is no one optimal strategy applicable to all firms or all situations. Companies differ in the resources and skills they possess, industries located in different countries vary in terms of structure and technological complexity, while countries themselves vary in terms of their industrial and market structures, stages of economic development, as well as levels of maturity.

Figure 2.6 The choice of foreign market servicing mode

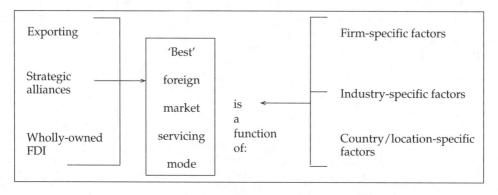

Accordingly, it is necessary to adopt an appropriate servicing strategy in the light of individual circumstances as they exist at present and to consider altering the company's servicing mode in the light of changing firm, industry and country circumstances. Consider the following configuration by way of example. Firm-specific factors (the company has an innovative product but lacks capital); industry-specific factors in the target market (the industry lacks product sophistication and has a complex distribution channel) and country-specific factors (the country is a low-wage economy and has high tariffs on imports). The only practical choice of servicing this market appears to be licensing. The company's lack of capital rules out wholly-owned FDI (although a joint venture might be considered). High tariffs rule out solo exporting and co-marketing alliances. Licensing an established in-market player to produce the company's product locally requires no capital outlay and gives immediate access to the distribution channels of the licensee. (Readers are invited to draw up their own possible permutations.)

CASE 2.1

Auto MNCs focus on Asia: Expansion and alliance – GM to form alliance with Suzuki Motors

General Motors Corp, eager to bolster its line-up of inexpensive cars for potentially high-growth emerging markets, announced a global alliance with Japan's biggest mini-car maker.

GM will become Suzuki Motor Corp's top shareholder, raising its stake to 10 per cent from 3.3 per cent by purchasing 42.27 billion yen (S$558 million) worth of new shares.

"It's become clear that Eastern Europe, Latin America and Asia-Pacific would provide growth where more mature markets would not," GM chairman John Smith said.

"The developing world is clamouring for even more affordable vehicles than we offer currently. Suzuki is the leader in the small and mini sector of the market, and in many places we needed to be, Suzuki was already there," he said.

The news comes less than a week after GM and Isuzu Motors Ltd, another second-tier Japanese car maker owned 37.5 per cent by GM, said they would build a US$320 million (S$556.8 million) plant in Ohio to make diesel engines for GM pick-up trucks.

Suzuki Motor president Osamu Suzuki said his deal with GM grew out of talks during a trip to Detroit in May that, purely by chance, coincided with the announcement that Germany's Daimler-Benz and Chrysler Corp planned to merge.

That merger helped spur a global consolidation in the industry, including Toyota Motor Corp's decision last month to buy out mini-car affiliate Daihatsu Motor Corp in a bid to beef up its small-car operations.

Suzuki and Daihatsu are Japan's two biggest makers of mini-vehicles, a unique segment in the Japanese market featuring small 660 cc engines and special tax breaks.

In stark contrast to Toyota's buy-out of Daihatsu, however, GM said it wanted Suzuki to remain independent and had no intention of boosting its stake beyond 10 per cent.

"It's independent and free-thinking and runs very fast and lean," he said. "Why would anyone want to change that?"

Mr Smith said GM's first joint efforts with Suzuki were likely to be small, inexpensive vehicles for emerging markets, such as an urban personal transport car and a farm utility vehicle that could also power water pumps and other agricultural equipment.

He added that, although Asia would take a few years to begin growing again after the recent financial crisis and was unlikely to regain the feverish pace of the past decade, it would in the long term be a key region for growth in the car industry.

Source: Reuters, *The Straits Times*, 17 September 1998

❖ ❖ ❖

Ford will proceed with Asia expansion plans

Ford Motor Co said it will go ahead with plans to expand its operations in Asia, despite the region's financial crisis in 1999.

Meiwei Cheng, a Ford vice-president, said the US automaker's expansion projects are continuing in at least six countries, including China, Japan and the Philippines.

"Rather than abandoning our customers or any country in the region, we have fine-tuned our expansion strategy. We are not slowing down," Mr Cheng said at an international conference in Manila on Asia's financial crisis.

In China, Mr Cheng said Ford last year began selling vehicles developed and produced at Jiangling Motors Co, which is partly owned by Ford.

Ford, which owns one-third of Japan's Mazda Motor Corp, has also formed a joint venture with Mazda in Thailand for an assembly plant with the capacity to produce 135,000 small trucks for the local market and for export. An assembly facility also has been established in Vietnam, he said.

In the Philippines, Mr Cheng said Ford is continuing with a project, which began in late 1997, to set up a car-assembly plant that is scheduled to open by the end of the year.

The plant can produce 25,000 vehicles and car engines a year and require purchases of more than $200 million of Philippine parts and components, he said.

Source: *The Asian Wall Street Journal*, 26–27 February 1999

GM to rely more on Suzuki for small cars

General Motors Corp, trying to meet its goal of winning a 10% market share in the Asia-Pacific region by 2006, will increasingly turn to Japan's Suzuki Motor Corp for help, especially in boosting its presence in the region's small-car segment, Rudolph A. Schlais Jr, a GM executive, said in an interview.

Suzuki, which is 10%-owned by the US automaker, is "our leader on minis and small cars," Mr Schlais said. And one area Suzuki is likely to make an immediate contribution is coming up with a strong GM entry into a market for what Mr Schlais calls "Asian value vehicles" – affordable subcompacts and mini-cars with engines between 0.8 liter and 1.3 liters in capacity.

One candidate for that car is a one-liter-engine mini GM is developing jointly with Suzuki for a launch in Europe next year. There is "a very distinct possibility" of selling this mini in Asia, including Japan, under an Opel nameplate, said Mr Schlais.

The agreement GM has with its Japanese affiliate, he said, is that "Suzuki will focus on minis and (small cars) and General Motors will provide platforms to Suzuki in larger vehicles."

Source: *The Asian Wall Street Journal*, 13 May 1999

Case Discussion Issues and Questions

1. What are the factors driving auto MNCs to further internationalise their operations?

2. Analyse from a competitive perspective the rationale for expanding operations during an economic downturn.

3. Discuss the relative merits of the two different auto MNCs' approaches to maintaining their competitiveness.

4. Discuss possible justifications for Toyota's decision.

5. How do you see the global auto industry in a decade?

2.2 THE MULTINATIONAL CORPORATION

A firm may simply source some of the inputs it requires from abroad by importing and supply its overseas markets by exporting, thus remaining anchored in a single national market. Increasingly, firms are using international strategic alliances and FDI to expand their businesses on a multi-country basis. Foreign direct investment, its operationalisation and management, is what distinguishes the MNC from a purely national company. A multinational corporation is a business incorporated in one country (the home or source country) but which owns income-generating assets – mines, component and manufacturing plants, offices, sales subsidiaries – in some other country or countries (host countries). Table 2.1 gives details of the leading multinational or transnational companies in 1995. These, and other prominent MNCs, are mainly domiciled in the 'triad' areas of North America, Western Europe and the Pacific Basin that is Japan. Globally, American and European MNCs are predominant while the largest international firms in Asia are overwhelmingly dominated by Japanese MNCs. Box 2.1 gives details of the world-wide subsidiaries of the UK pharmaceutical company Glaxo before its merger in 1996 with Wellcome. In addition to a manufacturing, marketing and research presence in many countries through FDI, Glaxo also exports to a large number of other countries through market intermediaries such as agents and distributors.

However, it is not only these giant corporations which have chosen the multinational route (Box 2.2). Many small- and medium-sized companies also have developed an international presence through overseas investment.

Operationally, MNCs may run each of their overseas businesses on a standalone basis or these businesses may be linked together as part of a complex global sourcing, production and market-servicing operation. In the former case, the manufacturing plants of the MNCs in a number of countries may, for example, be run basically as separate units but with some profits being repatriated to the controlling parent company. In the latter case, a MNC may, for example, use a subsidiary company making components in country A as an input source for a manufacturing plant operated by it in country B. Likewise, a MNC manufacturing

Table 2.1 The top 30 multinational corporations ranked by foreign assets, 1995

Rank/Corporation	Country	Industry	Foreign assets	Total assets ($ billion)	Foreign sales	Total sales
1 Royal Dutch/Shell	UK/Netherlands	Oil, gas and energy	79.7	117.6	80.6	109.9
2 Ford Motor Company	US	Automotive	69.2	238.5	41.9	137.1
3 General Electric	US	Electronics	69.2	228.0	17.1	70.0
4 Exxon	US	Oil, gas and energy	66.7	91.3	96.9	121.8
5 General Motors	US	Automotive	54.1	217.1	47.8	163.9
6 Volkswagen AG	Germany	Automotive	49.8	58.7	37.4	61.5
7 IBM	US	Computers	41.7	80.3	45.1	71.9
8 Toyota Motor Corp	Japan	Automotive	36.0	118.2	50.4	111.7
9 Nestlé	Switzerland	Food	33.2	38.2	47.8	48.7
10 Mitsubishi Corp	Japan	Diversified	30.1	79.3	51.0	124.9
11 Bayer AG	Germany	Chemicals	28.1	31.3	19.7	31.1
12 Asea Brown Boveri	Switzerland	Electrical equipment	27.2	32.1	29.4	33.7
13 Nissan Motor Co	Japan	Automative	26.9	63.0	24.9	56.3
14 Elf Aquitaine SA	France	Oil, gas and energy	26.9	49.4	27.8	42.5
15 Mobil Corp	US	Oil, gas and energy	26.0	42.1	48.4	73.4
16 Daimler-Benz AG	Germany	Automotive	26.0	66.3	45.6	72.1
17 Unilever NV	UK/Netherlands	Food	25.8	30.1	42.7	49.7
18 Philips Electronics	Netherlands	Electronics	25.2	32.7	38.4	40.1
19 Roche Holding AG	Switzerland	Pharmaceuticals	24.5	30.9	12.0	12.5
20 Fiat Spa	Italy	Automotive	24.4	39.1	26.3	40.6
21 Siemens AG	Germany	Electronics	24.0	57.7	35.5	62.0
22 Sony Corp	Japan	Electronics	23.6	47.6	30.3	43.3
23 Alcatel Alsthom	France	Electronics	22.7	51.2	24.2	32.1
24 Hoechst	Germany	Chemicals	21.9	36.7	13.4	36.3
25 Renault SA	France	Automotive	21.2	44.6	19.1	36.8
26 Philip Morris	US	Food/tobacco/drinks	19.5	53.8	27.7	66.1
27 British Petroleum	UK	Oil, gas and energy	19.3	28.9	34.8	57.0
28 DuPont	US	Chemicals	17.8	37.3	20.6	42.2
29 BASF AG	Germany	Chemicals	17.6	29.3	23.5	32.3
30 Seagram Co Ltd	Canada	Beverages	17.5	21.4	9.5	9.7

Sources: *World Investment Report 1997*, United Nations Conference on Trade and Development; company data.

Box 2.1 Glaxo Holdings Plc: Principal Subsidiary Companies (Prior to 1996 Regionalised Structure of GlaxoWellcome Merger)

Location	Activities
Europe	
UK (8 companies)	Co-ordinating and holding company: exporting; research: research co-ordination; production and marketing
Austria	Marketing
Belgium	Marketing
Denmark	Marketing
Finland	Marketing
France	Research; production and marketing
Germany (2 companies; one 50% owned)	Research; production and marketing
Greece	Production and marketing
Ireland	Production and marketing
Italy (2 companies)	Research; production and marketing
Netherlands	Marketing
Norway	Marketing
Portugal	Marketing
Spain	Research and marketing
Sweden	Marketing
Switzerland (3 companies)	Research and marketing and trading
Turkey (87% owned)	Production and marketing
Americas	
Argentina	Production and marketing
Bermuda (4 companies)	Finance and insurance
Brazil	Production and marketing
Canada	Research; production and marketing
Columbia	Production and marketing
Ecuador	Marketing
Mexico	Production and marketing
Panama	Marketing
Peru	Marketing
Puerto Rico	Marketing
Uruguay	Marketing
US (3 companies)	Administration and holding company; finance; research: production and marketing
Venezuela	Production and marketing

Box 2.1 (*cont'd*)

Asia-Pacific

Australia	Production and marketing
Bangladesh (70% owned)	Production and marketing
Hong Kong (2 companies)	Marketing (including China)
Japan (2 companies; 50% owned)	Research; production and marketing
Malaysia	Production and marketing
New Zealand	Production and marketing
Pakistan (70% owned)	Production and marketing
Philippines	Marketing
Singapore (5 companies)	Trading and holding company; Finance, Production and marketing
Sri Lanka (78% owned)	Production and marketing
Taiwan (90% owned)	Production and marketing
Thailand (2 companies)	Production and marketing

Africa

Egypt (69% owned)	Production and marketing
Kenya	Production and marketing
South Africa	Production and marketing

NOTE: All are 100% owned unless otherwise indicated.

---

a product in country C may choose to market the product in other countries (D, E, etc.) through its own sales subsidiaries rather than through independent agents or distributors.

Box 2.2   How Much Internationalisation?

Conventionally, the label multinational company (MNC) is attached both to a company whose overseas investments are limited to only a few foreign countries (for example, Hanson, whose overseas subsidiaries are almost exclusively based in the US) and companies which have an extensive network of overseas subsidiaries (for example, GlaxoWellcome).

The extent to which a company internationalises its operations depends largely on its corporate mission and how product and geographic diversification is viewed as a means of both reducing the company's exposure to risk and providing a platform for enhanced competitiveness and additional sales and profits opportunities.

In the case of Northern Telecom, Canada's leading supplier of telecommunications equipment and systems, its mission is to establish the company "as the preferred global

---

Box 2.2 (*cont'd*)

resource for designing, building and integrating a world of dynamically evolving information, entertainment and communications networks". Having broken into the US market in a big way in the 1960s and 1970s, the company has increasingly shifted its centre of gravity away from the North American market. In 1994, 32% of its revenues were earned outside North America and the company aims "to increase non-North American revenues to 50% of total global revenues before the turn of the century" (President's statement, *Company Report and Accounts*, 1994).

- In contrast, Matsushita of Japan, the world's largest consumer electronics group, has indicated that it will limit its overseas operations to a maximum of 25% of total group output in order to maintain its integrity as a Japanese company and to preserve the critical importance of its home-based research capabilities. Matsushita, a long time foreign investor, considers that the need to nurture research and development limits the extent to which it should internationalise production: "Traditionally, the most 'market-orientated' new product ideas have come from its factories around Japan rather than from basic research in Osaka, its research HQ – which is why 90% of Matsushita's R&D staff work in product design in the business units." "Move too many factories abroad," argues Mr Yamamoto (Managing Director), "and Osaka will lose touch with its shopfloor inventors" (*Financial Times*, 6 April 1995).

- BBA, the UK automotive components and specialist electrical products group, is an international company that obtains 80% of its turnover overseas. However "there are significant geographical imbalances which the Group needs to put right. Nine-tenths of our sales are made in Europe and North America. Our presence in East Asia and Latin America is minimal. Yet these are the fastest growing markets in the world, and any company with global aspirations must ensure that the whole of its product range is on sale in both regions" (Chief Executive's report, 1994).

In practice, many firms pursue a networking policy using multi-supply sources for their inputs, multi-production bases and multi-sales subsidiaries to handle marketing channels and distribution, linked together in a web of internalised transactions. For example, Nissan, the Japanese car producer established its UK assembly plant in 1986. This currently produces the Micra small car and Primera family saloon car models. Components are sourced both 'in-house' from Nissan's UK and Japanese parts plants and as well as from a multitude of European suppliers. Before 1986 Nissan cars had been exported to the UK from Japan and were distributed initially by Nissan UK, an independent distributor which operated a network of dealer franchises. In 1992 the company set up its own sales subsidiary, Nissan GB, to handle distribution and marketing. The UK plant, together with Nissan's assembly plant in Spain, are used primarily as an export platform to supply other European markets. Around 80% of UK-built Micras and Primeras are exported to the rest of Europe as well as to Japan and selected Southeast Asian markets. In France, distribution is handled by a wholly-owned sales subsidiary that was acquired by Nissan in 1991. Nissan's networking is illustrated in Figure 2.7. Overall, the available alternative growth trajectories for a firm are indicated in Figure 2.8.

Figure 2.7   Networking: Nissan

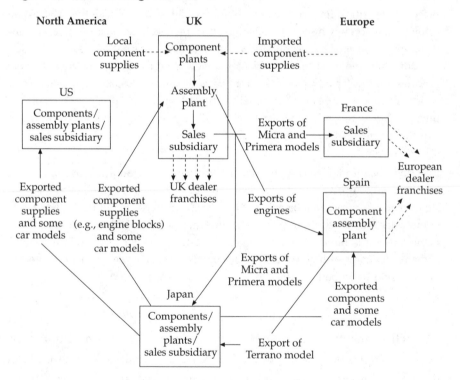

More specifically for FDI, Brooke and Buckley (1998) suggest that there are three main motives for such investments. They are:

- Market-oriented investment, for example, to gain access as a domestic supplier.
- Cost-oriented investment in assembly plants, for example, in developing countries to access cheap labour.
- Vertical investment to secure raw material resources or a distribution channel.

Figure 2.8 Classification of domestic and international growth alternatives for a firm

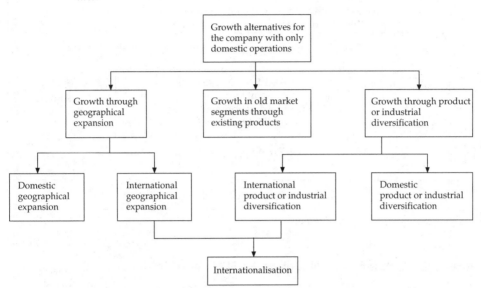

Source: Luostarinen (1979).

Additionally, there are a number of secondary motives for FDI. These include the following:

- The business and investment climate of the host country.
- The firm's responses to external approaches.
- Push factors in the home country.

According to Brooke and Buckley (1988) the general motives for operating internationally are as shown in Figure 2.9.

The Brooke and Buckley schema of motives for FDI is outlined in Table 2.2, while Box 2.3 gives some examples of recent internationalisation initiatives. It should be remembered that the motives need not be mutually exclusive.

MNC advantages over national firms

The MNC, distinct from firms that undertake their international operations exclusively from a single home country, may be in a position to enhance its competitive position and profitability in four main ways:

Figure 2.9 Motives for operating internationally

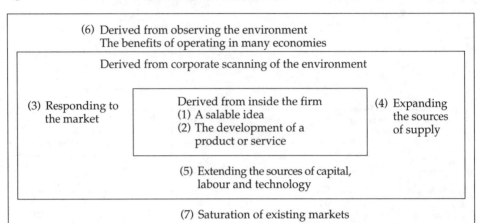

Source: Brooke and Buckley (1988).

Table 2.2 A classification of motives for FDI

1 Host market-oriented factors	2 Cost-based factors
Host market size	Cheap labour
Market growth	Availability of labour including skilled
Investment is better than alternatives	labour
To meet local demand more effectively	More profitable operation
Maintain/increase market share	Lower input costs
Trade barriers (including import	Lower transport cost
controls)	(Government) financial inducements
To use host country as an export base	Lower inflation
Defence of market	Access to technology
	Low taxation
3 Vertical integration	**4 Investment climate**
Availability of raw material inputs	Political stability
Lower cost material inputs	Cultural closeness to home country
Need to ensure supplies of inputs	Infrastructure provision
	Tax structure
	'Environment' generally
5 Response to an external approach	**6 Push factors (parent-country related)**
From government (usually host	Underemployed resources
government)	Difficulties at home
From local agent/distributor/licensee	Diversification of risk
From customer	Difficulties in using other methods
From supplier	Need to exploit advantages abroad
From competitor	'Exchange of threat'
	Multiple sourcing

Source: Brooke and Buckley (1988).

Box 2.3   Motives for FDI: Some Examples

- *Cost reduction*. Thomson Consumer Electronics, the leading French manufacturer of audio and video equipment, switched production of its cheapest video cassette recorders from Berlin to its plant in Singapore in 1992 in order to take advantage of lower labour costs in Southeast Asia. Similarly BMW, the German luxury-car maker, established a manufacturing plant in the US, its biggest market, partly because of the high costs of production in Germany compared to the US (and partly to decrease the distance to its largest market and thus serve it better).

- *Market presence*. ICI announced in 1993 that it was to establish a new green-field manufacturing plant in Belgium to produce a meat substitute product specifically to service mainly European markets. In 1993 the UK frozen food group, Iceland, entered the French market by purchasing Au Gel, a frozen food store group, thereby obtaining a base for expansion through establishing cold storage facilities and shops. In 1992 PepsiCo and General Mills, the US food groups, merged their subsidiaries in Belgium, France, the Netherlands, Greece, Portugal and Spain, to form the second largest snack food business in the European Union (EU). In 1998 Deutsche Bank acquired Bankers Trust to expand its presence in the US.

- *Market access*. Nissan Motor, the Japanese car producer, established a green-field manufacturing plant in the UK in 1986 and followed this by establishing a manufacturing plant in Spain. These investments were undertaken partly in response to the EU's protectionist stance on Japanese car imports, in particular the limitations imposed by the EU–Japanese export restraint agreement. Similarly, Toyota opened a green-field plant in UK in 1992 to produce models for the European market. In 1998 General Motors formed an alliance with Suzuki Motors of Japan, taking its equity stake to 10% from 3.3%, to gain improved access to the mini-vehicles market. Similarly, in 1998 Keppel, a Singapore government-linked firm, merged its shipping interests with that of Hitachi Zosen to pursue investment projects jointly in the region under the dynamics conditions of Asia's economic crisis.

- *Control of distribution*. In 1991 Nissan Motor, the Japanese car producer, acquired its French importer and distributor, Richard Nissan, which had been selling the company's cars since 1971. In the UK Nissan replaced its independent distributor by a green-field company-owned distribution subsidiary.

- *Access to technology*. In 1992 Toray, the Japanese synthetic fibre company, and Shimadzu, a precision-equipment maker, jointly acquired Therma-Wave, a US company which produced measuring and inspection equipment for the semiconductor industry. The acquisition enabled Japanese technology to gain access to Therma-Wave's patented technology. In 1993 First National Computer, owned by the Wang conglomerate from Taiwan, acquired Everex Systems (a Fremont,

---

Box 2.3 (*cont'd*)

California innovative computer maker in Chapter 11). Similarly, in 1996 Glaxo acquired Wellcome for its assets in pharmaceutical research and development.

- *Brand acquisition.* In 1991 Grand Met, the UK drinks company, acquired Kaloyannis of Greece which makes Ouzo 12, a leading aniseed-flavoured aperitif; and Sankyo of Japan took over Daks Simpson, the fashion house 'with an internationally-recognised brand name'. In 1992, Grolsch, the Dutch lager brewer, took over Ruddles, the UK real ale brewer, to expand its product portfolio.

---

1. The MNC can take advantage of differences in country-specific circumstances. Given a world economy that consists of a spectrum of countries at different stages of economic evolution (some industrially advanced, others mainly primary producers), certain general country advantages may create or augment firm-level competitive advantages which the MNC can exploit on a global basis. For example, the MNC may locate its research and development establishments in a more technologically advanced country in order to draw on that country's existing scientific and technological infrastructure and skills to develop innovative new processes and products. Similarly, MNCs may locate their production plants in a less developed country in order to take advantage of lower input costs, in particular the availability of appropriately skilled labour at cheaper costs. Alternatively, the MNC may choose to continue to produce its outputs in its home country but seek to remain competitive by sourcing key components from subsidiary plants based offshore, again taking advantage of lower labour costs.

2. The MNC can benefit from the flexibility of being able to choose an appropriate mode of servicing a particular market. In some cases, exporting to a market may be the preferred option as the market may be too small to support a local manufacturing presence. Strategic alliances such as co-marketing agreements and joint ventures with established local companies may offer advantages by enabling the MNC to capitalise on partners' distribution systems to gain higher levels of market penetration. In other cases, direct investment in production and sales subsidiaries may yield on-the-ground presence advantages – faster deliveries, control of local marketing, provision of after-sales service back-up, etc. – and may be the only viable way of servicing a market in the face of tariff and other obstacles to exporting.

3. Internalisation of the MNC's operations across countries by direct investment provides an opportunity for the firm to maximise its global profits by using various transfer pricing policies, for example, to ensure that profits are declared in countries where corporation taxes are the lowest.

4. An international network of suppliers, production plants and sales subsidiaries enables a MNC to introduce a new product simultaneously in a large number of markets (an important consideration in the case of products having a relatively short life cycle and patent protection) in order to maximise sales potential. Equally importantly, it spreads the risk of consumer rejection across a diversified portfolio of overseas markets so that failure in one market may be offset or perhaps more than compensated for, by rapid acceptance in another. In this respect, transnational product development is an important component of a risk management policy. Additionally, it enables the MNC to develop a global brand identity (as with, for example, Coca-Cola, Foster's lager and Sony) or, alternatively, more effectively customise a product to suit local demand preferences.

CASE 2.2

Going regional: Keppel inks new deal with Hitachi Zosen

It will also form an alliance with the Japanese parent company to pursue regional investment projects

Keppel Corporation signed a revised deal to merge its shipyard with Hitachi Zosen Singapore on improved terms in late 1998.

The government-linked firm has also agreed to form an alliance with Hitachi Zosen Corporation of Japan – the parent of Hitachi Singapore – to pursue investment projects jointly in the region.

The new deal values Hitachi Singapore shares at 52 cents each, a figure that is close to the shares' average market price in the last three months. On the stock market yesterday, the shares ended at 52.5 cents, down half a cent.

In March, Keppel Corp and Hitachi Singapore signed a deal in which Keppel Corp was to have transferred the assets and business of unlisted subsidiary Keppel Shipyard – which owns its Tuas shipyard – to Hitachi Singapore in exchange for new Hitachi Singapore shares priced at 59 cents apiece.

As the merger of the shipyards involved a swap deal valuing Keppel Shipyard in Tuas at $265 million, the lower valuation of Hitachi Singapore means that Keppel Corp will get more shares.

Instead of 56 per cent, Keppel Corp will end up with 59 per cent of the enlarged Hitachi Singapore.

Hitachi Zosen Corp's interest in Hitachi Singapore will be reduced to 29 per cent from 71.4 per cent.

Both Keppel Corp and Hitachi Singapore – which will be renamed Keppel Hitachi Zosen – are listed on the mainboard of the stock exchange.

For the minority shareholders Hitachi Singapore, the revised terms come as bad news since Keppel Corp will now have to pay only 52 cents instead of 59 cents a share in its unconditional takeover offer.

Under the Code on Takeovers and Mergers, Keppel Corp must make an unconditional offer for the remaining Hitachi Singapore shares it does not own.

Hitachi Zosen Corp has agreed not to accept the offer or sell its remaining stake in Hitachi Singapore for 18 months.

The takeover offer will be tabled after Hitachi Singapore shareholders and the relevant authorities give the merger the nod, which is expected by November.

Professor Bernard Tan will be made chairman of Keppel Hitachi while Mr Charles Foo will become its managing director.

Its board will consist of seven directors from Keppel Corp and three serving directors of Hitachi Singapore.

The make-up of the new boardroom underlined the strategic alliance between Keppel Corp and Hitachi Zosen Corp. Both companies yesterday signed a memorandum of understanding to pursue and work on investment projects jointly in China, Indo-China, India and ASEAN countries.

"Keppel is always on the look-out for like-minded and reputable partners like Hitachi Zosen to expand our business in the region," said Keppel Corp managing director Loh Wing Siew.

Source: *The Straits Times*, **11 September 1998**

Case Discussion Issues and Questions

1. What competitive pressures may be behind Keppel's move?

2. Classify the possible motivations for the alliance's FDI.

3. Discuss the motives driving the new deal into serving the land-locked Indochina market.

4. What potential challenges confront the alliance?

CASE 2.3

Local hero making good: Dickson Concepts looks for more British aisles

Dickson, a retailer of up-market fashion and accessories, has a significant regional and increasingly prominent international presence. In the UK it owns the well-known retail brand name Harvey Nichols – a department store outlet specialising in designer brands in clothing and household accessories. Hong Kong retailer Dickson Concepts (International) Ltd plans to spend £20 million ($32.9 million) on a new Harvey Nichols store in Scotland, its third in Britain.

The company said it conditionally agreed Friday to lease a property in Edinburgh. The agreement hinges on "the timely receipt of planning consent acceptable to Harvey Nichols Group PLC and the developer, Coal Penslon Properties Ltd."

The new store will have about 6,750 square metres of retail space, and should open in the second half of 2002. The store will be occupied under a 125-year lease at "a peppercorn rent," the company said, but gave no further details.

The company already operates a Harvey Nichols store in London, England and another in Leeds.

Dickson Concepts is a fashion retailer with outlets in Hong Kong and in Southeast Asia. It operates Warner Brothers Studio Stores, the Seibu department stores and Polo/ Ralph Lauren outlets in Hong Kong, Harvey Nichols in Britain and S.T. Dupont SA in France.

Source: *The Asian Wall Street Journal*, **12 January 1999**

Case Discussion Issues and Questions

1. Discuss the motives for Dickson's continued international expansion in the UK.

2. What competitive factors have drawn an Asian retailer such as Dickson to Europe (Britain and France)?

3. Suggest options for Dickson to develop its business further.

2.3 Trends in the Global Economy: International Trade and Investment

The dynamics of the international environment are also important for understanding internationalisation imperatives. Perhaps the most significant changes for MNCs is the emergence of global markets and global competitors. The supply of many products (for example, automobiles, chemicals, electrical appliances, computers, telecommunications and pharmaceuticals) are now dominated by a core of global oligopolistic producers engaged in head-to-head competition in some key markets, while in others they have forged strategic alliances with particular rivals to enhance their competitiveness against similarly partnered and non-aligned, competitors. Thus, for example, the US food groups, General Mills and PepsiCo, while competing aggressively against each other in the US market, merged their subsidiaries in Belgium, France, the Netherlands, Greece, Portugal and Spain in 1992 to form the second largest snacks food business in the European Union after the UK company, United Biscuits. In contrast, BT and AT&T, while dominant in their respective domestic markets, in 1998 struck up a strategic alliance to service global customers.

The growth of the global market has been propelled by a complexity of factors including the long-term breaking-down of barriers to trade and capital movements and advances in communication technologies (computer-linked telecom-munications data and voice transmission networks in particular) which have made the world a smaller place in logistical and management terms. International trade has been liberalised both multilaterally, through the work of the General Agreement on Tariffs and Trade (GATT), World Trade Organisation (WTO) and the United Nations Conference on Trade and Development (UNCTAD), and regionally by the formation of various free trade blocs such as the European Union and the North American Free Trade Agreement (NAFTA). The progressive removal of tariffs and other obstacles to trade (quotas, subsidies, etc.) by the main industrial countries through various GATT rounds culminating in the Uruguay Round (1987–93), has not only stimulated greater flows of exports and imports in general, but has aided MNCs which use particular countries as export platforms as part of a network of multi-country production plants and marketing subsidiaries. For example, the Nissan and Toyota-car assembly plants in the UK not only service the UK market but are used to supply European markets alongside imports from the parent plants in Japan. In part this example also serves to emphasise the impact of regional blocs. Unlike general trade liberalisation, regional free trade blocs contain an element of tariff and quota discrimination against non-members. For this reason companies may wish to establish a direct presence inside the fortress to ensure that they remain competitive against established in-market players. Moreover, in the European Union, for example, the initial removal of internal tariffs has recently been augmented by the Single European Market (1992) which involves a move to a much deeper integration of members' economies including the establishment of common technical standards and specifications, systems design, labelling and packaging, etc. The progressive liberalisation of capital movement by many countries which operate 'open door' policies has likewise played a significant role in increasing the flow of foreign direct investment. This is particularly true of Southeast Asia at least up to the Asian crisis of mid-1997.

The growing economic strength of the newly-industrialised countries of Asia (Taiwan, Thailand, Korea, Malaysia, Hong Kong, Singapore, etc.) and the opening up of China and Eastern Europe have provided an added stimulus to multinational activity. The triad configuration of Western Europe, North America and the Pacific Basin (principally Japan), however, continues to dominate MNC operations. The general prosperity of these regions, reflected in their rapidly increasing high levels of per capita income, their growing intra-regional trade dependency and their sophisticated technological and scientific infrastructure make them especially attractive to global companies. The Asian crisis has not diminished the appetite of MNCs; if anything their commitment to the Asian region has been reinforced by greater opportunities of cheaper assets created by the crisis.

International trade

International trade involves the exchange of goods and services between countries through exports and imports. Strictly speaking, of course, in the case of the *market* economies it is not countries that trade, but rather a multitude of private enterprise firms. This is an important distinction for while countries remain relatively fixed entities over time, firms, specifically multinational firms, can deploy their resources *between* countries replacing, for example, arm's-length exporting to a foreign market by investment in manufacturing capacity in that market.

Cross-frontier trade is generally based on the comparative advantages which countries have in supplying particular products, providing the basis of an international division of labour (location of production). Inter-country variations in comparative advantage are reflected both in terms of their differential cost structures (i.e., price competitiveness) and different skill levels (i.e., product differentiation competitiveness). These, in turn, are determined in large measure by the country's basic factor endowments (natural resources, labour and capital) and degree of economic maturity (level of per capita income, general cost and price levels, scientific and technical skills, etc.). Availability of resources and skills indicate the product range which a country is technically capable of supplying, while *relative* cost, price and product differentiation factors dictate which of these products it is economically appropriate for the country to produce, i.e., for those products that it enjoys a comparative advantage over other countries.

Over the long term, rising per capita incomes in the leading industrial countries, the continuing industrialisation of many developing countries and governments' commitment to free trade policies have all served to increase international trade. Table 2.3 gives details of the growth in world exports of merchandise trade (that is, trade in goods) in value and volume terms for the period since 1960. Although the recessionary impact of the oil price increases of 1973 and 1979 served to slow down the rate of growth of international trade in the 1980s, world exports have continued to expand at a more rapid rate than world output.

International trade in goods is dominated by the developed countries, a situation explained largely by the preponderance of manufactures in world

**Table 2.3 World merchandise trade and output, 1960–97
(average annual percentage change)**

	Exports value	Export volume	Export output
1960–69	9	9	6
1970–79	20	6	5
1980–90	6	4	3
1990–96	7	6	1.5
1996	4	5	2.5
1997	3	9.5	3

Source: WTO (1997).

exports and imports. Since 1950, the developed countries have increased their share of total world trade from 61% in 1950 to 71% in 1992 with a slight fall to 67% in 1996. The only interruption to this trend occurred in the 1970s when the oil price increases of 1973 and 1979 temporarily boosted the world market share of the oil-exporting developing countries and the growth of the Asian Tiger economies (Table 3.1 and Table 8.1). Western Europe, particularly the European Union bloc, has increased in relative importance and in 1996 accounted for around 43% of total world trade. Japan too has significantly increased its share of world trade.

Table 2.4 gives details of the 25 leading exporters and importers of goods in 1979 and 1996. Together these countries accounted for some 84% of total world exports and 80% of total world imports. A number of countries increased their merchandise export ranking substantially between 1979 and 1996; these were mainly the newly-industrialised countries of Asia and the Pacific Rim – China, Hong Kong, Korea, Taiwan, Singapore and Malaysia in particular. The older industrial countries, however, still continue to dominate the higher rankings. In general, the leading importing countries are those countries (US, Germany, Japan, France, UK, Italy, the Netherlands and Canada) that are also the major exporting countries, a fact explained largely by an increased degree of intra-product specialisation in manufactures.

Table 2.5 indicates the extent to which a particular region's exports comprises *intra-regional* trade (that is, trade between the various countries making up that region) compared to *inter-regional* trade (that is, trade between different regions). It will be noted that in the case of the world's largest region in international trade, Western Europe, 68% of Western European countries' exports were intra-regional

Table 2.4 Leading exporters and importers in world merchandise trade, 1996 (US$ billion and percentage)

	Exporting					Importing			
Rank	Exporters	1979 rank	Value	Share	Rank	Importers	1979 rank	Value	Share
1	US	1	625	11.8	1	US	1	818	15.1
2	Germany	2	521	9.9	2	Germany	2	456	8.4
3	Japan	3	411	7.8	3	Japan	4	349	6.4
4	France	4	291	5.5	4	UK	5	288	5.3
5	UK	5	262	5.0	5	France	3	276	5.1
6	Italy	6	251	4.8	6	Italy	6	207	3.8
7	Canada	10	202	3.8	7	Hong Kong	21	201	3.7
8	Holland	8	198	3.7	8	Holland	7	181	3.3
9	Hong Kong	27	181	3.4	9	Canada	10	175	3.2
10	Benelux	11	169	3.2	10	Benelux	8	158	2.9
11	China	34	151	2.9	11	S. Korea	15	150	2.8
12	S. Korea	29	130	2.5	12	China	11	139	2.6
13	Singapore	32	125	2.4	13	Singapore	20	131	2.4
14	Taiwan	22	116	2.2	14	Spain	13	122	2.2
15	Spain	19	102	1.9	15	Taiwan	24	101	1.9
16	Mexico	37	96	1.8	16	Mexico	16	90	1.7
17	Sweden	12	85	1.6	17	Switzerland	25	79	1.5
18	Switzerland	13	81	1.5	18	Malaysia	18	79	1.4
19	Malaysia	38	78	1.5	19	Thailand	44	74	1.4
20	Russian Fed.	—	69	1.3	20	Austria	12	67	1.2
21	Australia	28	61	1.1	21	Sweden	29	67	1.2
22	Saudi Arabia	9	59	1.1	22	Australia	19	65	1.2
23	Austria	25	57	1.1	23	Brazil	—	57	1.1
24	Thailand	41	56	1.1	24	Denmark	30	45	0.8
25	Denmark	30	51	1.0	25	Indonesia	—	43	0.8
	Total of above		4,428	84.0		Total of above		4,327	79.8
	World		5,270	100.0		World		5,420	100.0

Source: WTO (1997).

(the same as in 1986) while in the case of the world's second largest region in international trade, Asia, 52% of Asian countries' exports were intra-regional (up from 37% in 1986). The growing proportion of intra-regional trade, fuelled by regional trade alliances and their discrimination against non-members (for example, the European Union's Common Agricultural Policy) has led to fears in GATT that further polarisation of trade flows may undermine attempts to develop a broader-based multilateral trade framework.

Table 2.5   Shares of intra- and inter-regional trade flows in each region's total exports for selected regions, 1996 (percentage)

	Destination					
	North America	Latin America	Western Europe	Africa	Asia	Others
Origin						
North America	36	14	19	1	26	4
Latin America	50	21	16	1	10	2
Western Europe	8	2	68	3	10	9
Africa	15	3	52	9	15	6
Asia	23	2	16	2	52	3

Source: WTO (1997).

The relative importance of various trade partners for *individual* countries can vary substantially, reflecting traditional historical associations, the commodity composition of a country's exports and imports as well as membership of a free trade area. For example, UK exports to other European Union countries accounted for 57% of total UK exports in 1996 (up from 42% in 1979).

Table 2.6 gives details of the product composition of world merchandise trade. Around one-quarter of world merchandise trade in 1996 consisted of primary products, principally foodstuffs and fuels, while manufactures accounted for nearly three-quarters of total merchandise trade. Within the manufactures sector it will be noticed that over one-half of trade consisted of machinery and transport equipment. Over the long term, trade in primary products has declined in relative importance while trade in manufactures has increased. These developments are a reflection of changed patterns of demand and the introduction of new technologies and products.

Demand has become more diverse and sophisticated with rising per capita income in the older industrialised countries, and their industrial structures have become more specialised. This in turn has led to trade flows being increasingly characterised by the interchange of differentiated manufactured products within the same product group. Thus, for example, as Table 2.7 shows, the US and Germany are both substantial exporters and importers of automotive and textile products. Trade in manufactured goods has been greatly facilitated by the removal of tariffs and other obstacles at the GATT level and the establishment of free trade areas.

Although world trade continues to be dominated by exports and imports of merchandise, international trade in commercial services (principally

Table 2.6   Composition of world merchandise exports by product, 1992

	%
Agricultural products	11.5
Food	9.0
Raw materials	2.5
Mining products	*11.2*
Ores, minerals and non-ferrous	–
Metals	3.1
Fuels	8.1
Manufacturers	*73.3*
Iron and steel	2.7
Chemicals	9.3
Other semi-manufactures	7.7
Machinery and transport equipment	38.8
Textiles	2.9
Clothing	3.2
Other consumer goods	8.7

Source: WTO (1997).

transportation, tourism, business and financial services) has increased in importance and in 1997 accounted for around 19.6% of the value of total world merchandise and commercial services trade (up from 17% in 1979). In part this mirrors the structural changes that have occurred in the national economies of the US and Japan.

European Union and other leading countries (where the services sector of respective economies has expanded relative to the industrial sector), dominate but, again, this is also due to the creation of more open trading conditions between countries. Table 2.8 lists the 25 leading exporters and importers of commercial services in 1979 and 1995. Nine countries improved their ranking substantially (including Singapore, Hong Kong, Taiwan, Thailand and China). Changes were even more pronounced on the import side with Nigeria, Iran, Venezuela, Brazil, South Africa and Yugoslavia who were in the top 25 importers in 1979 dropping out in 1995 to be replaced by Taiwan, Hong Kong, Singapore, Thailand, China, Malaysia and Indonesia. It should be noted that the same group of leading countries (US, Germany, Japan, France, Italy, UK and the Netherlands) which dominate merchandise trade are also the most prominent exporters and importers of commercial services.

Table 2.7 Leading exporters and importers of automotive and textile products, 1996 and 1980

Exporters	Share in world exports (%)		Importers	Share in world imports (%)	
	1996	1980		1996	1980
Automotive products					
Germany	18.5	21.0	US	23.1	20.3
Japan	15.9	19.8	Germany	9.6	6.2
US	11.7	12.7	Canada	7.0	8.7
Canada	9.5	6.9	UK	6.8	5.7
France	7.3	9.9	France	5.9	5.5
Spain	5.4	1.8	Benelux	4.9	5.4
Benelux	5.3	4.9	Italy	4.2	5.6
UK	5.1	5.8	Spain	3.8	0.9
Italy	4.1	4.5	Japan	2.6	0.5
Mexico	3.2	0.3	Holland	2.3	2.6
Textile products					
Hong Kong	10.5	3.2	Hong Kong	11.4	5.1
Germany	9.0	11.4	China	7.6	2.0
Italy	8.8	7.6	Germany	7.2	12.2
S. Korea	8.5	4.0	US	6.8	4.5
China	8.1	4.6	UK	5.1	6.3
Taiwan	8.0	3.2	France	4.5	7.3
US	5.3	6.8	Italy	3.9	4.7
France	4.9	6.2	Japan	3.9	3.0
Benelux	4.9	6.5	S. Korea	2.4	0.7
Japan	4.6	9.3	Benelux	2.4	4.2

Source: WTO (1997).

Foreign direct investment

Foreign direct investment constitutes the aggregate of corporate economic activity that forms part of the financial account of a country and is recorded in IMF balance of payments statistics. It comprises: (1) the net acquisition of share and loan capital through mergers or takeovers, joint ventures, and the establishment of new greenfield subsidiary companies; (2) profits of overseas subsidiaries which are reinvested abroad and (3) parent to subsidiary capital transfers. Economically, FDI is to be distinguished from 'portfolio investment' (investment in corporate stocks and shares, government stocks, etc., mainly by investors and financial institutions such as pension funds and insurance companies) insofar as FDI represents the maintenance and creation of real, productive assets (a factory, office, etc.) whereas

Table 2.8 Leading exporters and importers in world trade in commerical services, 1995 and 1979 (US$ billion and percentage)

	Exporting					Importing			
1995 rank	Exporters	1979 rank	1995 value	1995 share	1995 rank	Importers	1979 rank	1995 value	1995 share
1	US	1	190	15.9	1	Germany	3	132	10.9
2	France	2	96	8.1	2	US	1	128	10.6
3	Germany	5	81	6.8	3	Japan	2	122	10.1
4	UK	3	71	5.9	4	France	4	77	6.4
5	Italy	4	65	5.5	5	Italy	7	65	5.4
6	Japan	6	64	5.4	6	UK	5	58	4.8
7	Holland	8	47	4.9	7	Holland	6	45	3.8
8	Spain	7	40	3.3	8	Benelux	9	33	2.7
9	Hong Kong	18	36	3.0	9	Canada	10	29	2.4
10	Benelux	9	34	2.9	10	Austria	20	29	2.3
11	Austria	10	33	2.8	11	S. Korea	12	28	2.3
12	Singapore	17	29	2.5	12	China	34	25	2.0
13	Switzerland	12	26	2.2	13	Taiwan	13	24	2.0
14	S. Korea	19	25	2.1	14	Spain	11	22	1.8
15	Canada	14	21	1.8	15	Hong Kong	26	22	1.8
16	China	32	18	1.5	16	Russian Fed.	–	19	1.6
17	Australia	26	16	1.3	17	Thailand	30	19	1.5
18	Taiwan	22	15	1.3	18	Sweden	27	17	1.4
19	Sweden	13	15	1.3	19	Singapore	32	17	1.4
20	Denmark	16	15	1.2	20	Australia	15	17	1.4
21	Thailand	51	15	1.2	21	Norway	23	17	1.4
22	Norway	11	15	1.2	22	Switzerland	8	15	1.3
23	Turkey	20	15	1.2	23	Malaysia	36	14	1.2
24	Malaysia	33	11	0.9	24	Denmark	19	14	1.2
25	Russian Fed.	–	10	0.8	25	Indonesia	34	13	1.1
	Total of above		1,003	83.6		Total of above		1,001	82.4
	World		1,200	100.0		World		1,215	100.0

Source: WTO (1997).

portfolio investment merely transfers the ownership of a *financial asset* from one individual or institution to another.

There has been a prolific growth in direct investment flows in recent years as Table 2.9 shows. Despite discrepancies in reported outward and inward FDI by individual countries, total FDI flows increased from US$91 billion in 1986 to over US$238 billion in 1990 before falling back to US$192 billion in 1992. Thereafter, outward FDI increased significantly by an average of 19% year on year to 1995. In 1996, outward FDI increased by 3.6% compared to 1995. Absolute flows have increased each year except during the global downturn years of 1991–92.

Table 2.9   Global outward FDI, 1990–98 (US$ billion)

Year	1990	1991	1992	1993	1994	1995	1996	1997	1998
FDI	238.3	194.1	191.7	223.4	252.4	321.5	333	424	430–440*

* Estimated.

Source: *IMF Balance of Payments Statistics Yearbook (Part 2)*, Vol. 48, 1997; UNCTAD WIR 1998.

According to the latest figures flows of inward FDI increased to US$644 billion in 1998, which is an increase of 39% over 1997 values. The major part of in-FDI was composed of cross-border mergers and acquisitions drawn by the need to capture competitive advantages in industrial sectors where economies of scale are key determinants of success.

Table 2.10 shows the changing pattern of sources of, and hosts to, FDI since the mid-1980s. The industrialised countries accounted for 97% and 94% of outward FDI over the period 1986–92 and 1990–96, respectively. Japanese MNCs which accounted for nearly one-fifth of total outward FDI over 1986–92 had lost share to 10% by 1990–96. The MNCs from Japan, the US and UK made these three source countries together account for 46.5% of total outward investment, with the top 12 countries accounting for 92% of the total between 1986–92. Until 1992 notable developments include the fall in the share of total outward investment accounted for by the US and an increase in the Japanese share. The period 1990–96 shows significant changes. The total share of outward FDI by industrialised countries dropped to 94%. Whereas Japanese MNCs accounted for most outward FDI in 1986–92, American MNCs dominate the 1990–96 period of international business and its competitive activity with 24.5% share. The top 12 outward FDI source countries accounted for 89% of the total. This is reflected in the share of world stock market capitalisation by MNCs in the 1980s and 1990s. In 1990 the top 10 companies by market capitalisation were six Japanese MNCs, three US MNCs and one EU MNC. By the end of 1998 the top 10 companies by market capitalisation were all American MNCs bar one, Royal Dutch/Shell Group.

A significant feature of inward FDI flows over the period 1986–92 is the changing predominant position occupied by the industrialised countries. They increased their combined share of total inward FDI from an average of 72% in the period 1974–80 to some 79% in the period 1986–92, then suffered a decline to 70% in 1990–96. Table 2.10 highlights the predominant position of the US as a host for FDI although its share fell from 27% to 20% between the periods 1986–92 to

Table 2.10 World outward and inward foreign direct investment flows, total and distribution, 1986–92 and 1990–96 (US$ million)

Location	1986–92		1990–96		
Outward FDI flows	Total 1,212,754	Rank	Total 1,739,514	%	Rank
Industrial countries (%)	97.0		1,632,116	93.8	
Developing countries (%)	3.0		107,433	6.2	
of which					
Japan	17.2	1	177,380	10.2	2
US	15.3	2	425,749	24.5	1
UK	14.0	3	203,675	11.7	3
France	11.4	4	178,711	10.3	4
Germany	9.7	5	166,343	9.6	5
Netherlands	6.1	6	113,553	6.5	6
Sweden	3.9	7	49,677	2.9	9
Canada	3.3	8	49,307	2.8	10
Belgium-Luxembourg	3.2	9	50,801	2.9	8
Switzerland	3.1	10	62,294	3.6	7
Italy	2.8	11	48,707	2.8	11
Australia	1.7	12	18,307	1.1	12
Subtotal	*91.7*		*1,544,504*	*88.9*	
Inward FDI flows		Rank	Total 1,642,426	%	Rank
Industrial countries (%)	81.0		1,092,966	66.5	
Developing countries (%)	19.0		549,459	33.5	
of which					
US	27.4	1	327,018	19.9	1
UK	13.5	2	144,355	8.8	3
France	7.3	3	131,361	8.0	4
Spain	5.3	4	69,770	4.3	6
Netherlands	4.1	5	60,767	3.7	7
Australia	3.8	6	43,117	2.6	10
Belgium-Luxembourg	3.5	7	73,098	4.5	5
Germany	3.5	8	21,680	1.3	12
Canada	3.2	9	45,698	2.8	8
China	2.8	10	156,340	9.5	2
Singapore	2.5	11	43,370	2.6	9
Italy	2.4	12	27,710	1.7	11
Subtotal	*79.3*		*1,144,284*	*69.7*	

Source: *IMF Balance of Payments Statistics Yearbook (Part 2)*, 1993 and 1997.

1990–96. The attractiveness of the US over the first period has been underpinned by the weakness of the US dollar and the consequent cheapening of US-based assets, reflected in a spate of takeovers of US companies. The second period reflects the strengthening of the US dollar. In 1986–92 the UK was ranked number two as a host country, and benefited particularly from its attractiveness to Japanese MNCs as a production base from which to service the single EU market. In addition to the UK, six other European Union countries are ranked in the top 12 host countries for FDI, which also includes two newly-industrialised countries, Singapore and China. The period 1990–96 saw changes in nearly all hosts to FDI. The most significant, however, was the dramatic increase in share of inward FDI by China from under 3% in 1986–92 to over 9% in 1990–96. Most of this FDI were located in, or adjacent to, the special economic zones of the country's southern coastal region. A notable omission from the inward investment listing is Japan. In sharp contrast to its prominent position in outward investment, the restrictive industrial structure of Japan limits to only 0.4% its share of total inward investment over the periods 1986–92 and 1990–96. These trends have continued since the early 1990s and Box 2.4 illustrates the expectations of international business in the next decade.

Box 2.4   Asian Tech Industries Could See Over US$1t Flowing In

More than US$1 trillion may be invested in technology industries in Asia in the next decade as the region latches on to the high-tech bandwagon, according to Morgan Stanley Dean Witter.

"Excitement overcomes fear; money follows enthusiasm," the US investment house said in a report, which predicted that a "tech tidal wave is stirring in the ashes of the Asian crisis".

It estimated the gross savings and investment rate in East Asia excluding Japan would average at least 30 per cent a year for the 'foreseeable future'.

Over the next decade, gross domestic product in the region was likely to double to US$4 trillion, implying US$10 trillion in investment, it said.

"All the tech talk means that US$1 trillion will be invested in technology-related areas with the blessing of governments," Morgan Stanley Dean Witter said.

It said many Asian governments believed the difference between their economies and that of the US was technology sophistication.

"Foreigners are fascinated by American tech companies and pay extraordinary prices for their stocks, supercharging the mighty dollar," the report said.

The US economy is surging with no inflation, while Asian economies are blighted with excess capacity.

In Asia, Hongkong has initiated a project to build a Cyberport to house high-tech firms, Malaysia has a Multimedia Super Corridor, China is calling for its population to 'revive the nation with science and technology' while Singapore may eventually be referred to as the 'cybercity', it said.

Box 2.4 (*cont'd*)

"The tech hype is evidently trickling down to all walks of life," it said. "Internet start-ups are popping up like bamboo shoots in spring."

The report cautioned Asian governments to avoid targeted investment and market protection, as competition was the only way to promote a technology-intensive economy.

In its last investment boom, Asia created too much capacity and had to write off the investment through major devaluations.

"It cannot afford to make the same mistake again," the report warned.—AFP

Source: *The Business Times*, 20 July 1999

CASE 2.4

Signpost China: AXA China region aims to enter Shanghai life-insurance market

AXA China Region Ltd plans to acquire a 49% stake in AXA China for 36.8 million French francs (US$5.9 million) from its ultimate parent AXA of France, paving the way for the Hong Kong insurer to enter the Shanghai life-insurance business.

AXA China, which was formerly known as National Mutual Asia Ltd, has long been trying to enter the potentially lucrative Chinese insurance business.

AXA China is 74% owned by National Mutual Holdings Ltd of Australia, which in turn is 51% owned by AXA of France.

AXA China owns a 51% stake in AXA Minmetals Assurance Co, a Chinese joint venture that was granted a coveted license to conduct life-insurance business in Shanghai. China has given out only a handful of insurance licenses to foreign insurers, many of which are hoping to gain access to the vast market.

AXA of France will continue to hold a 51% stake in AXA China after the deal.

AXA China's partner in the life-insurance venture is China National Foreign Trade and Financial Leasing Corp, a unit of China National Metals & Minerals Import & Export Corp.

Under the deal, as long as the company is part of the AXA group, AXA China Region has the option to acquire 49% of the equity interest held by AXA or any of its French units in any insurance company in China. AXA likewise, has the option to acquire 49% of any stake held by National Mutual Holdings or its units in any insurance company in China.

AXA China Region will provide a host of services to the joint-venture insurance company for three years from the granting of the insurance license in April. The services include underwriting support, actuarial services, information technology, agency support, administration, marketing, accounting and human resources. The company will charge fees at market rates.

Separately, AXA China Region said its net profit for the half to March 31 surged to HK$496.3 million (US$64 million), from HK$194.1 million a year earlier.

Revenue rose 8.5% to HK$3.05 billion, from HK$2.81 billion a year earlier. AXA China Region's dividend fell to 3.8 Hong Kong cents, from 5.9 cents a year earlier.

Source: *The Asian Wall Street Journal*, **26 May 1999**

Case Discussion Issues and Questions

1. Discuss the motives for foreign market entry with regard to China.

2. Analyse the rationale for acquisition as a means of entering the Chinese financial services market.

3. Discuss the potential competitiveness of the respective partners.

The large upsurge in FDI flows over recent years has been mainly associated with the expansion of multinational companies as they sought to enhance their positions in the three major Triad blocs – Western Europe, North America and the Pacific Rim. Foreign direct investment flows (and portfolio investment) have been greatly facilitated by the removal of exchange controls over capital movements and related income streams in many countries as well as various institutional arrangements encouraging inward investment. The UK, for example, abolished all exchange controls over capital movements into and out of the country in 1979, and there are no limitations on the repatriation of profits. There are no restrictions on the proportion of local equity that can be held by foreign direct investors, nor are there any selective controls on investment in particular industrial sectors.

The UK operates an open door policy towards FDI by actively supporting inward investment. The Invest in Britain Bureau (IBB) was established in 1977 to act as a facilitator and conduit for foreign investment in the UK. The IBB, part of the UK's Department of Trade and Industry, is able to offer companies practical assistance and detailed advice on all aspects of investing and locating in UK. Foreign companies are treated on an equal footing with domestic businesses with regard to, for example, financial backing if they locate in an 'assisted' region of the UK.

Similar moves to liberalise capital movements have been made by the UK's partners in the EU under the Single European Market initiative, and likewise by other major industrial countries. Developing countries have also sought to make inward investment easier and more attractive as a means of industrialising their economies. The efforts of countries in Asia have not been, in general, as comprehensive as those of Europe and North America and there are some concerns that the Asian crisis may make imposition of controls attractive for some countries in the region.

Aggregated data on the *global* geographical and product distribution of foreign direct investment are not available from the usual sources of international financial data (the IMF and the UN). However, an examination of the detailed balance-of-payments accounts of individual countries provides useful insights. Table 2.11, for example, shows the geographical distribution of UK and Canadian outward and inward investment. Like international trade patterns, the location of countries' investments tends to reflect traditional economic ties as well as responses to changing circumstances. Interestingly, in contrast to the situation of UK merchandise exports, the proportion of UK investment accounted for by the EU has fallen slightly while investment in North America, the US in particular, has increased markedly. In the case of inward investment, the proportion of investment accounted for by EU partners and other developed countries (mainly Japan) has increased substantially, while US investment in UK has declined in relative importance as US investment has become more diversified across the EU bloc as a whole. Canadian investment patterns, in contrast, conform to its merchandise trade profile, that is, notwithstanding old colonial ties to the UK, Canadian investment is still dominated by its dependence on the US, a dependency that is reinforced by NAFTA.

Table 2.11 UK and Canadian stock of outward and inward direct investment by region, 1978 and 1992 (percentage)

	UK				Canada			
	Outward		Inward		Outward		Inward	
	1978	1992	1978	1992	1978	1992	1978	1992
European Union	26	24	18	29	12	20	15	24
Other W. Europe	5	4	11	10	1	2	2	4
N. America	25	44	64	45	70	61	75	64
Other developed countries	24	11	5	13	2	3	5	5
Rest of world	20	17	2	3	15	14	3	3
	100	100	100	100	100	100	100	100

Sources: *Business Monitor* (UK), 1994 and *Statistics Canada*, 1994.

The product composition of outward and inward investment varies according to countries' comparative advantages, the importance of particular industries, and companies' use of the FDI mode to establish and enhance their own competitive advantages. Table 2.12 presents, again by way of example, details of the product composition of UK and Canadian outward and inward investment. Chemicals and food, drink and tobacco figure prominently for the UK in the manufacturing sector, and wood and paper and metal products in the Canadian manufacturing sectors. Financial services and the energy sectors are prominent areas of investment in the non-manufacturing sector for both economies.

Table 2.12   Composition of stock of UK and Canadian outward and inward direct investment by industrial activity, 1992 (percentage)

	Outward	Inward
UK		
Total manufacturing	34.4	36.2
of which		
Chemicals	9.4	7.7
Food, drink and tobacco	6.8	5.7
Total non-manufacturing	65.6	63.8
of which		
Energy	26.0	28.9
Financial services	13.4	18.0
Canada		
Total manufacturing	44.6	43.9
of which		
Wood and paper	11.7	7.4
Non-ferrous metals	10.8	4.5
Iron products	5.3	13.9
Total non-manufacturing	55.4	56.1
of which		
Financial services	27.6	20.9
Petroleum and gas	7.0	17.1

Sources: *Business Monitor* (UK), 1994 and *Statistics Canada*, 1994.

CASE 2.5

Taking on the competition: UPS plans to expand in China

United Parcel Service of America Inc aims to open 18 new offices in China this year as part of a push to expand its express-delivery service network on the mainland, executives said.

The new offices will be in addition to those UPS already has in Beijing, Shanghai and Guangzhou with its joint-venture partner China National Foreign Trade Transportation Corp or Sinotrans.

James Kelly, chairman and chief executive officer of UPS, said the US company is seeking to expand its partnership with Sinotrans, even though the Chinese company also has joint ventures with competitors. "It works very well for us in China and we will continue the relationship," Mr Kelly said.

In January, UPS signed an agreement to invest, transfer information technology and management expertise to the 50–50 joint venture with Sinotrans as the 18 additional offices are set up. UPS executives declined to provide details of the investment plans.

China groups UPS and other foreign express couriers into the freight-forwarding industry, an area of restricted investment. The Chinese government prohibits controlling stakes in joint ventures and limits the local partners from which to choose. Both UPS and DHL Worldwide Express Inc have teamed up with Sinotrans.

In its drive to join the World Trade Organization, China has promised to phase out such restrictions. Mr Kelly and other UPS executives plan to meet with top Chinese leaders during a two-day trip to lobby for these changes.

Source: *The Asian Wall Street Journal*, **5 May 1999**

Case Discussion Issues and Questions

1. Discuss the possible motives for UPS plans.

2. From the perspective of UPS what competitive advantages and disadvantages characterise China's inward FDI regime?

3. Suggest alternatives to the organic growth UPS intends to pursue.

2.4   CHAPTER REVIEW

International business encapsulates the overseas operations of a firm with respect to the sourcing, location, production and marketing of goods and services, and their networked and spatial distribution. These operations, which comprise different types of economic transactions, are performed by organisations – multinational corporations – that demonstrate a unique ability to project cross-border managerial control over multiple FDIs.

International business is critically important because emerging patterns in economic relations between countries and between companies today are increasingly dominated by competitive and strategic considerations. Furthermore, the trend towards deregulation and liberalisation, notwithstanding the Asian crisis of mid-1997, has made world markets more readily accessible by both large and small firms.

International business strategy is concerned with the formulation of plans that enable the firm to sustain continued attainment of its business objectives over the long term. These objectives are parsimoniously revenue and profit related but may have dimensions as varied as market share and access to particular technologies. These plans invariably incorporate different aspects of the business – financial management; organisational and human resources management; research, design, development and production; marketing, sales and distribution management in a coherent manner. The corporate decision-making that is involved with formulating these long-term plans possesses two critical dimensions – strategic direction and competitive strategy (competitiveness). On the one hand, strategic direction focuses on what the firm is going to do with its products and where its markets are. The set of choices that faces the firm involves the possible combinations of new and existing products and new and existing markets. On the other hand, competitive strategy focuses on the firm's understanding of the dynamics that drive economic activity in industries and markets and the firm's ability to position itself advantageously to exploit relative balances of power within industries and markets. The results of analysis lead to foreign market servicing choices involving decisions not only concerning where the firm obtains its inputs and where it sells its outputs but also how the firm performs and manages these functions.

Firms with extensive international operations are known as multinational corporations. They are structured essentially as inter-organisational networks. Their network structure gives them advantages over local firms and renders them uniquely suited to perform and manage functions of sourcing, locating their production plants and marketing internationally. Evidence of the nationality, structure and operations of MNCs indicates on the one hand that they are predominantly from the US and Europe with relatively few from Japan among the top 30, and on the other hand just how much internationalisation there is in today's globalised economy.

Although the forms of operating internationally are many, firms in general, and MNCs in particular, are motivated to internationalise their activities by a limited set of motivations. These motivations may be classified according to the different factors that concern the configuration of costs, the availability of inputs and market access. The motivations may be classified as: (1) host market-oriented factors; (2) cost-based factors; (3) vertical integration factors; (4) investment climate factors; (5) response to external factors; and (6) push factors.

Trends in world trade and investment indicate that international business, in terms of export values, volumes and output, has grown tremendously since the 1960s. International trade and investment are dominated presently by the developed countries (North America, Europe and Japan). However, between 1972 and 1997 the newly-industrialised regions and countries of Asia, notably southern coastal China, South Korea, Taiwan, and most notably Hong Kong and Singapore, increased substantially their share not only of FDI and world merchandise exports but also of trade in commercial services. Furthermore, shares of intra- and inter-regional flows point to definite patterns in the regionalisation of world trade.

The strategic and competitive postures of MNCs in international business manifest itself ultimately in FDI, which is of growing significance in the world economy. Foreign direct investment has been partly responsible for the tremendous growth in Asia's newly-industrialised countries. Foreign direct investment comprises the ownership of income generating assets in one or more foreign countries. Three forms of ownership are possible either separately or in combination: (1) the acquisition of share and loan capital through international mergers and takeovers, joint ventures between two or more partners, and the establishment of subsidiaries; (2) profits of overseas subsidiaries that are re-invested abroad; and (3) parent company to subsidiary transfers of capital. Economically FDI is distinguishable from portfolio investment by the nature of ownership – the possession, maintenance and business management of real productive assets whereas portfolio investment involves the transfers of ownership of financial assets and instruments.

2.5 QUESTIONS FOR DISCUSSION

1. What determines the manner in which a firm will internationalise its operations? What options are available for the international firm in servicing its foreign markets?

2. What are the motivations for international business? To what extent are these motives mutually exclusive?

3. How may the alternatives for the international growth of the firm and the network structure of the MNC give rise to different strategic postures?

4. How may the emerging trends in international trade and investment be related to the operations of MNCs?

**Table 3.1 Performance profiles of selected Asian exporters
(US$ billion and percentage change)**

Country	1997	1998*	1999*	Major exports and direction of exports
China	182.7	+5.0	−6.0	Textiles, garments, shoes, mechanical & electrical products, toys: 19% to US, 15% to EU, 16% to Japan, 39% to Asia
Hong Kong	188.1	−5.9	−5.8	Clothing, electrical appliances, textiles, office machinery, watches: 22% to US, 32% to EU, 5% to Japan, 41% to Asia
Indonesia	53.5	−4.5	+2.0	Oil, natural gas, textiles & garments, plywood, shoes: 13% to US, 13% to EU, 18% to Japan, 34% to Asia
S. Korea	138.6	−6.7	−5.0	Vessels, semiconductors, autos, metals, chemicals: 16% to US, 13% to EU, 9% to Japan, 22% to Asia
Malaysia	61.2	+27.0	−1.0	Semiconductors, disk drives, consumer electronics, oil & gas, wood products: 21% to US, 16% to EU, 11% to Japan, 45% to Asia
Philippines	25.2	+12.5	+10.6	Electronic equipment & parts, garments, machinery & transport equipment, mineral products, coconut products: 34% to US, 15% to EU, 17% to Japan, 19% to Asia
Singapore	125.0	−16.0	+9.4	Computer disk drives, PCBs, ICs, refined oil, electronic components, crude oil, food, electric generators, aircraft & ships: 20% to US, 18% to EU, 6% to Japan, 47% to Asia
Taiwan	122.1	−8.0	+1.0	Machinery, electronic products, textile products, IT products, metal articles: 26% to US, 17% to EU, 9% to Japan, 37% to Asia
Thailand	56.7	−6.5	+4.5	Computers & parts, electrical appliances, textiles, ICs, rubber: 21% to US, 18% to EU, 14% to Japan, 35% to Asia
Vietnam	8.9	+10.0	N/A	Crude oil, rice, coal, textiles, garments, marine products: 4% to US, 30% to EU, 27% to Asia

* Forecast.

Source: *The Asian Wall Street Journal*, "Asian Economic Survey 1998–99", 26 October 1998.

Table 3.2 Export modes

Export mode	Exporters' control over sales and marketing
Indirect	
1. Export houses • Buy exporters' product and sell abroad on their own account • Handle all exporting functions (e.g., documentation, physical movement, selling and marketing)	None
2. Confirming/buying houses • Buy exporters' product on behalf of foreign firms on a commission basis • Handle all exporting functions	None
Direct	
3. Agents • Generate customers for the exporters' product on a commission basis (but do not take title to goods)	Potentially high but efforts may be impaired if market coverage is handles competing products
4. Distributors • Take title to goods and earn profit from mark-up on product • Handle some exporting functions, in particular local distribution and marketing	Low or none; overall sales potential may be impaired if market coverage is limited or handles competing products (Box 2.2)
5. Co-marketing • Exporters access the distribution channels of a local supplier, the product being jointly marketed	Medium/high depending on division of responsibilities
6. Direct selling • Exporters supply direct to final customers who order from catalogues, trade directories, etc.	Potentially high but lack of in-market presence may impair sales efforts
7. Sales office • Exporters own sales personnel in target markets engaged in customer generation • Handles all exporting functions from home country	Medium/high. In-market presence helps develop sales potential (but may be too small to cover the whole market)
8. Sales and marketing subsidiary • Company-owned local subsidiary providing a dedicated market operation	Total but lack of investment resources may limit market coverage

Box 3.2   Control of Distribution/Marketing

The world's leading spirit producers radically changed their distribution arrangements in the late 1980s switching from using market intermediaries to developing company-owned distribution networks. In 1987 United Distillers (owned by Guinness) controlled only 25% of its distribution; by 1990 this had increased to 80%. International Distillers (owned by Grand Metropolitan) has increased the proportion of its business handled by its sales and marketing subsidiaries from 13% to 94% over the period 1986–90, while Hiram Walker has similarly increased in-company control over distribution from 50% to 88% over the period 1985–90. Behind these moves was the recognition that control of distribution was critical to competitiveness and the key element in maintaining and building international brands. United Distillers, for example, found after its takeover of DCL that the firm's brands were being handled by 244 agents in Europe 'all doing their own thing' and often in fierce competition with each other. Johnnie Walker Red Label Whiskey, the most international of its brands was supported by seven advertising campaigns each with a different message. Control of prices and margins has now enabled the company to decide which proportion of the margin should be put behind the brands and how it should be spent.

Remy Martin decided to create its own distribution network in 1975: "We had great difficulty in getting some of our agents to follow our marketing strategy. They wanted to go for volume, sell at a discount and did not give a fig for the brand's image." (Ralph Browning, Chairman, Remy and Associates, the Group's distribution company.) Acquiring distributors has not only enabled Remy to co-ordinate and control its marketing efforts more effectively but has produced other benefits: "Without our own distribution system we would never have been able to expand into champagne and rum. The real cost of acquiring new brands is reduced if you can put them through an existing distribution system."

Source: *Financial Times*, 29 November 1990

Flymo, the UK producer of lawnmowers, is a subsidiary of the Swedish multinational Electrolux. The company's 'hover' mower, its leading product in the UK, was initially distributed in Europe by a number of Electrolux's sales subsidiaries. Export potential was being harmed, however, by over-pricing. The sales subsidiaries supplied independent wholesalers who sold to specialist retail stores at mark-ups, which effectively doubled the equivalent UK price on average. In response to this situation Flymo altered its distribution arrangements in the early 1990s. The sales subsidiaries began selling directly to retailers which enabled overheads and prices to be reduced. The retail network itself was enlarged from one comprising only specialist outlets to include also mass distribution retailers such as hypermarkets. Importantly, Flymo took over managerial control of distribution. A central sales organisation based in the UK and run by Flymo was established with those staff in the European sales subsidiaries

---

Box 3.2 (*cont'd*)

responsible for Flymo products now reporting directly to the UK headquarters and not to Electrolux. This more focused and dedicated approach to marketing the company's product has produced a large increase in European sales.

Source: *Financial Times*, **25 May 1993**

On the other hand, the firm could be put at a competitive disadvantage if host governments impose import restrictions such as tariffs and quotas, if exchange rates become unfavourable, or if the firm loses touch with changing host country market conditions. Furthermore, where the firm makes use of agents or distributors then it can exercise little control over the marketing and distribution of its products and in some cases its ability to penetrate the market may be impaired by the fact that its distributors are also handling competitors' products. For these reasons a firm may choose to replace channel and market intermediaries by a wholly-owned sales and marketing subsidiary (Box 3.2).

3.2 STRATEGIC ALLIANCES

Strategic alliances may be defined as inter-firm collaborations over a given space and time for the achievement of mutually defined goals. Strategic alliances can cover a wide variety of arrangements between alliance partners. Broadly, they fall into two categories: knowledge sharing arrangements which involve mainly the transfer of basic know-how and co-operation arrangements covering marketing, production, etc., which are usually characterised by a more comprehensive association between the partners.

Licensing

Knowledge sharing arrangements include licensing, franchising and various technical exchange agreements. International licensing, for example, is a contract between two firms in different countries in which one firm (the licensor) provides technical information (including the rights to use its devices, patents, brands and trade-marks) to another firm or firms (the licensee[s]) in return for an agreed lump sum payment and/or royalties on sales. The licensee takes responsibility for investing in facilities for production and/or marketing that embody the licensed technology and/or the licensed brand.

A number of practical issues are involved in licensing including (1) the *identifiability* of the advantage that forms the basis of the licensing deal. For example, is it 'tangible' and 'embodied' in a machine, or patented product; (2) technical *transferability* of the process or product; for example, have potential licensees the capital and skills necessary to produce (and market) the product, or does the licensor have to provide extensive back-up? (3) drawing up contract agreements with licensees involves various *transaction costs* – seeking out partners, agreeing terms and conditions, defining mutual responsibilities and policing the agreement to ensure compliance.

For an innovating firm with limited financial resources for investment abroad (see the Pilkington example on page 66) licensing offers a means of obtaining extensive international sales and a quick return on its know-how or brands. Furthermore, licensing offers a relatively safe return on the firm's technology or patents since it avoids head-to-head competition with established firms in similar industries in foreign markets. A direct investment or exporting entry may disturb the oligopolistic status quo, causing price competition, the threat of vertical integration and reduced profit potential. In addition, licensing provides a means of gaining market entry to countries where exporting is difficult or impossible because of trade restrictions such as tariffs or quotas and 'tied' distribution systems and where FDI is prevented by host country restrictions on inward investment.

However, licensing has several potential disadvantages. The production and marketing standards of the licensee may be difficult to control so that inadequate licensees may undermine the value of the licensor's know-how or brands. Licensing may involve the under-exploitation of profit potential (that is, the royalties obtained may be much smaller than the profit which the firm could have generated by its own investment). Finally, there is a danger that the firm, by providing actual and potential (long run) competitors with its know-how and brands will lose control of core technology and products to rivals, with licensees turning into competitors. In part this threat can be countered by a cross-licensing arrangement whereby any subsequent development of the original technology or product is shared between the firms.

Licensing is a characteristic feature of many global industries including automobiles and components, computer software, telecommunications equipment, pharmaceuticals and food and drinks. As noted earlier it may be deployed to obtain access to restricted markets. Thus, for example, many foreign lager brews have found their way into the UK and the growing Asian beer market through licensing agreements with local brewers owning distribution outlets. Budweiser, the US brewer Anheuser–Busch's leading brand, is brewed under licence in the UK by Fosters as are the US brewer Miller's Millers Lite, and German brewer Henning's Hofmeister. Heineken (of the Netherlands) and Stella Artois (Interbrew of Belgium) are both brewed under licence by Whitbread, while Australian lagers, Castlemaine and Swan Light, are brewed under licence by Carlsberg-Tetley. Notably, Heineken brands are produced in Singapore by Tiger Breweries for distribution throughout Asia.

A good example of how licensing can be used as a platform for establishing an international business is provided by Pilkington which has licensed its 'float glass' process world-wide. The revolutionary float glass process invented by Pilkington and protected by patent rights became a commercial reality in the early 1960s with the building of a new float glass plant in the UK. For the world-wide exploitation of the invention two broad strategic options confronted Pilkington: it could either license established overseas manufacturers to produce and sell float glass, or it could itself invest in new float glass capacity abroad. In the event, the FDI option was initially rejected on both financial and strategic grounds. At this time Pilkington was still a private unquoted family business (it did not get a public stock exchange quotation until 1970) and had strained its financial resources to the tune of some £4 million in developing the float process. There was thus a serious question mark surrounding its ability to raise capital to establish a new plant even on a joint-venture basis. Also to be considered was the likely reaction of local producers to the entry of Pilkington into their established markets bringing with it the threat of cut-throat competition and also the likelihood that the invention would be pirated raising attendant policing costs. The option of licensing, therefore, appeared to be far more appealing, while at the same time leaving Pilkington room for FDI initiatives at some future time as its finances improved. This then was the broad strategy, which turned out to have been the right choice, pursued by Pilkington. The company placed heavy emphasis initially on licensing producers in the older industrialised markets and subsequently producers in the newly-industrialised countries. These were augmented, as time went on, by FDI presence with new green-field plants in Canada, Australia, South Africa, New Zealand and Scandinavia and by acquiring Flachglas (Germany) and LOF (US).

Box 3.3 gives details of the licensing agreements concluded by Pilkington for the float process over the period 1962–86. The terms of these licences, in broad terms, were as follows: the payment of an initial lump sum to Pilkington in exchange for know-how and a production royalty for a given period (normally the

Box 3.3   Licences Granted by Pilkington for the Float Glass Process, 1962 Onwards

Licensee	Country	Date licence granted
Pittsburgh Plate Glass (PPG)	US	1962
Boussois Souchon Neuvessel (now PPG)	France	1962
Glaverbel (now Asahi)	Belgium	1962
St Gobain	Italy	1963
Glacerie de St Roch (now St Gobain)	Belgium	1963
Libbey-Owens-Ford (now Pilkington)	US	1963
Asahi Glass	Japan	1964
St Gobain	France/Germany/Spain	1964
Ford Motor Company	US	1964
Nippon Sheet Glass	Japan	1965
Vidrio Plano (now Vitro Plan)	Mexico	1965
Sklo Union	Czechoslovakia	1966
Pilkington Brothers (Canada) now Ford Motor Co	Canada	1967
V/D Technoproimport	USSR	1967
Central Glass	Japan	1968
Combustion Engineering	US	1970
Guardian Industries	US	1971
ASG Industries	US	1971
Pilkington-ACI (a Pilkington subsidiary)	Australia	1972
Vetreria di Vernante (now PPG)	Italy	1972
Societa Italiana Vetro (SIV owned by Italian Govt)	Italy	1972
Fourco Glass	US	1973
Pilkington Floatglas (a Pilkington subsidiary)	Sweden	1974
Polimex-Cekop	Poland	1975
Pilkington Bros (S. Africa) (a Pilkington subsidiary)	South Africa	1975
Turkish Glass Works	Turkey	1976
Hankuk Glass	South Korea	1977
VE Industrientlagen-Import	East Germany	1977
Cebrace	Brazil	1980
Vitro Flotado (now Vitro Plan)	Mexico	1980
Taiwan Glass (Pilkington has a small stake)	Taiwan	1980
Asahi Glass	Indonesia/Thailand	1982
Nippon Sheet Glass	Malaysia	1983
SYO Glass (Pilkington has a small stake)	China	1983
Covina	Portugal	1984
Continental Float (Pilkington has a small stake)	India	1985
Lahti (a Pilkington subsidiary)	Finland	1985
Guardian Industries	Venezuela	1986
	Luxembourg/Spain	

Source: Pilkington.

life of the patent, which is 20 years) on all net sales of the licensed products. In those countries where Pilkington already had manufacturing operations, the use of patents was reserved to its own subsidiary or associated companies. In other countries, Pilkington has licensed indigenous producers on a non-exclusive basis allowing them to sell freely on world markets (so as not to infringe GATT rules), including the UK.

The majority of the licences taken out in the 1960s have expired and this has led to a fall in Pilkington licensing income from a peak of £35 million to £40 million in the early 1980s to under £15 million in the 1990s.

CASE 3.1

Extending the product, extending the market: Samsung licensed to manufacture Motorola's flex protocol decoder chips

Motorola announced in 1998 that Korean-based Samsung Electronics Co Ltd licensed the FLEX™ protocol decoder chip set to offer a more complete wireless messaging solution to its customers. The FLEX protocol decoder chip sets, combined with Samsung's own IF/PLL-based, MCU-based, LDI-based and EEPROM-based products, is expected to expedite the growth of Asia's FLEX pager market as the market transitions from POCSAG technology to FLEX protocol paging.

Through the licensing of Motorola's FLEX protocol for decoder chip sets, Samsung expects to offer its customers a complete chip set solution to more easily enable manufacturers to develop FLEX-based products.

"The addition of Samsung as a FLEX decoder chip licensee further extends the global impact and reach of this wireless messaging standard," said Elizabeth J. Altman, director of Licensing & Strategic Alliances, Motorola's Messaging Systems Product Group. "This licensing agreement further opens the door for expanded development of FLEX-based products throughout Asia."

"The Asian market has embraced the FLEX protocol as a standard for wireless messaging," said Dr Daejae Chin, executive vice-president & CEO, Samsung Electronics, Co. "We view the integration of the FLEX protocol chip set with our Samsung products as the most efficient way to serve our customers while increasing revenue."

The FLEX™ protocol, created by Motorola, is the global *de facto* standard for high-speed paging. It has been adopted by 18 of the top 20 US service providers, as well as by market-leading providers in Canada, Latin America, Asia, Africa, the Middle East and Europe. The FLEX protocol is the national standard for high-speed paging in Japan and Korea, and is also a national standard in India and Russia. In addition, it has been adopted by China's Ministry of Posts and Telecommunications (MPT) as its nationwide high-speed paging standard and it is included in an International Telecommunication Union (ITU) Recommendation. FLEX protocol-based operators are in all of the world's top ten largest paging markets. There are over 160 FLEX technology-based systems in commercial operation in 37 countries, which represent 94 percent of the world's paging subscriber base.

Motorola is a global leader in advanced electronic systems and services. It liberates the power of technology by creating software-enhanced products that provide integrated customer solutions and Internet access via wireless and satellite communications, as well as computing, networking, and automotive electronics. Motorola also provides essential digital building blocks in the form of embedded semiconductors, controls and systems. Sales in 1997 were US$29.8 billion.

Samsung Electronics Co Ltd, a US$13 billion (1997) flagship company of Korean-based Samsung Group, is a world leader in electronics, with operations in more than 50 countries and 75,000 employees worldwide.

Source: World Reporter, *Business Wire*, 8 December 1998

Case Discussion Issues and Questions

1. Analyse the respective competitive advantages that accrue to Samsung and Motorola from this licensing decision.

2. Discuss the extent to which Motorola's decision is a licensing move and Samsung's decision is a strategic alliance. Who stands to gain the most?

3. Given the extensive use of joint ventures and strategic alliances in the international electronics components industry, discuss the potential for inter-firm conflicts of interest. What are the major implications for management?

Another form of licensing is *franchising*. This involves the granting by one firm to another firm, or number of firms, the rights to supply its products on a royalty basis. Franchises (for example, McDonald's and Kentucky Fried Chicken food chains) are a form of co-partnerships offering mutual benefits. They allow the franchisor to expand sales rapidly and widely, often on a global basis, without having to raise large amounts of capital, by building on the efforts of a highly motivated team of entrepreneurs. Franchisees are usually required to contribute the bulk of the investment in physical assets and hence have a personal interest in the success of the venture. On the franchisees' side, the business obtains access to an innovative product or novel selling method with the franchisor providing back-up technical assistance, specialised equipment and advertising and promotion.

In 1991, Mothercare, the UK baby wear company, established a franchise agreement with Negoro, a Japanese wholesaler, under which Negoro is to open 20 Mothercare stores in Japan selling a product range sourced from the UK.

Co-operation arrangements

Co-operation alliances between firms (each of which continues to retain its own individual identity) can enable them to obtain access to technologies, know-how, capital and markets to augment their own resources and capabilities. Pairing resources and capabilities in this way allows strategic partners to achieve synergistic benefits otherwise unobtainable on an individual basis, while allowing each partner to focus and concentrate its efforts on its core business strengths. Co-operation alliances are seen as a particularly effective way of expanding internationally as an alternative to solo exporting and FDI. Partners can contribute established marketing and distribution systems, production and research and development (R&D) facilities and local knowledge of the markets they serve. They can ensure that products get to the market more quickly and more effectively, particularly where products need to be modified to meet local regulations covering product standards and packaging, and the preferences of local customers.

Co-operation alliances can take a variety of forms including the following:

- *Joint production agreements* in which partners co-operate to make components or complete products. These agreements enable partners to optimise the use of their own resources, to share complementary resources and to take advantage of economies of scale, for example, through joint purchasing or each agreeing to specialise in the production of particular components or finished products.

- *Co-marketing or co-promotion agreements* in which partners co-operate to market or promote each other's products. Again these agreements enable partners to maximise their marketing efforts by obtaining wider sales coverage through wholesale and retail outlets and the benefit of partners' local marketing expertise.

- *Joint R&D agreements* in which partners co-operate in undertaking basic research and development of products. Such agreements facilitate the input of different mixes of technical expertise and know-how in solving problems and in completing projects, allowing partners to reduce the expense and risks involved in R&D work.

- *Joint venture* which involves the formation of an independent business through the co-operation of two or more parent firms. The central characteristic of a joint venture is that it is an equity-based relationship, with ownership split in a variety of ways, for example, two firms: 50 : 50 or 60 : 40, three firms: 50 : 25 : 25. Forming a joint venture is usually undertaken if the nature of the business or project is such that it is deemed necessary to involve partners in a deeper commitment to the business or project than can be allowed for within the confines of a contractual agreement.

Co-operation agreements, like licensing, need careful planning and nurturing and involve 'agency costs' in negotiation, securing and monitoring the associated contractual arrangement. Joint ventures go some way to implementing a stronger link between partners, but fall short of the full impact of internalising those commitments by merging with, or taking over, the partner.

CASE 3.2

Needs must: Singapore Airlines, Rolls-Royce start venture

In early 1999, Singapore Airlines entered into a joint venture with Rolls-Royce PLC and Hong Kong Aero Engine Services Ltd to overhaul and maintain Trent aircraft engines.

The national carrier will take a 50% stake; Rolls-Royce will take a 30% holding; Hong Kong Aero will hold the remainder. The joint venture will work on aircraft engines for Rolls-Royce customers in the Asia-Pacific region.

The joint venture, expected to be operational in 2002, will be capable of handling 200 engines annually, the company said.

Singapore Airlines said it will have the option of acquiring another 10% from Hong Kong Aero Engine Services, which is a joint venture between Hong Kong Aircraft Engineering Co and Rolls-Royce.

The Singapore company said new premises will be set up at Singapore Changi Airport to incorporate the latest technology in Trent aircraft engines. The center will initially repair and maintain the Rolls-Royce Trent 800 aircraft engines currently installed in the Singapore Airlines' Boeing 777 fleet.

Meanwhile, the Economic Development Board on Monday said Singapore's aerospace industry grew 24% to S$2.38 billion (US$1.37 billion) last year despite the region's economic woes.

Source: *The Asian Wall Street Journal*, **16 March 1999**

Case Discussion Issues and Questions

1. Analyse the typology of the co-operation; how well does it conform to the available classifications?

2. Discuss the competitive factors driving co-operative forms of business in the international airlines services industry.

3. Discuss the advantages and disadvantages of pure contract between the principals and contract with co-operative forms.

Some notable examples of international alliances

- **Market entry and development – manufacturing**

  In 1984, Volkswagen, the leading European car maker, entered the Chinese car market through a joint-venture company Shanghai Volkswagen Automotive (SVA) in which VW has a 50% equity stake. SVA produces the Santana and Jetta models. In 1988 VW licensed a local company, First Automobile Works (FAW), to produce the Audi 100 model, partly from imported kits supplied by VW. In 1994, VW set up a joint-venture company with FAW in which it has a 40% equity stake to produce a modernised version of the Audi 100 (with VW continuing to supply kit parts) and a version of the Seat Cordoba car (from kits supplied by Seat, the group's Spanish subsidiary). In the period 1984–94 VW produced some 453,000 cars in China built by the two joint-venture companies and a further 71,000 Audis built under licence by FAW. VW is seeking to increase co-operation between the two joint ventures, in particular, in engine production, with exchange of key components between the two concerns. Camshafts and crankshafts are to be made by SVA while FAW will produce connecting rods and crank cases.

  In 1998 British Aerospace (UK) and Dasa (Germany) and DaimlerChrysler entered into talks to ally their non-defence businesses to develop non-defence related markets in the EU.

- **Market entry and development – services**

  In 1994 Gartmore, the UK fund manager, formed a joint venture with Nations Bank, the US's third largest bank, which will allow it to sell international fund management expertise to US retail and pension fund investors. Nations Bank is the US's second largest bank distributor of mutual funds and Gartmore is seeking to take advantage of NB's wide distribution network. NB has been less successful than other big US banking groups at developing and selling its investment products and hopes to benefit from access to a stronger product portfolio.

  In 1994 Dusit Thani Group (Thailand), having saturated its domestic market for top-end hotel services, formed a joint venture overseas to manage the 75-year-old Melrose Hotel in Dallas, Texas.

- **Joint production**

  In 1994 Mitsubishi, the Japanese car producer, established a joint-venture company with the Swedish car producer, Volvo, and the Dutch Government (each having a one-third stake), which will produce a new Mitsubishi car model at plants in Nedcar and Born, Netherlands. The venture is Mitsubishi's first European production base and its new model, a five-door hatch-back car, is aimed at the large family car sector of the European market. The Volvo version of the new car is expected to replace the current Dutch-built Volvo 400.

- **Joint production and marketing**

  Ford, the US car maker, agreed in 1994 to supply Mazda, the Japanese car producer (in which it has a 25% stake), with a Mazda-badged version of its Fiesta model for sale through the Japanese group's European dealer network. Mazda is the last of the leading Japanese car groups to secure a European production source. The deal for Ford cars to be sold under the Mazda brand name in Europe is a reversal of the two companies' long-established arrangement in Asia where some Mazda cars are sold as Ford cars; for example, the Mazda 626 is sold as the Ford Telstar.

- **Product development and co-marketing**
  In 1994 Astra, the Swedish pharmaceutical company, and Merck, the largest US drug maker, established a 50 : 50 joint-venture company. The new company will take over the marketing of one of the biggest prescription drugs in the US, the anti-ulcer drug Prilosec. The drug, developed by Astra, has been sold in the US by Merck since 1991 under an agreement between the two companies (which provided for Astra to buy a 50% stake in a new US joint-venture company once sales by Merck of Astra products reached a specified level). The new company will develop and market new drugs from Astra and from the other pharmaceutical companies.

- **Technical collaboration**
  In 1994 Rover, the UK subsidiary of BMW of Germany, entered into an agreement with Kia, the second largest Korean car producer, to jointly develop a new range of engines to be built in the UK and Korea. Initially the agreement is intended to develop a range of V6 engines which in Rover's case will replace the Honda V6 engine currently imported from Japan. The Kia version of the V6 engine will be produced in Korea for use in a new range of Kia executive cars under development.

- **Technical co-operation**
  NEC of Japan and Samsung Electronics of Korea, two of the world's largest memory chip manufacturers, agreed in 1994 to extend their existing co-operation agreements to jointly develop next-generation 256-megabit D-RAM chips. The cost of developing the new chips is expected to run into tens of billions of yen and this accord is seen as a way of spreading the risk, sharing the financial costs and facilitating mutual supply by unifying product specifications.

- **Technical standards**
  In 1994 General Magic, the US multimedia communications software company, added five new partners to its technology alliance. Cable and Wireless of the UK, Northern Telecom of Canada and Mitsubishi, OKI and Sanyo of Japan each took a small minority stake in General Magic. The new partners will licence General Magic's Telescript software, which enables users of personal computers (PCs) and personal digital assistants to access a communications network to deliver messages, retrieve information or shop. The alliance (which also includes AT&T, Apple Computer, Motorola, France Telecom, NTT, Philips, Fujitsu and Toshiba) is aimed at establishing its technology as a world-wide standard for multimedia communications.

CASE 3.3

Building up muscle: Fuji Heavy to begin talks with GM, Ford over tie-up

Subaru maker says they will explore technology alliance

Fuji Heavy Industries, the maker of Subaru cars, will soon begin talks with General Motors (GM) and Ford Motor on the formation of a technology alliance.

Fuji Heavy executives in 1999 met with GM and Ford officials and agreed to explore such a possibility, the Japanese automaker said in a press release. Fuji Heavy is also open to such negotiations with other automakers, the statement said.

Tokyo-based Fuji Heavy denied a *Nihon Keizai* newspaper report that it's seeking a capital infusion from either of the world's two top automakers. The company's shares rose by their daily limit of 100 yen, or 10 per cent, to 1,063 yen on 19 July 1999.

Fuji Heavy, an affiliate of Nissan Motor, is in talks with the US companies to sell up to 20 per cent of its equity, the *Nihon Keizai* newspaper said, without citing sources. Fuji Heavy is seeking cash to finance its development of vehicles that are more efficient and emit fewer pollutants, the paper said.

Fuji Heavy spokesman Shinichi Murata said President Takeshi Tanaka visited the US and met with US auto executives. Mr Murata declined to elaborate on the content of the talks, which follow the sale in May of a 37 per cent stake of Nissan to Renault SA, France's second largest automaker.

Hiro Tanabe, a spokesman for Ford Motor (Japan), declined to comment. Masaaki Gotsubo, a spokesman for General Motors in Japan, said Fuji Heavy officials have met with GM executives to discuss alliances. Yet GM doesn't have any plan to buy Fuji Heavy shares, he said.

Nissan's move has put Fuji Heavy in an awkward situation, said analyst Shinji Kitayama of New Japan Securities Co, who rates Fuji Heavy shares 'neutral'. The company, established in 1953, is increasingly concerned that it might become a target of a hostile bid unless it finds a partner, he said.

Any purchase of a Fuji Heavy stake by either US automaker would provide Fuji not only the needed capital for development, but links with other Japanese automakers as well.

General Motors holds a 9.9 per cent stake of Suzuki Motor and 49 per cent of Isuzu Motors while Ford owns 33.3 per cent of Mazda Motor.

While Japan's overall auto sales are falling, Fuji Heavy is enjoying solid earnings thanks to strong sales of its Legacy station wagons and small passenger cars.

Fuji Heavy reported record group net income of 33.7 billion yen (S$474 million) for the year ended March 31, up 9.8 per cent on the year. Sales were 1.35 trillion yen, up 3.7 per cent.

Source: Bloomberg, *The Business Times,* **20 July 1999**

Case Discussion Issues and Questions

1. Discuss the factors driving Fuji Heavy industries' decision.

2. Analyse the production network advantages that may accrue to the parties involved.

3. Discuss the possible competitive reactions to the proposed technology alliance.

3.3 FOREIGN DIRECT INVESTMENT

Foreign direct investment usually involves the establishment of the firm's own control over raw materials, components, production, distribution and marketing facilities abroad. Such investment may be undertaken by establishing new (greenfield) operations from scratch or by taking over, or merging with, established businesses overseas. FDI can be undertaken, as noted earlier, on a joint-venture basis, or it can be a wholly-owned investment.

Firms engage in FDI because of its potentially greater efficiencies from lower cost of inputs, increased profitability and higher cost-effectiveness in servicing markets. This is achieved through the direct presence in a number of locations rather than relying solely on a single home base and on imports and exports as the basis of their international operations. For example, with FDI a firm is able to supply 'just-in-time' from in-market plants and provide better back-up services such as maintenance and repair.

A firm may possess various competitive advantages over rival suppliers in the form of patented process technology, know-how and production skills, or a unique branded product that it can better exploit and protect by establishing overseas production or sales subsidiaries. A production facility in an overseas market may enable a firm to reduce its distribution costs by reducing distance to market and allowing it to keep in touch more closely with local market conditions such as changes in customer tastes, competitors' actions, government regulations, etc. Moreover, direct investment enables a firm to avoid governmental restrictions on market access such as tariffs and quotas and the risk problems of currency variation. For example, the growth of protectionism by the European Union and the rising value of the yen have been important factors leading to increased Japanese investment in the EU, particularly in the UK (Chapter 7, Box 7.2). By the same token, firms may be able to benefit from the availability of grants and other subsidies given as part of the host government's investment regime to encourage inward investment. Again, Japanese investment such as Nissan's car manufacturing plant at Washington has been attracted into the UK by the availability of regional selective assistance. In Asia, Singapore has been able to bring substantial inward investment through its attractiveness as a location by providing infrastructure incentives to MNCs.

In the case of sourcing, direct investment allows the MNC to enhance their international competitiveness by matching their advantages with those of some countries', i.e., lower labour costs or local firms that provide them with access to superior technological know-how (Figure 3.1). Moreover, direct investment by internalising input sourcing and market servicing within one organisation enables the MNC to avoid various transaction costs of using the market. That is, FDI avoids the costs of finding suppliers of inputs and distributors and negotiating contracts with them, as well as the costs associated with imperfect market situations, e.g., monopoly surcharges imposed by input suppliers, unreliable sources of supply and restrictions on access to distribution channels. Thus, FDI is an important means of maintaining the *real* competitiveness of firms. In addition, the MNC is able to take advantage of the internal transfer of resources at prices which allow it to secure various *treasury* and *fiscal* benefits from its multi-currency, multi-country operations such as tax savings (Chapters 6 and 7).

In some cases, a multinational company may favour offshore production, producing some components overseas which are then exported to be incorporated into the final product at the firm's local assembly plant (Box 3.4); or producing final products overseas to be marketed through the firm's local sales subsidiaries. Alternatively, some areas of the production process may be subcontracted to outside firms. Offshore production is undertaken primarily to enable the firm to maintain its international competitiveness by taking advantage of the lower labour costs of host countries and the financial subsidies offered by their governments. An illustration of this is provided by tremendous growth of Maquiladora firms (often subsidiaries of MNCs) operating on the Mexico–US border. These firms specialise in assembling components (automotive sub-assemblies, electronic goods, etc.) from parts imported from the US. The semi-finished or completed parts are exported back to the US or other destination for further production processing. The important fact to bear in mind is that MNCs take advantage of Mexico's lower labour costs relative to that of the US for labour intensive stages of manufacturing. In Asia the illustration is provided by the growth in export processing zones (for example, in China's southern coastal area and Subic Bay in the Philippines) that do much the same type of processing.

**Figure 3.1   Citibank's sourcing of Internet-based
payments system based in Singapore**

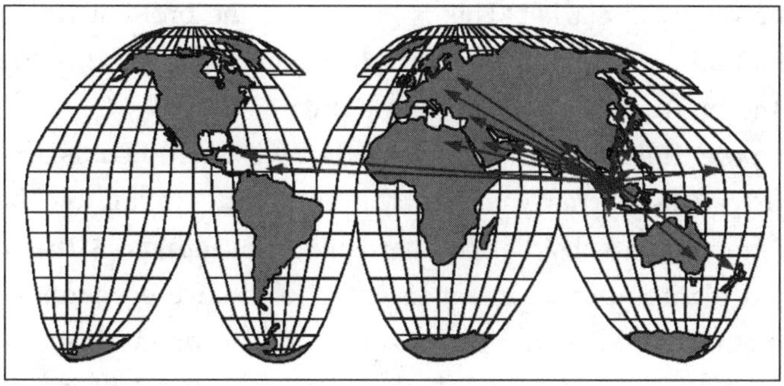

Source: *The Business Times*, 16 September 1998.

Box 3.4   International Sourcing

In procuring inputs for its production operations a firm has two basic choices: make or buy. In the former case the firm obtains some or all of the materials and parts required to manufacture its product from plants the firm itself owns as part of a vertically integrated business. The firm's component plants may be located either alongside the firm's main assembly plant or located overseas. In the latter case the firm purchases its input requirements from other suppliers (outsourcing) locally and overseas based.

Self-supply in general can produce cost savings and enable a firm to co-ordinate the production process more effectively; on the other hand buying inputs on the open market may be cheaper if supply conditions are competitive and obviates the need for the firm to invest in ancillary as opposed to 'core' operations. Domestic sourcing may yield logistical benefits (for example, just-in-time deliveries), but international sourcing may enable the firm to obtain inputs at lower costs or to obtain components that local suppliers are unable to supply.

Many MNCs rely extensively on a network of foreign suppliers; for example, Toyota's UK car-assembly plant, while drawing on its own in-house (UK and Japanese) supply of engines and some other parts, sources the bulk of its components from some 150 outside suppliers to both increase its cost-effectiveness and enhance product sophistication. Similarly, Ford's production of its Fiesta model sources from suppliers in 12 different European country locations. In a different vein, within the internationalised services industries, Citibank sources its Internet-based payments systems from across the Asia-Pacific region (India, Pakistan, Thailand, Indonesia, the Philippines, Taiwan, Guam, Japan, Hong Kong, Korea, Australia, New Zealand) to reach the Middle East (Turkey, United Arab Emirates, Saudi Arabia, Egypt), parts of Eastern Europe (Poland, the Czech Republic, Hungary) and the Caribbean (Puerto Rico).

Finally, in the case of some products (e.g., flat glass, metal cans, cement) decentralised local production rather than exporting is the only viable way a MNC can supply an overseas market. This is because of the prohibitively high costs of transporting a bulky product or the need, for competitive reasons, to market high volumes of the product at a relatively low price.

A main potential disadvantage of wholly-owned FDI is that it can be expensive in capital terms (despite the sometimes available host country government grants and subsidiaries), particularly in industries that require large investments in plant and equipment in order to achieve economies of scale (for example, a petrochemical complex or a semiconductor fabrication plant). This investment may be exposed to risk higher than an equivalent investment in the domestic market. This is because of the extra commercial risks of operating in an unfamiliar foreign market that is characterised by different business practices, consumer preferences, languages, customs and cultural differences, as well as the extra political risks of expropriation, profit and dividend repatriation limitations, price controls, etc. encountered in some countries (Box 3.5).

Box 3.5   Host Country Issues: FDI and Political Risk

In India a planned US$2.8 billion power project in the state of Maharashtra was put in jeopardy by a change of government. The newly installed BJP and Shiv Sena – Hindu nationalist parties in coalition-government reviewed and cancelled the first phase US$920 million Dabhol power project by Enron Development Corporation of the US that was agreed under Maharashtra's former Congress Party administration. It is the biggest single direct investment project in India since the country's 1991 liberalisation of FDI laws that allowed foreign companies to invest in its core industries. The Dabhol project is part of a two-phase operation to build a large power station. Enron has an 80% equity stake in the project, with US partners Bechtel (10%) undertaking construction and General Electric (10%) supplying turbines. When the State government cancelled the project, Enron had already spent US$300 million on civil construction work.

The controversy over the project was sparked off by the Hindu government claim that the original deal negotiated by the central government of Congress (I) Party had been open to corruption and that the electricity it is to produce would be too costly. Earlier, the Congress Party had gone out of its way to attract foreign capital into the sector, conscious both of the urgency of installing new power capacity to deal with India's increasing power shortage and of the availability of public funds. It sought negotiated deals, rather than tendered competition, for reasons of speed: "We need early winners" (India's commerce minister), hoping that these would inspire other

---

Box 3.5 (*cont'd*)

private contractors to follow. As a further incentive, the government agreed to underwrite the obligations of the state electricity boards to pay for power from eight selected fast track projects, of which Dabhol was the first.

At projected power prices and a 90% capacity utilisation rate the project will offer a return on capital of just over 20%, lower than for many other foreign power projects. Enron's calculations involved a significant risk premium for setting up not just a generator plant, but India's first foreign 'power generation business'. "Few other investors in 1992 would have considered India as an investment opportunity" (Enron's chief executive).

Should the inexperienced Hindu government decide to continue the cancellation of the project then this is likely to have an adverse effect on wider FDI commitments. While the Hindu government is claiming this to be a 'special case' of foreigners overstepping the mark its 'unsympathetic' attitude *towards foreign investors has been duly noted.*

The BJP State government held up the US$2.8 billion project from 1992 until 1996 when the dispute was eventually resolved after arbitration and several local and international court cases which Enron won. Part of the settlement was the enticement of a further US$20 billion FDI by Enron in India's energy, power and distribution infrastructure system.

In part, these disadvantages can be overcome by joint-venture arrangements which share investment expenditure, and hence risk, between partners and so pool the commercial and political risks involved. Indeed, when the joint venture involves an alliance with a *local* partner rather than another overseas partner then these commercial and political risks can be reduced by capitalising on the partner's local identity. In the case of Enron (Box 3.5) this did not happen to the detriment of Enron's local influence and image. Asian firms in general and Japanese MNCs in particular have favoured, almost exclusively, the joint-venture mode of entering foreign markets. However, as with contractual alliances, problems can arise over communication difficulties and differences in the objectives and commitment of partners in international joint ventures, thus reducing the competitiveness of the joint venture and negating the purpose of entering the joint venture in the first place.

Another way of reducing the risk attendant on moving into a foreign market is to enter that market by merging with, or taking over, a local firm with established business relations and well-developed marketing and distribution networks rather than establishing a green-field operation. This helps overcome the cultural problem of learning the way of doing business in an unfamiliar market. It also facilitates more rapid entry into the market by buying market share and providing a vehicle for the acquiring company to introduce and consequently establish its *own* products in that market. Such a competitive strategy does not disturb the equilibrium of the market as market shares remain unchanged at least in the short term. On the other hand, mergers and takeovers of foreign companies may pose significant 'inheritance' problems because of differences in objectives, management style and organisation structure between the acquiring HQ and acquired foreign subsidiaries.

Case 3.4

Grabbing territory: MCI WorldCom bids for OzEmail

At the end of 1998, US long distance company MCI WorldCom Inc launched a A$520 million (S$528.2 million) takeover bid for OzEmail Ltd, one of Australia's biggest Internet service providers.

Jackson, Mississippi state-based MCI WorldCom has already secured 14.9 per cent of OzEmail for about A$70 million through the issue of new stock at US$20 per American depositary share (ADS). It will bid US$22 per ADS for the balance of the company, compared to OzEmail's closing ADS price on Friday of US$20.87.

"The Asia-Pacific region is of key strategic importance to us and the synergies between OzEmail and MCI WorldCom are clear," said MCI WorldCom vice-chairman John Sidgmore. MCI WorldCom unit UUNET Holdings Pty will undertake the bid. Internet use is exploding in Australia, with nearly 18 per cent of the population having access to the Net as of August. OzEmail says the volume of electronic mail it processes for its subscribers has doubled in the past 90 days.

MCI's UUNET WorldCom offers Internet services to more than 70,000 businesses and Internet services providers in more than 76 countries.

Source: Bloomberg, *The Business Times*, 15 December 1998

Case Discussion Issues and Questions

1. Discuss the risk profile of MCI's market entry.

2. Discuss the possible inheritance problems that MCI may face. How may MCI reduce these?

3. Compare alternative decisions and locations for MCI's entry into Asia with the current decision.

❖ ❖ ❖

Some notable examples of wholly-owned FDI

- **Market entry**

  Citibank, the US banking group, is entering the retail banking market in the UK for the first time. Citibank already has a £1.3 billion residential mortgage portfolio in the UK, making loans through intermediaries. The operation is initially a toe-hold investment (six branches are planned for 1995, four in London) aimed at providing a niche service 'for professional persons who travel widely', but may be expanded in the UK to provide a more comprehensive global branch banking network. The bank has around 500 branches in Europe, including 300 branches in Germany, 96 branches in Spain and 62 branches in Belgium.

- **Market penetration**

  Toyota is to build a second car-assembly plant at Cambridge, Ontario, Canada with a capacity to produce 120,000 cars a year. In 1993 output at its current plant in Cambridge was 85,000 cars a year and its total North American output of cars and light trucks is around 533,000 vehicles. The main model to be produced at the new plant will be the Corolla small family saloon. This model is already assembled at Toyota's Ontario plant and at the New United Motor Manufacturing Inc (NUMMI) plant at Freemont, California, Toyota's joint venture with General Motors. Exports of the Corolla from Japan to North America will cease when the new plant comes on-stream. North American produced vehicles are expected to account for 60% of Toyota's sales in the US and Canada in 1996 compared to 46% in 1993. Toyota is also increasing its car exports from North America, chiefly to Japan, Taiwan and Western Europe. In 1993 50,000 cars were exported from the US. The appreciation of the yen is encouraging Toyota to relocate production out of Japan to its main markets.

- **Market penetration and extension of product portfolio**

  In 1994 Kenwood, the UK household appliances group, acquired Ariete, an Italian household appliance producer and distributor. "Ariete has a complementary range of products and an established position in the Italian market. The opportunities for growth in international markets with Ariete's existing product range and new ranges under development will be substantial" (T. Parker, chief executive, Kenwood). Ariete's main products include coffee-making machines and steam irons. Some of Kenwood's products will be branded under the Ariete name in Italy as Kenwood intends to exploit Ariete's distribution network in the Mediterranean area.

- **Market access**

  In 1994, following the rejection of Norway's entry into the European Union, Frionor, Norway's leading fish processor, announced its intention to shift production to Denmark or Sweden because it faces EU duties of up to 20% on *processed*, ready-to-eat fish products. According to a company spokesman, "The EU has prevented us from building a value-added market. We were aiming at more of these products because it is becoming more difficult to defend our market position on raw materials." (UK import duties on raw fish are only 1.7%.)

Nissan's automobile production FDI in Sunderland, UK, before the completion of the Single European Market is another example of market access.

- **Design and development**

  In 1994 Sony Electronic Publishing established a new base in Liverpool as its European centre for the design and development of computer and video games. The move followed Sony's acquisition in 1993 of Prygnosis, a Liverpool computer games software company.

- **Brands**

  In 1994 Hasbro, the US toys and games group, acquired the games division of Waddington of the UK including the world-famous Monopoly board game. Hasbro already held a licence to market Cluedo, owned by Waddington, outside the UK, and the acquisition of Waddington will add some 60 games to its product portfolio.

  Ford Motor Company's acquisition of the British Aston Martin and Jaguar racing car brands in the mid-1990s and BMW's 1998 acquisition of the luxury Bentley and Rolls-Royce marques are typical examples of the value of brands with 'a history' to the consumer.

- **Control of distribution**

  In 1994, Suzuki, the Japanese car and motorcycles group, took over the distribution of its vehicles in the UK by buying out the interests of its former distributor, Heron International. The assets acquired included an import and distribution centre at Sheerness and a parts centre and administrative offices at Crawley, and gave Suzuki full control over the development of its dealer franchises. The Suzuki takeover is another example of attempts by international car groups to assume control of UK distribution of their models: Nissan established Nissan GB to replace the independently run Nissan UK (Chapter 6, section on tax planning and transfer pricing), Volkswagen took back its UK franchise from Lonhro, Volvo from the Ibex Service Group and Fiat took Alfa-Romeo back from Inchcape's TKN subsidiary.

- **Sourcing**

  Nissan, the Japanese car maker, is to construct an axle manufacturing plant to come on-stream in 1996 as part of the further development of its UK car-assembly complex at Washington. When completed, Nissan UK will source all its car component requirements (except engine blocks and gearboxes imported from Japan) either from its own local plants or from other European suppliers.

3.4 CHOICE OF OPTIONS

Companies can operate internationally in a variety of ways: exporting through market channel intermediaries such as agents and distributors or company-owned sales offices; strategic alliances such as contractual co-marketing and co-production agreements or joint ventures with local firms, and by go-it-alone investments in production and marketing subsidiaries. As noted in Chapter 2, the modes that will be selected either singly or in combination will depend on an amalgam of factors. For example, nature of the product, locational advantages, distribution arrangements, etc., that impinge upon the firm's cost structure and marketing effectiveness and hence its ability to compete successfully against international and domestic rivals in targeted markets. There is no one optimum mode of servicing international markets given the diversity of firm, industry, market and country characteristics. Hence in their competitive strategy, MNCs must be pragmatic and flexible in their attention to the needs of particular markets as the following cases demonstrate. Moreover, as we shall discuss in Chapter 4, dynamic changes in firm, industry, market and country circumstances may require the MNC to alter its mix of options, switching between servicing and sourcing modes as required and as befits its chosen strategic direction.

CASE 3.5

Into the big league: Renault builds global growth plan with stake in Nissan

Tokyo – Louis Schweitzer, chairman of French automaker Renault SA, arrived in Japan late Thursday, 25 March 1999, in hopes of sealing his company's bid to purchase a 35-percent stake in the ailing Nissan Motor Corp.

A Renault-Nissan partnership would be the latest in a series of international automotive mergers and acquisitions – a trend that picked up speed last May, when Daimler-Benz AG and Chrysler Corp announced they would merge.

In addition to giving Renault a controlling stake in Nissan's passenger car division, the deal would give Renault a 23-percent equity stake in Nissan's faltering truck-making affiliate, Nissan Diesel Motor Co. Nissan's board of directors is expected to meet Saturday to vote on Renault's $5.08 billion bid.

But Renault's offer is more than just another example of consolidation among far-flung companies trying to create economies of scale. A linkup with Nissan is a key step in Renault's global growth strategy. The Paris-based automaker, which spent much of the '90s mired in bureaucracy and debt, has staged a monumental recovery over the past two years and racked up record sales and profits in 1998 – a stunning turnaround that is largely unknown outside Western Europe, where Renault has passed Volkswagen to become the leading brand.

Acquiring control of Nissan would vault Renault, now the world's tenth largest automaker, to the No. 4 spot among world automakers – ahead of Toyota but still behind General Motors, Ford and DaimlerChrysler.

The move also would enable Renault, which now derives 85 percent of its annual sales from Western Europe, to tap Nissan's extensive dealer networks in Asia and North America. This could enable Renault to return to the US, the world's largest automotive market, after an embarrassing retreat in 1987, when the company closed all its dealerships and left its few American customers scrambling to find mechanics to service their Le Cars, Encores and Alliances.

Renault recently began building its most popular model – the Megane Scenic compact mini-van – at a new plant in Brazil, and the company is keen to increase sales in South America and elsewhere.

Buying a controlling stake in Nissan also would give Renault access to the Japanese company's extensive research into more environmentally friendly engines – one of the few bright spots in Nissan's otherwise bumbling business.

The demise of Nissan – the vaunted nemesis of Detroit's humbled automakers in the 1970s and 1980s – is the latest symbol of the failure of Japan Inc. The nation has been unable to shake an eight-year-old recession that has crippled the largest economy in Asia, forcing debt-laden Japanese companies to grovel as wealthy Western suitors acquire them at fire-sale prices.

Up to $37 billion in debt and losing money for six of the last seven years, Japan's No. 2 automaker has little choice but to accept Renault's offer. The Asian economic meltdown has devastated sales at home, and a lacklustre product line-up in North America – Nissan's second largest market – is further sapping revenue.

Nissan's debt was downgraded to junk-bond status by Moody's after DaimlerChrysler AG, which hired German accountants to pour over Nissan's finances earlier this year, backed away from a tie-up that company officials had been plotting for more than a year.

But while Renault has succeeded in turning itself around, it isn't clear that buying a 35-percent stake will give the French company enough clout to restructure Nissan's hidebound bureaucracy and corporate culture.

"Nissan's problem is that they aren't building cars people want to buy and the question is, can these Renault people really turn it around?" said Tokyo-based analyst Peter Boardman of UBS Securities. "The question isn't simply whether they can cut costs. The question is, in three or four years' time, can these people build cars people want?"

A 35-percent stake in Nissan would give the French – and the French government, owner of 40 percent of Renault – at least three seats on the Nissan board, while Nissan president Yoshikazu Hanawa would get a seat on the Renault board.

Trimming Nissan's bloated bureaucracy and restructuring its debt could eventually pave the way for profits at the combined company, experts say. The two companies, which overlap in the subcompact and compact model range, could share platforms and use their increased size to cut better deals with suppliers.

"If this deal gets finalized, you're talking about a much stronger balance sheet, significantly improved or reduced debt burden and you've given Nissan some more flexibility than it has now," said Steve Usher, an auto analyst for Jardine Fleming Securities in Tokyo.

But even the most optimistic merger advocates say financial health for Nissan is years away, and the possibility of failure is great. Other automakers – from Italy's Fiat to Sweden's Volvo – have shunned the French automaker because they believed it to be too hierarchical and ego-driven.

"There's going to be enormous cultural friction," said Tsuneo Akaha, a professor of international studies at the Monterey Institute of International Studies in Monterey, Calif. "The Japanese approach is much more consensual and decisions take much longer than in France, where bosses take control and others are willing to give up responsibility to one leader. Renault will have a lot to get used to."

Source: World Reporter, *Detroit Free Press,* **26 March 1999**

Case Discussion Issues and Questions

1. Discuss the extent to which Renault's move is opportunistic or strategic.

2. Analyse the range of competitive challenges Renault faces in this stake.

3. Discuss the competitive advantages and disadvantages for Nissan and Renault. What factors will give Renault long-term capabilities as an automotive industry player?

Notable examples of foreign market servicing by UK MNCs

- **GlaxoWellcome** is a leading global pharmaceutical producer. The company has established production and sales subsidiaries in the major markets of North America, Europe and Japan (Chapter 2, Box 2.1); smaller markets are serviced in the main through wholly-owned sales subsidiaries and strategic alliances with local partners.

    Direct investment is the company's general policy in markets where presence is important in dealing with the regulatory authorities over drug approval and in developing customer contacts (especially medical practitioners). In these cases local management is given a high degree of autonomy in running the subsidiary companies.

    The company's foreign market servicing strategy in its main markets is based on a distinction between 'primary' and 'secondary' production and the advantages of presence effects, especially in marketing. Primary manufacture consists of the production of patented active ingredients, which for competitive reasons were initially produced exclusively in the UK (they are now also produced in Singapore) and then exported to secondary manufacturing plants located around the world where they are incorporated into the final products and marketed through sales subsidiaries. Given local preferences, packaging adaptations are necessary in most markets (design, size and instructions, colours and capsules versus tablets, etc.). A comprehensive sales force on the ground is also considered to be an important competitive advantage as marketing pharmaceuticals is critically one of 'selling quality to professionals'.

- **Lucas Automotive** is a major company supplying components to the global automobile industry. In the last decade the company has been progressively restructured to broaden its international base and to focus on growth markets and technologies with greater applications scope. Two imperatives guide the company's strategy: one is technological leadership through continuous product innovation; two, close collaboration with major customers in vehicle design and construction is becoming ever more important as its customers' own competitive success increasingly hinges on reducing product development lead times and the introduction of reliable, high-performance vehicles. This means an international presence in customers' R&D and manufacturing locations have centred in Europe, North America and Japan.

  Lucas' policy is to have manufacturing facilities in its main customer bases – Europe (Germany, France, Belgium and the UK) and North America (US) – and service companies to support exports to other markets (e.g., Canada, Japan, Mexico, Ireland). Service companies carry stocks, and act as distributors. In the main their activities are confined to 'aftermarket' operations (i.e., the supply of replacement components and parts). In addition, sales and marketing subsidiaries operate in the company's main markets.

- BT was formerly British Telecom, a state-owned monopoly supplier of tele-communication services to the UK market with no overseas operations. Since privatisation of the company in 1984 and the liberalisation of the UK telecom-munications market, the company has had 'to learn to compete'. Growth prospects for the company in the UK had been stunted by a combination of regulatory controls and the emergence and entry of new competitors, and this has led to an increasing emphasis on international expansion as shown in Table 3.3.

  BT's competitive advantages lie in its telecommunications expertise, particularly in operating conventional telephone network systems and in the provision of a range of innovative telecommunication services such as cordless (that is, mobile) telephones and voicemail. Vertical (backward) integration was once seen as offering benefits through having an in-house captive supply of telephone equipment, but its interests in this area have now been divested. The company's present strategy is based on the exploitation of its competitive advantages in offering differentiated packages of high value-added telecommunication services, particularly to business customers with global interests, i.e., MNCs. This requires presence in major user markets through the establishment of sales offices, subsidiaries and strategic alliances to provide ongoing customer contact: 'Global customers require global servicing'. In this respect, a presence in the North American market, the US in particular, is seen as crucial since the area is home to many of the world's largest multinational companies.

GLOBAL PRODUCTION AND MARKETING: THE STRATEGIC OPTIONS

Table 3.3 BT's main overseas investments

Company	Activity	% held	Date acquired (or established)	Cost (£m)	Status
CTG	Canada-based distributor of IT products	100	1986	not disclosed	sold
Mitel	Canadian telecoms manufacturer	51	1986	156	sold
Dialcom	US-based message handling	100	1986	not disclosed	merged with BT North America
JAL	US-based global airport and telecom services	100	1986	not disclosed	continuing
Gib Tel	Gibraltar telecom services	50	1988	not disclosed	continuing
Voicecom	US voice messaging	28	1988	not disclosed	continuing
Belize Telecom	Telecom services	25	1988	not disclosed	continuing
Metrocast	US paging	80	1988	16	closed
McCaw	US cellular	22	1989	907	exchanged for equity stake in AT&T
Tymnet	US data communications	100	1989	231	merged with BT North America
Syncordia	US-based global telecommunications	100	1991	not disclosed	continuing
AT&T	Pooling of international operations	50	1998	US$10b	continuing
SingTel	'Concert' Alliance to provide global service	undisclosed	1998	undisclosed	continuing

Source: Company reports.

Additionally, BT is involved in a strategic alliance with AT&T of the US and KDD of Japan, which provides advanced digital links for business users; the company has established a Japanese subsidiary and has minority stakes in two Japanese telecommunication service providers, Nippon Information Services and Global van Japan. BT is also part of the Pan-European 'europage' paging consortium.

3.5 CHAPTER REVIEW

There are three major competitive strategies for sourcing, production and marketing in order for a firm to provide goods and services to its overseas customers. In their various forms these involve: exporting; co-operating with other firms (in strategic alliances); and foreign direct investment (FDI). Exporting, the sale of a firm's goods produced in one country and sold in another, may be thought of as an independent form of foreign market servicing in that the exporting firm, to be successful, does not necessarily need extensive relationships in the export destination country. Co-operative forms of international business – strategic alliances – come in various types ranging from simple contractual arrangements (licensing for example) to complex multiple partner equity-based joint ventures for exploiting a particular technology. International joint ventures in the automotive, aerospace and electronics industries are often of the latter type. In *wholly-owned subsidiary* production, the firm sets up a FDI operation in a particular location to benefit strategically from specific advantages available only in that country. This form of foreign market servicing is clearly dependent on the location chosen for the operations, and selection is made according to various factors that influence the firm's strategic decision-making. Multinational corporations utilise all three modes of foreign market servicing in different combinations and at different levels of intensity for different countries.

There are indirect and direct techniques in exporting. Each provides the exporter with a different measure of strategic control over the process that results in different levels of competitiveness for the exporter. In general, the more direct the exporting technique the more control is exerted by the exporter and hence the higher the level of competitiveness that the firm can hope to attain. Exporting may be relatively inexpensive and, as a consequence, is usually favoured by small- to medium-sized enterprises or those firms beginning their international expansion. However, the initial relative low cost does not mean that it is risk free or remains low cost.

Strategic alliances, or inter-firm collaborations, have been growing in importance for international firms and are designed in a variety of forms. The simplest forms – licensing and franchising – comprise the contractual codification and packaging and transfer of proprietary information (brands, blueprints, patented processes, trade-marks, etc.) to another firm (or group of firms) in exchange for fees. These are nowadays being complemented by newer, more complex forms. These newer forms may be non-equity-based co-operation or equity-based joint ventures, for sourcing or production, between two or more firms either using similar technologies or in the same industry. Escalating costs not only of technology and product development in the leading sectors such as biotechnology; materials for automotive, aerospace and semiconductor industries; telecommunications; and computers but also for global marketing and promotion are driving firms to seek partnerships and alliances that confer additional strategic capabilities and competitive advantages. Some key issues to be addressed in strategic alliances involve: the selection of the 'right' partners for collaboration; the spatial and temporal terms and conditions of co-operation; building and maintaining appropriate levels of trust between partners; sharing developments in know-how and 'know-why' between partner firms. The judicious choice of alliance partners along with the form of collaboration can lead to sustaining long-term strategic advantage in foreign market servicing as in the example of Pilkington Glass.

Foreign direct investment through a *wholly-owned* or *majority subsidiary* operation confers to the firm control over the entire range of input and output functions (raw materials, semi-finished components, manufacturing, distribution) that has to be managed in order for the firm to service its customers overseas. Whereas the first two strategies of foreign market servicing involve external market intermediaries to a considerable extent, FDI, involving total control over all the firm's functions, either eliminates or internalises these intermediaries (and associated risk) and thus renders operations more cost-efficient and effective. The competitiveness that accrues to MNCs from having this level of control enables them to sustain strategic advantage over endogenous firms in the country where the subsidiary is located.

The choice of global sourcing and production options depends on an amalgam of factors (the nature of the product and where it is in its product life cycle, the advantages specific to the locations available, and arrangements for distribution, etc.). These factors impinge on the firm's cost structures and marketing effectiveness and hence its abilities in competing internationally. It is important to realise that there is no perfect mode, or combination of modes, for foreign market servicing given the diversity of firms, their industry characteristics and the differences there are in countries. As a result of dynamic changes in the nature of the firm, technological advances in industries and the circumstances of countries, the decision-making process in MNCs, while based on objectives and planning, is increasingly pragmatic and flexible. Multinational corporations need to be able to switch between options for foreign market servicing.

3.6 QUESTIONS FOR DISCUSSION

1. What are the characteristics of the generic strategies for global production and marketing?

2. What are the advantages and disadvantages of the different strategies for foreign market servicing?

3. What are the determinants for selecting options for foreign market servicing by MNCs?

4. How do the different strategies for foreign market servicing confer competitive advantages on the firm's international operations?

CHAPTER
4

Competitiveness and Internationalisation

CHAPTER OUTLINE

- Competitive advantages
- The dimensions of competitive advantages
- Understanding industry structures
- Understanding industry dynamics
- Formulating competitive strategies
- Competitiveness and foreign market servicing strategies
- Operationalising competitiveness in international business
- Competitiveness and strategic alliances

CHAPTER OBJECTIVES

After studying this chapter you should be able to:

- Categorise the key dimensions of competitiveness.
- Identify the relationships between the sources and characteristics, of competitive advantage.
- Explain the structure of industries.
- Comprehend the relationships between the structure and dynamics, of industries.
- Explain the relationship of competitiveness to foreign market servicing strategy.
- Distinguish the characteristics of international strategic alliances.
- Design different internationally competitive strategies appropriate to different industries.

INDUSTRIES, WHICH ARE generally supply-oriented, or markets which are generally demand-oriented, are defined as a group of goods and services possessing similar product characteristics and which buyers regard as substitute products. They constitute the particular arenas in which companies do business. No matter how few or how many business activities a company undertakes, its competitiveness and hence corporate prosperity will depend fundamentally on how well it succeeds in the individual product markets making up its business portfolio. It is thus important for companies to understand the underlying characteristics of the markets in which they compete (or which they are likely to enter). It is vital that companies comprehend fully 'the forces that drive, and the dynamics of, competition' in those markets in order to become corporate winners, achieving above-average profit returns on their investments. To be successful a firm must possess some specific form of competitive advantage over rival suppliers, either an ability to offer customers products at prices lower than equivalent competitors' products or to offer customers product qualities, attributes and sophistication not provided to the same degree by competitors.

Spatially, an industry or market may be local, regional, national or international in scope. In recent years many industries have taken on a global dimension with the removal of trade barriers and the expansion of foreign investment that have come about through long-term trends towards deregulation and liberalisation. Many industries are now dominated by a core of oligopolistic multinational companies that confront each other in many national markets. Thus, for example, Ford, General Motors, Toyota and Nissan compete against each other in the European, North American and Japanese car markets. The same is true in telecommunications where AT&T, BT, Deutsche Telecom, France Telecom, MCI, Sprint and STET compete separately and in strategic alliances to provide global services across the Triad. Another example is the pharmaceutical industry. Competition in global industries (Porter, 1986) is similar to localised competition based on *firm-specific* competitive advantages (for example, innovative products) but with the added dimension that firms which have established multinationality can draw on and exploit *country- or location-specific* advantages (for example, a sophisticated scientific infrastructure) to enhance their competitiveness.

The discussion below is based extensively on the pioneering works of M.E. Porter (1980, 1985, 1986 and 1990) augmented by the model of competitiveness developed by Buckley *et al.* (1992).

Figure 4.2 Determinants of national competitiveness

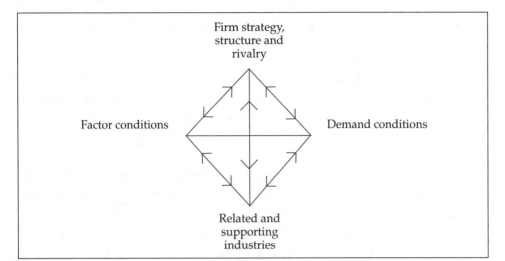

Source: Porter (1990).

- Human and social capital: quality, skills and cost of different categories of personnel resources.
- Physical resources: the abundance, quality, accessibility and cost of land, power, raw materials, climatic conditions, location and geographic size.
- Knowledge resources: the stock of scientific, technical and market knowledge in universities, research institutes, private research facilities, trade associations, etc.
- Capital resources: the amount, risk characteristics and cost of capital available to finance industry.
- Infrastructure: the type, quality and user costs of infrastructure available that affects competition, including the transportation system, the telecommunications system, capital and banking systems for funds transfer, health care, housing stock, cultural institutions, the quality of life and attractiveness of a location as a place to live and work.

Porter also identifies hierarchies among factors as follows:

- *Basic* (e.g., natural resources, climate, unskilled and semi-skilled labour, debt capital, etc.) and *advanced* (telecommunications infrastructure, graduate engineers, university research institutes, etc.).
- *Generalised* (the highway and transportation system, a supply of debt capital, a pool of well-motivated and qualified employees, etc.) and *specialised* (personnel, infrastructure and knowledge bases with specific skills, etc.). Factors that are

advanced and specialised will give a lasting competitive advantage; generalised and basic factors can easily be matched.

- *Created* (e.g., through investments made by individuals, firms or governments in telecommunications or transport systems, etc.) or *inherited* factors (natural resources, location, etc.). Created factors that are continually upgraded give the greater competitive advantage.

- Competitive advantage can grow out of innovation in overcoming disadvantages in some factors. Pressure, not abundance, often leads to new solutions, so long as pressure does not lead to paralysis.

Demand conditions. With regard to demand conditions it is not so much the *size* of the home market (although it is accepted that a large home market may be necessary to underpin economies of scale in lowering supply costs and prices) as its dynamic *nature* that matters. Porter emphasises the importance of the presence of sophisticated and demanding buyers in stimulating the innovation and introduction of new products capable of being transferred into global markets.

Related and supporting industries. The quality and category of related and supporting industries provide an important bedrock for competitive success by providing a network of subcontractors and input suppliers and commercial infrastructure.

Firm strategy, structure and rivalry. The pattern of rivalry in domestic industries has a significant role to play in the process of innovation. Strong domestic competition between firms creates pressure on firms to improve cost structures, accelerates innovation and forces firms to look for higher order competitive advantages than their rivals, thus providing a springboard for international success.

All of these factors, it is suggested, are interrelated, creating a 'virtuous circle' of resource generation and application and sensitivity in meeting customers' demands.

Of course, in the last analysis competitiveness applies as a general rule to *companies* not nations. While, for example, a country which is price uncompetitive in world markets because of inflation may attempt to correct this by devaluing its currency, whether this is sustainable or not will depend ultimately on the cost-effectiveness of a range of individual suppliers. This said, nation-specific factors provide an important background for the creation and enhancement of company, and hence industry, competitive advantages on a global basis. For example, companies may establish a research and development subsidiary in a more technologically advanced country in order to tap into that country's embedded scientific and technological infrastructure to innovate and develop new processes and products. This is illustrated by Japanese pharmaceutical companies that established R&D facilities in the UK and the US. Alternatively, companies may set up extraction and manufacturing plants in less developed countries in order to access essential raw materials and cheap labour (Box 4.3).

Box 4.3   Competitive Advantage of Countries

Labour Costs

Factor input costs differ between countries, reflecting differences in relative factor endowments and the general level of economic maturity attained by different countries. Table 1 shows labour costs per hour for a number of leading industrial countries. The labour cost gap is even more pronounced between the mature industrial countries and the **newly-industrialised** countries of the world. Table 2 shows industrial labour costs in selected Asian countries. Increasingly, high wage costs in the Japanese textile industry have encouraged companies to go offshore to lower cost locations elsewhere in Asia. Similarly, UK textile companies have moved production overseas. S.R. Gent, the UK textile group, for example, shifted 50% of its production to the Far East over the period 1990–95. Siemens, the German engineering company, moved the manufacture of its car wiring systems from Germany to Turkey, where labour costs at DM6 per hour are DM34 lower than in Germany.

The appreciation of the yen and Deutschemark in the early 1990s encouraged more Japanese and German companies to relocate production (for example, Nissan and Toyota established car-assembly plants in the UK and BMW and Mercedes established assembly plants in the US).

Table 1   Labour costs in world manufacturing, 1996 (US$)

	Labour costs per hour	Direct pay	Social costs
Germany	32	18	14
Switzerland	28	18.5	9.5
Sweden	24.5	14.5	10
Japan	22	13	9
France	20	11	9
US	17	12	5
Italy	16.5	9.5	7
Great Britain	14	11	3

Source: *The Economist*, 24 May 1997.

Box 4.3 (*cont'd*)

Table 2 Asian industrial labour costs, 1996 (US$ per hour)

Country	
Hong Kong	5.14
Taiwan	5.93
Singapore	8.32
S. Korea	8.09
Sri Lanka	0.48

Source: US Department of Labor, Bureau of Labor Statistics (1998).

Skills and Competencies

The presence in a country of a highly trained labour force and of a sophisticated scientific and technological infrastructure provide companies with the foundation on which to engage in technically demanding manufacturing operations and access the skills and expertise necessary to develop innovative new products. GlaxoWellcome, the UK pharmaceutical MNC, for example, established an international network of R&D centres including those in the UK (respiratory, cardiovascular, anti-infectives, viral diseases, rheumatoid arthritis, biotechnology and genetics), US (cancer, metabolic diseases, diabetes, obesity, osteoporosis, viral diseases and genetics), Japan (respiratory, dermatology), France (cardiovascular), Italy (anti-infectives, genetics), Switzerland (bioinformatics, disease models), and Spain (anti-microbial, anti-fungal). Additionally, it enters into strategic alliances, joint ventures, academic links and research contracts to undertake collaborative programmes with centres of excellence (universities and research institutions) to tap into the latest scientific ideas and developments.

In 1994, Daewoo, the Korean car producer which currently has no production presence in Europe, established a technical centre in the UK which now employs 750 people. The UK centre is near to completing the design and development of a new range of cars specifically for the European market, working in collaboration with Daewoo's main technical centre in Pupyung via interactive digital data links.

4.2 COMPETITIVE STRATEGY

As observed in the introduction a firm's corporate prosperity depends funda-mentally on its strength as a competitor in the industries in which it operates. The firm has to make strategic choices on *which* industries to operate in and how to

Lufthansa, SAS and United have anti-trust immunity from Washington, which means they can operate as if they were one airline, setting fares and doing their marketing together. They are still waiting for clearance from Brussels, however.

KLM and Northwest have anti-trust immunity in the US and BA and Qantas have clearance from the Australian authorities to co-operate closely. Those alliance partners which do not have regulatory clearance can co-operate to a more limited extent, as the Oneworld partners do: they can pool their frequent flyer programmes and share airport lounges, for example.

But joint purchasing requires no regulatory approval. So why haven't the alliances made more progress? "We've adjusted a lot of our IT systems," says Jurgen Weber, chairman of Lufthansa. "We're investing $100 million this year in common IT." The Star Alliance has appointed a full time co-ordinator for its purchasing teams. Mr Weber says the alliance has the potential to save $1 billion a year. He admits, however, that Star Alliance is at present achieving only a fraction of those savings.

Mr Weber prefers to talk about areas other than joint procurement. "The most important achievement of the Star Alliance is we provide seamless transport to our customers to more than 700 destinations in the world. This means we have co-ordinated our schedules. The second is we offer a joint mileage programme." This means that a frequent traveller regarded as a valuable customer by one alliance partner receives the same recognition from the others. "Another achievement is joint lounges at several hundred airports," Mr Weber says.

Robert Ayling, chief executive of BA, says: "I think there are two different things alliances can do on the cost side. The first is to plan activities together. With BA and Qantas, we have joint management in many parts of our network in Asia. If you go to Singapore, the BA manager is also the Qantas manager. He can spread his costs over a bigger operation."

"We can learn best practice from each other. We can clearly do that sort of thing in other markets." This is only possible, Mr Ayling says, in markets where partners do not compete or where one is overwhelmingly stronger than another. But the partners can co-operate where they are of more or less equal strength.

Like Star Alliance, Oneworld intends to invest in joint information technology systems. Mr Ayling says: "The next generation of IT technology will need huge investment. If that can be spread across eight companies rather than be borne by one that will be in everyone's interest. There would be one standard and much lower costs."

Of the possibility of the Oneworld partners buying aircraft jointly, Mr Ayling says: "It's possible, but it's not a priority." BA has just made a large purchase of Boeing 777 long-haul jets and Airbus single-aisle regional aircraft. BA might still buy short-haul jets with fewer than 100 seats, but Mr Ayling says he does not expect to make any further substantial aircraft orders during his time at BA.

So what are Oneworld's priorities? "We have four priorities," Mr Ayling says. "The first is our global frequent flyer programme. The second is our IT development cost savings. The third is sharing airport facilities, like lounges. The fourth is joint marketing, where we're free to do it."

Source: *Financial Times,* **1999**

Case Discussion Issues and Questions

1. Discuss the competitive dynamics of the international airlines according to the Porter model of industry analysis (Figures 4.2 and 4.3). In which force directions do the major factors lie?

2. Discuss the relative gains in competitiveness that accrue to the various participants.

3. Discuss the dynamics of the value chain(s) involved in these alliances. Who wins, who loses?

❖ ❖ ❖

The formulation of competitive strategy

Porter (1980) advocates that the aim of a competitive strategy should be to create a profitable and sustainable position in an industry against competitive forces by either defensive or offensive action.

The aim for any firm should be to develop a distinctive competence greater than its competitors. Distinctive competence is concerned with identifying those particular strengths that give the company an edge over its competitors and those areas of particular weaknesses which are to be avoided at all costs. Porter (1985) identifies *three generic strategies* for achieving above-average performance in an industry, as shown in Table 4.1.

Table 4.1 Competitive generic strategies

	Strategic advantage	
Strategic target	Uniqueness perceived by the customer	Low-cost position
Industry-wide	Differentiation *General Motors*	Cost leadership *Nissan*
Particular segment only	Differention Focus *Mercedes*	Cost Focus *Skoda*

Source: Adapted from Porter (1985).

Cost leadership. The aim of this strategy is to become the lowest cost producer in the industry. "If a firm can achieve and sustain overall cost leadership, then it will be an above-average performer in its industry provided it can command prices at or near the industry average. At equivalent or lower prices than its rivals, a cost leader's low-cost position translates into higher returns" (Porter, 1985). A cost leadership strategy does not mean that the company should ignore the bases of differentiation. In fact, this strategy to be successful must be based on a product that has to be perceived as comparable or acceptable by buyers, otherwise the cost leader will be forced to discount prices well below the competitors' to gain sales, thus eroding the benefits of its favourable cost position.

A low-cost producer must find and exploit all sources of cost advantage such as economies of scale, vertical integration and, in the international context, the sourcing of inputs and finished products from offshore locations.

There are, however, a number of potential vulnerabilities in the cost leadership strategy. In particular, if the firm's management concentrates on cost they may fail to perceive product or marketing changes and thus may fail to adapt their products and marketing strategies to meet shifting market requirements. Such marketing myopia may cause the firm to concentrate excessively upon what Drucker (1989) terms 'efficiency' (doing things right) rather than 'effectiveness' (doing the right thing).

Differentiation. In a differentiation strategy, a firm seeks to be unique in its industry along one or more dimensions valued by its customers. A differentiator aims at the ability to demand a price premium based on the perceived value added by differentiation. A firm that can achieve and sustain differentiation on its products will be an above-average performer in its industry if the extra costs incurred in being unique are lower than the price premium charged for the uniqueness. "A differentiator, therefore, must always seek ways of differentiating that lead to a price premium greater than the cost of differentiating" (Porter, 1985).

The means for differentiation are peculiar to each industry and can be based on the quality, design and sophistication of the product itself, the means of delivery or the 'image' of the product cultivated by brand advertising.

Again, Porter warns of certain risks associated with the differentiation strategy, for example, the price differential between low-cost competitors and the differentiated firm's product may become too great for differentiation to succeed in defending market share. Here buyers sacrifice some of the features; services or image possessed by the differentiated firm in return for large price savings.

Focus. The cost leadership and differentiation strategies generally seek competitive advantage across the whole industry while focus strategies aim at either a cost or a differentiation advantage, but within particular segments of the market. This strategy involves purposely selecting a narrow scope, with the focuser selecting one or a group of industry segments and tailoring its business to serving them to the exclusion of others. The intention is to achieve competitive advantage within target segments, despite having no overall competitive advantage.

Both variants, cost focus and differentiation focus, rely on the differences between the target segments and the other segments in the industry. The target segments must have buyers with special needs or else the production and distribution systems that best suit the target segments must differ from those of other industry segments. The focus strategy implies that the target segments are poorly served by broadly targeted competitors.

However, over time the cost differential between broad range competitors and the focuser may narrow to eliminate the cost advantages of serving a narrow target or the differences between the customer requirements of the market segment and those of the overall market may diminish.

Case 4.2

Keeping the competition guessing: World-class port bags S'pore quality award – first local MNC to win the Business Excellence award

If any company has reason to look back contentedly on its own achievements, then PSA Corporation must surely be one of them.

Here's a short sample of the multinational port operator's successes: it has been voted by shippers and shipping lines worldwide as the best terminal operator in Asia for 10 years. Singapore has also been voted the best seaport in Asia for 11 years. And last year, PSA handled 15.1 million 20-foot equivalent units (TEUs) at its container terminals here, making Singapore the world's number one container port, surpassing Hong Kong, Kaohsiung and Rottterdam.

Now, PSA has yet another feather to add to its cap. The company has just won the Singapore Quality Award (SQA) for Business Excellence – the first local multinational to do so in the award's five-year history.

However, PSA chairman Yeo Ning Hong is well acquainted with the dangers that come with being top dog. "We realise how human we all are – how vulnerable to complacency we can be," he told BT in an interview. "We deliberately stretch and push ourselves forward, so that we can avoid all the areas that lead us to become complacent."

It is this constant drive for improvement that has helped PSA win the SQA. Said Dr Yeo: "We are already a world-class port and we want to go beyond that. Our goal is to become a world-class company with a network of ports and related business all over the globe."

Winning the SQA represents another milestone in PSA's efforts to become a company recognised internationally for its quality service, he said.

One of the keys to PSA's success lies in the attitude the company adopts towards its employees. "We believe that every one of our workers, given the opportunity, has the ability to be creative and make a contribution to the success of the organisation," said Dr Yeo.

He said PSA strives to create an environment conducive for employees to participate in productivity programmes. The company must be doing something right: Since 1996, the staff participation rate in quality circles has been sustained at 100 per cent. Even the workers at the lowest level are not neglected. Supervisors speak with these workers regularly to find out about their ideas for improvement, Dr Yeo said.

PSA, whose employees take part in over 600 quality circles, also has a staff suggestion scheme which has enjoyed a 98-per cent participation rate since the start of this year. In addition, the company has a 'waste-busters' programme which looks for ways to cut wastage within the company. Dr Yeo noted that these three programmes help PSA save more than $18 million a year.

To sustain the success of its staff involvement programmes, PSA spends a fair bit of money to train its employees. For the past three years, PSA has invested an average of $16 million a year or 4 per cent of its annual payroll – on staff upgrading. "Continuous improvements to our workforce means continuous improvements to the organisation," said Dr Yeo. "Better trained workers are more productive and also more confident in coming up with new ideas for improvement."

Beside PSA's efforts to boost productivity internally, the company also places a lot of emphasis on being customer-oriented. "We keep in touch with our customers and communicate with them at every level to make sure that we know what they want," said Dr Yeo.

Every year, Dr Yeo leads a delegation of senior executives to the headquarters of PSA's major customers worldwide. "This is to hear from them first-hand about their needs and strategies, as well as to find out how PSA can meet their requirements," he said.

PSA's co-operation with its customers extends to the nitty-gritty operational details too. In 1990, the company pioneered the concept of joint quality circles with its customers, suppliers and external agencies to effect work improvements and increase productivity for its business partners. Last year, PSA saved its customers about $4.5 million, said Dr Yeo.

To provide faster and more personalised service to its customers, PSA's senior port operations managers act as 'key customer managers' to look after customers' needs. Customers need only deal with their key customer manager to arrange for all their requirements to be met. Said Dr Yeo: "We exist to serve our customers. Ultimately, they are our employers."

The port operator's commitment to its customers was clearly shown during last year's economic turmoil. Although PSA handled 7 per cent more container volume in 1998, overall revenue growth was flat because the company gave substantial rebates to all its customers to help them lower their operating costs. Last November, PSA announced another package of rebates, totalling $25 million on various cargo-handling and rental charges for the whole of 1999.

Indeed, PSA, which was corporatised in October 1997, has much to be proud of. Now with the SQA under its belt, what are the company's plans?

Striking a blow at complacency, Dr Yeo said: "Our plans are never to rest on our laurels. We want to keep running, moving and getting better. At the end of the day, it is what our customers say about us that matters the most."

Source: *The Business Times*, **23 July 1999**

Case Discussion Issues and Questions

1. Discuss the strategies that PSA is pursuing. How does PSA drive its competitiveness?

2. Analyse the inherent challenges in internationalising a business such as a port.

3. Suggest strategic options for PSA to follow in the future.

Global competitive strategies: Some notable examples

Cost leadership. BBA, the UK multinational, recently reorganised itself to establish a more tightly focused group, all of whose businesses are expected to conform to one of two criteria. They must be either substantial and efficient competitors in the global marketplace or companies which occupy strong positions in specialist markets where they can earn above-average margins.

The company is a leading supplier of automotive components, particularly disc pads, brakes and clutches. Global sourcing of components by multinational vehicle assemblers has increased competition between suppliers to win "more new car business on price and technology. The consolidation of buying power is pressing on our and our competitors' profit margins" (Group Chief Executive, *Annual Report 1994*). This has forced suppliers to reduce costs, improve productivity and invest heavily in new machinery and new facilities to remain price competitive. BBA has set itself a target of achieving an average margin on sales of 10% on its components business. A first priority has been to reduce the cost of labour.

The company aims to reduce the total size of its workforce by a tenth – around 2,000 people from all levels of the organisation. Payroll costs were reduced to £46 million in 1994. The job losses were mainly in BBA's European operations, where the combination of relatively high wages and generous welfare provisions had made labour costs 'excessive'. Uncompetitive operations or plants with excess capacity (such as the company's Belgian and Dutch plants) were closed and production transferred to more efficient plants in the UK, Germany and Spain. In Spain, one of three plants was closed down while BBA's Canadian friction materials plant, with high production costs, was closed and production transferred to a new green-field plant in the US with lower production costs.

New investments have also helped reduce costs. At the Borg and Beck brake subsidiary in the UK, for example, the introduction of cellular manufacturing has increased productivity by two-thirds. BBA's Italian clutch subsidiary recently inaugurated a £2 million automated assembly line. The new machinery, which incorporates 14 industrial robots and eight electronic control points and can be operated by only three people per shift, enables production to be switched rapidly between the 23 different 'families' of clutch required by local customers.

Differentiation.   Nestlé, the Swiss multinational, pioneered the UK soluble coffee market in 1949 with the introduction of Nescafe. Over the years it has added to its brand portfolio and is represented in all the main market segments. General Foods, a subsidiary of Kraft of the US, entered the UK market in 1947 by acquiring a UK supplier, A. Bird. In 1954 it launched its main US brand, Maxwell House, in the UK and has become a full range supplier. Brooke Bond is a subsidiary of Anglo-Dutch group, Unilever. The company does not offer a speciality brand. Coffee brands are differentiated by product quality, by product formulation (whether they are regular versions of the product or decaffeinated) and by media advertising and promotions (Table 4.2).

Table 4.2   Coffee brands – differentiation profiles

Sector brands	Nestlé brands	General Foods brands	Brooke Bond brands
Economy	Nescafé Fine Blend	Birds Mellow	Choice
Quality	Nescafé Maxwell House	Master Blend	Café Mountain
Premium	Nescafé Gold Blend Nescafé Blend 37	Café Hag Kenco	Red Mountain
Speciality	Nescafé Cap Colombie Nescafé Alta Rica	Café Hag Select	

Cost focus. Cott Corporation, the Canadian specialist own-label soft drinks supplier, has taken on the giants of the cola world, Coca-Cola and PepsiCo. In Canada, Cott produces Presidents Choice for food retail chain Loblaws, the company's own-label cola brand. A 750 ml bottle of Presidents Choice cola sells for 49 cents, compared with 79 cents for Coca-Cola and Pepsi.

Cott has signed supply agreements with 90 retail chains around the world, including Wal-Mart, the largest US food retailer, J. Sainsbury, the UK's second largest food retailer and Continenta, the Spanish food chain. Sainsbury's Classic Cola was launched in April 1994 and quickly took over store leadership from Coca-Cola and Pepsi. Cott expanded its Canadian canning and bottling plant to service its American customers. In the UK, Cott took a 51% stake in an established canner and bottler, which it supplies with a range of specially prepared concentrate to be made up into particular customised own-label products. Cott has also signed up Cadbury-Schweppes (which bottles Coca-Cola in the UK) to bottle its drinks in continental Europe.

As a cost-focuser Cott has two main advantages over PepsiCo and Coca-Cola. Firstly, its marketing and advertising expenses are minimal by comparison. By providing retailers with their own-label brands, Cott has no need to spend millions of pounds on promoting a national brand. Secondly, Cott piggybacks on retailers' centralised warehouse and distribution facilities. The same supermarket trucks that carry products from warehouses to stores bring Cott soft drinks from the bottler back to the warehouse.

Coca-Cola and PepsiCo have responded to Cott's challenge in North America both by lowering wholesale prices and widening retailers' margins and by putting even more money behind promoting their brands in the hope that product differentiation advantages will 'offset' differentials.

Differentiation focus. ICI, the UK chemical multinational, 'succeeds by understanding what customers want and being fast on its feet to meet their needs'.

- In Japan, household baths have traditionally been made of stainless steel. Realising that consumers wanted something new and different, Japanese bath producers such as Matsushita Denko and Cleanup Corporation saw a market opportunity based on new materials that ICI was to introduce to Japan. Working closely with its customers, ICI developed a new formulation of Asterlite artificial marble. "We chose Asterlite because it offered design flexibility and an excellent range of colours and textures. These features helped us to develop our own unique products" (Kyoichi Inoue, President, Cleanup Corporation, Japan). ICI also provided technical assistance to help its customers switch their manufacturing to the new material.

Motors in 1990, without which SAAB might have had to exit the automobile business. Another example pertinent to Asia is Shinawatra of Thailand forming a strategic alliance with SingTel of Singapore to provide paging services to Thailand.)

3. Remain

The business is *peripheral* in the firm's overall business portfolio but the firm is the market *leader* in their particular business. In this case strategic alliances can be used to consolidate the firm's leading position in the sector particularly, in situations when the parent firm is not prepared itself to fully back non-core activities. (Lorange *et al.* cite the example of Ericsson's 1989 strategic alliance with General Electric in the cellular radio field.)

4. Restructure

The business is *peripheral* in the firm's overall business portfolio and a *market follower* in this particular business. In this case strategic alliances can be used not only to improve the competitive position of the firm in its sector but also increase its relative importance in the firm's overall business portfolio (Lorange *et al.* cite the example of Bulten, the once ailing fasteners subsidiary of the Kantinal Group.)

In the view of Lorange *et al.* "the parents' desires regarding input and output resources are the basic determinants of the type of strategic alliance a firm is going to enter into." Resources committed typically include physical, human, financial and organisational elements and may be provided on a limited or extensive basis; output considerations include the extent of value added generated and how the output of the alliance is to be shared between two partners. Lorange *et al.* identify four main types of strategic alliances determined according to the parents' input of resources and parents' retrieval of output, as shown in Figure 4.6.

Figure 4.6 Archetypes of joint ventures and strategic alliances

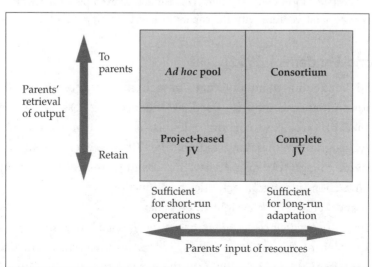

There are four types of strategic alliances:

1. *Ad hoc* **pool**

   The characteristic feature of this form of alliance is the commitment of a minimal set of complementary resources, usually over a temporary basis, with all of the output (profit, know-how, etc.) accruing to the parents. (Lorange *et al.* cite the example of ship owners who pool their ships in a time charter agreement.)

2. **Consortium**

   In this form of alliance parents put in more resources than in an *ad hoc* pool but with all of the output still accruing to the parents. A good example of this is provided by joint researchers development alliances. Each partner subscribes its technologies, facilities and scientists, with any output (scientific discoveries, new product ideas, etc.) being disbursed back to the parents.

3. **Project-based joint venture**

   The characteristic feature of this form of alliance is the commitment by the parents of a minimal set of input resources into a common organisation 'the child', but the main output is retained by the child with the parents receiving a financial return (dividends, royalties, etc.). Lorange *et al.* suggest that this form of alliance is particularly useful as a means of facilitating an initial toe-hold entry into foreign markets.

4. **Complete joint venture**

   In this form of alliance the parents provide a substantial input of resources but again with most of the output being retained by the alliance itself with the parents receiving a financial return. Lorange *et al.* cite, by way of example, the case of the Swedish firms ESAB and AGA which set up a joint-venture concern, GCE, pooling their resources in the wedding, the merging of the transportation divisions of GEC and Alcatel to form GEC Alsthom. This is another example of the establishment of a focused joint venture with the capabilities of becoming a global player.

Urban and Vendemini (1992)

Urban and Vendemini point out that strategic alliances, or to use their term 'co-operative alliances', may be used to enhance business effectiveness and performance of three key corporate levels: *activity* (for example, product, technology, geographical area targeted); *function* (that is, every operation the firm has to provide to carry out an activity); and *company*, responsible for organising, directing and co-ordinating all activities and functions.

Urban and Vendemini highlight three generic forms of co-operative alliances between firms: *Adaptation co-operation*, based on the need to ensure a competitive position for each of the firm's activities; *functional co-operation*, justified by the quest for an essential congruity between the various functions within an activity and at company levels; *co-ordinated co-operation*, suggested by the congruity of the combination of activities within a company (p. 91). These concepts are analysed by Urban and Vendemini in the particular context of how firms might adjust to the formation of the Single European Market.

1. **Adaptation co-operation**

   Adaptation co-operation is aimed at increasing the competitiveness of a firm at the level of the activity, both by facilitating access to supply quantitative positions (increasing supply capacity and improving market share) and better qualitative positions (control, development and acquisition of key factors of success). "Consequently, adaptation co-operation is aimed especially at accelerating the development skills (sales and distribution) and of upstream skills (technology)." (p. 123).

   Co-operative agreements in the area of sales and distribution offer one means of entering foreign markets and increasing market penetration. It may be preferred to the use of market intermediaries (e.g., export agents) and a direct siting when alliance partners can offer comprehensive and deep market coverage in local marketing expertise. Urban and Vendemini suggest that in the face of growing costs of funding technological developments and the shortening of technological life cycles, collaboration between alliances that offers firms a means of sharing development costs is becoming increasingly significant.

2. **Functional co-operation**

   Functional co-operation seeks to reduce the cost of one or more functions within an activity and within the firm, or a whole set of functions can be performed as a standalone operation in respect of a simple activity or a function may be shared between several activities. Urban and Vendemini suggest that alliances with partners provide scope for potential cost reductions in all functional areas of a business. Some examples include purchasing (joint purchases of supplies, common external logistics, routing of supplies) technology (joint development work); production process (joint manufacture, specialisation and pooling of components for common assembly), and distribution and sales (shared customers, combined sales force, joint penetration of a new market).

3. **Co-ordinated co-operation**

   Co-ordinated co-operation occurs in the range of activities undertaken by a firm which can be narrowly focused (specialisation) or comprehensive (diversification), and is aimed at enabling firms to expand within their current activities (or to adjust to changed circumstances within that activity) or to develop new activities. In the case of specialisation, Urban and Vendemini suggest that alliances provide one important route to increased capabilities by, for example, sharing R&D work, reducing investment costs and avoiding duplication and competition between investment projects.

In the case of diversification, in particular 'linked' diversification (when a firm is able to use its existing expertise to develop other activities), Urban and Vendemini suggest that collaboration can reduce the investment entry fee to a new activity and by providing scope for blending together complementary competencies provide a platform for the development of innovative new products.

Urban and Vendemini identify 11 main forms of co-operative agreements. The 11 forms of co-operative agreements are:

1. *Research contract* in which one firm pays some other firm to undertake research on its behalf. This can help a firm access new ideas and enjoy economies on in-house research work.

2. *Joint research agreement* in which participants collaborate in specified research work. Such collaborations can reduce costs, achieve alliance critical mass and cross-fertilise each other's technologies.

3. *Joint purchasing agreement* in which firms combine their purchasing power in order to achieve better procurement terms (especially bulk buying discounts).

4. *Sub-contracting agreements* in which one firm contracts some other firm to undertake part of a production and/or service process units on its behalf. This can save on the need to initial in-house capacity and access the skills and competencies of the contracted firm.

5. *Engineering contract* in which a firm contracts some other firms to provide particular services covering the start-up installation of various types of industrial plant and equipment. Again this type allows a firm to access the superior know-how and expertise of specialists.

6. *Joint manufacturing agreement* in which firms undertake to participate in the manufacture of one or more specified products, either using a common unit of production or each firm specialising in a particular production task. This can lower production costs by enabling economies of scale to be achieved and also to undertake a costly manufacturing process that the firms cannot undertake alone.

7. *Patent licence* in which one firm assigns the rights to a patented technology, product, etc., to some other firms in return for the payment of royalties. Such licences may include clauses that require that licensees who make improvements to the original technology or product make the advances available to the licensor. This aspect may be underscored by a cross-licensing agreement whereby each party shares technical advances.

8. *Trademark licence* in which one firm, the trade-mark holder, permits some other firms to use it in return for a fee. In some cases the trade-mark licence is the main element around which a more extensive co-operation is built as, for example, in franchising.

9. *Agreement for the communication of expertise* is a so-called 'knowledge agreement' in which the holder of the rights to a process passes on his expertise to some other firm which assists it to manufacture a product or provide a service. Again, as with licences and trade-marks, co-operation provides access to a wide pool of technology, etc., than can be achieved solely from in-house efforts.

10. *Consortium agreement* in which the firms undertake joint marketing of their products. This can be particularly effective in penetrating foreign markets in the case of first-time entrants who can ally with established local or foreign firms in the target market.

11. *Distribution contract* in which one firm undertakes the physical distribution of some other firms' product and making available itself or contracts retailing to provide points of sale. Such distribution arrangements can provide wide market coverage and in the case of foreign markets, distributors can use their local knowledge and contacts to enhance sales potential.

CASE 4.3

Seizing the market: Nippon Mining agrees to join LG Metals in copper venture

In early 1999, Japan's Nippon Mining & Metals Co and South Korea's troubled LG Metals Corp reached a basic agreement for LG Metals to split off its copper operations and transfer them to a joint venture to be set up in Korea by both companies.

Nippon Mining signed a memorandum of understanding with LG Metals a day earlier; the agreement valued the copper operations at $638 million.

LG Metals said it would sell its copper smelting and refining plants in Onsan and Changhang to the joint venture for $638 million after due diligence by Nippon Mining.

The working capital of the two plants will also be handed over to the joint venture as additional charges, LG Metals said.

A consortium of Nippon Mining, Mitsui Mining & Smelting Co and Marubeni Corp will have a 50% stake in the joint venture, while the Korean side will also have a 50% stake.

LG Metals will merge with LG Industrial Systems Co on April 1.

LG Metals and Nippon Mining said that after due diligence they expect a contract to be formally signed in the middle of this year.

LG Metals said that as a result of the alliance with Nippon Mining, the two companies will produce a total of 900,000 tons of copper cathode per year, comparable to the production of the world's largest copper smelter, Chile's Corporacion Nacional del Cobre de Chile or Codelco.

The joint venture will be the only copper smelting and refining company in Korea.

LG Metals said it has been in talks with Nippon Mining since October 1998 as the Korean company suffered losses due to the depreciation of the won, economic turmoil in

Korea and financial burden from construction of a plant.

Nippon Mining proposed in January 1999 that a joint venture take over the copper smelting and refining operations of LG Metals.

LG Metals said it chose Nippon Mining as a partner because of its competitiveness in the copper business and its close location to Korea. It said the alliance will help LG Metals restart its business with a 'greatly enhanced financial structure and improved cutting-edge production technology'.

Both companies said they expect to benefit from synergies in such areas as raw-material procurement, production, research and development and overseas sales.

Nippon Mining is Japan's largest copper producer and a world player in the nonferrous metals industry. LG Metals is a nonferrous metal-smelting and base-materials company.

Source: *The Asian Wall Street Journal*, **3 March 1999**

Case Discussion Issues and Questions

1. Analyse the industry competitive factors driving the proposed joint venture. To what extent is the co-operation a viable solution? Describe the Korean copper industry dynamics after the joint venture.

2. Discuss the competitive strategy inherent in the joint venture. In which category does it fit?

3. Analyse the source of resources for the joint-venture partners. To what extent are they sustainable?

Porter and Fuller (1986)

Porter and Fuller identify two distinct forms of strategic alliances which they categorise as X-type and Y-type coalitions. In X-type coalitions activities are divided between the partners, whereas in Y-type coalition activities are shared. These two types involve various forms of co-operations, the most common being the technology-, marketing- and production-based ones.

The form of collaboration and the strategic objectives underlying co-operation between companies may vary substantially. Technology-based co-operation is aimed at reducing the costs and sharing the risks associated with technology development. In pooling of R&D and/or technology, transfer between the partners is involved. In marketing-based co-operation the main objective is to gain market access through using local marketing expertise and distribution channels and other marketing and sales and service facilities. Production-based co-operation is aimed at improving manufacturing and production efficiency through sales and/or learning benefits, transferring manufacturing know-how, joint purchasing and taking advantage of country specific comparative advantage (for example, cheap labour).

In X-type coalitions, value-adding activities such as production, marketing and technology are divided with one partner undertaking one value activity and the other partner performing some other value activity. Porter and Fuller cite by way of example the alliance between US concern AT&T and Dutch company Philips in the area of telephone exchange switching equipment. AT&T was seeking a partner to market its innovative digital public-exchange systems in foreign markets where it had never previously been sold. Philips, which had market contacts in a number of countries, was in need of a digital public-exchange system to update its product line which had hitherto been based on mechanical switching systems. By the alliance, AT&T gained immediate market access in a number of countries and Philips gained immediate access to digital technology.

In X-type coalitions, the fact that complementary activities in manufacturing new technologies and product are shared and access to other countries, distribution channels and market are secured, can provide competitive advantages rapidly to a company against global rivals. The need for vertical integration or to strengthen a weak link in a company's value-adding activities makes X-type alliance particularly attractive. Companies that find themselves weak in manufacturing, for example, often resort to this type of coalition to compensate for an inability to make a product or the high expense of local production (Lei, 1989).

In Y-type coalitions the partners share the performance of one or more value-adding activities such as joint R&D production, marketing and purchasing. This option is common where a partner seeks the other partner's technology or production skills. The motives are risk sharing and pooling of resources to achieve economies of scale and learning curve advantages. By facilitating the cross-fertilisation of technology and new product development, Y-type coalitions can provide particular scope for establishing competitive advantages over rival suppliers. For example, in 1992 IBM of the US, Toshiba of Japan and Siemens of Germany formed a joint venture to develop advanced computer memory chips for the twenty-first century. In recent years the number of such international alliances has increased dramatically as firms sought a 'global position' in pursuing economies of scale and scope and market penetration.

Potential benefits and drawbacks of strategic alliances.   In this section, we will discuss various possible benefits of strategic alliances and draw attention to problems associated with alliances.

of strategic alliances include the following:

cases and shared production in others, can enable firms to achieve the volumes necessary to take advantage of economies of scale in procurement through bulk buying, discounts through cost savings in research and product development, in production by centralised assembly operations and distributions through the use of common logistic systems and the wider and deeper international marketing of joint products (Jain, 1987). The pursuit of economies of scale in the key areas of production and marketing can be of critical importance in remaining globally competitive (Porter, 1986).

2. **Technology development**

   Greater technological complexity encourages collaborative efforts since few companies can control all elements of technology internally. Through alliances, companies can contribute their experience in producing separate parts of components or jointly developing them to make a product, thus enhancing their technology and product competencies. Cross-fertilisation and exchange of technology between partners can lead to the emergence of new technologies in products. Companies can have a quick access to technological, production and product know-how which take a long time to develop by going it alone or may even be impossible to generate internally. In fast changing industries speed can be a critical factor in remaining globally competitive (Porter, 1986).

3. **Costs and risk reduction**

   Strategic alliances that allow pooling of resources and sharing of risks enable partners to undertake projects beyond the separate capabilities of either party. In the commercial field, a new global car model can cost up to US$2 billion to develop and establish manufacturing facilities; a new semiconductor wafer design and fabrication plant can cost beyond US$2 billion, and a new telecom switching system can cost up to US$1 billion to research and develop. Similarly, in the defence-related fields new weapons that have the potential for global sales cost billions of US dollars to design, research and develop. Costs and risks on this scale can put a severe strain on a company's internal resources and put a question mark over its very survival if a new product proves unsuccessful in the market against competition. Thus, it is no coincidence that strategic alliances are gaining prominence in fields such as pharmaceuticals, computers, telecommunications and automobiles when the pace of technological advance is fast, product life-cycles are shortening, and wide and deep international marketing is an imperative to maximise profit streams (Lei, 1989).

4. **Sharing competition**

   Alliances between firms operating in the same product area can reduce competition. Alternatively, they may enable collaborating firms to embrace new technologies, develop new products and enter new markets, thus increasing the competitive strength of the partners.

5. **Neo-protectionism**

The increasing 'regionalisation' of international trade is evident with the formation of various trade blocs. The most significant, the European Union, the North American Fee Trade Agreement and in Asia the progress of the Association of Southeast Asian Nations (ASEAN) towards an ASEAN Free Trade Area and ASEAN Investment Area, have encouraged the establishment of alliances between 'outsiders' and 'insiders' in order that firms from non-member countries can secure market access. Alliances enable outsiders to breach the 'fortress' and adjust to changing internal conditions (for example, the harmonisation of technical standards, packaging requirements within the European Union under the Single European Market initiative).

6. **Learning experience and skill building**

Partners can learn from each other and strengthen links in their own value-adding activities. Companies can obtain access to new technologies and products and develop new core skills. Collaboration provides an opportunity to internalise the other partner's skills and capitalise upon them to enhance the firm's own 'best practice' (Doz and Prahalad, 1989). Additionally, strategic learning allows knowledge of what competitors are doing and understanding of their corporate culture and likely competitive responses.

CASE 4.4

Searching for excellence: Toyota car maker seeks technology alliances

Toyota Motor will seek technical alliances with companies to gain access to technologies that have proved difficult for it to develop on its own, according to Fujo Cho, the car maker's new president.

Japan's largest car maker is ready to do deals with companies with which it does not have alliances already, Mr Cho told the *Financial Times* in one of his first interviews since replacing Hiroshi Okuda as president in June.

"Toyota, Daihatsu (an affiliated car maker that specialises in mini-cars) and Hino (the truck maker) will run the core business together. But as far as development of environmental technologies is concerned, this will become an extremely important issue for global car makers, including Toyota. It will become necessary to have various technologies.

"Right now, we have alliances with companies like GM and Exxon, but if there were the need for other technologies in the future, we would tie up with other companies," he added. Toyota also has a non-capital alliance with Volkswagen.

Mr Cho declined to specify which areas had been identified as potential candidates for an alliance. However, Toyota officials said Mr Cho had mentioned batteries and fuel-related technology as areas for co-operation with a non-car maker. Tsuyoshi Mochimaru, analyst at Dresdner Kleinwort Benson, said diesel engines was another area where Toyota might need a partner.

Environmental technologies, such as fuel cells, electric vehicles and low-emission engines, are among the critical areas of research for car makers in order to meet stiffer emissions regulations in the future.

While cash-rich Toyota has avoided equity alliances, the car maker has linked with General Motors for joint development of electric, hybrid and fuel cell vehicles and Volkswagen for intelligent transportation systems, recycling and marketing. It also has a tie-up with Panasonic EV Energy for batteries.

Mr Cho said recently that Toyota was studying the feasibility of expanding its relationship with Volkswagen to include joint parts purchasing and development.

Toyota was also considering expanding its credit operations, an area Ford Motor has cultivated as part of its effort to be [a] consumer services company, but that has been slower to develop in Japan.

Mr Cho said: "There are many car-related businesses – customer finance, car monthly payments, car insurance and credit car – and we are already doing a little bit in these areas. In the future, I think we will need to do a bit more in car-related businesses."

Source: *Financial Times*, wysiwyg://11/http://www.ft.com/hippocampus/q11a3e6.htm

Case Discussion Issues and Questions

1. Analyse the rationale underlying Toyota's strategic decision. Suggest potential alliance partners.

2. Discuss the competitiveness Toyota stands to gain from its decision. What are the specific implications of the options under consideration?

3. Suggest reasons why Toyota has avoided equity alliances to date.

The following potential drawbacks to strategic alliances have been identified by Jain (1987) and Porter (1986). Some of these are discussed further in the next section on Formation and Management of Strategic Alliances.

1. **Insufficient contribution by partners**
   Strategic alliances involve mutual dependency whereby each partner is dependent on the other's contributions and inputs, including commitment and motivation. This aspect could give rise to difficulties if one partner's contribution is insufficient or, to put in terms of game theory, 'defective'.

2. **Outcome uncertainty**
   Most strategic alliances are established as long-term projects. As such, results are difficult to predict. Uncertainty about the outcome makes it difficult to compare the

value of strategic alliances against the alternatives available, such as, for example, a wholly-owned operation.

3. **Big requirements on management time and effort**

Strategic alliances by their very nature tend to be costly in terms of top management's time and effort. Finding which strategic alliance and negotiating mutually beneficial agreements can be protracted while, operationally, shared decision-making can be a slow process and subject to conflicts.

4. **High co-ordination costs**

Co-ordination costs refer to the time and effort involved in managing divergent interests between alliance partners and attempting to integrate coalition activities into the broader global strategies of each company. These costs can be substantial as more careful and close co-ordination will be necessary in cases where partners do not trust each other's long-term motives. However, co-ordination costs may fall over time as partners gain experience in working with each other and trust is established and developed.

5. **Conflict between partners**

There is the risk of conflict and disagreements over major decisions, distribution of benefits, allocation of inputs, etc. The need to compromise decisions may impair the efficiency of the alliance and possibly undermine the whole venture. Due to asymmetries (resources, information, managerial, etc.) partners to the coalition may find themselves in an adverse bargaining position with respect to each other. This is especially so if one partner, due to its specialised or irreplaceable contribution, attempts to dominate the venture to achieve its own specific strategic objectives. Furthermore, communication and interpersonal problems can arise. In international strategic alliances there is the risk of misunderstanding as a result of language differences and socio-cultural barriers.

6. **Erosion of competitive position**

In an alliance there is the potential of dissipating sources of competitive advantage and undermining industry structure. Either new competitors may be created or existing competitions may become more formidable through the transference of expertise such as the provision of market access. A partner may enter an alliance with the strategic interests of global industry leadership, using the alliance as a stepping stone in the process of building, adding and laying sources of competitive advantage. According to Doz and Prahalad (1989), Japanese companies in particular have used networks of joint ventures and strategic alliances to improve their global competitive positions. Somewhat cynically they suggest that many Japanese companies form alliances in order to take over their partners' core skills, ultimately pushing partners into a position of dependency.

Case 4.5

Between dependence and independence: Japan Airlines doesn't plan to join alliance

Japan Airlines doesn't plan to joint the fledgling Oneworld alliance of airlines because doing so might jeopardize profitable bilateral agreements it has with carriers outside the group, a spokesman said.

The Oneworld alliance was formed in February and includes British Airways, AMR Corp's American Airlines, Canadian Airlines, Cathay Pacific Airways, Qantas Airways, Finnair and Iberia.

JAL already has separate agreements with American Airlines, British Airways and Cathay Pacific to sell seats or cargo space on one another's flights, an arrangement known as code-sharing. Airline executives have speculated that JAL would soon join Oneworld. But JAL also has code-sharing deals with a number of other airlines, including three members of the rival Star Alliance grouping – Thai Airways International, Lufthansa and SAS.

"We already have our own little world," said JAL spokesman Geoffrey Tudor.

Mr Tudor said the airline wasn't completely ruling out the possibility of someday joining a group such as Oneworld. He said executives at JAL are waiting to see how exclusivity clauses in the agreements might affect JAL's ability to strike separate deals of its own. "It's easier to see where the benefits are for each party with a bilateral alliance," he said.

Source: *The Asian Wall Street Journal*, **2 March 1999**

Case Discussion Issues and Questions

1. Analyse the competitive dynamics of the international airline business. What are the major factors driving competitive strategy?

2. Given the avowed advantages and benefits of strategic alliances, discuss reasons for Japan Airlines' reluctance to exploit potential gains. Is the company justified in its decision?

3. Discuss the dangers in the strategic alliances depicted.

❖ ❖ ❖

4.6 THE FORMATION AND MANAGEMENT OF STRATEGIC ALLIANCES

Strategic alliances as we have noted in the previous section can offer partners many *initial* advantages. However, the mutual forebearance inherent in alliances means that turning potential into performance is not always a straightforward affair. Selecting the right partner is absolutely critical; holding the relationships

the potential benefits. An emphasis on control through equity can poison the relationship (Ohmae, 1989). It can deter development of inter-company management skills, which are critical for success in today's global environment. The attitude is not who is to control whom, but to work together successfully. Therefore caution must be exercised in this aspect of control in an alliance.

In joint ventures, key issues are the structure of the board and who should have control. It has been found in practice that, where management of the venture is dominated by one partner or is independent of both partners, the chances of success are much greater than if both partners are involved in day-to-day management. The reason is that when two sets of management are involved, many decisions get referred to the respective boards. This alone slows down the decision-making process and stifles initiative. If the two boards have different corporate cultures and styles, which affect the speed of reaction and information requirements, the result can be disastrous.

The essence of an alliance is 'You win and I win'. Lynch (1989) and Lorange and Roos (1992) emphasise that successful alliances are built on the fundamental premise that all the partners must be winners. Without the presence of this condition, no strategic plan, no formal agreement and no operational schedule will overcome such a fundamental deficiency. A partner that believes it is losing will not perform well and may eventually undermine the alliance itself. The win-win condition means an equitable share of benefits, arising from the relationship. Dominant partners can be tempted to expropriate much of synergistic benefits, arguing that they control or determine the overall success of the alliance. For the win-win condition to be realised, good management of the alliance is crucial.

Good management in this instance is difficult to generalise about. Both large and small corporations can develop strong cultures. Today national characteristics may be blurred but are still highly differentiated. Companies with differing competencies increasingly find themselves working together, the perceptions of those involved differ, etc. Many alliance and joint-venture failures have been due to strong and incompatible cultures. All such factors mean that specific alliances vary greatly. This must be appreciated and management should adopt a sensitive and self-aware approach in handling other participants. Commitment is another crucial element. Many alliances have failed because of lack of commitment. This aspect is even more crucial when Western and Japanese companies are involved because of socio-cultural differences. The lack of commitment from the Western partner is a major complaint from the Japanese side (Turpin, 1993). A further important element is organisational learning. Both partners have to learn from each other in order to see that they are gaining from the venture. Again in the case of Japan, many alliances have failed because the learning opportunities that a joint venture can bring were either not understood or poorly exploited by the Western partner (Doz and Prahalad, 1989).

As an aid to managing alliances, Devlin and Bleackley (1988) defined some very general guidelines indicating management issues and commitment, as follows:

1. Clearly defined goals and objectives
2. Allocation of sufficient resources to alliance
3. Allocation of accountability and responsibility
4. Transfer of key people to partnership
5. Enhance career prospects of alliance employees
6. Monitor progress of alliance
   - Regular reporting
   - Revision of alliance agreement
   - Duration of alliance
7. Recognise limits of alliance

Defining objectives and communicating them within all partner and alliance type structures are critical. Objectives have to be clearly defined in measurable terms. An example follows. A and B companies establish a joint venture in 1990 to use A's patented laser technology and B's proprietary instrumentation and process control systems to manufacture and market laser welding systems for the precision-tool industry with the intention of capturing 25% of the market by 1995 at a 15% pre-tax profit margin.

In addition, staff involved in the venture have to understand the intent of the venture and accept the possibility of conflicting responsibilities. This issue of loyalty has to be tackled by all companies and individuals involved.

Sufficient resources, money and people must be devoted to the venture. It is regarded as any other investment, with cash flows and cash requirements projected, discounted, and decisions based on acceptable investment criteria. High-quality staff should be committed as they are the eyes-and-ears of their respective organisations and must be sophisticated enough to ensure that goals are achieved and consistent. Diplomatic skills are especially important in international partnerships. Those working in the alliance should have their career prospects enhanced and not as a sideways move. The new setting is a dynamic one, with challenge, a mix of loyalties and cultures. Teamwork is necessary and vital. Personnel should be kept long term. The reason Japanese firms have managed to learn more from alliances than their Western partners is because they keep their personnel long term in the alliances, so as to observe and learn key skills from their partners. This provides an opportunity to form a critical mass of knowledge. In conclusion, the people involved have to be well equipped and be responsible to manage the venture for the long term.

In the area of responsibility and accountability, allocation of work has to be appropriate and accountable. One necessity to make alliances work is a shift from a focus on return on investment (ROI) to a focus on return on sales (ROS). This means that managers will concern themselves with the ongoing business benefits of the alliance and not just wait for a healthy return on their initial investment. Employees will have to be responsible for not giving out too much information to their alliance counterparts as well.

A proactive management kept informed through high levels of contact (formal and informal); formal reporting and regular monitoring are vital. Apart from ensuring that the venture follows the agreed and prescribed path, management needs to monitor goal achievement and any tendency towards unintended dependencies. Regular reporting will keep management informed, allowing awareness of how the alliance is going. While there may be problems, management must not forget the benefits involved as well. Understanding of this kind enables sustained enthusiasm and persistence, which are required for success in alliances. In summary, it is the people involved, their actions, attitudes and commitments, that will make or break an alliance.

In conjunction with the step-by-step recommendations above, the following general guidelines developed by Doz and Prahalad (1989) for managing effective strategic alliances should be borne in mind:

1. Partnerships are second best solutions and, therefore, should be entered into carefully and limited to situations where they are clearly needed.

2. Partnerships are strategic. Therefore, managers should be careful that seemingly sensible decisions that maximise results in the short run do not undermine their competitiveness in the long term.

3. Partnerships are dynamic with active management, in a clear strategic context, being as important as initial negotiations and contractual provisions. Active management is essential to prevent strategic encroachment.

4. Partnerships should be closely monitored by top management for signs of drift in unplanned directions.

5. Partners should constantly replenish their inventory of core skills which will increase the value of their contribution and, therefore, their bargaining power within the partnership.

6. Partners should regulate the flow of their contribution in order not to contribute too little (which may result in coalition failure) or too much (which may result in an imbalance in contributions).

7. The partner's organisation should be made more receptive to the venture in order to successfully assimilate and use the new knowledge obtained.

4.7 CONCLUSION

As a result of the emergence of global markets and global competitors, stimulated by a global liberalisation of trade and capital movements for investments, many firms have found it necessary for both defensive and opportunistic reasons to internationalise their operations. The formation of various regional trade blocs such as the European Union and the North American Free Trade Agreement, which contain elements of discrimination against non-members and hence potential protectionism, have also encouraged firms to position themselves within these areas to remain market competitive. Rapid changes in technology and the need to take full advantage of a wide and deep market coverage to amortise large R&D expenditures and shortening product life-cycles have fuelled the inter-nationalisation movement. Many firms in a whole range of industries are dealing with these developments by entering and exploiting strategic alliances.

Strategic alliances enable partners to gain the advantages of synergy between the resources, skills and competencies of the combined firms in particular product areas as well as becoming a global player, all at lower costs and risks than going it alone. Strategic alliances enable firms to obtain member market access, technology and other core skills, and launch global products in a more effective way. Alliances allow smaller and threatened firms to join forces with other firms to combine strength, to leverage their internal advantages and thus to combat larger competitors.

One cautionary note however; it must be emphasised that alliance partnerships are inherently relationships and invariably pose problems and need to be managed carefully.

The establishment of a 'win-win' situation with partners requires particular attention to the identification of suitable partners, their strategic 'fit' in terms of resources and skills, structuring of the alliances and commitment and trust. The strategic direction of the alliance over time needs careful handling. Shared knowledge skills with actual and potential competitors inevitably poses the problem of loss of competitive advantage should the alliance disintegrate.

4.8 CHAPTER REVIEW

Competitiveness in international business is highly dynamic and depends on wrestling advantages, from within the firm and from the external environment of the firm, that are unique to the firm or at least not readily copied or attained by others, and applying those advantages strategically over different international locations. When critical amounts of advantages accrue to significant numbers of firms within a particular industry within a particular country, that country is deemed to project national competitiveness in comparison with other nations regarding that particular industry or technology.

The hierarchy of sources of advantage are as follows:

- The firm's capabilities and capacities with regard to its assets.
- Its attributes and how it manages the performance of various functions.
- The cost structures of the firm with respect to industry averages.
- The differentiated qualities of the products the firm has to offer.

These sources of advantage from within the firm are complemented by sources of advantage from the external environment of the firm. These are as follows:

- The extent and intensity of rivalry among companies in the firm's industry.
- The availability and quality of input factors accessible by the firm for its operations.
- The nature and qualities of demand that the firm tries to satisfy.
- The network of related and supporting industries comprising suppliers and sub-contractors as well as the economic and trading infrastructure that enables the firm to operate commercially.

Importantly, the first and last external sources can be repositories of potential partners for strategic alliances and joint ventures.

The competitive strategy that emerges from the basis of the firm's advantages is based on two key strategic considerations: *which industries to operate in* and *how the firm positions itself* to maximise high profit returns. In resolving the challenge, the firm must understand fully the forces that drive industry competition and hence the behaviour and reactions of companies with respect to the relative bargaining power of suppliers and customers, the threat of substitute products, and companies poised to enter the industry. The balance of bargaining powers and threats in conjunction with the firm's array of advantages determine ultimately those industries that may be entered profitably and the position the firm should adopt for maximising returns as well as which industries should be avoided. Profitable industries are those in which the threats of either entry or substitute products are low and in which the firm enjoys superior power in its supplier and customer relations and in which the level and intensity of rivalry are minimal.

The firm may adopt one of three strategic positions or a combination of them, for its portfolio of products or subsidiaries. Cost leadership strategy enables the firm to be the lowest cost producer, thus creating above-average profits in comparison with the industry average. Differentiation strategy enables the firm to be unique in the industry with respect to product, technology or 'branding' – so permitting the firm to command premiums not attainable by its rivals. While cost leadership and differentiation are strategic positions across the whole of an industry by a firm, the third position – a focus strategy – aims at either cost leadership or differentiation in a limited number of specific segments in the industry or market. A focus strategy, because it caters for niche segments other companies are willing to ignore or unable to service, enables a firm to command premium prices of supply. At the international level, MNCs have to configure and co-ordinate their activities. In other words, they have to decide not only on the geographical locations of each, or groups, of their value-chain functions but also on how the locations are to be managed coherently and cohesively in terms of communications, co-ordination and control.

Examples of competitive strategies by MNCs indicate a variety of industries and possible strategic positions. It is important to remember that among the key factors that drive industry competition are changes in technology. Innovations in materials, manufacturing and process control enable firms that are competitive to adjust in a timely manner their strategies with respect to industry entry and exit as well as positioning.

No single measure of competitiveness can fully explain the nuances of competitiveness as a dynamic process. Hence operationalising competitiveness is only pragmatic in terms of potential, process and performance measures as well as choice of foreign market servicing mode. In this regard, each of the choices delineated in Chapter 3 – exporting, strategic alliances and foreign direct investment – must be weighed according to the firm's array of advantages with respect to the selected industry and strategic position.

The diversity of arrangements for and advances in management of, strategic alliances formed nowadays by MNCs make them exceptionally powerful weapons of competitiveness. The motives for entering and types of, strategic alliances provide competitive benefits in the following areas: economies of scale and scope; technology development; reductions in costs, risks and effects of competitive destruction; as well as organisational learning and building on core skills. However, strategic alliances are not problem-free. On the contrary, they require close attention by the firm's top management from formation right through to the maturing of the partners' relationship. Hence selecting the most appropriate firm, with the proper set of advantages, as alliance partner is the most crucial of managerial issues. Without diligence and prudence in the formation, the human resource dimensions and management of strategic alliances, potential drawbacks (including insufficient partner contributions, high co-ordination costs and conflict between alliance partners) can erode the effectiveness of the alliance as well as the firm's own competitiveness.

4.9   QUESTIONS FOR DISCUSSION

1. What are the determinants of competitive advantage at the level of the firm? How do these translate into competitiveness at the level of countries?

2. What are the options in devising competitive strategy with regard to industry dynamics and the strategic position of the firm?

3. How are the measures of competitiveness related?

4. How do strategic alliances confer competitiveness on a firm's international operations? What are the potential dangers in entering strategic alliances?

CHAPTER
5

Foreign Market Entry
and Development

CHAPTER OUTLINE

- General considerations for entering markets
- Strategic options for foreign market entry
- Organisational considerations in foreign market entry
- Foreign market entry illustrations – competitive aspects
- Switches in foreign market servicing mode – competitive aspects

CHAPTER OBJECTIVES

After studying this chapter you should be able to:
- Identify the different options for foreign market servicing.
- Demonstrate an understanding of the competitive advantages in each strategic option for foreign market servicing.
- Recognise and compare the different competitive aspects of entry conditions.
- Analyse the strategic options for foreign market entry with respect to different firms.
- Characterise switching modes in foreign market servicing.
- Select appropriate foreign market entry and servicing strategies for different firms.

important factors in building market share over the long run. Green-field investments allow the firm to 'customise' its overseas operations and to dictate the scale and pace of subsequent expansion. However, market penetration may be impaired because the firm's products are unknown and untried. Mergers and takeovers may be more attractive in this respect since the firm buys established production facilities and well-known brands. Although this enables the firm to make a quick entry, considerable management attention may be required to integrate the two business and secure the future development of the business.

Case 5.1

Anatomy of a buy-in: Why did a Canadian communications company decide to take a stake in an ailing Korean wireless telephone provider?

When the Asian flu hit Korea in December 1997 sending the won down to the 1,800 to the dollar level, sending the country to the International Monetary Fund for assistance and causing newly-elected president Kim Dae-Jung to declare an economic disaster, Hong Kong-based John Cheh took notice.

As the vice-president, Asia, for Bell Canada International Inc. (BCI) the international investment of Bell Canada Enterprises Inc., Canada's largest communications company, Mr Cheh is responsible for exploring investment prospects in Asia for his company. Its focus – identifying strategic investment opportunities for an overseas telecom project.

"When everything was breaking apart, we felt that Korea among all the Asian countries, given its history, culture and the fact the Korean people were very much united in their determination to overcome their difficulties, would pull out faster than any other country," said Mr Cheh. "So to pick a place in Asia, Korea came very much at the top of the list."

A former commercial counselor at the Canadian embassy in Seoul in the mid-1980s, Mr Cheh was not without personal knowledge of his chosen investment target. "My recommendation to our chairman, Derek Burney, was, 'Let's take a look'." Some nine months later, that recommendation led to BCI investing 210 billion won (US$153.75 million) in wireless telephone provider Hansol PCS Co Ltd, then experiencing financial difficulties. In addition, US-based insurer and BCI investment partner American International Group Inc. (AIG), a co-investor with BCI in telecom projects in Mexico, Colombia and China, invested a further 140 billion won (US$102.49 million) in Hansol. The investments were a mixture of common and convertible preferred stock and convertible debentures, which gave BCI and AIG stakes of 9.8 percent and 6.5 percent, respectively. On conversion, these vehicles would allow the two investors to enlarge their stakes to 23.6 percent and 15.8 percent, respectively. BCI also got to place several executives on the board of Hansol PCS, including the deputy chief executive officer and chief financial officer.

The decision would be just the latest of a series of strategic investment partnerships BCI had been forming around the world. In March 1994 BCI joined with Cable & Wireless PLC to form Britain's largest cable TV company. Three years later, BCI exercised its right to convert debentures in the Brazilian Canabras Communications Corp to take a 51 percent stake in the group which holds a controlling interest in a cable TV company.

In this case Mr Cheh's recommendation struck a particular resonance with the BCI chairman. Mr Burney had served as Canada's ambassador to Seoul in the late 1970s. "There was a personal angle, but eventually it was a corporate decision," said Mr Cheh who prior to the Asian contagion had checked out projects in Southeast Asia but decided not to proceed because of the absence of necessary corporate value. The crisis in Asia prompted Mr Cheh to look anew at the region and Korea stood out as presenting the best medium- to long-term possibilities.

Relationship-building. Not too long before the crisis hit Korea and the subsequent election of the government of President Kim, the wireless telephone market had undergone an upheaval. The market had been dominated by cellular providers SK Telecom and Shinsegi Telecom. Prompting later criticism of excess, the previous administration in 1997 auctioned off three licences to provide the newly-emerging Personal Communication System wireless technology in the fall of that year. The licences were awarded to wired service provider Korea Tel, which marketed its service under the name KT Freetel, to major conglomerate, or chaebol, subsidiary LG Telecom and to minor chaebol, Hansol. "In January 1998 I came to Korea and met with all the operators," said Mr Cheh. "I think in those meetings we very quickly found Hansol as the company we'd like to focus on."

By March 1998 BCI had decided to do a deal with Hansol and start due diligence. Both companies launched teams to handle all matters – legal, technical and financial – pertinent to the deal.

Why Hansol? Much had to do with Hansol's top executives, especially the brothers Dong-Kil Cho, vice-chairman of Hansol Paper, Henry D. Cho, vice-chairman of the Hansol Group and particularly, D.M. Cho, vice-chairman of Hansol PCS. "Hansol, being a very young company, not having KT's strength, a small chaebol, 14th in size, we found the Cho brothers very open and very flexible," said Mr Cheh. "For BCI there's a real importance attached to relationship-building. There has to be a strong relationship and partnership feeling and we felt our dealings with Hansol had that aspect." He added: "We were also impressed by the technical performance of their network."

Mr Cheh ascribed perseverance of both sides in reaching a deal to BCI chairman Mr Burney. "You could say that in BCI under his leadership, we looked beyond when everything looked gloomy because of his firm belief in the Korean economy and people."

Things did indeed look gloomy as negotiations continued. The credit crunch bit deeper, the demands of creditors mounted and the competition raged ever fiercer. On top of this, the company was suddenly the subject of a money-for-PCS licences bribery investigation which proved not to be a 'deal-breaker', according to Mr Cheh. "The allegations were certainly exaggerated," said Len J. van der Heyden, former BCI vice-president for Human Resources and Corporate Services and now Hansol PCS deputy CEO and chief corporate officer. "If there had have been any grounds, we would've walked."

A memorandum of understanding was finally signed in Seoul in April 1998 with Mr Burney acting for the BCI side, during which visit the BCI chair met with President Kim and his senior advisors who reaffirmed their commitment to foreign investment and restructuring. In fact, Mr Cheh credits key officials from the Ministry of Foreign Affairs and Trade, the Ministry of Commerce, Industry and Energy and the Ministry of Finance and Economy for their support in helping realize the deal.

Two-way street. However, while the MOU established a target of June or July for closure, negotiations on financing carried on through the summer largely because the industry practice of subsidizing subscribers meant the proposed investment requirement by BCI was getting larger by the day. A contract was finally signed in August 1998 which led to the injection of capital and the dispatch of a BCI senior management team to Hansol which included Mr van der Heyden, Jim Wilkinson as chief financial officer and a number of network-dedicated technical personnel.

The BCI/AIG stake is presently under the 33 percent ceiling permitted foreign ownership and will not exceed that limit until after July 1st when such strictures are removed and the investors begin to convert their holdings into additional equity. "Even after the changes our stake will be over 33 percent but we still won't take control. It's very Canadian," said Mr Cheh who is also a BCI board member of Hansol PCS. "It shows how sensitive we are to local practices."

Mr van der Heyden said the key elements for BCI in the deal were "obtaining a good, strong partner who understood the local culture and having three to five key people occupy key positions," while from the Korean side the benefits were financial oversight and corporate governance. BCI envisioned its association with Hansol as more than a straight financing-for-market access arrangement. Mr van der Heyden said from the beginning BCI looked on the association as a two-way street. "Where it's a one-way street is in the area of finance and accounting reporting; where it becomes a two-way street is in the area of technology," pointing to Hansol's leading edge network and management and billing systems. "We felt we could utilize the know-how of Hansol's outstanding technical team, in terms of engineering, operation and maintenance for our operations in North and South America and in Europe. Korea is on the leading edge of CDMA (Code Digit Multiple Access) which we believe is the technology of the future."

So what shape was Hansol at the time its new partnership was formed? "The company would have gone bankrupt if not for the capital injection," said Mr van der Heyden. "The Hansol Group didn't have the resources." In July 1998, the cash-strapped group's pulp and paper division sold its Chonju newsprint mill plus its 53 percent stake in a Chinese newsprint operation for US$1 billion to a joint venture comprising another Canadian investor, Abitibi-Consolidated, in league with Norwegian company Norske

Skog. Hansol PCS's financial situation had continued to worsen through the due diligence period and the word on the street was the company was in trouble.

"Ours was a case of managing investment in a difficult environment and managing difficult challenges in striking a deal. Now we feel we have a very solid base to profit from," said Mr Cheh. "In the meantime the economy has upturned and Korea's debt has been upgraded. So far, we say, 'hey, our original intention to look at Korea was well-founded.'"

Source: World Reporter, *The Financial Times Limited,* **1999**

Case Discussion Issues and Questions

1. Characterise the buy-in as a market entry mode. To what extend does this fit into the typology of strategic options?

2. Analyse the rationale behind BCI's decision. To what extent is it strategic or tactical?

3. Given the nature of competition in the Korean domestic market discuss possible options for BCI to develop its business.

5.3   INTERNATIONALISATION

The process of internationalisation by a firm requires it to analyse its own resources and capabilities to undertake overseas expansion, investigate target markets and select an appropriate initial mode of market entry. Over time the firm will often modify its foreign market servicing strategy as it 'learns' from experience more about foreign markets and the need to adapt to changes in competitive and market conditions.

Welch and Luostarinen (1988) have developed a framework to analyse the state of internationalisation of a given company. Their model, as illustrated in Figure 5.1, has six dimensions which relate the organisational capacity of the company to the market opportunities facing the company. The three variables identified by Welch and Luostarinen to characterise the organisational capacity, although critical, are not exclusive. Nevertheless, they can efficiently cover most of the areas that are needed to characterise the internal capacity of the firm for internationalising its business.

Organisational capacity

Organisational capacity is concerned with the company's internal factors that are resultant from, and reflect, the degree of internationalisation. It also forms the

Figure 5.1   Dimensions of internationalisation

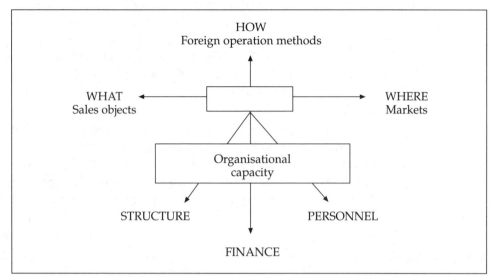

Source: Welch and Luostarinen (1988).

foundation for additional steps forward in the overall process. The organisational capacity in this model is assessed by three variables: the firm's financial resources, its human resources and its organisational structure. These three variables together determine the organisational capacity of the firm for expanding overseas.

1. **Finance**

   International operations require the availability of funds to support the various activities. The nature and extent of the company's financing requirements for international activities can range in sources and in sophistication depending on the degree of internationalisation of the company. Some firms may have to rely exclusively on internal funding, using the profits of the parent to finance its overseas operations. For capital constrained smaller companies, exporting or contractual strategic alliances may be the only viable options initially since the amount of capital investment required to support these activities is generally small. At the other extreme, larger well-established MNCs may use a mix of internal and external funding (for example, Eurobond loan finance) to establish green-field manufacturing plants or to take over some other firms.

2. **Personnel**

   The success of internationalisation for any company depends heavily on the type of people both initiating and carrying through, the various steps in the process, as well as the firm's overall personnel policies. In certain types of international operations where co-operation is required, such as joint ventures, human resources play a major role in the success of the venture. The background of the people involved, such as foreign experience, education and language training, can be critically important to the success of the firm in the internationalisation process. In many cases the employment of foreign personnel (local people who are fully conversant with local market conditions) will be preferred, whether they be agents, distributors or the firm's own workforce; for example, in the case of Kodak's Japanese subsidiaries all but 1% of the company's employees are Japanese.

3. **Organisational structure**

As the firm's international operations expand, administration and organisational demands tend to increase. This is particularly the case when firms establish overseas subsidiaries. Subsidiaries may operate on a decentralised standalone basis with limited parental control or they may be fully integrated into a networking operation requiring good communication and organisational compatibility and strong central direction (see Chapter 6).

What: Sales objects

As the involvement in international operations increases, the company tends to offer a wider and diversified range of products. This typically includes attention to product adaptation and customisation to meet the local needs, requirements and preferences of particular markets.

Where: Target markets

The choice of the foreign markets is a strategic decision that can have a strong impact on the success of the internationalisation process. There is a basic tendency for companies, particularly in the early stages of internationalisation, to approach markets which appear simpler, more familiar and less costly to penetrate. These are most commonly those markets which are closest in physical and cultural terms (Buckley, 1989).

How: Operation method

The internationalisation decision is usually a complex and gradual process due to the higher risks it represents to the firm. Often a firm will go through a number of intermediate stages before engaging in a total commitment to foreign markets, as illustrated by Buckley (1988) in Figure 5.2. This gradualist approach allows a deepening investment as success occurs and the learning process takes place, while reducing the risks of failure.

Figure 5.2   Routes to a foreign production subsidiary

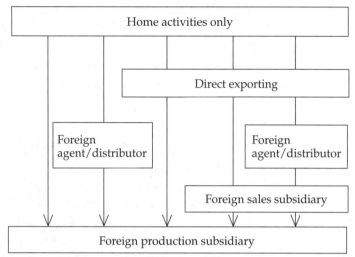

Source: Buckley (1988).

The gradualist approach emphasises that by starting with direct exporting, firms gain knowledge of the foreign market, specifically the identification of which products are to be sold and the adaptation requirements on products and selling techniques. At this stage the company becomes familiar with transportation problems, exporting formalities and distribution difficulties. As foreign sales grow, more intense contact with the target market is needed. The use of locally-based agents and distributors is commonly the next step. This allows a further penetration of the target market through on-the-ground representation and distribution channels. However, agents and distributors may handle other firms' products and this may constrain sales potential. Once local business volume reaches a certain level (or fails to do so because distributors underperform) the firm may then switch to a wholly-owned sales subsidiary to provide a more dedicated marketing effort facilitating an even deeper penetration of the market. Finally, local sales may reach substantial levels and justify an investment in a local manufacturing plant so as to provide a more effective and integrated in-market production and marketing capability.

Considerable empirical support has been found for the 'incrementalist' approach to international expansion (see next section and Buckley *et al.*, 1988). However, there is no set formula and in many cases firms may find it advantageous to move from no or little international presence to FDI in order to exploit innovative technology or products.

The prescribed theoretical basis for foreign market entry and development when reflected by what international firms actually do point to the complexity of these decisions. The sections that follow, descriptive of foreign market entry activities and development by MNCs, illustrate some of the various routes to the establishment of an overseas presence that is substantial (Box 5.1). They portray European and Asian aspects of foreign market entry and development.

Box 5.1   A Note on Cooperation in Foreign Market Entry

Corporate Marriages Are Not Made in Heaven

Business pages of American newspapers trumped the society pages in announcing weddings in 1998. Travelers went to the altar with Citicorp, Chrysler with Daimler-Benz and big fat Exxon announced its nuptials with pleasingly plump Mobil in the first day of December. The combined dowries of these last two were valued at over US$86 billion by stock markets on the day of the announcement. That's the biggest such hitch-up ever.

Indeed, 1998 was phenomenal for mergers and acquisitions involving US companies, with the activity by far exceeding any other year in the history of mankind. The stock value of the players was nearly US$1.68 trillion, 85% greater than the previous record of US$906.5 billion, set a year earlier.

Worldwide, M&A activity totaled over US$2.33 trillion, mainly because of the added, recently awakened interest in the game among European CEOs. Expectations of the new marketing opportunities that will be opened by a single European currency helped fuel the excitement. But the Europeans were shopping abroad as well as at home, as the big 'Daimler' wedding signified, along with such other monster tie-ups as British Petroleum and Amoco and Deutsche Bank and Bankers Trust.

The euro came into being yesterday, the first business day of the new year, and there are widespread expectations that the Europeans will be at it again as soon as they get their bookkeeping figured out. The watchword in such tradition-bound countries as Germany these days is 'restructuring'. Juergen Schrempp of Daimler and Rolf Breuer of Deutsche Bank thought one good way to restructure was to get a piece of the American action. Mr Schrempp admired Chrysler's marketing skills and Mr Breuer saw the BT purchase as a way to get a better foothold in investment banking, where there is a lot of action to be had in helping other companies arrange and finance deals.

There is a whole range of other explanations to be had for why companies merge, about as many as there are mergers or acquisitions. The oil companies say they are linking up in search of greater efficiencies to help them cope with depressed, US$10-a-barrel oil prices. If one partner is strong, say, in crude oil reserves and production, and the other in refining and marketing, there is synergy to be had, or so the saying goes. There also are people to be dispensed with. BP and Amoco announced after

Box 5.1 (*cont'd*)

completing their US$49 billion merger on the last day of 1998 that there will be more job cuts than the 6,000 originally expected.

The Traveler's-Citicorp deal envisions one-stop financial services shopping for the merged firms' customers, who will be able to finance a house and take out life insurance with a single all-purpose agent. More synergies and more weeding out of superfluous hired help.

But while mergers and acquisitions always are accompanied by logical-sounding arguments about synergies and efficiencies, the record shows that very often neither is achieved. Much has been written about the internal civil wars provoked by attempts to meld together two very different corporate cultures. There are many doubts, for example, about whether the wheeler-dealers at Bankers Trust can accept the Teutonic logic of their new German masters. Germany's BMW has not been at all happy with results from British Rover, which it acquired five years ago. Not a few marriages, even within nation-states, end in divorce after prolonged and unproductive periods of crockery flinging.

What Are They Adapting To? And Are the M&A Guys Making the Right Adaptations?

McKinsey & Co, the management consulting firm, evaluated 115 mergers and acquisitions in the early 1990s involving US and British companies and found that only 23% could be rated 'successful' in terms of return on capital. For the rest, the results were at best ambiguous. Although many big mergers have worked out OK over the years, such findings are not uncommon, particularly for the short term.

But why was 1998 such a spectacular year? More than likely, it had to do with something other than synergies and efficiencies, opportunities for which have existed in past, less frantic periods. The most obvious explanation comes from a quick glance at the Dow Jones Industrial Average. The market prices of corporate stocks soared through the first seven months of 1998, dipped and then recovered, ending the year at near the summer peak. CEOs have been looking for ways to cash in on their highly valued capital. One very tempting way is to use it to buy into other businesses or sometimes even better, buy out a competitor.

Fortune magazine notes in its latest issue that in last year's mergers, 67% of the wherewithal used was in the form of stock rather than cash, compared with only 7% in the M&A wave of 10 years ago. It also observes that 96% of the deals were friendly, whereas 24% of the link-ups in 1988 involved a hostile takeover.

Further evidence that the stock market has been driving the M&A explosion can be seen in what happened during the August–September market slump. M&A activity slowed markedly then picked up again after markets began to recover in October. Circumstantial, to be sure, but it all adds up.

Box 5.1 (*cont'd*)

Which makes some people wonder about all those 'logical' explanations. It is one of the wonders of capitalism, to be sure, that corporations adapt to changing circumstances. Economic Darwinism decrees that those who don't die. But the question always is, what are they adapting to? And are the M&A guys making the right adaptations?

Another interesting thing is happening in the US and Europe. Stocks are up but corporate earnings are beginning to slip. Stock prices relative to earnings, the so-called p-e ratio, are climbing to troubling levels. The economists who argue that we have been moving into an era of asset inflation sound a bit more plausible than they did a year ago. And if the stock market goes into another 'correction' on the order of the one last year – or maybe larger – will the wedding partners have made the right or wrong choices?

The answer to that question may very well be found in whether they will be too preoccupied trying to make the marriage work to take the necessary measures to deal with an economic downturn. In other words, are they stronger or weaker? It's just possible that time will tell.

Source: *The Asian Wall Street Journal*, 5 January 1999

NOTE: The quest for competitive advantages in economies of scale for foreign market servicing through cooperative forms of internationalisation is far from risk free. In some cases, IJVs, ISAs and mergers and acquisitions, if not managed appropriately, can lead to loss of competitiveness in international business.

The plasterboard and coffee market examples from the UK illustrate the importance of initial entry conditions and the significance of national economic developments that MNCs have to consider in terms of the impact on the subsequent ability to develop their foreign market servicing. The scientific instruments and pharmaceutical examples characterise the importance of initial entry conditions and the significance of wider regional economic trends for the further development of foreign market servicing. Both sets of illustrations underscore the dynamic nature of competitiveness in foreign market servicing.

The selected cases illustrate European MNCs' engagement with Asian business in markets similar to, and contrasting with, earlier examples – relatively simple and stable (tobacco and retail) on the one hand and relatively complex and dynamic (telecommunications and financial products) on the other hand.

These examples and cases bring to the fore the practical dimensions of competitiveness in foreign market servicing through diversified types of entry and their various development in terms of the need to change competitive positions as markets alter their characteristics. The examples demonstrate that the management of the foreign market servicing part of international competitiveness is an activity that is rarely unambiguously defined and circumscribed. They also show the optimism with which top management approaches these matters – a necessary prerequisite but one that belies the bewildering complexity of competitive decisions in international business.

5.4 NOTABLE ENTRY CONDITIONS ILLUSTRATED: THE UK PLASTERBOARD AND COFFEE MARKETS

Initial entry into a market may be easy or difficult depending upon the existence of various obstacles in the way of potential entrants. The UK plasterboard and coffee markets provide useful examples of international entry. The entry issue is developed further in the next chapter in the context of building a sustainable and profitable position in a target market over the longer term.

The plasterboard and coffee markets have both been investigated by the UK competition authorities and the discussion below is based largely on data forming part of the Monopolies and Mergers Commission (MMC) reports on these industries in 1990 and 1991, respectively.

The UK plasterboard market

In 1989, BPB Industries was the sole UK manufacturer of plasterboard, accounting for upwards of 95% of UK supplies of plasterboard. Import penetration was limited by the low value-added nature of the product and high-shipping costs relative to product value.

Over the years, BPB has expanded into mainland Europe and is a leading producer of plasterboard in Italy, Germany, France, the Netherlands, Spain and Austria, as well as having interests in gypsum mining and plaster production. The company is now the largest plasterboard manufacturer in Europe.

However, in April 1989 and September 1989 two new producers, Knauf and RPL, respectively, opened up green-field manufacturing plants in the UK. RPL was a joint-venture company owned 51% by Redland, a UK-based supplier of building materials (roof tiles, bricks, aggregates, etc.) and 49% by CSR, which is the largest producer of plasterboard in Australia. The company's first plant, at Bristol, came on-stream in September 1989, with RPL intending to build a second plant at some future date. RPL had already begun to build up its sales and distribution network in 1987 to prime the market, and supplied this operation by importing plasterboard from its joint-venture companies in the Netherlands and Norway. (The business was sold in 1993: see below.)

Knauf, with its headquarters in Germany, is the second largest plasterboard manufacturer in Europe, after BPB. It has three plants in Germany and one each in Austria, France, Greece and Spain. Knauf started importing plasterboard in August 1988 in order to prime the market before production at its first UK plant, at Sittingbourne, came on-stream in April 1989. A second plant was opened at Immingham in September 1990.

Market entry: Background to the decision to set up UK capacity.   RPL told the MMC that it had decided to enter the UK market "because they believed that, given the existing high margins, unpopular monopoly conditions and prospects for future growth, there would be considerable potential for a *second* supplier to establish a sound and profitable business in the market". When RPL announced its decision to enter the market in September 1987, "it was not aware that Knauf also intended to begin production".

RPL had intended to establish two plants to give it national coverage, but Knauf's entry put it in a dilemma by causing overcapacity and BPB had to cut prices: "RPL believed (when it had originally planned its entry) that the addition of 60 million square metres of plasterboard could be absorbed by the likely growth of the market". This had exacerbated its losses during its start-up phase and raised a question mark over the viability of setting up a second plant.

Knauf had been eyeing the market for some time, but the "acquisition of a German competitor by BPB in 1987 had probably accelerated its decision to enter". Knauf, like RPL, was interested in establishing two UK plants. At the time of the MMC report the company's second plant had been given the go-ahead and was under construction.

Potential barriers to entry.   The UK plasterboard market is characterised by a number of potential barriers to entry, including the *capital* costs required to build an optimal-sized plant (estimated at US$40 million to US$60 million) and the need to acquire *technical expertise* in producing plasterboard. These were not particular problems for RPL or Knauf, which were both backed by deep-pocket parents, while in the case of Redland plasterboard know-how was provided by its joint-venture partner (with Redland providing marketing expertise and established contacts in the building materials market).

company with no external borrowings, took a long-term view of its investments; it did not expect a payback on investments for between 12 and 15 years. It was, thus, not going to be pressurised into leaving the market.

Overall, the MMC concluded on the entry issue:

> Even in the face of keen competition by BPB, RPL and Knauf may be expected to remain viable competitors. They have invested substantial capital in starting up manufacture; the financial position of their parents is strong; and each of them has built up a sound customer base. We conclude that BPB's latest price-cuts were not predatory. BPB's resulting realised prices exceed total average costs; the cuts are explicable as a competitive action by BPB in a market which is under threat, particularly at a time of excess capacity; and having regard to the structure of the market it is implausible to suppose that BPB considered that the cuts were likely to drive out either RPL or Knauf.

Redland's exit from the market. In 1990 Redland ended its joint venture with CSR, exchanging its 51% holding in RPH for a 20% stake in a new joint-venture company, Lafarge Plateurope, formed in association with Lafarge Coppee, a French building materials supplier. At the same time the new joint-venture company acquired CSR's 49% holding in RPH for cash. "Our plasterboard operations could not escape being squeezed between falling demand and a marked increase in total industry capacity. In these circumstances we decided it would be preferable to broaden our competitive position in this activity (by forming a joint venture with a major European-based supplier)" (Annual Report, 1990). In 1991, however, after incurring further losses, Redland sold its stake to Lafarge Coppee, thus exiting the plasterboard market.

The UK coffee market

The supply of instant coffee in the UK is dominated by Nestlé, whose Nescafé portfolio of brands accounted for some 47% by volume and 56% by value of total retail sales in 1990. For a while, in the 1960s and 1970s the company's market share came under threat from other brand suppliers, in particular by General Food's Maxwell House and Brooke Bond's Red Mountain and the emergence of a plethora of retailers' own-label brands. At the end of the 1970s Nestlé's market share had been reduced to under 40%, but it has since regained its preponderant position in the market by astute marketing and new product launches. Entrants to the UK coffee market are discussed in the following paragraphs:

- *Nestlé* which is Swiss-owned, pioneered the establishment of the industry in the UK in 1939 when it launched its original Nescafé brand. Over the years it has added to its brand portfolio and is represented in all the main market segments (brands: Nescafé; Nescafé Gold Blend; Nescafé Blend 37; Nescafé Alta Rica; Nescafé Cap Colombie; Nescafé Find Blend; Nescafé Elevenses; Nescafé Nescoré). The company has production plants at Hayes and Tilbury.

- *General Foods*, which is American-owned, entered the UK market in 1947 with the acquisition of an established coffee producer, Alfred Bird. In 1954, it launched its main US brand, Maxwell House, in the UK. In 1981 it added to its UK brands by acquiring Hag AC, the Dutch supplier. The company became a subsidiary of the tobacco group Philip Morris in 1985 and was reconstituted in 1989, following Morris's acquisition of the Kraft food group (brands: Maxwell House; Cafe Hag; Masterblend; Mellow Bird; Brim). The company has a production plant at Banbury.

- *Brooke Bond*, an established UK supplier of tea, entered the coffee market in 1965 with the launch of Crown Cup. In 1985 Brooke Bond was acquired by the Anglo-Dutch food and detergents group, Unilever. The company's main brand is Red Mountain, launched in 1982 (other brands: Cafe Mountain; Brazilian Choice). Brooke Bond imports made-up coffee from Europe and Brazil which it then packages at its Redbourn and Trafford Park factories for retail sale.

- *Lyons Tetley*, is a subsidiary of Allied Lyons, the UK brewing and food group. Lyons entered the market in 1962 with Lyons Instant Coffee. The product failed, however and in order to use the spare capacity at its Greenford plant, the company turned to supplying own-label brands. In 1965 Lyons acquired Sol Café, another own-label supplier and in 1982 it purchased Tenco, an American-owned company, which packaged own-label brands. The company is the largest UK own-label supplier. In February 1994 Allied sold the business to General Foods in order to concentrate on its more successful tea interests.

- Other suppliers include: *Find Foods International* (German-owned) is the largest of the minor suppliers; it sources coffee from its parent company ready packed and supplies own-label retailers. *Gold Crown Foods* (UK) imports coffee which it packages at its Liverpool factory for sale as own label. S. Daniels (UK) entered the market in 1978 selling under the brand name of Vendona; the company imports coffee, which it has packed in its UK factories since 1989. The *Food Brands Group* (UK) supplies coffee under the Percol brand name, which was launched in the UK in 1989; coffee supplies are sourced from the Swiss company Jacobs Suchard (now owned by Philip Morris). *Douwe Egberts* is a subsidiary of the Dutch concern Sara Lee/DE NV (itself owned by Sara Lee of the US); the company entered the UK market in 1984 with its Moccona brand which is imported from the Netherlands.

- The main own-label retailers are the leading supermarket groups: *Sainsbury, Tesco, Safeway, Gateway* and *Asda*.

The conditions of entry. As noted above, a number of new suppliers have entered the market, the latest being Douwe Egberts and Food Brands, as well as an increasing number of own-label brands (for example, Aldi of Germany, a recent entrant to the UK market, offers four types of own-label).

The ease of entry into the industry depends on the method of entry adopted. Entry by establishing a new green-field instant coffee plant would require a capital investment of some US$60 million to US$100 million for a spray-dried coffee plant and some US$70 million to US$120 million for a freeze-dried coffee plant, although these figures would be reduced if a plant was installed at an existing food manufacturing site. These sums would not be a problem for a deep-pocket entrant. Nestlé indicated that the minimum efficient scale of operation for a spray-dried plant was in the order of 5,000 tonnes per annum, equivalent to around 10% of the UK market. An alternative entry strategy would be to import ready-made coffee for packaging in the UK or importation of the complete product, as have Food Brands and Douwe Egberts.

In either case, large-scale entry into the main market segments would (given a relatively static overall demand for coffee) require an entrant to win market share from established firms. In this context, it was suggested to the MMC that advertising posed a particularly serious problem for entrants. Advertising and promotion costs for a typical national launch were in the order of US$9 million, but this in itself would not be a particular problem for a deep-pocket entrant, nor is it out of line with those for any other branded grocery product. Smaller newcomers such as Food Brands and Douwe Egberts have not sought to compete head-to-head with Nestlé in the main market segments but have focused on the premium sector, obtaining widespread distribution for their brands without heavy television advertising. At the other end of the market, major food retailers have launched their 'captive' own-label brands into mainly the low-price sector. The development of the own-label sector has provided coffee producers with greater opportunities for entry as a specialist supplier of own-labels, as was the case with Sol Café.

The MMC concluded that it was not so much the high level of advertising in the industry *per se* which represented a serious barrier to entry, but the need for entrants' brands to match or exceed the quality of Nescafé's brands which was the key factor in successful entry. The fact that major new brands such as Red Mountain and Maxwell House failed to undermine the dominant position of Nescafé, despite heavy advertising support, was due to their inability to outperform Nescafé in terms of quality and value-for-money attributes. A number of coffee suppliers indicated that there were proprietary methods of manufacture which enabled some existing suppliers to produce coffee of superior quality: "Most suppliers agreed that the quality of Nescafé products could not be easily replicated by other manufacturers".

CASE 5.2

Breaking into Korea: Europe's Allianz takes over Korea's First Life

Acquisition marks first full control of Korean insurer by foreign firm

European insurance giant Allianz AG absorbed First Life Insurance Co yesterday, marking the first full foreign acquisition of a South Korean insurer, officials said.

The acquisition was completed when the Cho Yang Group transferred a 72 percent stake in First Life to the German firm. The debt-stricken shipping group agreed to turn over the remaining 28 percent in August.

First Life is South Korea's fourth largest prime insurer with 3.8 trillion won (S$5.5 billion) in assets as of March. It recorded 1.66 trillion won in premium income for 1998 and has in-force business worth 27.7 trillion won.

"We are one of a few profitable insurance firms here. The transfer was prompted by heavy debts at its parent group," a First Life official said. First Life officials refused to disclose the value of the deal with Allianz.

Insurance firms now form the second line of targets for reform in South Korea's limping financial sector, following moves to clean up banks and financial institutions of their massive bad debts.

"I am confident that with the excellent reputation of First Life and the international experience of Allianz we will be able to offer the highest quality standards to our customers," Michael Diekmann, a board of management member of Allianz AG, said in a statement. First Life said the acquisition represented "a cornerstone in the strategy of Allianz in Asia" as it will bring the German group "an important step forward" in sourcing 5 percent of its premium income from the region.

Allianz, a leading composite insurance and asset management group in Europe, has already been active in the South Korean market through France Life which it acquired as part of the 1998 merger with the French Group AGF. The Munich-based Allianz Group operates in 17 markets in the Asia-Pacific region.

"This is the first instance of full control of a South Korean insurance firm by any foreign firms," said an official at the Financial Supervisory Commission, which has led the restructuring of South Korea's debt-stricken insurance market.

Talks are under way between the government and foreign firms on the sale of Korea Life Insurance Co Kookmin Life Insurance Co and other insurers.

Source: AFP, *The Business Times,* **21 July 1999**

Case Discussion Issues and Questions

1. Discuss the entry mode choice by Allianz for serving the Korean domestic insurance market.

2. Analyse the likely problems that Allianz will face in developing the Korean insurance market.

3. Discuss the respective competitive advantages for the parties to the acquisition.

5.5 Switches in Market Servicing Mode: UK Scientific Instruments and Pharmaceutical Companies

Having successfully entered a target market the firm will need to consolidate its position. In order to increase market penetration the firm may need to change its mode of servicing the market. The case studies on page 168 will highlight the fact that whatever the initial mode of entry, the situation needs to be reviewed pragmatically in the light of experience and this may well necessitate a switch in market servicing mode. Although some foreign market entry decisions may be opportunistic, lasting success depends crucially on the adoption of a flexible and long-term market servicing strategy. A company must also be mindful of the opportunities and threats posed by changes in its business environment occasioned by, for example, the formation of regional economic blocs such as the European Union and the North American Free Trade Agreement (NAFTA) or the forthcoming ASEAN Free Trade Area.

In this section we report the experiences of a number of UK scientific instruments and pharmaceutical firms entering overseas markets (Buckley *et al.*, 1992). These two sectors are illustrative of the competitive advantages highlighted in Chapter 4, namely cost and product differentiation advantages.

The scientific instrument industry supplies a wide range of low-to-high technology products for use in research, healthcare, defence and industrial process control and automation. Although there are a number of major international suppliers, the industry remains highly fragmented with small- and medium-sized companies competing successfully in the more specialised areas. The major production centres and user markets are the US, the European Union (France, Germany, UK in particular) and Japan. The sample of five firms operate mainly in the low-technology end of the market where their main competitive advantage internationally is low costs.

In contrast, the sample of five pharmaceutical companies operate mainly in the research-driven sector of the industry, ethical drugs, where firms seek to secure competitive advantages through product differentiation, specifically first-mover advantages through the introduction of new patent-protected drugs. The main markets for pharmaceuticals are the US, Japan and the EU (where again France, Germany and the UK are prominent). In each of these markets the government plays a critical role both as an 'approver' of new drugs (new drugs being subjected to protracted and expensive safety and efficacy trials before they can be released on the market) and as the preponderant purchaser of drugs. Lengthy trials often reduce the effective patent life of a drug (nominally 20 years in Europe and Japan, 17 years in the US) by about a half so that firms are under a strong imperative to recoup R&D expenses and make profits by rapid and extensive international marketing. Additionally, firms have come under increasing pressure from governments' attempts to reduce their health-care spending by cutting the prices of drugs. Procurement bias by governments favouring local supply sources has encouraged many firms to set up local manufacturing plants. Patented drugs are sold at premium prices, reflecting their product uniqueness. However, once a drug goes 'off-patent' then the tendency is for generic producers to offer rival versions of it, competing primarily on the basis of low prices. Thus, the major producers are under a constant imperative to bring out a succession of new products to augment or replace those whose patent protection has expired.

Table 5.2 presents details of our sample firms' initial entry mode into the target markets indicated and subsequent moves to improve their market positions. In-depth interviews were conducted with representatives of the firms and some of their comments are recorded in the case citations below.

Scientific instrument firms

Firm A specialises in thermo-analysis equipment and small scale 'free testing' equipment. Because of its restricted product range it is at a disadvantage in competing for customers requiring a full line of items to equip a complete laboratory. However, the firm's focused approach confers a number of advantages. In particular it offers a wider range of thermo-analysis equipment than most competitors and it has a price advantage stemming from the fact that its equipment which performs two key analytical functions is cheaper on a pro rata basis than competitors that offer these functions in two separate pieces of equipment. The firm's price competitiveness is underpinned by its policy of

Table 5.2 Market entry and subsequent switches in market servicing mode for UK scientific instruments and pharmaceutical companies

Company	Market entered	Initial mode of entry (switch in mode)
Scientific instruments		
A	US	Exports via agent (FDI – takeover and establishment of green-field sales subsidiary)
	Germany	Exports via distributor
B	US	Exports via distributor (direct sales)
	France	Exports via distributor (new distributor)
C	France	Exports via distributor (FDI – joint venture)
	Germany	Exports via distributor (FDI – green-field sales subsidiary)
	US	Exports via distributor (FDI takeover and establishment of green-field sales subsidiary)
D	US	FDI – sales subsidiary (then takeover of local producer)
E	France	Exports via distributor
	US	Exports via distributor
Pharmaceuticals		
F	Japan	Licensee (FDI – joint venture)
	Australia	Exports via distributor (FDI – takeover of local producer)
G	France	Direct exports (FDI – green-field producer)
H	Mainly EU	Direct exports
I	US	Exports – co-marketed through sales subsidiary of European pharmaceutical firm (FDI – takeover of local producer, followed by major green-field investment)
	Japan	Exports via agent (FDI – joint venture)
J	US	Exports via agent

centralised production in its UK plant, enabling full advantage to be taken of economies of scale. An additional benefit from centralised production is a more effective control of product quality.

Two foreign market entry initiatives and subsequent change in market servicing mode are reported as part of this survey, one in the US, the other in

Germany. Initially Firm A exported its products to the US through an agent, but this arrangement proved to be 'unsatisfactory'. The hoped for rapid expansion of sales and profits did not materialise; the agent was considered by Firm A 'not to be sufficiently committed to selling the company's products'. Firm A then switched to a sales subsidiary having become convinced that presence effects were important in developing sales, particularly the need to convince customers that the company was 'here to stay' and could provide a prompt and reliable maintenance and repair service. Direct entry into the market was effected by the takeover of a firm selling related spares and equipment (but not original equipment), i.e., it was a form of piggy-back entry aimed at capitalising on the acquired firms' knowledge of the market and extensive customer base.

The sales subsidiary is supplied by exports from the UK so as to maintain the cost advantage of centralised production (although Firm A intimated that it would be prepared to set up a manufacturing plant in the US 'if exchange rate movements undermined profitability'). However, given the nature of user requirements some (usually minor) product modification is frequently required. In this regard the sales subsidiary provides both a vital pre- and after-sales supplier-customer linkage.

The switch in market servicing mode has had a dramatic effect on company performance, described as a quantum leap in terms of its ability to penetrate the market and expand sales and profitability.

This situation contrasts markedly with Firm A's position in Germany. Presently the firm exports to Germany through a distributor who undertakes marketing and sales promotion, servicing and maintenance but not stockholding. The distributor's performance has been unsatisfactory and Firm A's sales manager was sent to work alongside the distributor to provide more 'commitment' and 'closeness to customer benefits'. Clearly, as in the US case, a switch to a sales subsidiary could prove beneficial, but there appears to be some internal problem in this regard. The view is that a sales subsidiary would be 'too costly to bear' at the moment and that exporting provides a means of building up a customer base which 'will enable them to generate enough demand to sustain a sales subsidiary'. Alternatively, however, it might be suggested that an immediate investment in sales subsidiary would pay for itself quickly in increased turnover and profits.

Firm B specialises in liquid analysis equipment which is sold as original equipment mainly to laboratories and to other manufacturers who put it into their own systems. As a general policy the firm's UK production base needs to be supported by overseas sales so that full advantage can be taken of economies of scale. The company offers the same product line in all markets, but these are adapted to meet specific user requirements. The ability to compete on price, high-product quality and flexibility in meeting customer demand are seen to be key competitive advantages. Presence on the ground is also vitally important: sales mostly depend on getting a foot in the door during the time the client is making decisions.

Two foreign market entry moves are reported in this survey, one in the US the other in France. Initially, Firm B exported its products to the US through a distributor but this was not a success due to 'a lack of commitment on the part of the distributor' and 'poor communications' between the two parties. However, the change in exporting mode to direct sales to endusers equally has had only a minor impact on performance. Sales promotion is seen to be a particular problem. The firm advertises in US trade journals, relying on enquiries from potential customers to add to its existing client list. However, close customer contact (i.e., presence in the form of a sales subsidiary) is often more effective in this regard. As the interviewee acknowledged when commenting on a major competitor's position in the market: "They are able to develop and work at contacts rather than merely follow up remote lead." Additionally a sales subsidiary would help in respect of service back-up on the ground. Currently Firm B sends personnel from the UK to attend to customers with inevitable delays. It would appear, however, that a possible switch to a sales subsidiary is contingent on a sufficient expansion of US demand via exporting to justify the investment, again a somewhat myopic view of the likely impact of the US-based operation.

The situation facing the company in France is no less problematic. To begin with, Firm B exported its products through an independent distributor, but this arrangement proved to be 'unsatisfactory'. Firm B then appointed a new distributor, one of its former employees who had set up business independently but is committed to the company, knows the policies and procedures. This distributor operates a sales office, undertakes physical distribution, servicing and maintenance of equipment. The new arrangement has helped boost sales and profitability, but performance has been limited by the relatively small scale of the distributor's network and lack of funds. Firm B has 'considered buying him out' but its own resources are limited and 'could be put to better use at home'.

Firm C is a supplier of air-conditioning products for specialist 'closed room' applications such as computer terminal rooms. Centralised production in the UK helps keep costs down and the firm's price competitive in European markets, but the US market is now serviced from a local production plant. An important competitive advantage is product quality and design, including energy-saving features. The firm makes strenuous efforts to keep up-to-date with the latest technology, but is more involved with development than basic research. Overseas markets are highly competitive and the firm is up against powerful rivals (especially US concerns) whose scale of operations and extensive sales coverage give them substantial market penetration.

Three foreign market entry and market servicing mode switches are reported for the French, German and US markets. In France, Firm C competes against around 30 companies and is ranked number four in market share terms. The market leader (a US company) operates through a distributor who sells to regional commissioned agents, as do most other firms. Firm C, too, initially operated through a distributor who had approached the company seeking representation. This arrangement proved 'unsatisfactory': When working with distributors you can only advise and persuade them to go out to specifiers and endusers, but at the end of the day they are only concerned with getting orders and short-term sales. This experience in France (and elsewhere) convinced Firm C that a on-the-ground presence would provide greater commitment and visibility in developing the business long term. In 1989, Firm C established a joint-venture sales subsidiary with a local company, taking a 75% stake in the business. The sales subsidiary is supplied from the UK (Firm C's systems are made to order and generally require four to six weeks' delivery time which can be handled efficiently from a UK base, so that there is no particular advantage in producing locally). The sales subsidiary is managed by the French partner and this has caused some initial communications problems: a 'them and us' situation. An exchange of staff programme has been instituted to bring about greater goal congruence and organisational identity. Sales volume has increased, but a stronger market penetration and profitability has yet to show up.

A similar situation arose in Germany. The firm first entered the market by employing the services of an exclusive distributor based in Hamburg, but he was not prepared to develop a network of regional offices. Firm C then switched to a wholly-owned sales subsidiary in 1988, taking the view that this provided greater commitment and control in expanding the business. However, the rebuilding of turnover has been slow and it is only now achieving the kind of performance originally achieved using the distributor (i.e., a market share of around 5%). The sales subsidiary acts as an autonomous unit (obtaining its products from the UK parent) and carries out a variety of selling and distribution functions. Marketing is seen to be a problem. Firm C currently sells through five regional dealers (installers), but feel they need 25 to 30 dealers to be fully effective. Overall, competition is intensive and the firm is up against local producers and MNCs (mainly US concerns). Presence on the ground gives the firm a German identity and underscores the necessity of 'chipping away', building up new contacts and cultivating repeat customers.

The company initially entered the US market by exporting through a distributor and developed a modest toe-hold in the market. However, adverse exchange rate movements together with the payment of high rates of commission to the distributor made this uneconomical. Firm C then bought out the distributor and established a sales subsidiary, but even this was insufficient to restore profitability. The firm took the view that this was too big a market to pull out of and accordingly set up a production plant in 1988. The firm's long-term future in this market, however, remains problematic. At the moment it is losing money and has been unable to achieve critical mass in marketing coverage to rival established local suppliers. A key factor with regard to its future prospects is considered to be its ability to secure contracts with major inter-state installers who offer clients whole package deals.

Firm D is a global supplier of analytical instruments used in the manufacture, for example, of oil and chemical products and by public and commercial laboratories. The firm's competitive advantage has been built up on its ability to offer customers a range of good quality products, sustained over time by heavy investment in research and development. Until recently, the company has pursued a policy of centralised manufacturing in the UK and a foreign market servicing strategy based on the establishment of sales subsidiaries in Europe and the US and exports through agents in Japan. A shift in market sales towards low-technology products, however, impressed upon the firm the need to develop its distribution beyond the sales subsidiary format.

In 1988 Firm D entered the US market by acquiring a manufacturing firm. The acquisition of this company was partly opportunistic (the company was losing money and looking for a buyer), but had the merit of a product range which was complementary to that of Firm D. Thus, the products manufactured in the US were seen as providing an extension of Firm D's product portfolio and not as an alternative form of market servicing. The US plant also enabled the firm to achieve a stronger presence in the market and gave them an American identity. The acquired company is still making losses, partly due to the higher operating costs stemming from a greater attention to pre- and after-sales services and there have been problems between the parent and its US managers. The chairman of the company spent six months at the subsidiary to 'improve communication and commitment' and institute policies designed to restore the long-term profitability of the business.

There is also some general concern in the company regarding the optimal means of competing in foreign markets. The preference is still for centralised production in order to exploit economies of scale and control quality, but the sales subsidiary approach may be 'too narrow' to exploit growth opportunities in the low-technology sector. One interviewee suggested that sales subsidiaries were ideal for 'big ticket' sales (involving expensive and complex items of equipment requiring customisation) because of the high degree of client liaison required. However, low-technology items like flanges which sell in large volumes and which have a wide and diverse target market require availability if they are to succeed. In such instances, the optimum course to follow is perceived to be 'catalogue sales' supplied from an extensive network of contracted distributors.

Firm E is a major supplier of equipment used in 'closed environments' (incubators, sterilising units, etc.). It also sells 'factored' lines supplied by other brand manufacturers as a means of offering a fuller product range to customers. The company has 'no overall general policy on foreign market servicing'; strategies are developed country by country depending on circumstances. It is currently concentrating on developed countries where the firm's position is relatively weak.

The company operates mainly in the low- to medium-technology sector and is relatively small compared to market leaders. Although the company considers that it has good technical products in its specialist areas, its products lack uniqueness (i.e., product specialisation is not sufficient enough for customers to actively seek them out). Its larger competitors tend to have entrenched market positions, underpinned by extensive distribution networks and customer bases.

Two foreign market entry situations are considered in this survey, both distributorships – one in France, the other in the US. As with the companies discussed above, centralised production in the UK is favoured because of economies of scale, with exports providing 'good profit returns' if handled effectively. The company currently exports to France through a long-standing distributor, who approached them in the late 1940s. The distributor principally acts in a selling capacity, but also provides technical support and after-sales service to customers. The company's performance in France has been steady rather than spectacular. Firm E is considering the establishment of a sales subsidiary, recognising that they will make little progress without stronger marketing of their products and the ability to offer customers a more credible service back-up. This view has been reinforced by the fact that the distributor has started a manufacturing operation and may well pose a competitive threat to the company in the future. As with Firm A, however, financial considerations have caused hesitation. Although it is recognised that a FDI commitment requires the company 'to take short-term risks for long-term gains', there is some serious doubt that the firm could attain the critical mass of sales estimated (around 300,000 units annually) to be necessary to support a sales subsidiary. Considering their weak position at the present time against domestic manufacturers, the size of the investment required seems difficult to justify.

In the US, the company entered the market through a distributor in which it has an equity stake. Despite this, control and commitment have been lacking and the company describes its performance to date as trivial: a market share of under 0.5% and low profitability. The distributor is under no compulsion to sell the company's products (although sales persons receive high commissions). Distributors are viewed as 'wheeler-dealers who will sell anyone's products, including competitors, so long as they make a profit'. To describe this distributorship as 'not to have been the right choice' is perhaps a classic understatement! Ideally, a wholly-owned sales subsidiary is seen as the way forward. Non-US companies that have wholly-owned subsidiaries have sales and promotion muscle and are advantaged in terms of technical support and after-sales service. They are not faced with the same problem of competing for salesmen's time as is this company. But, as with the French situation that this action has not been taken already is due to the companies' 'financial constraints'.

Pharmaceutical firms

Firm F is a global supplier of ethical drugs. Its product portfolio consists of a number of patented drugs as well as generics. As is the case with other firms operating in the ethical drug sector, the company's competitive advantage depends fundamentally on discovering and patenting new drugs. Generally, the company aims to produce in the UK and export through sales subsidiaries. Centralised production protects key proprietary technology and local sales subsidiaries are seen as the most effective means of marketing its products, including product adaptations to meet local preferences. Manufacturing is undertaken in some countries, however, because of government buy-local policies. Licensing is generally avoided in order to protect know-how except, occasionally, in servicing small markets or 'difficult' markets (e.g., Japan).

Two foreign market entry initiatives and subsequent changes in servicing mode are included in this survey, one relating to Japan, the other Australia. The company first entered the Japanese market in the early 1950s, acquiring two companies producing agro-chemical products. In the 1960s it was approached by a leading Japanese pharmaceutical company who was interested in obtaining the Japanese rights to one of the company's recently patented respiratory drugs. As a result the Japanese concern became Firm F's licensee. Under the deal the local company manufactured the drug in Japan, incorporating the 'active ingredient' (i.e., the core technology) which was produced in the UK and customised the product for local use. The Japanese company was responsible for selling the product and handled the critical price negotiations with doctors and officials of the Ministry of Health and Welfare. This arrangement worked extremely well and performance results were impressive. The company sees 'long termism' as a key factor in tackling the Japanese market: "A long corporate relationship is important when dealing with the Japanese ... setting and working towards long-term objectives, without being greedy for short-term profits.... market presence requires building and sustaining a local infrastructure over time." Notwithstanding the trust element in the original arrangement, Firm F felt that there was some danger that once the product went off-patent its licensee would make their own version of the product with the technology and experience they had gained. This problem was headed-off by replacing the licensing arrangement with a 50 : 50 joint venture covering local manufacture and marketing. Performance results have been good and market penetration enhanced. However, the company is now considering establishing a wholly-owned subsidiary in order to capitalise further on its ongoing patented drug portfolio.

The company initially exported patent drugs to Australia through a local distributor. However, government pressure began to threaten the research based sector of the industry by stipulating that the pricing of pharmaceuticals should be set at the value of the ingredient cost plus 10%. The mark-up available to firms consequently did not allow them enough leeway to recoup the cost of their R&D. Normally, during the patent life of a product, the initial mark-up is necessarily high and despite the fact that the price falls over time it continues to be relatively high in order to pay for the research over the short marketable patent life. Australia, however, wanted original brands at generic prices.

Australia was the first market exposed to government pressure for generics. This had the effect of expanding the generics market and putting others off launching generics in Australia. In order to maintain a presence in the market

effect of the switch to FDI has been strongly positive, leading to a substantial increase in sales and profitability.

Notwithstanding the Single European Market initiative, the company feels that a local presence will remain important given different market preferences. However, in view of the harmonisation of various rules and regulations governing trucking, whether a continuing manufacturing presence as distinct from a sales subsidiary is necessary in major markets is something which needs to be investigated closely. In the case of France, buy-local procurement policies by the French health-care authorities have been a factor favouring local production. This is an attitude the Single European Market initiative is designed to break down, but it is likely that chauvinistic buying behaviour will continue to assist those firms with a French identity.

CASE 5.4

From Taiwan to Ireland: Hon Hai Precision Industry Co

In early 1999, the Irish Government said Hon Hai Precision Industry Co of Taiwan plans to invest I£8 million (US$10.8 million) and create 500 new jobs in the Irish Republic.

The company will operate in Ireland as Fortex Engineering (Ireland) Ltd. It intends to set up two industrial projects in Country Westmeath, the government said.

In one project, Hon Hai Precision will invest I£4.5 million in a plant to manufacture casings for personal computers. The company expects to create 350 new jobs within the next four years at the plant.

In the second project, Hon Hai Precision will invest I£3.5 million in a design-and-production unit for specialized electronic components, including cable assemblies and connectors. Hon Hai Precision will employ 150 people at the second plant over the next three years.

Source: *The Asian Wall Street Journal*, **19 May 1999**

Case Discussion Issues and Questions

1. Discuss the possible rationale for Hon Hai's FDI decision.

2. Analyse the potential motives for this type of green-field FDI.

3. Discuss the pros and cons of green-field FDI by this Taiwanese firm.

Firm H is a generics specialist, currently focused on the UK which undertakes only incidental exporting. The company supplies both unbranded and branded generic products to retail pharmacies, unlike its main competitors who sell primarily to wholesalers. The competitive advantages of Firm H are based on a combination of low prices, fast delivery and, in particular, the efficiency of its sales force. Increasingly it is facing tough competition from a number of research-based companies who have themselves moved into the generic sectors to counter 'me-too' rivals.

Hitherto the company has felt unable to develop an overseas operation because of lack of resources and as such has contented itself with meeting the occasional unsolicited export order. The 1992 Single European Market initiative, however, has acted as a catalyst and the company now intends to put exporting on a firmer basis, possibly employing an agent before moving on to a sales subsidiary format. The agent would have to be someone who could offer an efficient on-the-ground facility (i.e., warehousing, selling contacts and support services). A key factor in the UK is delivery times (two to three days) and this would need to be replicated abroad. The agents would sell from stock, carrying an extensive range of items. The services offered 'would depend on those being offered by competitors'. The company 'expects a long learning' in this respect being aware, from its UK operations, of the problems in managing and motivating an effective sales team. Ideally, the company sees a wholly-owned sales subsidiary with a distribution facility as being the most effective means of building overseas sales. The company's lower production costs, combined with the availability of higher margins in many European markets, indicate plenty of scope for market penetration and profit opportunities. For example, in the UK generic drugs retail at around 20% of brand leader prices whereas in Germany they retail at around 75%.

Firm I is one of the leading global pharmaceutical suppliers and because nowadays it has no other business it is much more focused in its commitment to developing its pharmaceutical interests than many of its competitors. The company has established production and sales subsidiaries in the major markets of the US, Japan (a 50 : 50 joint venture) and Europe; smaller markets are serviced in the main through sales subsidiaries. The initial international success of Firm I was based largely on one patented product which has proved to be a massive seller; this, in turn, has financed a sustained R&D programme which has extended the company's patented product portfolio and has provided it with the resources to establish a large network of wholly-owned production and sales subsidiaries. Investment in R&D is mainly undertaken in the UK as a means of keeping tight control over proprietary technology, although the company has set up a number of overseas

R&D establishments, notably in the US, to tap into the latest developments. However, research in the UK is considered to be 'better value in relation to spend than it is in the US'.

The company's foreign market servicing strategy in its main markets is based on a distinction between primary and secondary production and the advantages of presence effects, especially in marketing. Primary manufacture consists of the production of patented active ingredients which for competitive reasons are produced exclusively in the UK and then exported to secondary manufacturing plants located overseas where they are incorporated into final products and marketed through sales subsidiaries. Given local preferences, packaging adaptations are necessary in most markets (design, size and instructions, colours and capsules versus tablets, etc.). A comprehensive sales force on the ground is also considered to be an important competitive advantage as marketing pharmaceuticals is critically one of 'selling quality to professionals'.

Two changes in foreign market entry initiatives and later changes in market servicing mode are recorded in this survey, one in the US, the other in Japan. The company had started exporting to the US in the 1930s through an agent, but this was only a small operation and related mainly to non-pharmaceutical products. In the 1980s the launching of a major new drug (described as a product breakthrough) propelled the company into the big league. Initially this product was co-marketed in the US (from July 1983) with a European pharmaceutical company which had its own established US sales subsidiary. This, however, was only a springboard into the market and was soon followed, in 1984, by the establishment of a combined green-field manufacturing, sales and R&D operation. Having a FDI presence has helped the company in dealing with the US authorities over drug registration and 'given it a closeness to the market which enables them to tailor products to local needs'. FDI has given the company an American identity that has been important in cultivating contacts at the general practitioner level. All in all, FDI has had a significant impact on the company's market share and profitability and its competitive potential has been enhanced further by its US R&D facility.

In the case of Japan, the company's products were originally sold through an agent who dealt with a number of local pharmaceutical companies. In the late 1960s the company established a 50 : 50 sales subsidiary with a prominent Japanese company as a means of securing greater market penetration. The development of a comprehensive sales force, however, has been slow (the company has recruited people mainly straight from university and trained them up) and this requires further augmentation. The product breakthrough mentioned above was the key factor that led the joint venture to establish a green-field manufacturing plant. The latter is engaged in secondary manufacturing and customisation of products for the local market. As with the US operation a direct presence in the market has helped in the critical matter of obtaining new product registrations with the Ministry of Health and Welfare. The company's sales and profitability have steadily improved. Market share, however, at around 1.4% in what is the world's second largest market is considered to be still too low and compares unfavourably with its position in the US and the leading European markets.

Firm J is a relatively small one producing branded and unbranded products which are sold over the counter rather than on prescription. It was acquired by Firm I in 1961, but became independent again in 1986. At the time of writing, its international operations are limited to exporting, being confined in the main to the US. Around one-fifth of its turnover is accounted for by exports which are considered essential to ensure that its three UK factories work to capacity. The company produces good quality products and offers an extensive product range 'which enables them to target a large number of market niches'. Product development rather than basic research is an important means of updating the company's product portfolio, but resources are limited in this respect.

For a company of its size, exporting is seen as a relatively risk free and inexpensive means of expanding sales. The company uses a number of agents and distributors in the US and it has an export director, an American with a deep knowledge of the market, who co-ordinates the company's efforts. Careful attention is paid to the identification of market segments for the company's products and the selection of appropriate intermediaries to handle the products. Key factors in this respect are their position in the relevant market areas and their ability to provide the right kind of support for the product. The company reports 'good' relationships with its distributors. Exports have made an important contribution to the company's profitability. Further expansion abroad is being contemplated, particularly in Europe where the company is currently under-represented. The US market is seen to be especially attractive and the company is likely to establish a FDI operation 'in the near future', depending on the availability of financial resources.

CASE 5.5

'Casinos' and supermarkets: Thai and French firms link up

Big C Supercenter PCL has tied up a deal with French retailer Casino Guichard Perrachon SA that will give it much-needed financial support.

Although the injection of capital for new shares by Casino won't immediately solve sales declines at supermarket operator Big C, most analysts believe it will clear up high-debt levels and benefit Big C's stock.

The planned sale is the latest in a number of deals involving foreign strategic partners and Thai retailers, which are being squeezed by falling consumer demand. Big C has suffered more than most because it sells cheap products in bulk at its warehouselike supermarkets. With declining volumes, Big C's cash flow has come under pressure, making it difficult to meet payments on debt of six billion baht (US$159.4 million), analysts say.

Through issuing 530 million new shares at 11.50 baht each or about 68% of equity to Casino's Netherlands-registered unit, Geant International BV and Thailand's Saowanee Holding Co, Big C should clean up its balance sheet.

SG Asia Securities changed its recommendation on the stock to a buy on the premise that Big C will no longer have to shoulder the burden of one billion baht in interest payments every year. "This is good news for Big C," SG Asia Securities said, forecasting net profit of 504 million baht in 1999, compared with a loss of 126.58 million baht last year.

Other analysts said Casino's arrival should benefit Big C in terms of management experience. Casino has a sprawing retail empire in France and the US including retail, restaurant, food-processing, wine-bottling and real estate businesses. "The coming of the Casino group will support Big C in terms of technical know-how," said Natanee Savirasarid, an analyst with Capital Nomura Securities.

"With a foreign company coming in, their operations could improve quite a bit." The deal underlines just how much financial pressure Big C's majority stakeholder, Central Group, is under as consumer demand in Thailand continues to slump.

Analysts say Central has bowed to economic reality by selling its Big C stake. Before the deal, Big C's principal shareholders were the Chirathivat family of Central with a 35.4% stake. After the issue of new shares, the family will own 8.4%.

According to analysts, Casino will take a legal maximum 49% stake directly, with the remainder through Saowanee Holding. Big C, however, hasn't made the details of this clear.

According to SG Asia Securities, Casino is effectively getting a majority stake in Big C's 20 stores for only six billion baht. The estimated cost of opening a new store is one billion baht, SG Asia said.

On the negative side, analysts say Thailand's consumer demand isn't set to pick up for at least another year and higher margin competitors will do better than Big C.

Market talk is that Casino may help Big C raise further loans to expand operations, but the Thai company also may be able to use future cash flow to help fund expansion once its debt burden has been reduced.

Source: *The Asian Wall Street Journal*, 5 April 1999

Case Discussion Issues and Questions

1. Discuss the rationale behind the choice of developing the Thai food mass retailing market by CGP.

2. Suggest a strategy for expanding operations in Thailand.

3. Analyse the potential for Big C to internationalise its operations.

5.6 CHAPTER REVIEW

Competitiveness in international business ultimately depends on the quality of a firm's foreign market entry and the competence displayed in the management of its development. In this, the firm has to weigh a number of general and specific considerations before decision-making. Among these considerations are: the competitive advantages the firm possesses; the various obstacles that may present themselves prior to and at, market entry (costs, low-distribution capacities, etc.); the structural characteristics of the target market; and host country investment and trade policies (import and export restrictions, limits on foreign ownership, incentives, etc.).

As the strategic options for foreign market entry and their development have particular characteristics that confer or reduce competitiveness, firms have to consider carefully the balance of advantages and disadvantages. Whereas an export entry strategy may have an apparent low risk profile, the possibility of divided loyalties by the firm's agents, given a social culture unfamiliar to the firm, may render the strategy unworkable. The attractiveness of strategic alliances in reducing costs may be outweighed by the costs of losing technological 'know-why' and know-how to the joint-venture partner resulting in a new competitor being created instead of in increasing the firm's competitiveness. A firm's solo effort in penetrating a market, while it gives total control, may be compromised by the fact that the firm is unknown in the target market.

The careful balancing of advantages and disadvantages and subsequent selection of appropriate strategy cannot be operationalised without attention to functional managerial requirements. These involve the organisation, financing, assigned personnel and organisational structure for the entity that will implement the market servicing in the overseas location.

Market conditions and the degree of ease or difficulty of entry vary enormously over different markets in different places. Hence, the competitive dynamics at entry and the way those dynamics are configured subsequently by the firm's strategy are critical to success. It is also important for the firm to consider barriers to entry (and exit). Barriers to entry may vary in form from limited access to input factors and large capital requirements, to limited access to customers. It is just as important to consider the competitive reactions of incumbent firms. Competitive reactions depend in turn on the structure and dynamics of the industry. On the one hand, firms in relatively simple and slow changing industries with many players are less likely to react in an intensely competitive manner. On the other hand, firms in complex and fast changing industries with fewer players are more likely to react in an intensely competitive manner.

It is crucial to bear in mind that activating a particular strategic option carries consequences for industry structure. For example, whereas the direct investment through establishing a green-field operation adds capacity and changes structure by virtue of a new entrant, mergers and acquisitions, although they do not change capacity, may potentially alter industrial structures due to monopoly considerations. The competition policy that pertains in a particular country may limit such activity.

Foreign market entry and servicing is an activity that changes over time. Modes of entry rarely remain unaltered in the face of dynamic changes in industries. The implication is that firms have to develop their market servicing by switching between the different modes. Illustrations of various firms, from different industries, point to the learning dimension of foreign market entry and servicing. The majority of firms in the scientific and pharmaceutical industries enter foreign markets via exports and most of them switch to other modes of market servicing. These switches give the firms either more control over operations or added competitive capabilities such as benefiting from the technology owned by other firms through joint ventures.

5.7 Questions for Discussion

1. What factors should a firm take into consideration before deciding on the best strategy for entering and servicing a foreign market? What other considerations should a firm pay attention to?

2. What determines entry conditions for a firm targeting overseas markets? What kinds of barriers to entry may face a firm when entering foreign markets?

3. What advantages and disadvantages accrue to a firm in switching modes of foreign market servicing?

4. How would a firm decide on which strategy to employ in entering a targeted foreign market? How might the firm manage the development of its foreign market servicing over time with respect to changing conditions?

CHAPTER
6

Aspects of Managing MNCs

CHAPTER OUTLINE

- Organisational structures
- Managing international mergers and acquisitions
- Treasury planning in multinationality
- Communications in multinationality
- Co-ordination in multinationality
- Examples from multinational corporations (MNCs)

CHAPTER OBJECTIVES

After studying this chapter you should be able to:

- Identify the different structures for organising internationally.
- Recognise the competitive characteristics conferred by different organisational structures.
- Demonstrate an understanding of the competitive advantages derived by MNCs from organisational structures.
- Characterise post-acquisition match of organisational culture and operations.
- Identify the competitive dimensions of corporate treasury and tax planning.
- Demonstrate an understanding of structures for communications between, and co-ordination of, components of multinational organisations.
- Explain the communications and co-ordination differences among multinational organisations from different sources.

ALL COMPANIES NEED to:

- ensure that resources are effectively allocated within the organisation;
- co-ordinate the activities of different sub-units and functions in the company;
- provide an early warning of things going wrong with operations;
- assist with evaluating the performance of various sub-units or subsidiaries;
- help with evaluating the performance of individual managers; and
- provide a means of motivating managers.

Decentralisation adds to the difficulties of co-ordinating the activities of sub-units in order to achieve overall company goals. In delegating responsibility to subordinates, top management needs to define the various responsibility centres that have control over costs, revenues and profits. These management tasks become more complex where a company operates across national frontiers. Geographic distance may preclude frequent personal contacts between headquarters managers and sub-unit managers, and can even slow down the transmission of formal written communications, so that prompt feedback about sub-unit performance is hindered. Culture distance arises from socio-cultural differences and language difficulties between parent company managers and local sub-unit managers. Institutional backgrounds also differ with differences in national economic systems and policies, distribution arrangements and financial institutions.

6.1 ORGANISATIONAL STRUCTURES

Companies can be organised in a number of different ways, in particular management activities may be grouped by function, by product group, by geographical area or by a holding company arrangement.

Functional or unitary structures

Functional or unitary structures group activities into departments by management functions (production, marketing, etc.) with formal co-ordination of these activities being undertaken at the apex of the pyramid-shaped organisation, as shown in Figure 6.1. Top management is responsible for directing and co-ordinating all the functional activities for all the firm's products in all of the firm's markets.

Such structures provide a generally effective means of co-ordination, both within departments and across the organisation as a whole when there is a single product and single market being targeted. However, functional structures become less effective when an organisation supplies a number of different products and

Figure 6.1 A functional organisational structure

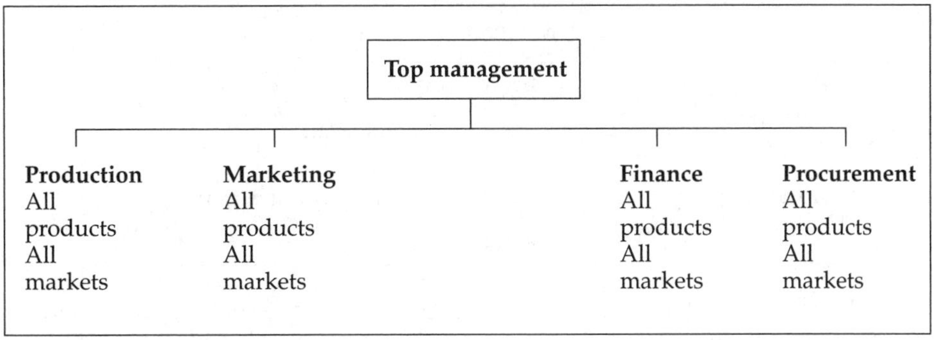

```
                          ┌──────────────────┐
                          │  Top management  │
                          └──────────────────┘
        ┌───────────┬───────────────┴──────────┬──────────────┐

   Production      Marketing              Finance        Procurement
   All             All                    All            All
   products        products               products       products
   All             All                    All            All
   markets         markets                markets        markets
```

sells in a number of different countries. Co-ordination increases in complexity and may be impaired because managers are juggling too many balls in the air at the same time and are thus unable to provide dedicated attention to one. Worst still, centralisation of decision-making may mean the firm loses touch with local market conditions and is unable to respond quickly to changes in customers' demands, competitors' actions, etc.

Multi-divisional structures

In these structures separate groups or divisions of the firm are each responsible for a group of similar products or servicing a separate market. Each group or division has its own management team and its own separate production, marketing, finance, etc., functions, co-ordinated by the chief executive of the group or division. Each group or division will be usually autonomously run with regard to day-to-day operational matters and may exercise some discretion over strategic decisions. Ultimately, however, they are accountable to headquarters for financial results. Typically, headquarters executives will be responsible for the strategic direction of the company, the co-ordination of the activities of groups or divisions which are linked together in a networking operation, the allocation of investment funds, including mergers and acquisitions, and the appointment of divisional chief executives and the other key staff members. Figure 6.2 shows one possible multi-divisional configuration for a business with international operations. There are, of course, many variations on this theme depending on the breadth of the company's product range, the extent of its multinationality and networking (see page 197).

Figure 6.2   A mutli-divisional configuration for international operations

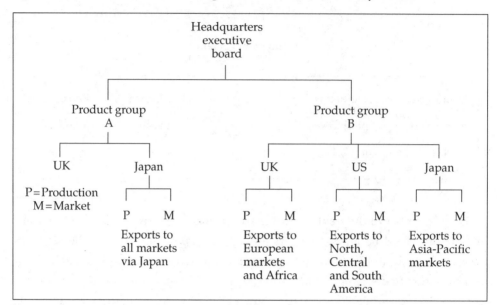

Although a multi-divisional structure involves duplication of management and some loss of economies of scale, it does have the advantage of a focused and dedicated approach to the management requirement of a particular product and its markets. It is, therefore, an appropriate organisational structure for a diversified business that supplies many products and operates on a world-wide scale. The locus of authority and co-ordination is at a relatively decentralised level (compared to functional structures), thereby providing for a potentially greater understanding of, and attention to, local market needs and an ability to react quickly to changing market conditions. A decentralised on-the-ground presence can be especially useful where customisation is an important competitive consideration. Where there are marked differences between countries in terms of consumer preferences and technical standards, firms may need to produce a wide range of products to meet these differing requirements and may need to market them in quite different ways using various combinations of marketing mix elements appropriate to particular market conditions. In such circumstances a critical factor in securing and maintaining competitive advantage is the employment of indigenous managers who are most familiar with the language, customs and cultures of their local communities.

Relationships between headquarters staff and divisional managers require careful handling to ensure goal congruence and a commitment to the interests of the group as a whole. The return on capital is often used as a yardstick for this purpose. With a central objective of return on capital it is possible to establish fairly clear-cut unequivocal targets in terms of return on capital expected for different divisions, making due allowance for different growth rates in different markets and the different degrees of risk involved. Senior managers at head office can then reward divisional managers and allocate capital resources to competing divisions on the basis of their performance measured in terms of return on capital. This may be appropriate where each division is run on a standalone basis. However, where divisions are networked and buy and sell to each other complications can arise if, for example, transfer prices are set at levels unrelated to actual operational and capital costs (see Section 6.3).

Holding company structures

Holding company structures are highly devolved multi-divisional structures in which constituent companies operate as independent companies. The constituent companies are completely or partially owned by a holding company. Little direct control is exercised by the holding company other than receipt of profits and the holding company confines itself largely to acquisitions and divestments. Figure 6.3 shows one possible configuration. An international holding company is based in, say, Switzerland (or any tax haven – see Unilever) with subsidiary companies in Canada, Spain, etc. The ultimate controlling company is based in the UK which receives profit reparations from the holding company secured by double taxation

Figure 6.3   Structure of a holding company

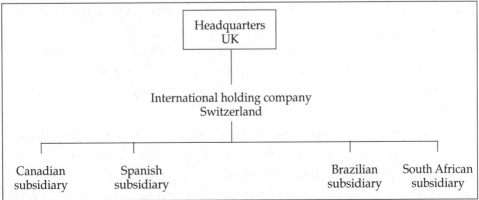

relief (i.e., under double taxation treaties between countries, profits which have already been taxed in one country are tax exempt when they are transferred to another country).

6.2 ORGANISATION OF MNCs

Unilever

Unilever, the Anglo-Dutch consumer goods group with a world-wide turnover of US$45.4 billion in 1994 (US$39.1 billion in foreign sales) and foreign assets of US$28.4 billion, provides a useful example of how a MNC can co-ordinate its cross-border activities. The Unilever group was established in 1930 when Margarine Unie (of the Netherlands) and Lever Brothers (of the UK) decided to merge their activities while retaining their separate legal identities. They are now incorporated as Unilever NV and Unilever PLC, respectively, and are the parent companies of a group which operates world-wide, with its corporate centre located in London and Rotterdam. Since 1930, NV and PLC have operated virtually as a single entity. They have the same directors and are linked by a series of agreements which bind the whole together. NV and PLC serve as holding and service companies. They co-operate in every way for the purpose of maintaining a common policy in every field of operations and exchange all relevant information regarding their businesses to ensure that all group companies act according to group policy.

In 1996 Unilever changed its organisational structure, in response to its changing business and external dynamics, from one based on product management groups and regional management groups to one based on business groups. Unilever's management structure 'is designed to be simple, effective and forward looking'. Unilever's organisation derives the maximum benefit from international co-ordination of its activities, while giving individual companies responsibility for their own operations. The top management structure consists of an Executive Committee that comprises directors: Joint Chairmen; Foods; Home and Healthcare; Strategy and Technology; Personnel; and Finance. The activities of the operating companies world-wide are co-ordinated by business groups and consumer groups (Figure 6.4).

Consumer goods business groups. There are 12 consumer goods business groups based essentially on geographical markets. In most geographical regions, all Unilever subsidiaries are organised into one business group. Business groups are headed by presidents. Larger geographical regions have more than one

Figure 6.4 Unilever's organisational structure

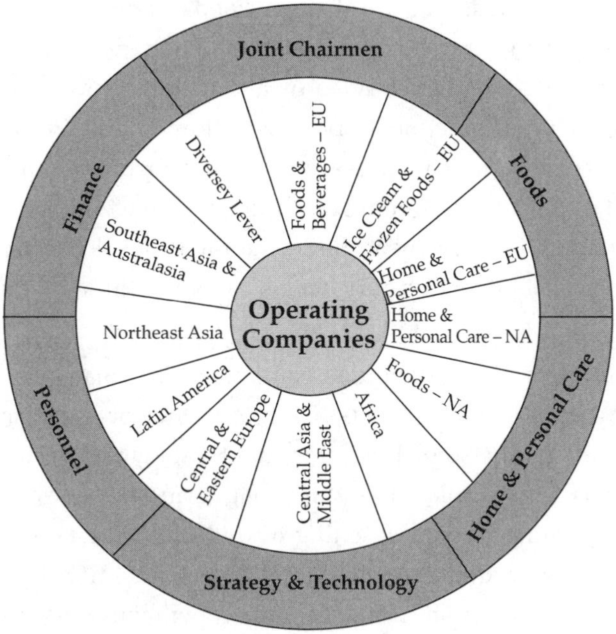

Source: Unilever.

business group, for example, Europe and North America. These business groups are responsible for overall profit policy created in two- to three-year cycle plans for the strategic development, production and marketing of Unilever's products. In the case of foods, three business groups – two in Europe, one in North America – are responsible for the performance of the business. All business group presidents are responsible for the profits of their businesses and act in an advisory capacity to subsidiary companies. The directors in co-ordination have global responsibility for the objective of ensuring both international and product synergy.

How the business groups operate. Presidents are responsible for overall group profit; development of regional strategies; processing market intelligence into headquarter decision-making; and executing corporate policy. Medium-term strategic plans are built on two- to three-year cycles monitored on an annual basis for each group. Plans are succinct containing one or two strategic targets and limited operational and financial targets. The emphasis is on a decentralised management of operations in the best judgement of business groups presidents. Performance is reported every quarter.

Product categories. Unilever identifies its core products in 13 categories – the Corporate Consumer Goods – in two streams. Foods, and Home and Personal Care that are present in several business groups. Each product category is the responsibility of a category team headed by a Category Senior Vice President. The category team includes functional specialists from marketing and technology liaising with research. The category team reports to one of the two Category Directors on the Executive Committee. Category Directors are responsible for strategy, brand equity management, innovation and development of world-class expertise in their category. Category teams network through the International Category Network informally and formally.

Executive committee. The committee comprises Chairman NV and Chairman PLC plus Category Director – Foods; Category Director – Home and Personal Care; Finance Director; Personnel Director; and Strategy and Technology Director. The committee is responsible for setting long-term strategies for: establishing priorities and allocating resources; setting overall corporate targets; agreeing and monitoring business group strategies and plans; identifying and exploiting opportunities created by Unilever's scale and scope; managing external relations; and developing future leaders.

De La Rue

Given the dynamics of the marketplace companies need to be mindful of the need for organisational changes (or business process re-engineering as it is now fashionably called; see Box 6.1) in order to remain competitive and responsive to customer needs. De La Rue, the UK-based world's leading cash to cards security printing, transactions and payments systems group with a global turnover of US$1,320 million in 1998 and a profit of US$146 million, provides an illustration of this.

Box 6.1 Business Process Re-engineering

Many international companies face the problem of overcoming functional barriers separating their sales and marketing departments and production and new product development departments. These barriers limit their effectiveness and speed of competitive response. Unilever's re-organisation in 1996 is a strategy to overcome these barriers. For some companies (see our discussion of De La Rue), overcoming this problem has involved a radical restructuring of their businesses based on an

---

Box 6.1 (*cont'd*)

international product division approach in which each division has central control over both production and marketing for a particular product group in all countries. In 1994, for example, Ford merged its North American and European vehicle businesses into a single grouping, Ford Automotive Operations (FAO). Within FAO, there are five vehicle programme centres (VPCs), with one located in Europe and four in the US. Each VPC has world-wide responsibility for product development, procurement, manufacturing, and sales and marketing operations for its vehicle models. The European VPC, for example, is responsible for small- and medium-sized cars: the Fiesta, Escort and Mondeo classes. Ford is seeking in particular to achieve major cost savings by eliminating duplication of effort in the value-chain, which in the past has seen the company developing similar cars, engines, etc., in parallel in North America and Europe. For the time being Ford's Asia-Pacific and Latin American operations are to remain separate.

By contrast, Electrolux, the Swedish electrical appliance producer, while restructuring the production side of its business has continued to operate a *cross-divisional* approach to local marketing. In 1992 the company restructured its production and new product development operations, abolishing its individual country management structure and establishing three Pan-European industrial divisions. The company's 'cold' products division (refrigerators, etc.) and 'hot' products division (microwave ovens, etc.) are based in Stockholm, and the third division, 'dry' or 'wet' products (washing machines, etc.), is based in Venice. These three divisions are responsible for planning and co-ordinating production operations for the whole of the European market. However, instead of transferring the country managers' power over national marketing to the new divisions these have been partly retained at the national level but are now planned and co-ordinated by a central marketing unit based in Italy. This unit controls all European sales and marketing through product portfolio managers in each country or sub-region. The reason for this approach is that trade customers expect the company's local sales offices to handle the *full* range of products and individual brands from all three divisions.

De La Rue has a decentralised structure with management devolved to the three operating divisions (Figure 6.5). There is a small central staff at the London head office, where strategy is formulated, budgets and operating targets are set and agreed with the divisions, and performance is monitored. A number of support functions are also controlled from head office including Human Resources, Legal and Public Affairs.

Each of the operating divisions is headed by a main board director who, in turn, delegates responsibilities to the managers of individual business units. Thus,

Figure 6.5   De La Rue's operational structure

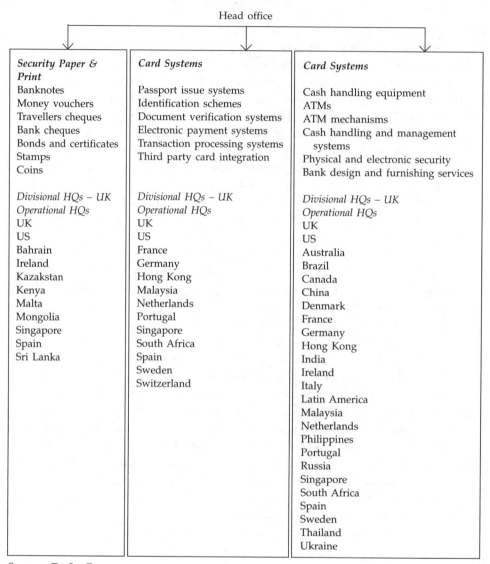

Head office

Security Paper & Print	Card Systems	Card Systems
Banknotes	Passport issue systems	Cash handling equipment
Money vouchers	Identification schemes	ATMs
Travellers cheques	Document verification systems	ATM mechanisms
Bank cheques	Electronic payment systems	Cash handling and management systems
Bonds and certificates	Transaction processing systems	Physical and electronic security
Stamps	Third party card integration	Bank design and furnishing services
Coins		
Divisional HQs – UK	*Divisional HQs – UK*	*Divisional HQs – UK*
Operational HQs	*Operational HQs*	*Operational HQs*
UK	UK	UK
US	US	US
Bahrain	France	Australia
Ireland	Germany	Brazil
Kazakstan	Hong Kong	Canada
Kenya	Malaysia	China
Malta	Netherlands	Denmark
Mongolia	Portugal	France
Singapore	Singapore	Germany
Spain	South Africa	Hong Kong
Sri Lanka	Spain	India
	Sweden	Ireland
	Switzerland	Italy
		Latin America
		Malaysia
		Netherlands
		Philippines
		Portugal
		Russia
		Singapore
		South Africa
		Spain
		Sweden
		Thailand
		Ukraine

Source: De La Rue.

the managers who are closest to the markets and customers are in a good position to optimise the commercial and financial performance of their team.

The three operating divisions have been restructured. For example, all the security paper and printing operations have been grouped within the renamed Security Paper and Print. This is designed to optimise the advantages gained by combining sales, manufacturing and technical resources for printing security documents with those for banknotes and travellers cheques.

Cash Systems now concentrates exclusively on the provision of automated solutions for the handling of cash, both for banknotes and coins. As this increasingly involves the design of systems and not just the supply and servicing of equipment, product groups have been reformed to facilitate the provision of systems solutions to customers.

The most significant structural change has been the formation of a new Card Systems Division. This brings together all those business units which play a part in the rapidly expanding markets for systems involving the issue of personalised plastic cards or identity documents, the use of electronic terminals for reading and authenticating them and computer-based integration systems. The growing number of applications for such systems includes identity card schemes, machine readable passport systems and a range of electronic payment systems.

Networking. Where a company owns a number of subsidiaries it can operate them on a purely standalone basis or it can link them together in a network of internalised cross-border transactions. As explained in earlier chapters the de-coupling of component supply, assembly of final products and the distribution and marketing of products usually occur to lower production costs, increase marketing effectiveness and product differentiation advantages as well as protect core know-how and products. Figure 6.6 shows two possible permutations (see also Chapter 2, Section 2.2). The company produces key components at home (to protect patents and avoid dissemination or loss of technical know-how, for example). In one case these (firm-specific advantages) are transferred to a

Figure 6.6 A networking configuration

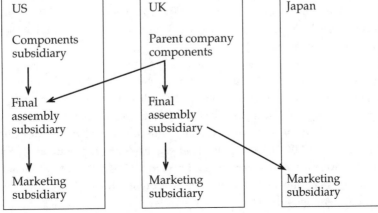

production plant in the US for assembly into the final product (which is produced locally for economies of scale reasons, for example). In the other case, Japan, the complete product is exported from the UK to a sales subsidiary which undertakes marketing (through company-owned distribution channels, for example). In both cases, a transfer pricing mechanism is required to support the transactions (Section 6.4). In addition to *vertical* linkages, networking can also be practised to good effect *horizontally* across business units located in different countries to produce group synergies (Box 6.2).

Box 6.2   Networking at Bowater

In addition to vertical linkages, networking can also be practised to good effect across related and diverse business units located in several countries as the example of Bowater, the UK packaging multinational, illustrates.

Bowater is an orchestrated collection of businesses. How well they play together determines whether we reap commercial benefits from the potential linkages. We encourage managers to network within the Group on every issue – from purchasing to marketing, and from the sharing of technology to the joint development of products. Joint purchasing of fibre, inks and resin is now routine. For example, designated resin specialists within Rexham Plastics (a US subsidiary) act on behalf of sister companies (in the UK, Canada, Germany, the Netherlands, etc.) to leverage the purchasing power of the Group, gain access to the latest polymer technologies and coordinate partnering arrangements with key suppliers. Collaboration on sales takes many forms. As an example of customer linkages, Rexham in the US introduced John Horn (a Scottish subsidiary) to Calvin Klein (the US cosmetics group), leading to a £1 million order for cosmetics packaging. Companies may network across very diverse business. Mulox (of the UK) which makes flexible intermediate bulk containers, drew on the computer skills of MiTek (a US subsidiary), which makes metal connector plates, to develop a database for customer presentations.

Bowater has set up a simple and pragmatic scheme to encourage companies within the Group to share technology, and help them take advantage of innovative developments. The scheme involves the creation of a 'hub' for developing particular technologies based on one company which then makes it available to others in the Group. For example, Cope Allman Plastics in the UK is taking the lead as the 'hub' for laminated object manufacturing systems which are used by various sister companies, including Reboul Cosmetique in France (Chief Executive's Review, *Bowater Annual Report and Accounts*, 1993).

Some notable examples of international networks

In 1994 Volkswagen (VW), the leading European car producer, expanded its presence in China by establishing a joint venture with a local company, First Automobile Works (FAW). VW has a 40% equity stake in the joint-venture concern, FAW-Volkswagen Automotive Company. A modernised version of the Audi 100 is assembled at the FAW-VW plant in Changchun, partly from kits supplied by VW from Germany. In addition, Seat (VW's Spanish subsidiary) Cordoba small car is assembled by FAW at its plant in Chunde from kits supplied by Seat. The car is sold in China as the VW City Golf.

In 1994 VW also established a joint venture in Taiwan with a local company, Chinfon Global. VW has a 33.3% equity stake in the joint-venture concern, Chinchun Motor, which produces light commercial vehicles. VW provides kits, technology and expertise, and Chinfon the facilities and management. The vehicles are marketed jointly. The assembly plant was scheduled to produce 30,000 vehicles per year by 1996 of which 20,000 would be sold in Taiwan and the rest exported to Southeast Asia and China. It is hoped that eventually more sophisticated parts made in Taiwan will be exported to supply VW's plants in China and completed engines made in China will be installed in Taiwan-made vehicles.

Komatsu, the Japanese producer of earthmoving equipment, has been increasing the sourcing of components from its overseas plants in order to keep costs down. In 1983 it began importing cast steel parts from its Brazilian subsidiary; in 1987 this was augmented by outsourcing cast steel parts from Samsung of Korea. In 1990 the company established two plants in Indonesia to supply casting and fabricated components, and in 1992 Komatsu set up a joint venture with Hokuriku in Indonesia to supply forgings for undercarriages. The company has continued its policy of switching its outsourcing of parts from Japanese suppliers to overseas companies; these include Berco of Italy (undercarriage parts), Kab and T-Mat of the UK (seats) and Gates of the US (hydraulic hoses).

In 1992 Nissan, the Japanese vehicle producer, launched its new estate car model, the Serene, for the European market. The car is assembled at Nissan Motor Iberica, Nissan's Spanish vehicle subsidiary in Barcelona, incorporating engines imported from its UK subsidiary in Sunderland. In 1994 Nissan, which already exports some 10,000 cars a year to Japan and Taiwan from its UK plant, commenced exporting its new Spanish-built Terrano II four-wheel drive vehicle to Japan.

In 1994 Mercedes-Benz of Germany began production of a new range of light-duty trucks in Indonesia as part of its Asian expansion programme. The MB700 range of light-duty trucks was developed to meet Asian cost levels with a system of global sourcing of components. The vehicles are assembled in Indonesia by PT German Motors Manufacturing, a joint-venture company in which Mercedes-Benz holds a 33.5% stake. Vehicles are supplied to the domestic market and for export to other countries in Southeast Asia and the Middle East.

Engines for the vehicles are assembled in Indonesia from components produced by Mercedes-Benz's commercial vehicle subsidiary in Brazil. Transmissions and front axles are supplied by Tata Engineering and rear axles are sourced from AAL, both of India. Brakes and shock absorbers are also supplied from India. Propeller shafts are supplied by Spicers of the US, Mercedes-Benz Argentina supplies mechanical steering systems, optional power steering systems are supplied by Koyo of Japan, and cab parts by Mercedes-Benz's Spanish subsidiary. Local companies supply other items such as tyres, truck bodies, exhaust systems and wheel rims.

Mercedes-Benz in 1996 subsequently established a joint venture with Singapore's Economic Development Board and sited its US$100 million automotive plant (small buses, light-duty trucks, cars) in Ho Chi Minh City to service Vietnam. Vietnam's projected annual transportation needs by 2000 will be between 20,000 and 40,000 commercial vehicles. The joint venture also provides a competitive platform and economies of scale for exporting to the near region.

6.3 MANAGING INTERNATIONAL ACQUISITIONS AND MERGERS: ACHIEVING GOAL CONGRUENCE, A COMMON CORPORATE CULTURE AND OPERATIONAL 'FIT'

International mergers and acquisitions (M&A) have grown tremendously and in 1997 sales and purchases totalled US$230 billion and US$300 billion respectively, for developed countries (Box 6.3). For developing countries totals were US$100 billion in sales and US$45 billion in purchases. The management of such asset values is critically important for the international competitiveness of the firms involved. In the late 1990s huge mergers and acquisitions have been announced in the oil and gas (BP and AMOCO, Exxon and Mobil, and TOTAL and Petrofina in 1998), banking and finance (Deutsche Bank and Bankers Trust in 1998) and pharmaceuticals (Glaxo and Wellcome in 1995) sectors.

Box 6.3   Britannia Rules the M&A Waves

1999 seen as bumper year, telecoms most active area in Q2, says KPMG poll. British firms dominated merger and acquisition activity during the first half of 1999, acting as the buyers in 48 per cent of deals totaling US$285 billion (S$486 billion) notched up during the second quarter.

The latest KPMG Corporate Finance survey – released yesterday – predicts a bumper year for M&A activity, outstripping 1998's record total.

The total value of international M&A activity during the first half of the year was US$409 billion, up from US$243 billion during the same period in 1998, the survey found.

"1999 looks set to beat easily the full year M&A volume of US$544 billion," KPMG Corporate Finance said in a statement.

A sector breakdown revealed telecoms as the most active area during the second quarter, with deals worth US$113 billion. This was followed by the chemical sector with some US$46 billion and oil and gas with US$17 billion.

Banking and finance – one of the sectors most hotly tipped for consolidation – came in at US$14 billion while the food, drink and tobacco sectors totaled nearly US$15 billion.

At US$285 billion, M&A activity during Q2 was up from the US$124 billion during the first quarter of the year, with British firms regaining the No. 1 slot as the most acquisitive, after losing it in the first quarter.

The UK Plc factor also boosted Europe's position as a major buyer of companies in other parts of the world. European Union firms bought firms worth a total of US$189 billion during the second quarter, some 66 per cent of the world total.

British companies were the buyers in deals worth a total of US$139 billion during the second quarter of the year, ahead of US firms with US$38 billion, Spain with US$19 billion and the Netherlands with US$9 billion.

"UK firms are clearly increasingly confident about their ability to handle market-transforming global acquisitions and are looking to make a real impact in overseas markets," said Stephen Barrett, head of M&A at KPMG Corporate Finance.

British firms put most of their cash into the US with 56 deals worth US$80 billion – some 50 per cent of the British total. Mr Barrett said the cultural compatibility between the two had not yet been replicated in British ties with European firms.

British firms were also active in Sweden, with purchases totaling US$38 billion, and the Netherlands.

In terms of inward investment, the US ruled the roost with deals worth US$145 billion – representing 51 per cent of the world total in Q2.

Sweden was the next biggest magnet for foreign money at US$42 billion, ahead of the UK which attracted only S$17.2 billion. But Mr Barrett sees the UK as a growing target for overseas acquisition in the coming months.

Source: Reuters, *The Business Times*, 20 July 1999

CASE **6.1**

Elf launches counterbid for TotalFina

France's Elf Aquitaine SA launched a 50-billion-euro (US$50.97 billion) cash-and-stock counterbid to acquire TotalFina AS, which on July 5, 1998 had announced a 42-billion-euro all-stock offer for Elf.

In what is known as a Pac-Man defense strategy, in which a target company turns around and makes an offer for its hostile bidder, Elf said its board decided late Sunday to offer three of its own shares and 190 euros in cash for every five shares of TotalFina. This, Elf said, was a 10% premium over TotalFina's closing price on Friday.

In response, TotalFina said that its bid "will go ahead once it has received authorization" from France's stock-market regulator. Under TotalFina's proposed deal, Elf shareholders would receive four TotalFina shares for every three Elf shares tendered.

In New York trading, Elf shares slipped to US$88.875 from US$90.625, while TotalFina shares rose to US$67.0625 from US$66.8125.

Philippe Jaffre, Elf's chairman, said in a statement that "together with our strong belief that we can deliver synergies exceeding twice those announced by TotalFina, our proposal combines a stronger industrial vision with a better value package for both sets of shareholders."

Elf said it expects to wring annual pre-tax savings of 2.5 billion euros within three years from the proposed merger. It also said it has a plan to realize more value by separating the two companies' oil and gas activities from chemicals, creating two separate companies.

Mr Jaffre earlier had hinted that the defense against TotalFina that he and his team of bankers were preparing was a 'major project'. In a speech to Elf managers, Mr Jaffre had pledged that "total's hostile bid will fail."

Ever since TotalFina's bid, and the implicit French government approval of it because it didn't involve a foreign company, Elf's choices have been limited. Industry experts reckoned a so-called white knight was out of the question because the large international oil companies that might be interested were all foreign.

Either way, a merger between TotalFina and Elf would create the world's fourth-largest publicly-owned oil company (after Exxon Corp, Royal Dutch Shell Group and BP Amoco PLC) with market capitalization of more than US$85 billion.

Mr Jaffre and his counterpart at TotalFina, Thierry Desmarest, had privately discussed the possibility of a friendly merger. But the talks broke down. Mr Jaffre has previously indicated that the two couldn't agree on what would happen to the overlapping business of the two companies following a merger. And the Elf chief suggested that instead of trying to resolve these differences, Mr Desmarest jumped the gun and made a hostile bid for Elf.

Now, Mr Jaffre says his plan would result in savings of more than one billion euros annually within three years from exploration and production activities, mainly by reducing production costs and through capital efficiencies. Another 950 million euros in savings would come from refining and marketing operations. And combining chemicals activities of the two companies could yield 200 million euros in savings.

The company said job losses under its plan would be no more than the 4,000 suggested by TotalFina in its bid. Elf said there would be selected asset sales, but only specifically identified disposal of 15% of the chemicals group Sanofi-Synthelabo.

Elf's offer hinges on its shareholders approving a capital increase, and the acceptance of at least 66.67% of TotalFina shareholders.

Source: *The Asian Wall Street Journal*, **20 July 1999**

Case Discussion Issues and Questions

1. Discuss the competitive implications of the wave of acquisitions and mergers in oligopolistic industries in the latter part of the 1990s. What are the main driving forces?

2. Analyse the potential competitive pressures on Elf and TotalFina.

3. Discuss the possible co-ordination challenges for Elf–TotalFina. Where are the main problems?

International expansion based on takeovers and mergers rather than the establishment of green-field subsidiaries poses the issue of goal congruence and unifying different corporate cultures (how alike the two companies' ways of doing business, organisational structures and reporting systems, etc., are). The diversity of corporate cultures arising from the companies' different business histories may be compounded by national differences in attitudes and customs. How are these differences to be handled post takeover or merger? In the case of takeovers the change may be only cosmetic, involving a change in ownership with the acquired firm operating more or less autonomously as a separate business unit or subsidiary, subject only to financial accountability to, and strategic direction from, headquarters. In other cases the two businesses will be integrated to varying degrees. This could involve the adoption of the acquirer's own corporate objectives, structures, practices and systems by the acquired organisation so that, over time, it becomes fully absorbed into the whole. In the case of an agreed merger, changes to *both* organisations may occur as part of a bargaining process to establish a mutually acceptable organisational structure and corporate philosophy. Obviously, there is no set formula for 'bonding' hitherto separate companies as the following examples demonstrate:

- Bowater, the UK packaging company, restructured itself in recent years to concentrate on four key packaging product areas. This has involved the company in a number of international takeovers to deepen its global operations. The assimilation of the acquired companies into the Bowater organisation is part of the company's policy of encouraging its business divisions to co-operate with each other to unlock product and market synergies.

  Thus, the company has been concerned to foster a well-understood corporate philosophy:

  > When you buy as many companies as we have, you need ways to bring together different cultures. Our new businesses have widely differing cultures embedded in their history. The first step is to install Bowater systems. Acquisitions adopt within the first 100 days our methods for reporting, budgeting, strategic reviews and other Group-wide matters. It takes longer for them to absorb our culture – to know instinctively how they need to behave if we are to realise our vision of becoming 'international manufacturers of high-quality, low-cost components for customers with high-value products'. The Bowater culture is based on three characteristics: the Group is taut, open and innovative. Being taut relates to the basic disciplines that govern the whole business.... Within a system of strong financial control we can delegate decisions to managers, and give them 'ownership' of their businesses. An open organisation does not manage culture change by diktat. We cannot impose an attitude; business units will adopt it once they realise that it makes sense. We expect constant innovation from our managers and our open structure puts the ball at their feet. We can now see that the Bowater culture is beginning to prompt profound changes in how people behave, in relation to quality, teamworking and productivity (Chief Executive's Review, *Bowater Annual Report and Accounts*, 1993).

- In 1995, Dresdner Bank of Germany took over Kleinwort Benson, the UK investment bank. The takeover was motivated by Dresdner's desire to become a leading investment banking group as the industry develops a 'super league'. Executives of Kleinwort retained a significant degree of control over the UK operation. A Dresdner senior executive took a management role at Kleinwort, becoming executive director and one of two deputy chairmen, but the chairman and the other deputy chairman were from Kleinwort. The two organisations' investment banking operations were kept separate. Kleinwort would manage mergers and acquisitions, absorbing Dresdner's small existing M&A team; Kleinwort will also run the combined equities business outside Germany; swaps and most fixed-income derivatives, where Dresdner is strong, would be run by the parent bank; bond and other fixed-income activities would remain separate. To preserve the UK investment bank's identity, it would be known as Kleinwort Benson, a member of the Dresdner Bank group. This standalone 'persona' arrangement is similar to that of Midland Bank, UK, following its acquisition by the Hongkong and Shanghai Banking Corporation in 1992.

How long Kleinwort remains autonomous remains to be seen. In the case of the acquisition of a UK investment bank Morgan Grenfell by German bank, Deutsche Bank in the early 1990s, after a 'transitional' period of independence in 1998 the former became fully integrated into Deutsche's own operations.

The current arrangement for running the Kleinwort business has been described by Dresdner's chairman thus: "Neither will we work on a parallel basis, competing against each other, nor will Kleinwort be absorbed." This middle of the road position contrasts markedly with the acquisition in 1995 of two other investment banks, SG Warburg and Barings by, respectively, Swiss Bank Corporation and Internationale Nederlanden Group, who took direct control of the acquired businesses and instigated an immediate programme of integration.

- In 1989, Plessey, the UK electronics company, was split up after being acquired jointly by Siemens of Germany and GEC of the UK, with Siemens becoming the sole owner of one business unit – Siemens Plessey Electronic Systems. The most radical change which occurred was in what has been referred to as 'Anglo Germany cultural differences'. Siemens is showing a commitment to the business and a readiness to invest long term that was all too lacking under British ownership: "What Plessey did most of the time was respond to the City of London's need for quarterly profit increases. The British electronics industry has not done well globally because they have had their eyes on the wrong ball. Sensible long-term plans were disrupted constantly by short-term considerations" (Company director, *Financial Times*, 13 April 1994). A case in point is the company's new £1.5 million radar test tower, one of three new key investment projects which owe their existence to the change in ownership. The radar project was first proposed in 1980 but rejected because it could not meet Plessey's normal criterion of a two-year payback. Under Siemens, a seven to ten-year breakeven horizon is typical on such projects.

  For operational matters, the business unit has a high degree of autonomy within 'certain parameters'. There was an early 'problem' when Siemens insisted on using its usual German consultancy on a British cost-reduction project. Things did not work out too well and now the UK unit has the discretion to select a consultancy themselves. Matters have also been helped by an 'inter-cultural training' course which introduced the Plessey management team to their Siemens counterparts. Language remains a barrier, however. While German executives 'are tolerant enough to break into their colleagues' language whenever the need arises', it is recognised that there needs to be more commitment from the UK side: "Not enough of us have found time to do a total immersion course. We need to – it's critical" (company director).

- In 1988, Nestlé, the Swiss multinational, acquired Rowntree MacIntosh, the UK's largest chocolate maker. Nestlé was already well-established in the UK as the country's leading coffee producer and was looking to enlarge its relatively small chocolate business by acquiring well-known brands such as Kit Kat. The integration of Rowntree took around four years and has involved the gradual shift of various aspects of managerial decision-making to Nestlé's Swiss headquarters. Operationally the Rowntree subsidiary has received strong support from Nestlé, including the instigation of a £120 million investment programme (which has expanded capacity and helped double Nestlé Rowntree's total exports from its seven UK plants) and the upgrading of its UK R&D facility (which has become Nestle's leading world-wide research centre for confectionery). This latter move has involved closing Rowntree's R&D centre in France and scaling down Nestlé's R&D work in Switzerland.

A key to the success of the takeover has been the fact that Nestlé took care not merely to leave Rowntree people in control of UK operations, but also to move them into senior jobs elsewhere within Nestlé. "Rowntree integrated into Nestlé with enthusiasm, partly because the Rowntree managers were left in charge" (Rowntree company director, *Financial Times*, 20 April 1994). Subsequently, some Rowntree senior and middle managers have been transferred to other Nestlé business units and HQ and a 'Nestlé man' (but British) has been appointed managing director of Rowntree. This two-way traffic is designed to develop a 'one-company' culture – after an acquisition this does not emerge 'unless you really do mix people up' (Rowntree company director).

- In 1990, Matsushita of Japan, the world's largest electronics company, acquired MCA, the Hollywood film studio for US$6.1 billion, the biggest single Japanese acquisition in the US. Like Sony's acquisition of Columbia Pictures a year earlier for US$3.4 billion, the strategic thinking behind Matsushita's move was the potential synergy deriving from the alliance of media systems deliverers with providers of entertainment products (compact disks, movie films and video cassettes, etc.). The marriage has not been a happy one, however. The studio's managers have grown increasingly frustrated with their owner's reluctance to fund expansion plans, while MCA has given Matsushita cause for concern with vastly expensive film projects. The nub of the problem is a clash in American-Japanese management styles, the former tending to be entrepreneurial, fast and short term in nature, while the latter tends to be based on consensus decision-making, and is slow and long term in nature. In the main, Japanese expansion abroad has been based on the establishment of joint ventures with green-field entry modes for operations (for example, Nissan's and Toyota's car assembly operations in UK). In this way, it has been possible to replicate Japanese corporate culture (quality circles, teamworking, etc.) by training up local workers to accept and implement Japanese working practices.

CASE 6.2

SembCorp Industries, Singapore: Aims to emerge fitter

In times of economic uncertainties exemplified by the Asian crisis, MNCs need to respond proactively if they wish to safeguard their competitive prospects. The following case illustrates the requisite responsiveness.

The key to success is not mere survival during the tough times but rather the ability to emerge stronger in order to benefit from the subsequent recovery.

This will be the guiding philosophy behind SembCorp Industries (SCI), the entity to be formed next month by the merger of Sembawang Corp and Singapore Technologies Industrial Corp.

SembCorp Industries deputy CEO-designate Tay Siew Choon said, "Obviously, the merger is not just about surviving the difficult times, but survival in the long term as well. We want to be able to grab hold of the opportunities that present themselves when the economy recovers."

Forward planning. The two companies have already started reviewing their various operations – ranging from infrastructure to construction and leisure to information technology.

The plan is to evolve into a leaner, meaner operation that will be put into motion the minute it gets the go-ahead from shareholders.

Key operations like STIC's and SembCorp's industrial park chain will be placed under a single management team to cut cost and increase efficiency.

Initial projections are that weeding out duplication will cut the SCI group's costs between 5 and 10 per cent in the first three to six months.

Net profit is forecast to grow by 15–20 per cent annually for the next three to five years, with profits expected to hit S$160–180 million.

This compares to consolidated net earnings of S$92.4 million booked for the year ended 13 December 1997.

Positive outlook. In an interview last week, Mr Tay said that despite the regional uncertainties the outlook for SCI remained good because of continued strong demand for some of its core businesses.

The new group will focus on four core areas:

- Infrastructure,
- Marine engineering,
- Information technology and
- Lifestyle.

SCI looks set to become one of the larger construction firms in ASEAN, with capabilities to design, build and manage large-scale projects regionally.

Its member companies will have a combined order book of about S$2.26 billion. Following the completion of the merger, SCI plans to better exploit Sembawang Engineering and Construction's capabilities in civil, mechanical and electrical engineering as well as Singapore Technologies' turnkey design and build capabilities in building and civil engineering work.

Merger prospects. In its merger prospectus, the group said it hoped to leverage on STIC's capabilities in the industrial parks business.

Specifically, it will draw on STIC's ability to provide a "range of services and choices as well as the ability to provide cost-effective services to its tenants and deliver above average returns to shareholders once an industrial park develops past its gestation period".

SCI plans to integrate its five industrial parks in Batam, Bintan, Wuxi, Vietnam and Karimun under one management team, resulting in marketing efficiencies, reduction in overheads as well as improved competitiveness.

The group's marine engineering division will enjoy access to one of East Asia's largest shiprepair yards – the Jurong Shipyard with a docking capacity of about 1.8 million deadweight tonnes.

It can also capitalise on Jurong Shipyard's capacity and capabilities to meet the anticipated demand for the construction of rigs and offshore platforms for the oil and gas industries, the group said.

Return on equity. SCI's overall plan is to "select and use resources and systems to enhance and build core competencies for regional dominance and achieve SCI's financial objective of a 12 per cent return on equity (ROE)". According to Mr Tay, many of the group's businesses were already operating above the 15–20 per cent ROE range. "We have lots of assets that we can leverage on for quality earnings," he said.

SCI's future. Many analysts are optimistic about SCI's future because of the combined strengths of the two companies.

"It's fundamentally a strong company despite the deterioration of the overall market," said HSBC Securities Associate Research Director David Leow.

"Generally speaking, I am quite positive about the whole merger because it makes a lot of sense for the group in Singapore to start specialising."

He said the merger would create "size and economies of scale, add complementary skills as well as increase the group's financial strength".

Regional turmoil. However, Mr Leow warned that a 'good proportion' of STIC's and SembCorp's income came from the region and this was cause for concern, given the growing regional uncertainties.

"Many of the countries in the region have gone into recession so that certainly is a worrying factor," he said.

SCI's management-in-waiting is keeping close tabs on the regional situation.

As Mr Tay puts it: "Let's be realistic. If the economic crisis takes a turn for the worse, we would be lucky to hold on to our current position, much less talk about growth. It really all depends on how the region performs over the next few years. One should not be too naïve to talk about growth rates."

But grow the company will, agree analysts and market watchers, citing the group's strong leadership.

Mr Leow said: "We all know that the success of any merger depends ultimately on the strength of the management."

Another analyst said: "The new SCI management, led by Mr Wong Kok Siew, should be able to pull through these tough times. He has spelt out his game plan which includes weeding out the unprofitable bits of the business, and that sounds promising." Mr Wong is SCI's CEO-designate.

Rationalisation.   Both companies have identified several subsidiaries that will either be sold off completely, or partially. These include the Delifrance chain, the group's regional hotel chain as well as other leisure-related businesses. "We have been talking to several foreign parties although these are still in preliminary stages," said Mr Tay.

Besides possible divestments, it is also seeking investments opportunities in engineering and infrastructure.

"If we want to be a significant engineering and infrastructural player, we should capitalise on this period when more competitive projects are available."

Mr Tay, however, noted that the group was taking a cautious stance because of the shaky regional economy.

"We are not just going to grab every project that comes along, of course," he said.

Set against this backdrop of rationalisation and consolidation, analysts say the future looks bright for SCI.

DBS Securities analyst Sebastian Heng said a lot depended on the completion of the rationalisation but things were looking up for the group, especially in the billion-dollar utilities business.

Major player.   "It appears that SCI is positioning itself to be a major player in Singapore's power sector, with a strong foothold in the regional utilities market," Mr Heng said.

SCI plans to leverage on ST Energy's expertise in power plant development, as well as the operation and maintenance of Sembawang Utilities and Terminals – currently Jurong Island's sole provider of utilities and chemical waste water treatment services for the petrochemical and chemical industries.

Source: *The Straits Times,* **14 September 1999**

Case Discussion Issues and Questions

1. Indicate the major dimensions of the situation that a company like SembCorp finds itself in.

2. Delineate the pressures that are driving on SembCorp to consider merger prospects.

3. Discuss, in relation to regional developments, the competitive dynamics that characterise the types of industries that SembCorp is in.

4. Given the nature of its business and the prospects going forward, develop a viable set of alternative competitive postures for SembCorp.

5. What dangers do you see with respect to the different competitive scenarios you have developed?

❖ ❖ ❖

6.4 TREASURY AND TAX PLANNING ASPECTS OF MULTINATIONALITY

Operating in many countries each with their own national currencies raises a number of issues for the management of MNCs' finances with regard to fiscal and treasury functions, cash flow, borrowings and investment allocation. There is also the matter of tax planning, i.e., in which countries the MNC should seek to declare its profits.

Exchange rate exposure

Exchange rate exposure, that is the extent of a firm's potential losses and gains on its overseas operations (measured in domestic currency terms) as a result of exchange rate changes, is a particular concern. The firm can be exposed to variations in exchange rates in a number of ways:

- *Translation or accounting exposure* arises when consolidating the assets, liabilities, revenues and expenses of overseas subsidiaries (expressed in foreign currencies) into the parent company's group accounts (expressed in the parent's domestic currency).

- *Transactions exposure* arises when a firm exports and imports products and borrows funds from abroad or invests overseas. For example, when a firm exports a product, invoicing the customer in terms of the customer's own local currency, and granting the customer 60 days' credit, then the firm is exposed to the effects of exchange rate variations during the 60-day credit period, which may decrease or increase the domestic currency value of the money due. Were the exchange rate of the foreign currency to fall dramatically *vis-à-vis* the domestic currency, then the exchange rate loss may completely eliminate any expected profit on the transaction.

- *Economic or cash flow exposure* is concerned with the impact of exchange rate variations on the future cash flows generated by a company's production and marketing operations. Long-term or dramatic changes in exchange rates may well force a firm to rethink its foreign market servicing strategy and raw material sourcing strategy. For instance, a firm which serviced its overseas markets by direct exporting from domestic plants might decide to establish local production units to supply these markets instead, if an exchange rate appreciation were to render its export prices uncompetitive.

There are a number of mechanisms whereby a firm can reduce its exposure to potential losses resulting from exchange rate changes. First, a firm can seek to prevent an exposed position from arising by using such internal exposure management techniques as *currency matching* (matching foreign currency holdings with equal foreign currency borrowings); *leading and lagging* (accelerating or delaying foreign currency payments and receipts where the exchange rate of the currency is expected to change); and *multilateral netting*, which involves subsidiaries offsetting their receipts and payments with each other, leaving a single net intra-company receipt or payment balance to be financed.

Second, the MNC can use external contractual arrangements to reduce or eliminate whatever exposure remains, hedging risks by, for example, entering into forward exchange contracts to buy or sell currencies at known prices for delivery at some future point in time, and factoring (selling the firm's trade debts).

It is beyond the scope of this book to go into the technicalities of financial planning in MNCs in a detailed way but two examples will help indicate some of the facets involved.

De La Rue. A summary of the cash flows of the company for 1997–98 is given in Table 6.1, which shows that the group's net cash balance decreased from £4.3

Table 6.1 Cash flow

	1998 (£m)	1997 (£m)
Cash flow from operating activities	72.8	80.8
Returns on investment and servicing of finance	23.9	17.8
Taxation	(19.2)	(28.9)
Capital expenditure and financial investment	(30.9)	(34.4)
Acquisitions and disposals	(53.9)	11.4
Equity dividends paid	(53.2)	(52.2)
Cash outflow before use of liquid resources and financing	(68.6)	(5.5)
Management of liquid resources	16.7	21.3
Financing	48.5	(11.5)
(Decrease)/increase in cash in period	(3.4)	4.3
Reconciliation of net cash flow to movement in net debt		
(Decrease)/increase in cash in period	(3.4)	4.3
Cash inflow from decrease in liquid resources	(16.7)	(21.3)
Cash (inflow)/outflow from (increase)/decrease in debt	(47.6)	12.5
Change in net debt resulting from cash flows	(67.7)	(4.5)
Loans and finance leases acquired with subsidiary	(7.1)	(5.2)
Translation difference	12.4	9.5
Movement in net debt in period	(62.4)	(0.2)
Net debt at start of period	(58.9)	(58.7)
Net debt at end of period	(121.3)	(58.9)

Source: De La Rue, *1998 Annual Report.*

million to minus £3.4 million. This net cash balance was held in various currencies. Table 6.2 shows the cash balances by currencies in 1994. The cash and borrowings denominated in currencies other than sterling relate mainly to working capital required for trading purposes or are held as part of De La Rue's balance sheet hedging policy (Table 6.2). All major deposits are placed with banks which meet stringent third party credit quality criterion.

Table 6.2 Cash and borrowings by currency

	Cash	Borrowings	Net (£m)
£	276	(7)	269
DM	29	(28)	1
US$	37	(43)	(6)
SEK	9	–	9
SFr	17	(25)	(8)
Other	7	(4)	3
Total	375	(107)	268

Source: De La Rue, *1994 Annual Report.*

For operational and other reasons not all of the balances are held in the UK. Table 6.3 illustrates this tendency.

Table 6.3   Net cash by country (£m)

UK	217
Switzerland	80
US	(29)
Germany	(14)
Sweden	6
Other	8
Total	268

Source: De La Rue, *1994 Annual Report.*

The company's policy is generally to protect the sterling value of assets denominated in foreign currencies by arranging borrowings in those currencies such that the value of the group's net assets measured in sterling does not fluctuate significantly as a result of changes in exchange rates. Exceptions are made to this policy for certain currencies when it is considered impractical or uneconomical to follow the policy. A comparison of the assets by currency, before and after the associated hedging, is given in Table 6.4.

Table 6.4 Assets by currency

	UK £	Other European* and Swiss Franc	US$
Pre-hedging	53	30	17
Post-hedging	75	19	6

* Mainly German Deutschemark.

Source: De La Rue, *1994 Annual Report.*

The group also generally protects against transaction risk by ensuring that, once a sale or purchase is confirmed which is in a currency other than the domestic currency of the business undertaking the transaction, equal and opposite commitments are made in the foreign exchange markets to protect against subsequent movements in exchange rates. Again, exceptions are made to this policy where it is considered impracticable or uneconomical to operate it.

The overall effect of these policies is three-fold. First, the movement on reserves as a result of changes in exchange rates is kept to a reasonably low level. Second, the forward sale and purchase of foreign currency tend to smooth the effect of movements in exchange rates over time while providing the group's operating companies with a stable environment in which to do business. Third, the fact that De La Rue generates profits in US dollars, Deutschemark and, to a lesser extent, other currencies as well as the sterling, means that group profits tend to increase when these currencies strengthen against the sterling and decline when they weaken.

De La Rue's treasury department acts as a service centre operating within clearly defined guidelines that are approved by the directors and against which there is regular reporting to the board. The range of financial instruments used is subject to board approval and may include swaps and the purchase of options. Under no circumstances will instruments be utilised which involve the group in assuming an unquantified risks.

Unilever. Unilever finances its operating subsidiaries through a mixture of retained profits, bank borrowings and loans from the parents and long-term debt raised in the international bond markets. Long-term borrowings, which form a substantial part of Unilever's current financial commitments, are raised in major trading currencies. Approximately half of the company's total borrowings are in US dollars and the remainder in various currencies including sterling, guilders and Swiss francs. The operation of this policy is bound to change in 2002 when the euro becomes Europe-wide currency. Unilever operates an interest rate management policy with the objective of minimising interest costs. Interest rates are fixed on a proportion of debt and investments for periods up to ten years using interest rate instruments such as swaps and forward rate agreements.

Unilever does not actively manage its balance sheet exposure to currency retranslation using financial instruments but seeks to match assets and liabilities in the same currency. This is achieved by a combination of direct borrowing and hedging of loans made to subsidiaries by parent companies. Over 70% of net assets are denominated in the currencies of the two (UK and Dutch) parent companies. The advent of the single European currency will simplify matters considerably for a MNC like Unilever.

Foreign currency transactions are generally hedged, although some flexibility is allowed within overall exposure limits. Hedging is primarily achieved by the use of forward foreign exchange contracts and, to a lesser extent, currency options.

The treasury function within Unilever is not a profit centre but exists to serve the needs of the business operations and to manage financial risks.

Tax planning and transfer pricing

Using tax planning tactics, MNCs can aim to incur most of their expenditure in countries with high-tax rates and generous depreciation and expenses allowances in order to gain maximum tax relief on expenditures. At the same time companies can aim to generate most of their revenues and profits in low-tax countries to minimise their tax bills. In the latter context companies can siphon off profits earned in high-tax countries to low-tax countries through inflated interest payments between group subsidiaries, high-royalty payments between group subsidiaries and high-intra-group management charges and consultancy fees. However, where subsidiaries supply components, goods and services to one another or supply is provided by the parent company, the latter will have an incentive to adjust the transfer prices at which such transfers are invoiced (see next section). By charging a low transfer price for components, goods or services moved from a subsidiary located in a high-tax country to another subsidiary located in a low-tax country, taxable profits in the first subsidiary will be reduced and those of the second subsidiary increased, thus serving to increase post-tax profits of the group as a whole. To obtain maximum benefits from such opportunities MNCs may also use tax havens. These are countries which seek to foster their economies (such as the Channel Islands, Cayman Islands, Bahamas, Turks and Caicos Islands) by offering permanent tax inducements to individuals and companies. Such countries generally have few tax treaties with other countries, so they are not obliged to furnish information about companies to other governments and exchange controls may be minimal or non-existent thus making it easy to move funds into and out of the country. Establishing a foreign holding company domiciled in a tax-haven country enables a MNC to use their 'shell' company to receive tax-free the profits earned by operating subsidiaries. Recycling of funds can allow operating subsidiaries to be financed by loans from the holding company, so that interest payments reduce the taxable income of subsidiaries in high-tax countries. In a similar way, patents can be assigned to the haven company allowing it to collect royalties from operating subsidiaries in high-tax countries, while management charges and fees could also be levied upon operating subsidiaries and invoiced to the haven country.

Objectives of transfer pricing.   Maximising global corporate profits is often cited as a primary goal of a MNC. Given differences between countries in terms of cost, tariff and tax structures, changes in exchange rates and in competitive pressures, internal transfer pricing as opposed to market-based transactions with intermediaries can provide an effective and flexible means of enhancing corporate profitability. Transfer pricing can be deployed in a number of contexts:

- **Taxation**
  Minimisation of the MNC's global tax liability by using transfer pricing to move products at cost out of countries with high corporate taxes and the generation of profits in countries with low corporate taxes.

- **Tariffs**
  Minimisation of the MNC's exposure to tariffs by using transfer pricing to lower product prices sold to countries with high-import tariffs.

- **Exchange rates**
  Transfer pricing can be used to reduce the MNC's exposure to exchange rate risks by, for example, moving funds out of weak currencies into strong ones.

- **Exchange controls**
  Transfer pricing can be used to move funds out of a country that operates exchange controls restricting the repatriation of dividends and capital.

- **Competitive pressures**
  Transfer pricing can be used to enable subsidiaries to lower prices to match or undercut local competitors, thus creating barriers to entry.

Transfer pricing methods. There are three basic methods of transfer pricing:

- **Market-based prices**

  With this method, the MNC prices the intermediate or final goods and services that it transfers between its business units at a price equal to that prevailing for similar or same goods and services on the open market. This is a form of arm's-length pricing insofar as intra-company transfers are priced the same as that charged to an external customer.

  This method has two main advantages for the MNC. Firstly, business units are able to operate as independent profit centres with the managers of these units being responsible for their own performance. This can increase the motivation of local managers while making it easier for headquarters to assess the actual operating performance results of its business units. Secondly, the market price method is usually favoured by the tax and customs authorities of both host and home countries as they will receive a fair share of the profits made. In this case the international trading of the MNC is transparent, so avoiding potential conflict with the authorities.

  In practice, however, the use of a market price as a benchmark is often difficult. There needs to be a competitive market which can provide a comparable price to which the transfer price can be matched, but for some items such as complex capital equipment or intermediate goods an external market may not exist, and for others prices may be distorted by monopoly elements. Moreover, a definitive market price may be difficult to determine as prices for the same product may vary considerably from one country to another. Changes in exchange rates, transportation costs, local taxes and tariffs can result in large variations in the selling price. In addition, a company will want to set its prices in relation to the supply and demand conditions relevant to specific country conditions to ensure that a business unit can compete in that country. In sum, these factors mean that there is unlikely to be a unique market price for the MNC to follow.

- **Cost-based prices**

  With this method the cost of a product or service, with or without a profit element, is used as a basis to determine the transfer price. The costs of a product or service are generally available from within the company and can be determined from the MNC's own accounting systems. This method is generally acceptable to the tax and customs authorities since it provides some indication that the transfer price approximates the real price of supplying the item, and that the authorities will receive a fair share of tax and tariff revenue. Cost-based approaches are, however, not so transparent as to totally remove suspicion that they have been 'massaged' since the selection of a *particular* type of cost method can significantly alter the magnitude of the transfer price.

  The issue is which cost approach to use: full actual costs, full standard costs, actual variable costs, or only marginal costs? Should R&D costs be included? How should fixed costs be incorporated? How should a profit element be entered into the calculation? Different cost permutations can yield widely differing transfer prices and hence raise a question mark over how the authorities view the legitimacy of such prices. From the MNC's perspective, cost-based methods can create difficulties with the selling unit as there may be little incentive for it to remain cost-effective if it knows it can simply recover increased costs by raising the transfer price. Without an incentive to produce efficiently the transfer price may erode the competitiveness of the final product in the market place.

- **Negotiated prices**
  In this approach buying and selling business units are free to negotiate a mutually acceptable transfer price. Since each unit is responsible for its own performance this will encourage cost minimisation and encourage the parties to seek a transfer price which yields them an appropriate profit return. However, this may result in sub-optimisation *overall* since no account is taken of such factors as differences in tax and tariff rates between countries, and hence the scope to increase the profitability of the group as a whole by deploying transfer pricing to minimise the MNC's global tax bill.

Constraints. Transfer pricing can be a highly flexible tool in achieving benefits for the MNC but there are several constraints on its use, both internal and external.

- **Internal constraints**
  The extent of decentralisation or centralisation may pose potential conflicts between the interests of the MNC and its various business units in terms of goal congruence, motivation and performance evaluation. Decentralisation and arm's-length pricing may encourage attention to cost efficiency and boost local pre-tax profits but may undermine the overall after-tax profitability of the MNC because of a failure to transfer most of the company's profits to a tax haven. On the other hand, a centralisation and manipulative transfer pricing may have negative effects on individual subsidiaries by harming local managers' morale and hiding operating inefficiencies, thus serving to undermine the company's longer-term competitive viability.

  The mechanics of implementing and maintaining the less open forms of transfer pricing can be complex and time-consuming. For a global MNC a vast amount of information on product flows, tax and tariff rates in individual countries, and changes to these, need to be ascertained. A control system is needed to collect, analyse and transmit the obtained data and 'mastermind' the network of transfer prices between subsidiaries and divisions.

- **External constraints**
  The use of transfer pricing procedures by MNCs impacts on the countries between which intra-company trade takes place. National tax and customs authorities quite naturally wish to ensure that trade is conducted in a 'fair' way and conforms to the

country's legal requirements. The problem of the private interest of the MNC versus the public interest of the country can pose difficulties. The under-recording of local profits through the use of manipulative transfer prices which 'transfer out' value added, for example, is one common area of confrontation between MNCs and both developed and developing host country governments. One way of combating this latter problem which has been widely canvassed (and is currently employed by the US State of California) is the use of a unitary taxation system. Under a unitary tax system, local taxation is based on a proportion of the *world-wide* profits of a company calculated on the size of its assets, employment, etc., in that country instead of only on the profits actually declared in that country. Table 6.5 shows a company having US$1 billion of assets both in country Y and country Z and total gross profits of US$200 million. Country Y taxes corporate profits at 50% and country Z at 20%. Under the conventional taxation system the company would pay a total of US$40 million in tax to the authorities in country Z. Under a unitary taxation system, although the country has declared no profits in country Y the assets located there are assumed to have generated one-half of the world-wide profits of the company. In this case the company's tax bill is US$90 million to US$50 million payable on the 'shadow' profits attributable to the company's assets in country Y and US$40 million on the actual profits declared in country Z.

Table 6.5 Tax liabilities under conventional and unitary taxation systems

	Country Y 50% tax rate company assets = US$1 billion	Country Z 20% tax rate company assets = US$1 billion	Tax liability
Taxation systems			
Conventional basis			
gross profits	0	US$200m	US$40m
Unitary basis			
gross profits	(US$100m) plus	US$200m	US$90m

CASE 6.3

EDB aware of transfer pricing by exporters

What Is Transfer Pricing?

Singapore companies, many with operations in Malaysia, send goods to Malaysia for re-export because the peninsula has declared this year tax-free for earnings.

"If companies are not allowed to make money, usually they will make it illegally ... It's very straightforward. Transfer pricing is not a crime."

Mr Yeo on Singapore's stand on the issue

The gap between Singapore's growing manufacturing output and sluggish exports could be due to exporters using transfer pricing, Mr Philip Yeo, chairman of Singapore's Economic Development Board (EDB) said.

Singapore companies, many with operations in Malaysia, have been sending goods to Malaysia for re-export because the peninsula has declared this year tax-free for earnings.

"Singapore has never bothered about transfer pricing. Other countries watch these people suspiciously. Our belief is that businesses are in business to make money.

"If they are not allowed to make money, usually they will make it illegally … It's very straightforward. Transfer pricing is not a crime," Mr Yeo told Reuters in an interview on the sidelines of a semiconductor equipment exhibition.

It was understandable that Singapore companies would find ways to maximise their bottom-line.

"I don't care about transfer pricing. If they make money, it doesn't bother me … As far as Singapore is concerned, if they are able to get lower cost materials and inputs to make higher profits, so be it," he said.

The issue of transfer pricing has become a hot debate among analysts trying to explain the wide divergence in Singapore's industrial output and exports in the first quarter.

Industrial output grew 6.5 per cent in the first quarter over last year, while non-oil domestic exports only inched up 0.7 per cent over the same period.

"My theory is that Singapore companies are marking down prices for export into Malaysia before they are exported again," Vickers Ballas economist Eddie Lee told Reuters earlier.

Higher output could otherwise lead to rising inventories which could dent manufacturing growth in the second quarter.

Mr Yeo also said it was too early to say if the robust growth in manufacturing for the first quarter was sustainable but the outlook should be clearer after the second-quarter data was out.

Electronics and chemicals were expected to be the two key growth sector drivers, he said. "When they recover, engineering will be the third sector to follow."

He said there were 11 new plants coming on-stream in Singapore's chemicals cluster on Jurong Island this year.

"The semiconductor equipment companies are expanding too … Precision engineering is lagging about three to four months. But it will follow the electronics and chemicals. So when they improve, it will follow too," he said.

Last year, Singapore's semiconductor industry achieved an output of nearly S$11 billion against S$10.7 billion in 1997 despite a global sector slowdown and the Asian crisis.

The EDB was still aiming to achieve its S$7.5 billion target in foreign direct investments this year, he added.

Source: Reuters, *The Straits Times*, 5 May 1999

Case Discussion Issues and Questions

1. Discuss the relative merits of the attitude of the Singapore Government towards international transfer pricing.

2. Analyse the motives that might drive international firms to transfer price out of Singapore. What relative benefits accrue to MNCs and Singapore?

3. Discuss possible ways for Singapore to reduce its fiscal losses due to international transfer pricing.

Some cases of transfer pricing abuse.   Transfer pricing is often implemented in ways that are difficult to discern and evaluate by outsiders not privy to key corporate information and decision-making processes. This is particularly the case with manipulative transfer pricing that is conducted in a clandestine way. In some instances host country tax authorities need to rely on 'whistleblowers' or a blatant transgression of national legal requirements to alert them to the possibility of abusive transfer pricing.

The US and Japanese tax authorities acted against various foreign multinationals for suspected tax evasion: the US against Nissan, and Japan against Coca-Cola, Roche, Ciba-Geigy and Hoechst. In addition to national litigation, the 17-year dispute between Barclays Bank and the US State of California over the application of unitary taxation was ruled on by the US Supreme Court in 1994. The Supreme Court upheld California's right to apply penalty taxes on foreign companies. The verdict means that California is now not required to refund Barclays and a number of other foreign MNCs around US$400 million (£267 million) it has already collected in penalty taxes and cancel another US$500 million it has assessed and which is still awaiting collection.

Britain: Inland Revenue versus Nissan UK.   The Inland Revenue's litigation against Nissan UK while not strictly a case of 'pure' internal transfer pricing provides useful insight into some of the general features of clandestine transfer pricing and its detection. In 1992 the Inland Revenue issued a demand for £237 million in unpaid taxes against Nissan UK, the former distributor of Nissan Japan's motor cars in the UK. Nissan UK is a private company controlled by Octav Botnar whose parent company is the Panama-incorporated European Motor Vehicles Corporation. The substance of the Inland Revenue's charge was that executives of Nissan UK in collusion with a Norwegian freight transport company had conspired to defraud the UK authorities of corporation tax. Transfer pricing, using 'falsely inflated' shipping invoices, had been employed to under-record Nissan UK's pre-tax profits over the period 1975–92. In 1971 Nissan UK obtained an exclusive franchise to import cars from Nissan, Japan. Until 1975 it paid for the cars with a single 'cost, insurance and freight' payment to Nissan Japan's transport division NMCC. From 1975 onwards it employed firstly the services of a Dutch freight forwarder, and then from 1982, Scansivis, a Norwegian shipping firm. Over this period freight charges for imported cars were overstated by 40%–60% by Scansivis which arranged for monies paid over to be 'laundered' into a Swiss bank account.

In 1991, the Inland Revenue acting on a tip-off mounted a dawn raid on Nissan UK, searching 13 locations, including the company's headquarters, the offices of several of its legal and financial advisers and the homes of a number of current and former executives of the company. Two directors of Nissan UK were subsequently found guilty at the Old Bailey of fraud, but the prime mover of the operation, Botnar, had already evaded arrest by moving to Switzerland.

US: US Internal Revenue Services versus Nissan Japan. In 1993 Nissan the Japanese car manufacturer agreed to pay 'penalty taxes' of Y17 billion (approximately US$210 million) to the US Internal Revenue Services (IRS) following an IRS investigation which concluded that Nissan had avoided US taxes by transferring part of its US profits to Japan in the early 1990s. The IRS's main contention was that Nissan had set transfer prices on its passenger cars and trucks imported from Japan at 'unrealistically' high levels and as a result declared lower profits in the US than it should have done. What constitutes a 'fair' or 'realistic' transfer price is, as we have indicated earlier, open to question. In the US, the common Japanese practice of charging relatively low prices to build market share over the longer term is viewed with some scepticism and hence has raised suspicions regarding 'unfair' transfer pricing practices. Although Nissan has in principle accepted that a proportion of the profits declared in Japan should have been recorded in the US through its agreement to pay the penalty taxes imposed, its view that these impositions were unwarranted has been supported by the Japanese tax authorities. Nissan contested the IRS ruling and the issue was referred to the National Tax Agency of Japan who have refunded Nissan the full amount of the fines.

Earlier, Nissan had been fined by the IRS for transfer pricing abuses in connection with trucks and motor cars exported to the US from Japan over the period 1975–84. The IRS imposed penalty taxes of Y62 billion (approximately US$808 million) on Nissan but the Japanese National Tax Agency set a precedent and signalled its disapproval of the IRS's stance on transfer pricing by refunding the fines in full to avoid double taxation.

Japan: National Tax Agency versus Coca-Cola, Roche, Ciba-Geigy and Hoechst. The controversial nature of the transfer pricing debate at the inter-governmental level was compounded in May 1994 by the decision of the National Tax Agency (NTA) to impose penalty fines on a number of prominent US and European companies, including Coca-Cola, the US soft drinks producer, the German pharmaceutical company Hoechst, and Roche and Ciba-Geigy, the Swiss pharmaceutical firms.

The NTA alleged that many US and European concerns had deliberately under-recorded profits earned in Japan both by charging excessive transfer prices to their local subsidiaries for materials imported from their parent companies, and by levying excessive royalty payments on their Japanese subsidiaries.

The NTA imposed a penalty tax of Y15 billion (US$192 million) on Coca-Cola for 'unfair' transfer pricing practices and for applying excessive brand and marketing royalty payments transferred to its US parent company over the period 1990–92, while Ciba-Geigy was charged a penalty tax of Y5.7 billion (US$76 million) and Roche Y10 billion (US$128 million) for engaging in manipulative transfer pricing over a similar three-year period. Hoechst was fined an undisclosed amount but appealed against it before a Japan–Germany inter-governmental tax authority.

Transfer pricing, because of its various possible permutations, will continue to remain a controversial issue. The suspected tit-for-tat confrontation between the US Internal Revenue Service and the National Tax Agency of Japan seems set for escalation against the broader trade dispute between the two countries on how to remove Japan's huge balance of payments surplus with the US. Transfer pricing, however, remains of wider significance both for other industrial countries, as well as the developing countries given the substantial expansion of MNC investment over the past two decades.

The reconciliation of the private interest (profits) of the MNC with that of the public interest (tax raising and welfare distribution) of host country governments is unlikely to occur until there is full international co-operation and agreement on acceptable practices and the establishment of appropriate arbitration mechanisms to resolve disputed cases.

Apart from the technicalities of fiscal and treasury functions and the minimisation of overall corporate tax liabilities and the maximisation of performance in terms of profits, a key aspect of managing MNCs concerns the culture of the corporate organisation, i.e., how the organisation does its business and relates internally and externally to the functions it must perform in order to deliver long-term sustainable competitiveness. Different MNCs have different approaches to this immense task of engendering a workable corporate culture that delivers high performance in all the aspects of the business right through to the ultimate goal of customer satisfaction.

CASE 6.4

Avoidance or minimisation: Keeping what's yours

Media tycoon Rupert Murdoch may run one of the most profitable businesses in the UK, but it appears that he has somehow managed to avoid running up a tax bill over the past 11 years.

According to *The Economist*, Mr Murdoch has saved at least £350m in tax – enough to pay for seven new hospitals, 50 secondary schools or 300 primary schools.

How he has done it remains a mystery – and News Corporation is certainly loath to give away any financial secrets.

But it appears that Mr Murdoch's tax accountants have surpassed themselves – making full use of tax loopholes to protect profits in offshore havens.

Mr Murdoch also has the luxury of shifting funds from country to country across his sprawling media empire to foil the taxman.

It is not just the Inland Revenue that has been left empty-handed by News Corporation's clever financial engineering.

Mr Murdoch 'hands very little of his profits to governments' according to *The Economist*.

Overall, News Corporation paid just £146m ($238m) in corporate taxes on profits of more than £2 billion.

In other words he's paying tax at a paltry rate of just 6%. That compares with normal company tax rates of 30% and upwards.

The financial secrecy that has characterised Mr Murdoch's empire could turn out to be a double-edged sword.

On the one hand he has managed to hold onto more money. But News Corporation's complex structure, which includes 60 incorporated tax havens, such as the British Virgin Islands and the Cayman Islands, has confused analysts and investors alike.

In the same opaqueness that characterises its tax affairs, News Corporation said it had no further comment to make on the issue.

The company told *The Economist*: "News Corporation and its subsidiaries, including News International, prepare and file tax returns in every jurisdiction in which they do business."

"The company's tax returns and payments are reviewed on a regular basis by relevant tax authorities."

Whether Mr Murdoch can continue to get away with such low payments is a taxing question. Governments may seek to crack down on loopholes and special havens.

One thing is for sure – the company's accountants and lawyers deserve a bonus.

Source: The BBC, News Online Network, 21 March 1999

 ❖ ❖ ❖

News Corp firming China ties will open an office in Beijing

In early 1999, News Corp will open a representative office in Beijing, marking a smoothing of relations with Chinese authorities after a rocky start to its China business.

Gareth Chang, News Corp's executive director and a board member, will attend the formal opening of the office in Beijing, said the company.

The Australia-based media company's investments in China include its Star TV joint venture, the Phoenix Satellite television channel and a joint-venture Internet publication with the *People's Daily*, the official newspaper of the Chinese Communist Party. The company also has a joint-venture television-production studio with Golden Mainland Productions Co in Tianjin.

The representative office opening for New Corp comes after its chief executive, Rupert Murdoch, apparently angered Beijing in 1993 by calling satellite television an 'unambiguous threat to totalitarian regimes everywhere'.

Mr Murdoch's comment was later blamed for News Corp's failure to find wider distribution in China for his Star TV network.

Since then, however, Mr Murdoch has sought to regain favor with Beijing. Early last year, News Corp's publishing unit, HarperCollins, dropped plans to publish a book by Chris Patten, the last British governor of Hong Kong, because of the book's criticism of China. In 1994, News Corp dropped the British Broadcasting Corp's news service from its Star TV service, reportedly because of Chinese complaints about programming.

But, Mr Murdoch's meeting with President Jiang Zemin at the end of last year seemed to indicate that the company had patched things up with the Chinese government.

Mr Murdoch said after his meeting with Mr Jiang that he was optimistic about News Corp's scope for cooperation in China.

Source: *The Asian Wall Street Journal*, 18 March 1999

Case Discussion Issues and Questions

1. Discuss the competitive mechanisms by which News Corp may minimise its fiscal exposure.

2. What measures are available to host governments to enhance their taxation of MNCs' operations?

3. Competitiveness in international business for host nations is crucial for economic growth. Discuss the conflicting choices in enhancing national competitiveness and increasing taxation revenues.

❖ ❖ ❖

6.5   ORGANISATIONAL CULTURE

The issues and technicalities of tax planning and transfer pricing that moderate some of the explicit aspects of managing the competitiveness of MNCs remain important. However, they should not lead one to assume that there are other less explicit aspects that are not equally important. Of these less explicit aspects, organisational culture, is probably the most significant. Clearly, in the final analysis, it is people who engage in the complexity of business in circumstances and environments that are widely different in many ways. This variety is cohered ultimately, in the widest sense, by culture and its consequences. Therefore, the competence with which MNC management deals with differences in, and conflicting demands of, culture and its consequences hallmarks success in international business. Culture is manifest at different levels with varying degrees of intensity within the nation and within the business organisation. The nature of international business transactions across national and ethnic boundaries renders the managing of culture and its consequences an imperative for the top management of MNCs.

The view of organisational culture, from the perspective of a Japanese MNC and an American MNC, is provided by the following exposition of the relationship in a co-operative venture. The co-operative venture was set up between Japanese MNC Anritsu (established in 1885) and American MNC Wiltron Corporation in 1990 as Anritsu Wiltron, to exploit the relative strengths in the manufacture and sales and marketing of a range of advanced electronic and telecommunications equipment (spectrum analysers). Revenues over US$1 billion (1999) came from regional operation centres in Japan, the US, Europe and Asia Pacific set up to support global customers. However, it was clear that the partners had different business approaches that stemmed from two contrasting national and organisational cultures. Mr Koshikawa, a Japanese manager, states, "Sales are aimed at penetrating the heart, requiring a unique philosophy and culture. So, it is necessary for sales personnel to be deeply rooted in the place where sales are conducted. Consequently, I feel that the top management should be local, i.e., the Japanese president of each company has to return to Japan." Differences occur also during the development conferences. The way of programming development schedules was completely different. At Anritsu, a bottom-up system is adopted, where development strategy and product planning are formed by managers, who in turn report to the top management.

Meanwhile, at Wiltron, a top-down system is adopted. When staff members holding equivalent positions in the two partner companies held discussions, they talked at cross purposes. Moreover, although product planning is carried out together with the marketing section at Anritsu, Wiltron's policy is not to leak information on new products to the marketing section. Therefore, trouble occurred when compiling a comprehensive product map of the two companies.

Although inconceivable problems invariably accompany any business undertaken where a foreign company is concerned, unless they are solved, little progress can be made. And this takes up much time.

The issue of organisational culture raises a number of questions. Can we identify cultures? Can culture be aligned with strategy? How can culture be managed or changed? The best place to start is by defining what is culture and explaining how it can be identified in organisations.

Culture is a set of values, guiding beliefs, understanding, and ways of thinking, which are shared by members of an organisation and are taught to new members as correct. It represents the unwritten, feeling part of the organisation. The purpose of culture is to provide members with a sense of organisational identity and to generate a commitment to beliefs and values that are larger than themselves. Traditional values enhance the stability of the organisation and provide new members with an understanding that can help them make sense of organisational events and activities.

Corporate culture exists at two levels in an organisation, as illustrated in Figure 6.7 according to Daft (1992). On the surface level are visible artefacts, which include the way people behave and dress, and the symbols, ceremonies, and stories that are shared among members. However, observable artefacts represent deeper values that reside in the minds of organisation members. The underlying values, assumptions, beliefs and thought processes are the true culture.

The attributes of culture display themselves in many ways but typically evolve into a patterned set of activities and behaviours carried out through corporate social interactions.

If one compares corporate cultures (Figure 6.7) of the Japanese, Americans and Europeans, one could say that Japanese MNC corporate culture is an implicit or high context social environment. The Americans in contrast live in and out of both

Figure 6.7 Levels of corporate culture

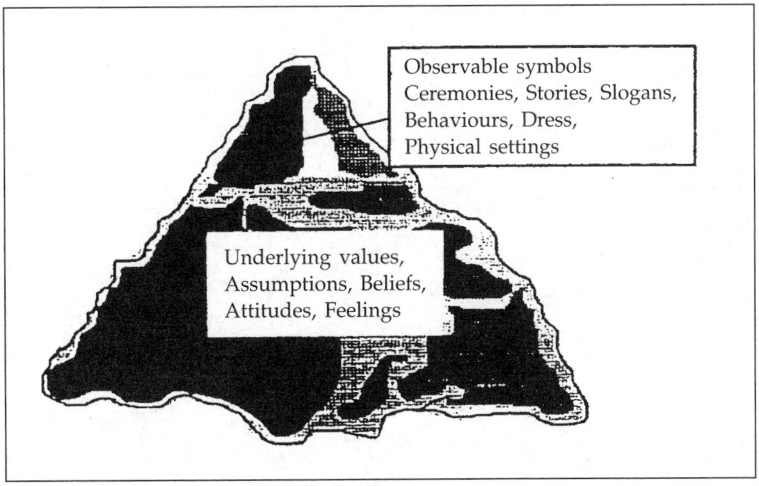

Observable symbols
Ceremonies, Stories, Slogans,
Behaviours, Dress,
Physical settings

Underlying values,
Assumptions, Beliefs,
Attitudes, Feelings

Source: Daft (1992).

the observable symbols and the underlying values, i.e., the mountain is totally free of water. In other words, American corporate culture in an explicit or low context social environment. The Europeans in contrast tend to handle both implicitness and explicitness and associated values carefully with tact and sensitivity.

Many people will probably be familiar with workplace phrases such as 'the way we do things here', 'it's not the sort of business we want to get into', 'we are different here' and so on. Such statements are often manifestations of the underlying values and culture held by the organisation and thus are powerful determinants of how an organisation behaves in international business and how it manages its competitiveness. Furthermore, on a macro level, there has been much debate of late, not least due the phenomenal rise of the East Asian economies (and their subsequent demise), in terms of national cultures and their effect on industrial prosperity.

Culture is a major determinant of managerial perceptions, which in turn affects recruitment, resource allocation and management, and organisational design, indeed, all aspects of an organisation. The McKinsey Seven-S framework and its relationship (Figure 6.8) explain the importance of shared values within an organisation.

Shared values have been termed superordinate goals (incremental) but essentially are sets of values and aspirations which underpin objective statements and as such are fundamental to beliefs deep-seated within the organisation.

Figure 6.8   The McKinsey Seven-S framework

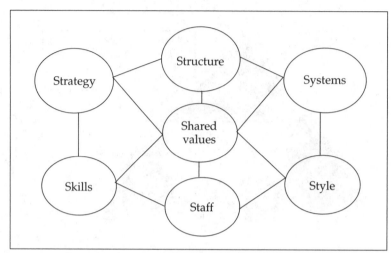

Source: Luffman *et al.*, *Business Policy: An Analytical Introduction*, 1987.

Whether formally expressed or not, they are omnipresent and often drive the other six "S" in the framework. Researchers like Minzberg and others have identified typologies of culture and their effect upon strategic decision-making. Organisations without clear explicit objectives tend to exhibit adaptive strategies that are often a function of conflicting goals held by senior managers.

6.6   COMMUNICATION DIFFICULTIES

In our example of the Anritsu Wiltron sales organisation, the differences in corporate cultures, organisations and systems resulted in a lack of smooth communication and thus it commenced business in a state of confusion. Within the European sales organisation as well, i.e., between the independent Anritsu Wiltron subsidiaries and the different agents, and with Anritsu Japan and Wiltron USA communications problems existed too.

The Organisation Configuration Models from Bartlett and Ghoshal (1992) provides good insights into the lack of communication within the Anritsu and Wiltron organisation, not only in the sales organisation.

Decentralised federation

Expanding abroad in a period of rising tariffs and discriminatory legislation, the typical European company found its budding export market threatened by local competitors. To defend their various market positions, they were forced to build local production facilities. With their own plants, various national subsidiaries were able to modify products and marketing approaches to meet widely differing local market needs. The increasing independence of these fully integrated national units was reinforced by the transportation and communication barriers that existed, limiting the ability of headquarters to intervene in the management of world-wide operations.

The emerging configuration of distributed assets and delegated responsibility fit well with the ingrained management norms and practices in many European companies. Because of the important role of owners and bankers in corporate-level decision-making, European companies, particularly those from the UK, the Netherlands and France, developed an internal culture that emphasised personal relationships rather than formal structures, and financial controls more than co-ordination of technical or operational detail. This management style, philosophy and capability tended to reinforce companies' willingness to delegate more operating independence and strategy formulation to their foreign subsidiaries. Highly autonomous national companies were often managed more as a portfolio of offshore investment rather than as a single international business (Figure 6.9).

The resulting organisation and management pattern was a loose federation of independent national subsidiaries, each focused primarily on its local market.

Figure 6.9   Decentralised federation

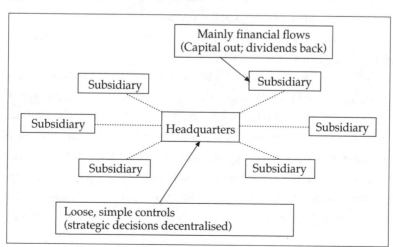

Source: Bartlett and Ghoshal (1992).

Co-ordinated federation

American companies, many of which enjoyed their fastest international expansion in the 1950s and 1960s, developed under very different circumstances. Their main strength lay in the new technologies and management processes they had developed as a consequence of being located in the world's largest, richest and most technologically-advanced market. After World War II, their expansion into Europe, then into Asia, focused primarily on leveraging this strength, particularly in response to demands generated by post-war reconstruction and the granting of independence to previously colonised nations. This pattern of internationalisation was so pervasive that it gave rise to the international product cycle theory.

Reinforcing this strategy was a professional managerial culture in most US-based companies that contrasted with the 'old boy network' that typified the European (especially British) companies' processes. The management approach in most US-based companies was built on a willingness to delegate responsibility, while retaining overall control through sophisticated management systems and specialist corporate staffs. The systems provided channels for a regular flow of information, to be interpreted by the central staff. Holding these reins, top management could control the free-running team of independent subsidiaries and guide the direction in which they were headed.

The main handicap such companies faced was that parent-company management often adopted a parochial and even superior attitude towards international operations, perhaps because of the assumption that new ideas and development all came from the parent. Despite corporate management's increased understanding of its overseas markets, it often seemed to view foreign operations as appendages whose principal purpose was to leverage the capabilities and resources developed in the home market.

Nonetheless, the approach was highly successful in the post-war decades, and many US-based companies adopted a co-ordinated federation organisation model as the template for their international strategy. Their foreign subsidiaries were often free to adapt products or strategies to reflect market differences, but their dependence on the parent company for new products, processes and ideas dictated a great deal more co-ordination and control by the headquarters than in the decentralised federation organisation (Figure 6.10). This was facilitated by the existence of formal systems and controls in the headquarters-subsidiary link.

Figure 6.10 Co-ordinated federation

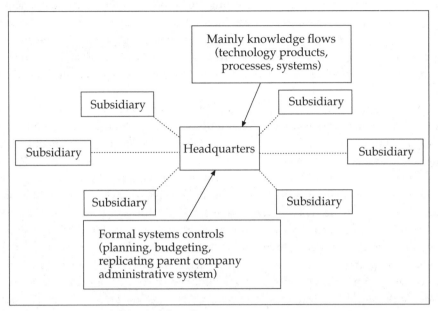

Source: Bartlett and Ghoshal (1992).

CASE 6.5

Excel or exit: Seagate has an unspoken message for suppliers

On 13 July 1999, the mood was jovial at Seagate's world-wide Supplier Day at the Shangri-La, but one could detect some nervousness amid the laughter greeting a senior official's quip: "It's not that we don't want to see you next year, but there's a good chance some of you won't be here next year."

Bringing all its 180 suppliers under one roof for the first time was part of Seagate's effort to be 'more open' and give more information to its vendors, a bid to counter the popular image of Seagate as some kind of pariah customer. This openness is part of Seagate's new mantras of 'time to market' and 'supply chain management'. More information and a closer working relationship are essential in a world of shortening cycle times and ever-thinning margins. To ensure seamless operations between Seagate, its suppliers and its customers, the new catchphrase is to 'manage information, not inventory'.

Closer, but fewer: In order to do this most effectively, Seagate is choosing to build closer relationships, but with fewer suppliers. And the unspoken message that Tuesday was clearly heard by its suppliers: meet our expectations, or get left behind.

Suppliers are expected to work with Seagate's engineers, right from the early design stages, to plan both components and manufacturing processes. This requires a greater time commitment than the current norm of visiting Seagate's overseas design centres once every few months. It could become a continuous process. The result: a component that works well and is designed to be made most efficiently and cheaply.

Changing the design of the part or the manufacturing process without Seagate's approval is a big no-no. And in line with the new just-in-time style of inventory management, suppliers are expected to cut their response time by more than half in some cases.

Seagate's moves are not unique to itself, but part of a wave that began two years ago when Dell Computer revolutionised the industry with its build-to-order model. Other computer makers have adopted this model, and the effects are now becoming obvious further down the supply chain.

In the disk drive industry, all this is also happening against a backdrop of drastic price cuts, which are hurting profits at all the listed US disk drive makers. Apart from the more obvious revenue repercussions, there are signs that unit demand is also coming under pressure. Research firm TrendFocus has recently adjusted its 1999 unit shipment growth down to 13 per cent. In February, its forecast was for 18 per cent unit growth.

It is important to note that the disk drive industry has been trapped in this downswing since mid-1996, when over-ambitious production plans caused drive prices to slide. Since then, the industry has seen short bursts of seasonal recovery, but larger forces have dominated. These have taken the form of all-out market-share fights, with upstart Asian drive makers slashing prices and boosting capacity.

Efforts to cut production plans and bring them closer to reality have not been successful, thanks to a *kiasu* mentality among drive makers. The latest round of profit warnings from drive makers are pointing to a chilling fact: one or two disk drive makers may have to go soon, either through bankruptcy or a merger.

When this happens, excess capacity will hopefully be siphoned off, and prospects will become brighter, especially for the stronger, listed local suppliers to the disk drive industry.

What to do: In the meantime, what can you do if you're a local supplier to the disk drive industry?

- Regionalise. If you haven't already set up plants in Malaysia, the Philippines or China to be close to your customers' overseas operations, it's time to act and harness the lower production costs there, while being headquartered in Singapore.

- Invest. Invest in highly-qualified design engineers capable of working with your customers' design labs; in additional staff dedicated to serving just one customer full-time; in advanced and specialised production processes aimed at shortening response time and keeping costs low.

- Collaborate. Team up with another supplier who makes a complementary part, and work together to produce sub-assemblies. The economies of scale may make a difference between survival and redundancy.

- Consolidate. The disk drive makers may be headed in that direction; why not bite the bullet and take the plunge? Two struggling metal parts makers may make a strong enough combination to muscle up against competitors.

Encouragingly, some listed Singapore companies are already market leaders in their area: Magnecomp comes to mind for its suspension assemblies, and base plate maker MMI Holdings last week won one of only four Outstanding Supplier awards from Seagate. It remains to be seen how other local companies navigate this sea-change.

Source: *The Business Times*, **20 July 1999**

Case Discussion Issues and Questions

1. Analyse the extent to which Seagate's supplier relations fit the co-ordinated federation model. What benefits accrue to the MNC?

2. Discuss the competitive advantages and disadvantages of increasingly closer ties in the value chain.

3. Discuss the implications of industry competition for suppliers in the electronic components industry.

Centralised hub

In contrast, the typical Japanese company (Figure 6.11), making its main international thrust in the 1970s, faced a greatly altered external environment and operated with very different internal norms and values. With limited prior overseas exposure, it chose not to match the well-established local marketing capabilities and facilities that its European and US competitors had built up. Indeed, well-established Japanese trading companies often had an easier means of entering foreign markets. However, the Japanese MNC had new, efficient, scale-intensive plants, built to serve its rapidly expanding domestic market, and it was expanding into a global environment of declining trade barriers. Together, these factors gave it the incentive to develop a competitive advantage at the upstream end of the value-added chain. Its competitive strategy emphasised cost advantages and quality assurance, and required tight central control of product development, procurement and manufacturing. A centrally controlled, export-based internationalisation strategy represented a perfect fit with the external environment and the company's competitive capabilities.

Figure 6.11   Centralised hub

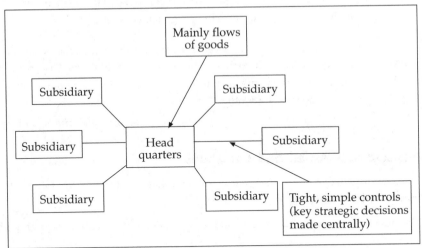

Source: Bartlett and Ghoshal (1992).

Such an approach also fit the cultural background and organisational values in the emerging Japanese MNCs. At the foundation of the internal processes were the strong national cultural norms that emphasised group behaviour and valued interpersonal harmony.

These values had been enhanced by the paternalism of the *zaibatsu* and other enterprise groups. They were also reflected in the group-oriented management practices of *nemawashi* and *ringi* that were at the core of the Japanese management of organisational processes. By keeping primary decision-making and control at the centre, the Japanese company could retain this culturally dependent management system that was so communications intensive and people dependent.

Cultural values were also reflected in one of the main motivations driving the international expansion of Japanese MNCs. As growth in their domestic market slowed and became increasingly competitive, these companies needed new sources of growth so they could continue to attract and promote employees. In a system of lifetime employment, growth (i.e., revenue growth through market share increases) was the engine that powered organisational vitality and self-renewal. It was this motivation that reinforced the bias towards an export-based strategy managed from the centre rather than the decentralised foreign investment approach of the European MNC. As a result, these companies adopted what we have described as a global strategy, and developed a centralised hub organisation model to support this strategy orientation.

Integrated network model

In the integrated network configuration, displayed in Figure 6.12, national units are no longer viewed only as the end of a delivery pipeline for company products, or as implementers of centrally-defined strategies, or even as local adapters and modifiers of corporate approaches. Rather, the assumption behind this configuration is that management should consider each of the world-wide units as a source of ideas, skills capabilities, and knowledge that can be harnessed for the benefit of the total organisation. Efficient local plants may be converted into international production centres; innovative national or regional development laboratories may be designated the company's 'centre of excellence' for a particular product or process development; and creative subsidiary marketing groups may be given a lead role in developing world-wide marketing strategies for certain products or business. The company becomes a truly integrated network of distributed and interdependent resources and capabilities.

Figure 6.12   Integrated network model

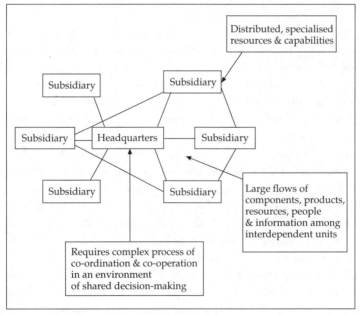

Source: Bartlett and Ghoshal (1992).

By summarising the key characteristics of the decentralised federation, co-ordinated federation, centralised hub organisation, and the shared values in the co-ordination of decision-making processes described in the preceding sections, we can identify the general cultures of MNCs. These structures reflect the cultural behaviour between the Americans: the world got told how to do it – here is the equipment, sell it, the Japanese: collecting only information – consequently producing general equipment for a world-wide demand, not country-specific ones, the Europeans: have tended to go their own way – with special customer-oriented products.

By implementing 'integration' into the company the cultural differences become less, and the communication within the company improves. Personnel will tend to respect each other more. This is the first step into a new culture and into global success for the company.

Case 6.6

Global reorganisation: Caltex is first multinational to move global HQ to Singapore

Shift will bring oil giant closer to customers: chairman. American oil giant Caltex Petroleum is moving its global corporate headquarters to Singapore from Irving, Texas – making it the first multinational ever to do so.

The global HQ relocation, which will become operational by March next year, will involve its top brass, including group chairman David Law-Smith and other executive management staff, being based here.

"The move to Singapore will position us centrally in the area where we do most of our business and allows us to be closer to our customers and serve them more effectively," Mr Law-Smith said in a statement out of Texas late on Tuesday. Besides, many of the group's key operations are already located in the Republic, he added.

Caltex is a joint venture between Chevron Corp and Texaco Inc. Elaborating on the rationale for the move, a Caltex spokesman in Texas said that the company obtains about 75 per cent of its revenue from Asia, making Singapore a more practical, centrally-located base for the 15 executives and support staff that will be coming here by March next year.

Caltex's decision is a significant feather in Singapore's cap. A Caltex spokesman here told BT that the company had considered other Asian sites like Hong Kong, Manila and Sydney before deciding on the Republic.

This highly significant shift of its world-wide corporate HQ to Singapore follows Caltex's establishment of its global oil trading HQ here. In January last year, it also started increasing its Singapore office's Asia-Pacific responsibilities by posting more of its key regional officials here.

As a measure of how much oil trading it does from here, latest available figures show that its world-wide trading HQ, Caltex Trading, based here, was Singapore's largest oil trader in 1996 with sales of US$9.9 billion (S$16 billion), or equivalent to about 12 per cent of Singapore's gross domestic product of $128.5 billion.

Under the latest reorganisation, Caltex's world-wide business units for trading, marketing, lubricants and new business development will also be based here.

Only two business units, refinery and aviation, will remain in Dallas, Texas, together with about 60 staff involved in treasury and tax, and supporting functions, the company's Singapore spokesman said.

The new global corporate HQ will be sited at Caltex House in Raffles Place, where Caltax Trading is located.

Under its world-wide reorganisation, which started in June, Caltex expects to save about US$50 million annually from the change in its operating structure, which will now focus on product types rather than geographical regions, the spokesman added. Only about 20 of its 7,700 world-wide employees will be retrenched as a result.

The reorganisation comes as an oil glut continues to pressure prices, pushing many companies to cut back on expenditures.

Shell, for instance, last month announced that it was merging its European refining and marketing operation with those of Caltex's parent, Texaco, from next year, in a bid to save on expenses.

A Shell spokesman said it expects this to result in cost savings of billions of dollars, similar in scale to that contemplated by British Petroleum and Amoco, which are merging in a US$54 billion stock swap. In Thailand, Caltex and Shell are also in a similar refining alliance to save on costs.

Reacting to the Caltex announcement, Economic Development Board chairman Philip Yeo yesterday said: "Caltex's decision affirms Singapore as an excellent headquarters location."

The EDB said in a statement that the move was 'most significant' and a milestone in Singapore's headquarters development history. It is testimony to Caltex's long-term confidence in Singapore despite the Asian crisis, it added.

"It means that the company's world-wide corporate management and control will reside here," the EDB said. "Board meetings will also be held here."

Caltex's other activities here include oil terminal operations, a retail chain operation of over 30 service stations, and also oil refining, where it is partner with BP and Singapore Refining Company's Pulau Merlimau refinery.

Last year, the Caltex group had gross sales of US$17 billion and commanded an 18 per cent share of the oil products market world-wide.

Source: *The Business Times*, **22 October 1999**

Case Discussion Issues and Questions

1. Discuss the potential competitive advantages that accrue to Caltex from its new organisation.

2. What kinds of effects might Caltex's decision have on the host nation?

3. Outline the challenges Caltex will face in its reorganisation.

6.7 STRATEGIC THINKING ON DECISION-MAKING AUTONOMY

A number of studies have been carried out in recent years on the processes which drive decision-making in MNCs, and the level of autonomy enjoyed by subsidiary companies. While much research has considered the issues of decision-making from the perspective of the parent company, limited work has been done from the viewpoint of the overseas-based subsidiary. Prahalad and Doz (1981) considered the shifts in the level of control in a head office–subsidiary relationship, as illustrated in Figure 6.13, which highlights the concern that MNCs have about allowing subsidiaries a greater degree of decision-making autonomy. The concern of MNCs with the development of a control gap derives from the fact that as subsidiaries mature and become increasingly autonomous over strategic resources, i.e., technology, capital, access to markets, management, etc., the parent's ability to control the strategies significantly diminish. In recent years, the parent companies of MNCs have experienced an increase in their sales and profits originating from overseas subsidiaries, and have committed a growing share of their assets to support the overseas operations. Increased capital investment in overseas

Figure 6.13   Shifts in control mechanisms in head office (HO)-subsidiary relationship

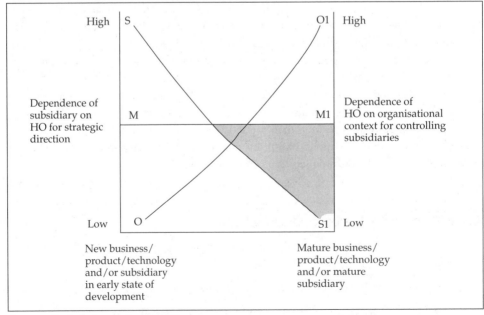

Source: Prahalad and Doz (1981).

subsidiaries, together with higher growth potential in overseas markets than the home market, strengthens the reluctance of parent companies to reduce their powers of control over the subsidiaries.

However, there is a growing call for parent companies of MNCs to relinquish more decision-making powers to the subsidiaries that operate in foreign markets, allowing greater autonomy to develop strategies to meet local market conditions more appropriately. The success in a global marketplace requires MNCs to be less bureaucratic and more market-driven, together with a requirement to decentralise decision-making and to develop a broader base of initiative-taking. There is also the need for MNCs to encourage the development of self-managing, empowered foreign subsidiaries if any sustainable competitive advantage is to be achieved. Analysis of parent-subsidiary relationships by Birkinshaw (1996) emphasises the point that a shift has taken place in the character of MNC subsidiary relationships. It was found that most of the MNCs considered in the research no longer merely controlled dependent units, but instead they managed a set of subsidiaries with mandates. Taggart and Hood (1995) identified some key variables which contributed to the evolution of subsidiary strategy, including nationality of parent, employment level in the subsidiary, technology level in the business, markets served, product range offered, and decision-making autonomy. However, a reluctance to relinquish control appears to be persistent in a number of international business cultures, which could continue to frustrate subsidiary managers on strategic issues in the long term and so affect their strategic competitiveness.

6.8 Decision-making Culture in US, Japanese and German Subsidiaries in Regional UK

In order to give form to the critical issues of corporate culture the decision-making culture focusing on US, Japanese and German subsidiaries, which have in combination a strong presence in Yorkshire and Humberside and industrial importance in the world economy, is examined. The main source of inward investment in the Yorkshire and Humberside region is from the US, with 239 subsidiaries (32.1%), followed by Germany with 113 subsidiaries (15.2%). Although Japanese inward investment represents only 4.6% of the total for the region, equating to 34 subsidiaries, the world-wide economic importance of Japanese industry warranted its inclusion.

US-owned subsidiaries

The US MNCs' approach towards the development of their overseas subsidiaries has been viewed as one of limiting the decision-making autonomy of the subsidiary. This reflects the results of other academic research in the area. The findings suggest that US MNCs' reluctance to encourage an increase in decision-making autonomy of the subsidiary, originates from the fact that while MNC managers tend to be highly focused on global strategic issues, they lack the ability to focus on host-country strategies. The result of having limited focus in host countries is that there remains a tendency on the part of US MNCs to centralise the decision-making process in the parent company.

The stance of US government policies on protectionist measures may also influence the decision-making culture of US MNCs. Since the US has relatively low protectionist policies, MNCs are required to develop more efficient organisations and strategies in order to compete effectively and profitably in the international market. Also, the structure of financing in the US, is usually based on stock ownership and public control of MNCs. The requirement of stockholders to receive healthy dividends on a regular basis force MNCs to concentrate on short-term profitability measures, which in turn require high levels of control across global operations in order to meet short-term objectives.

Japanese-owned subsidiaries

In contrast to the approach to the restrictive decision-making practices of US-owned subsidiaries, Japanese MNCs adopted a more liberal stance. The Japanese decision-making style reflects a high degree of consensus in the delegation of authority and responsibility of subsidiaries. The strategic thinking of Japanese MNC managers is focused on the global as well as the host-country situation, with the latter geared specifically towards greater responsiveness to local needs and demands than is noticed in US MNCs. One argument for the decentralised approach by Japanese MNCs is that the management philosophies adopted in Japanese companies have quality improvement as a cornerstone. This approach to management involves greater autonomy and decentralisation in decision-making, specific skills in market orientation, the ability to respond rapidly to customer needs, and a level of flexibility to operate in a proactive manner in dynamic environments.

The high level of protectionist measures adopted by Japan may allow MNCs to operate globally in a more stable environment, with the knowledge that their domestic market will remain a rich source of income. This confidence thus allows them to decentralise operations with a lower level of financial risk throughout the group as a whole. Since the main source of finance within the Japanese industry originates from banks (usually industrial group Keiretsu banks) instead of the equity markets, MNCs are allowed to concentrate on developing long-term strategies, in which more flexible policies on decision-making can be adopted at subsidiary level. The managers of MNCs realise that subsidiaries are better placed to co-ordinate strategies to meet the host-country market requirements, and to adjust their strategies to reflect changes in the external environment within which they operate.

German-owned subsidiaries

Limited research into decision-making and levels of autonomy has been carried out on the behaviour of German-owned subsidiaries in the UK. However, the work of Taggart and Hood (1995), although concentrating on a number of strategic issues relating to German-owned subsidiaries, does highlight a number of interesting characteristics in the decision-making process and level of automation adopted in the British Isles.

Their work identified five distinct groups of subsidiaries, based on a postal survey response of 102 companies (25% response rate), whose general characteristics were that of small and medium enterprises (SMEs) with average employee numbers of 178, and average sales revenue of £12.8 million, across a range of industries. The main focus on decision-making authority was related to market areas to be served and product range supplied. The results of the research are summarised in Table 6.6.

The results indicate a range of decision-making and autonomy, depending on the experience of the subsidiary, together with the markets and products served. Table 6.6 provides a useful basis for assessing the probable characteristics of German-owned subsidiaries in the UK. The research also suggests that the decision-making authority of German-owned subsidiaries has increased during the period 1989–94, together with a gradual increase in the overall autonomy of subsidiaries in the British Isles.

The issues of decision-making and level of subsidiary autonomy were also examined at a series of meetings between selected foreign-owned subsidiary companies within the Yorkshire and Humberside region to discuss support services and aftercare. The managing directors of six subsidiaries – two German owned, three Japanese owned and one owned by a US MNC – were interviewed.

Table 6.6 German-owned subsidiary groups and characteristics

Group	No. of firms	Title	Main characteristics
1	13	Integrated Branch Plant	Very high integration, low on decision-making, average in market-technology scope.
2	11	Strategic Independent	Highly autonomous, tightly integrated into parent networks: serving many markets with high levels of product and process technology.
3	31	Emergent Regional Supplier	High market-technology scope, low integration, average autonomy, but higher export dependency on EU markets.
4	22	Starter Plant	Almost directly opposite of group 2. Relatively low-level, small, initial manufacturing operations for host market.
5	23	Host-market Penetrator	High autonomy, very low market technology scope and average levels of integration. Mission largely to penetrate host markets with existing products and/or technologies. Very low dependence on exports.

Source: Taggart and Hood (1995).

An example of decision-making in a US subsidiary managed by the original management team of UK nationals is provided by the following. The decision-making structure on major capital expenditure, such as an extension of the plant, begins with the subsidiary presenting a proposal package, including a three-year profit plan and a five-year cash-flow forecast, to the parent company in the US. The response to the proposal – a formal analysis by HQs and defence by the UK management team – goes through several rounds of negotiations before acceptance and implementation protocols are agreed. There is competition among subsidiaries for the resources available from the centre of the multinational organisation.

Given the different approaches to managing decisions in different MNCs, among the most significant consequences of organisational culture in MNCs is formerly successful decision-making structures and organisational cultures losing their fluidity and becoming rigid and unresponsive – leading ultimately to a loss of international competitiveness. Once this occurs there is usually only one strategic response – radical reformation to shape the MNCs' organisation to match new industrial and market landscapes. A good example of such a process is illustrated by Unilever (Box 6.4).

Box 6.4   Restructure Shakes Unilever to Its Roots

UNILEVER yesterday announced the biggest top-level management and structural shake-up in the 65-year history of the Anglo-Dutch food and detergents group.

The triumvirate which has directed the group since it was formed is being scrapped along with the six-strong group of regional co-ordinators and replaced by a seven-man executive committee.

The existing businesses – with thousands of products ranging from Persil Power to Birds Eye, Walls Ice Cream and Elizabeth Arden – are being reorganised and 14 product and geographic groups created, headed by presidents. Sir Michael Perry, chairman of Unilever, and Morris Tabaksblat, his opposite number, will head the executive committee, which will be responsible for hammering out strategy.

The restructuring follows an in-depth review spearheaded by Niall Fitzgerald, who is due to succeed Sir Michael in September, after a series of marketing setbacks, including the Persil Power disaster, and criticism that the Unilever management structure was unwieldy and outdated. An input from McKinsey, the management consultants, was rejected as unacceptable.

But the radical shake-up will not extend to any break-up, demerger or reallocation of responsibilities between the London and Rotterdam operations. Sir Michael said that the businesses added "significant value" to each other while a complete separation would raise enormous tax problems.

No jobs will disappear under the restructuring, aimed at separating strategic and operational management.

The executive and business groups will meet quarterly under the umbrella of a new body, the Unilever executive council, to discuss strategy and policy issues.

Sir Michael said the change would produce a clearer focus inside the group, allow Unilever to take advantage of the changes in the business environment and allow local companies to react more speedily.

He said: "There is no such thing as a global consumer. Markets need to be dealt with on a personalised basis and this new structure will enable us to do it."

Source: *Financial Times,* **4 March 1996**

6.9   CHAPTER REVIEW

Co-ordinated management of the different operational elements (units, divisions, sub-units and subsidiaries) to maximise economic efficiency and optimise market servicing effectiveness, and thereby assure competitiveness, remains the most forbidding of challenges in the management of companies involved in international business. The complexity and diversity of functions within subsidiaries mean that resource allocation decisions have to be effectively communicated and co-ordinated within a command and control structure possessing a flexibility that maintains, and enhances, competitive advantages and yet simultaneously delivers coherence in overall corporate strategy. The organisational structure adopted by the firm, and adapted over time, determines how successfully intra-firm communication flows, how effectively the firm's subsidiaries communicate with headquarters and how well the management of their value chains are internationally co-ordinated.

Organisational structure enables a firm to manage competitively its diverse functional activities and international operations. There are many forms of organisational structures depending on the firm's strategic intent. The operations of the firm may be organised according to functions, product groups, geographical areas, or as a holding company with a sophisticated multi-divisional structure. When co-ordinated internationally, multi-divisional structures enable the firm to integrate some functions and disintegrate other functions and activities simultaneously while spreading those activities over different locations. This permits the firm to add value to sourcing and production in international locations that offer the lowest costs or best value-for-money for each of the firm's activities while servicing the customer optimally. A key aspect of the MNC is the networked structure that emerged recently as a result of business process re-engineering within organisations. International subsidiaries may be linked both vertically (outputs from one subsidiary as inputs for the next) and horizontally (similar outputs from similar manufacturing in different locations) to reduce risk profiles, smooth out fluctuations in economic cycles and between locations as well as create synergies among subsidiaries.

As indicated previously, the structural analysis of industry provides a basis for selecting the best foreign market servicing strategy, the optimum entry mode and the most appropriate positioning. The threat of new entrants can be actualised through international acquisitions and mergers activity. Whether the firm achieves entry most competitively or not will be determined by goal congruence and the corporate culture that is held in common and how these 'fit' with operations and strategy. In other words, within the increasing incidences of joint international business activities, what the parties want affects how they behave not only towards each other and vice versa but also operationally.

Having arranged subsidiaries into a suitable organisational structure that is dispersed, but inter-linked, across international borders to deliver competitiveness, the firm faces the challenge of maximising the returns on its treasury functions and minimising its tax liabilities. The issues herein concern how the firm manages its finances in terms of where it borrows, where it invests and in which tax jurisdiction it declares profits. As cash flows generated by international sales can be vast, treasury and tax planning dimensions of managing competitively MNCs become crucial to success.

The kind of attention the firm pays to exchange rate risk can increase or reduce its competitiveness. Likewise, the importance of transfer pricing (intra-firm transactions as well as manipulative) cannot be overestimated. Through transfer pricing on services or intermediate goods, exchanged between subsidiaries, the firm can elect to siphon off profits earned in high-tax locations to low-tax countries by inflated payments between subsidiaries, higher royalty fees and high intra-group management charges. MNCs may use tax-haven subsidiaries to invoice other subsidiaries and so minimise tax liabilities. Treasury, tax planning and transfer pricing enable the firm to project competitive postures by lowering prices and thus driving competitors out of the industry or lowering profit and so deterring the threat of potential new entrants.

Intra-organisational transfer pricing for intermediate goods that may not exist except inside the firm occurs on the basis of market-based or arm's-length prices, cost-based or negotiated prices. The important factor managers should bear in mind is the overall profitability profile of the MNC. Attempting to maximise the profitability of all subsidiaries might increase the group overall tax liability. Herein lie the internal and external constraints on transfer pricing. Internal constraints emerge when, on the one hand operating the arm's-length method, individual subsidiaries maximise profits to the detriment of the group tax liability. On the other hand, centralised dictation of transfer prices may lower the morale of subsidiaries designated as 'loss-making' (especially when strategy is not communicated).

The quality of decision-making and communication and co-ordination among firm group structures for sustaining competitiveness needs to be high. The form of organisational structure and the type of corporate culture therein determine this quality to a large extent. The decentralised federations of European companies have highly developed inter-personal cultures. US firms, tend to be more co-ordinated and possess more formal systems. In contrast Japanese MNCs are highly centralised Keiretsu structures. Increasingly, integrated networks that deliver greater functional flexibility are apparent among firms. This structure benefits from the fact that the entire network – individual units and the whole – is treated as a powerful source of ideas, capacity and capability for serving global markets.

Consequently, efficient local plants may be awarded world production mandates, or an effective regional research laboratory may become the firm's centre of innovation.

6.10 QUESTIONS FOR DISCUSSION

1. What are the advantages and disadvantages of different types of structures for MNCs to organise their international activities? In what ways do the different types confer competitiveness to the firm?

2. What mechanisms are used to achieve 'fit' in international acquisitions and mergers?

3. How do international firms set intra-firm transfer prices? What factors constrain an international firm's use of manipulative transfer pricing?

4. How do different organisational structures affect communications and decision-making in international firms? How do these differences manifest themselves among firms?

CHAPTER
7

Multinational Corporations and Their Impact on National Economies

CHAPTER OUTLINE

- Economic effects of outward direct investment
- Economic effects of inward direct investment
- Policies towards foreign direct investment (FDI)
- Country examples

CHAPTER OBJECTIVES

After studying this chapter you should be able to:

- Identify the dimensions of outward and inward direct investment.
- Characterise the effects of FDI.
- Analyse the balance of advantages and disadvantages to sources of, and hosts to, FDI.
- Discuss the viability of the different policies towards FDI with regard to economic development.

THE TENTACULAR PRESENCE of the leading MNCs in a large number of countries has not only prompted a reassessment of the importance to countries of traditional international trade, based on FDI, exports and imports, but also has focused attention on the MNC as an organisational powerhouse with an economic capability which transcends that of individual sovereign states. Specifically, a country is, by definition, a fixed entity; the MNC, by contrast, constitutes a bundle of resources which can be deployed between countries to achieve its corporate objectives. Such has been the global expansion of companies like General Motors and IBM of the US, Hoescht and Volkswagen of Germany, Sony and Toyota of Japan and ICI and Pilkington of the UK that their annual world-wide corporate revenues exceed the gross national products of many of the smaller countries in which they have invested. This has led to various questions being asked concerning the potential costs and benefits of such investment for source and host countries.

This chapter discusses the impact of MNC investment on host and source countries' economies in terms of resource transfers, domestic income and employment effects and balance of payments effects, and countries' policies towards foreign investment.

7.1 ECONOMIC EFFECTS OF OUTWARD DIRECT INVESTMENT

Balance of payments and trade effects

It is sometimes suggested that outward investment weakens a country's external position because it involves running down a country's foreign currency reserves and increasing overseas debt. However, it may well be that net capital outflows are financed out of current account surpluses so that there is no currency loss. The *fundamental* point to emphasise, however, is that outward investment, irrespective of whether it is financed by current account surpluses or by reserve drawings, adds to the country's stock of overseas assets, thereby increasing the country's external wealth and future income-earning capacity.

A number of industrial countries are net exporters of investment capital (Table 7.1). Some, such as Japan, finance overseas investment out of current account surpluses while others, such as the UK, use mainly reserves and borrowings.

Overseas investment in turn affects the current account position in two ways. On the negative side, there may be some displacement of exports of finished manufactured products as overseas markets come to be supplied from local plants.

Table 7.1 **Net FDI flows and current account position, selected countries, 1990–96 (US$ billion)**

Country		1990	1991	1992	1993	1994	1995	1996
Germany	FDI	−21.7	−19.6	−17.0	−13.1	−15.5	−26.6	−31.0
	Current account	+48.1	−17.9	−19.4	−14.1	−21.2	−23.5	−13.1
Japan	FDI	−48.7	−30.3	−14.6	−13.7	−17.2	−22.5	−23.2
	Current account	+44.1	+68.2	+112.6	+131.6	+130.3	+110.0	+65.9
UK	FDI	+13.1	−0.1	−2.9	−11.0	−24.6	−21.6	−12.2
	Current account	−32.5	−14.3	−18.4	−15.5	−2.3	−5.9	−0.5
US	FDI	+18.0	−9.4	−24.7	−29.0	−23.6	−19.2	−10.9
	Current account	−91.8	−5.8	−56.7	−90.6	−132.9	−129.2	−148.7
Belgium	FDI	+1.7	+3.1	−0.1	+5.9	+7.1	−1.3	+5.9
	Current account	+3.6	+4.7	+6.7	+11.2	+12.6	+14.7	+14.4
Singapore	FDI	+3.5	+4.4	+0.9	+2.7	+4.6	+4.2	+4.6
	Current account	+3.1	+4.9	+5.6	+4.4	+12.2	+14.5	+14.3

Note: − = net outflow; + = net inflow.

Source: IMF *Balance of Payments Statistics Yearbook (Part 1) 1997*.

However, additional export demands may be created in the form of machinery, materials or replacement parts as a continuing back-up to the original investment.

Thus the effect of foreign investment may be to change the composition of a country's exports away from some finished products to intermediate products rather than to eliminate them altogether.

On the positive side, foreign investment enlarges the stream of interest, profits and dividend receipts available to the country. Table 7.2 shows, for the UK, what a sizeable contribution net currency earnings can make to the current account.

Resource and employment effects

For the domestic economy, outward investment could be damaging to domestic output and employment if it was associated with a significant fall in manufactured exports but, for the reasons given above, this is unlikely to be the general case. Moreover, this possibility has to be considered alongside the scope for redeploying resources to alternative domestic uses, especially those activities not directly exposed to foreign trade and investment influences.

Table 7.2 UK and Singapore net earnings from foreign investment, 1990–96 (US$ billion)

Country		1990	1991	1992	1993	1994	1995	1996
UK	Net earnings from FDI	+15.5	+14.5	+14.4	+9.6	+18.2	+17.9	+20.0
	Current account	−32.5	−14.3	−18.4	−15.5	−2.3	−5.9	−0.5
Singapore	Net earnings from FDI	+1.0	+0.8	+1.5	+0.2	+1.5	+1.1	+1.7
	Current account	+3.1	+4.9	+5.6	+4.4	+12.2	+14.5	+14.3

Note: − = net outflow; + = net inflow.
Source: IMF *Balance of Payments Statistics Yearbook (Part 1) 1997.*

A point not always appreciated is that foreign investment is often undertaken to protect sales in overseas markets as direct exports fall due to increased local competition or the erection of trade barriers. In other words, a local production operation is substituted for exports as a more viable means of servicing that market. A further factor is that foreign investment often creates additional resource requirements by the home (parent) company especially for skilled personnel in such areas as research and development (R&D) as well as administration and finance.

A potentially more serious criticism of foreign investment centres on the possibility that it might *replace* home investment, thereby resulting in a *lower* overall level of domestic investment and consequent loss of output and employment. While *portfolio* investment (that is, investment in financial securities such as stocks and shares) can readily be switched from country to country at short notice in response to interest rate differentials and currency fluctuations, FDI in capital plant and associated assets differs because it involves the long-term commitment of resources in specific countries, a commitment not easily reversed once made. It could be argued, of courses, that any investment abroad could have been made at home instead but this is a superficial contention. The relevant question is: would the investment at home actually have gone ahead? The *fundamental point* is that FDI usually is additional to the MNC's domestic activities, representing a strategic response to an opportunity or threat in overseas markets. Thus FDI is normally seen as complementary to, rather than as a substitute for, domestic investment.

7.2 ECONOMIC EFFECTS OF INWARD DIRECT INVESTMENT

Superficially, the effects of inward investment might be thought to be a mirror image of outward investment. However, there are important differences, most notably in the impact on the domestic economy.

Balance of payments and trade effects

When the MNC establishes a foreign subsidiary, the capital account of the host country's balance of payments benefits from the initial foreign exchange inflow, although this may be a once-and-for-all effect if the subsidiary subsequently finances later expansion from local capital sources. Set against this is the continuing adverse impact on the current account representing the various payments of dividends, profits, interest, royalties and administration fees to the parent company. However, it is necessary to consider the wider trade flows associated with MNC investments to obtain a more complete picture of costs and benefits.

The operation of the MNC subsidiary may be highly import-intensive, with the subsidiary importing key raw materials and components from its parent or other geographically dispersed subsidiaries for local assembly. The so-called 'screwdriver' factories fall into this category. They are often used as a means of circumventing tariffs and other trade restrictions applied against imports of finished products. Consequently, they may well be opposed by host country governments not only for that reason but also because they may not deliver the kind of technology-intensive employment, necessary for skills upgrading, that the host government is looking for.

On the other hand, direct investment may involve import-substitution with inputs, or final products, now being sourced locally rather than being obtained from abroad. The European Union (EU), for example, currently applies particular pressure on Japanese motor car manufacturers (and other MNC producers) in the EU to increase the local content of their cars to a minimum of 80%. For finished products, the subsidiary may be used to supply both the host country market and export markets, in which case the visible trade effects of inward investment are likely to be strongly positive. Imports of finished manufactures will be reduced as they are replaced by home production, although there will be some stimulus given to imports of intermediate products.

A more significant impact, studies have shown, is on direct exports. In the case of the UK, inward investment is predominantly undertaken by US MNCs, but increasingly by the Japanese, who see the UK as a convenient and relatively cheap base from which to service European markets. In 1992, around 26% of UK exports were accounted for by foreign-controlled companies.

Host country government policies can materially affect the overall trade situation; for example, the extent to which their economic development programmes are inwardly orientated (i.e., focused on import-substitution) or outwardly orientated (i.e., focused on export promotion). Most newly-industrialised countries (NICs), in particular Singapore, South Korea, Hong Kong, Taiwan, and to an appreciable extent Malaysia and Thailand, have in fact favoured the latter strategy. They have done so because of its greater potential for improving economic growth. These Asian Tiger economies have encouraged the establishment of MNC subsidiaries and have used them primarily as export supply sources.

CASE 7.1

Improving performance: Jakarta to sell oil palm plantations to foreigners

Govt plans to raise US$600m; buyers will have to inject new technology. In a strategic move to raise much needed foreign currency, the Indonesian Government is looking to sell off more than 200,000 hectares of oil palm plantations in Sumatra, Kalimantan, Sulawesi and Irian Jaya. At a seminar on the privatisation of state-owned companies in Argentina, the Indonesian Government indicated its hopes to raise US$600 million (S$1 billion) from the sale of the plantations to foreign investors. The plantations are owned by PT Perkebunan Nusantara (PTPN), a company set up by the government to manage large plantations including rubber, tea and cocoa.

"These plantations have very good cash flow and we feel that foreign investors would be interested in buying them," noted Tanri Abeng, Minister for State Enterprises, adding that PTPN is expected to generate 2 trillion rupiah (S$290 million) this year.

But any foreign investor interested in buying up these plantations will have to contribute new marketing infrastructure and technology that will enable these companies to develop downstream products, Mr Abeng said.

Indonesia is the second largest producer of crude palm oil but it exports only a fraction of its output. It also lags behind Malaysia in the production and sale of downstream palm oil products, which include detergents.

"By 2020, I expect the palm oil sector to be a leading foreign currency earner but we need to build up a good marketing infrastructure before we can attract foreign investors and export more palm oil," he said.

Asked how the privatisation programme is progressing, Mr Abeng said the government is concentrating on restructuring the 12 state-owned enterprises slated for privatisation before taking the next step.

"My department has a three-pronged strategy to restructure, to make these companies profitable and then to privatise them," said Mr Abeng. He added that the government is in no hurry to sell off these assets as it hopes they would fetch a higher price. "We need to raise the share price of those companies that are listed on the Jakarta Stock Exchange before we can think of privatising them," he said, adding that the government will maintain the majority stake in these companies.

At the very least, these companies should be able to fetch a price equivalent to their initial public offer price but most of these companies are trading at about 30 per cent below their IPO price.

The office of the State Ministry of State Enterprises was set up early this year with the mission to restructure 159 state-owned companies, including privatising 12 of them to raise about US$1.5 billion in the current fiscal year.

State companies previously supervised by the related ministries are now under the supervision of the state enterprises ministry.

Source: *The Business Times*, **11 September 1999**

Case Discussion Issues and Questions

1. Discuss the motivations of the Indonesian Government. What are the key driving forces?

2. Analyse the competitive impacts on the local and national economy.

3. Discuss the balance of payment, and trade, effects of the decision to privatise the palm plantations. To what extent will transfer prices play a part?

Resource transfer

Another important component in the FDI package brought by MNC investment is embodied technology. For many host countries, particularly less developed countries, domestic ability to invent and innovate is strictly limited, not only by a lack of capital but also by lack of research institutions and scientists, technicians and other groups of skilled personnel. However, by adopting established technologies through the medium of MNC investment and the various entry modalities (joint ventures for example), host countries can by-pass the risky and expensive invention and innovation stages in developing commercially viable processes and products, thereby making a significant leap forward. Moreover, although it may be reliant initially on overseas personnel to instal and operate the new technologies, the host country may in time benefit considerably from the training and expertise acquired by the local labour force.

On the other hand, since know-how and technology are produced by MNCs to meet their own particular requirements, the advantages to be gained by host countries will depend on the suitability of the technology transferred and the price as well as the configuration and method of supply. This is a particularly sensitive area of MNC operations. Technological invention is such a prized asset that it is usually patented and jealously guarded by its instigators. Foreign direct investment, we have observed, is one way in which an MNC is able to recoup costly R&D as well as appropriate monopoly revenues from new processes and products. There is therefore a contention between technology transfer by source MNCs and capture by hosts.

CASE 7.2

German outpost in Singapore: Mercedes-Benz to design trucks and vans in Singapore

Singapore designed Mercedes-Benz light trucks and vans could well become a common sight in many Asian countries before the turn of the century.

Under an innovation development grant provided by the Economic Development Board (EDB) last week, Europe's largest industrial conglomerate, Daimler-Benz, plans to undertake vehicle customisation for Asia-Pacific in the Republic.

The grant to Singapore-based unit, Mercedes-Benz Asia, is intended to implement an 'innovative design process of vehicle customisation for Asia-Pacific'.

Mercedes-Benz is the first car manufacturer to be granted an award under the EDB's US$500 million innovation development scheme launched a year ago with the aim of developing Singapore into an innovation development hub.

Sources said the project – to be undertaken by the Asia-Pacific strategies unit of Mercedes-Benz – would cost about US$10.6 million, of which about US$3.7 million is provided by the EDB as part of an overall effort to promote innovation development.

The company's Singapore-based Asia-Pacific team will develop commercial vehicle concepts jointly with the global development project team based in Portland, US, said Mercedes-Benz's vice-president for Asia-Pacific, Mr Wolfram B. Geisler.

The focus will be on design and development of commercial vehicle concepts with the potential to be marketed and sold world-wide under the Mercedes-Benz name.

He said in an interview that this global development project – the company's first outside Germany – integrates teams with multi-disciplinary skills from various regions around the world.

The group has had a Mercedes-Benz concepts and strategies development unit here for the past few years.

Mr Geisler said that while the company's passenger cars were well-known throughout Asia, its commercial vehicles lagged behind even though they enjoyed a high market share in Europe and North America.

He said the company proposed to focus on developing a new commercial vehicle for Asian markets. The new concept to be worked on in Singapore would cover both light trucks and vans.

A team of about 12 experts was being assembled for the project, he added.

Source: *The Straits Times*, **25 February 1997**

Case Discussion Issues and Questions

1. Discuss the respective motives of host and investor. Who stands to gain the most?

2. Analyse the firm-specific sources of effects on the Singaporean economy.

3. Discuss the likely competitive advantages that might accrue to Singapore's industrial sector as a result of the FDI. To what extent are these static or dynamic?

Inward investment to exploit firm-specific advantages may confer very little in the way of technological spin-offs for the local economy. Moreover, it is argued that MNCs tend to centralise R&D in the parent company to protect secret know-how, so that subsidiaries become technologically dependent on their parents and are confined solely to local assembly operations. For these reasons, many host country governments insist on joint ventures between local companies and MNCs rather than exclusive foreign ownership and commitment to genuine technology transfer (Box 7.1).

Box 7.1   Technology Transfer

- In 1994 GEC Alstom, the Anglo-French group, won a contract to supply high-speed TGV trains to South Korea. GEC Alstom had to weigh the advantages of gaining its first entry into the potentially lucrative Asian market against allowing its consortium of Korean sub-contractors – Hyundai, Daewoo and Hanjin – to become an eventual competitive rival. The contract will enable Korea to make the TGV on its own once it acquires full rights to the transferred technology in 2002 and sell it to other countries. Initially GEC Alstom resisted the extent of Korea's technology transfer demands, citing patent and intellectual property rights. In the end, however, the company, facing stiff competition from two rival bidders (Siemens and Mitsubishi), agreed to provide design and manufacturing technology to enable the Korean sub-contractors to produce key components and provide them with the ability to upgrade the TGV in the future. "It's how the game is played" (company spokesman).

Box 7.1 (*cont'd*)

- In 1994 Ford Motor Company established joint ventures with two Chinese companies, Shanghai Automotive Industry Corporation and the Yao Hua Glass Works to produce motor components. China has told international automotive makers that before they become involved in vehicle assembly in China they must first show their commitment and willingness to upgrade local component supply sources by investment and technology transfer. Also in 1994, Lucas Industries, the UK automotive component group, entered into its first technology transfer agreement with China under which it is providing technology for braking systems to a joint-venture company, Hwa Heng, set up between Lucas' licensee in Taiwan and the Chinese company Wuhu Auto Parts.

- In 1993 a joint-venture concern involving two Japanese and three Malaysian companies was established to produce Malaysia's second national car to compete against the Proton model (a Malaysian-Mitsubishi of Japan joint venture). The new car is based on the existing Daihatsu Mira model. A key aspect of the venture is the 'total commitment' of Daihatsu of Japan to transferring technology to its Malaysian joint-venture partners. One of the principal reasons for the establishment of the new company was Malaysia's 'dissatisfaction' at the slow rate of technology transfer from Japan in the Proton car venture.

- In 1995 Honda of Japan won a licence to manufacture motorcycles in Vietnam in a joint venture with a subsidiary of the Ministry of Heavy Industry (MOHI) Vietnam.

CASE 7.3

Precision technology: Swiss investment is something to watch

The Swiss are not the biggest players here in Thailand in investment terms but, as Ambassador Bernard Freymond sees it, there is plenty of potential for growth.

The Thai people generally have a positive and tolerant attitude towards foreigners. Thailand has always integrated elements of other cultures into its own unique culture. This is true of religion, language, the arts and the renowned Thai kitchen. I arrived only two months ago, but already I have experienced the hospitality and sympathy Thai people share with locals and foreigners alike.

For a growing number of my fellow citizens, Thailand is not only an exotic and sunny holiday destination but also a fascinating country with a rich cultural heritage. After a steady increasing arrivals in recent years, the number of Swiss tourists has dropped by 10 percent in 1997 due to a stagnant Swiss economy. Next year however should see a stabilisation and an increase is expected over the next few years.

Today about 100,000 Swiss come to Thailand each year, while around 50,000 Thai visited my country in 1996. Thai tourists to Switzerland are business people who often extend their stay, group tourists on their trip through Europe and Thais married to Swiss.

Thailand accounts for the largest Swiss community in Asia with approximately 2,500 registered citizens, while the Thai community in Switzerland counts 4,000 to 5,000 people. Therefore, it does not come as a surprise that Swissair has recently introduced two additional flights to Bangkok, bringing the total number of flights per week to nine.

Cultural exchange through the local Swiss School and many other channels has become a regular feature between Thailand and Switzerland. Only two weeks ago, hundreds of Thai and expatriate music lovers applauded the first performance in Asia of the Swiss jazz band, Piano Seven.

In recent years, world-wide investment flows have grown considerably. They reflect the increasing importance of direct investment in a more and more globalised world economy.

Today, almost half of the world's trade activity is realised by multinational and transnational enterprises. Switzerland is one of the most important direct investors world-wide with a total stock of direct investment abroad of about 190 billion Swiss francs (approx 5,510 billion baht).

Switzerland is also the ninth investor in Thailand with far over 1 billion Swiss francs (29 billion baht) invested and a number of substantial projects taking shape over the last year. However, compared to Swiss investment in other countries, where Switzerland often ranks third, fourth or fifth, there is still large potential, especially in view of future markets in the wider Mekong region.

The positive effects of foreign direct investment go far beyond the return generated by invested financial capital, since the flow of private capital usually induces a transfer of technology and know-how, and gives employment to many local people. Such transfers are becoming more and more important to economic and human resources development, which is why Switzerland attaches great importance to the promotion of direct foreign investment.

The 'Agreement on the Promotion and Reciprocal Protection of Investment' to be signed on November 17 is the result of intense negotiations. It expresses the willingness of Thailand and Switzerland to create new opportunities for co-operation between entrepreneurs from the two countries. Confirming the existence of a positive framework for investment, the agreement will be of particular interest to small- and medium-sized Swiss enterprises that may want to invest in Thailand.

Finally, a Swiss investor, once he has taken a decision after a sometimes lengthy evaluation procedure, will stay in Thailand. The capital invested therefore will remain in the country and have its positive effects on the economy on a long-term basis.

Exports from Switzerland to Thailand mainly consist of machines, machine tools, watches and their components and pharmaceuticals (900 million Swiss francs [26.1 billion baht] in 1996) while Thailand exports jewellery, cut precious stones, watches and their components, agricultural products and shoes to Switzerland. After steady growth in recent years, the current economic slowdown has resulted so far in stabilisation of bilateral trade.

To illustrate how close economic ties between our two countries and within the globalised economy already are: a focus on the watch industry.

Various world-renowned Swiss and other manufacturers of timepieces, a labour-intensive industry, move some of their production bases to Thailand to take advantage of cheap labour. This relocation took place after it had become clear in the 1970s that traditional production methods with an expensive workforce in dozens of small- and medium-sized enterprises in Switzerland were no longer possible.

However, as in the textile industry, the advantage of labour costs in Thailand has since diminished, forcing low-end manufacturing industry to move to other countries with cheaper labour costs.

Nevertheless, large manufacturers prefer to remain in Thailand due to the fact that they have developed their technology to a level where they can engage in fully integrated production. Thai labour has, moreover, become more deft and skilful, and the country's infrastructure is more developed than in those places where cheaper labour prevails.

The export value of timepieces and parts has expanded rapidly, averaging annual growth of 40 percent until 1995. The only bilateral problem in this context is fake Swiss luxury watches, illegally produced and sold in Thailand and other countries. This remains a serious issue although the situation has improved somewhat recently.

Basic restructuring of the Thai economy towards more value-added output requiring better education will eventually make Thailand more competitive in international markets, a positive move that my government and the Swiss business community both welcome. High-quality products and services at competitive prices in a liberalised economy are the key to Thailand's economic future.

Although Thailand is no longer eligible for a "Priority Programme" for technical co-operation in the Mekong region, Switzerland remains committed to sustainable development in Thailand and throughout the region.

In order to support the Mekong riparian countries more efficiently, the Swiss Agency for Development and Co-operation is contributing to five regional centres located in Bangkok: the Mekong River Commission, the Asian Institute of Technology, the Regional Community Forestry Training Centre, the "Asdialand – Sloping Land" component of the International Board for Soil Research and Management and the Asian Vegetable Research Development Centre. Swiss contributions total several million Swiss francs each year.

Source: Chamber World Network International, *Bangkok Post***, 5 November 1997**

Case Discussion Issues and Questions

1. Discuss the potential industrial and non-industrial effects of such a significant Swiss presence in Thailand.

2. Analyse the evolving influence of Swiss FDI on Thailand's labour markets. Who benefits most – Thailand or Switzerland?

3. Discuss the potential derivative benefits from Swiss investments in Thailand.

❖ ❖ ❖

While, in theory, less developed countries stand to gain the most in terms of acquiring new technology through inward investment, developed countries, too, can benefit from a cross-fertilisation of ideas, know-how and technology transfer by MNCs. The UK, for example, has benefited directly from the rejuvenation of its motor industry deriving from the joint venture between Rover Group and Honda of Japan (which ended in 1994 when Rover was acquired by BMW of Germany) and Honda's own green-field investment in a car-assembly plant at Swindon. The UK has also gained from the green-field investments made by two other Japanese groups, Nissan, which established a car-assembly plant at Washington, and the Toyota investment in a car-assembly plant at Burnaston, near Derby (Box 7.2).

Box 7.2 Japanese Car Makers' Investment in UK

Nissan
- Assembly and engine plant in Washington, near Sunderland (opened 1986)
  Output: 400,000 cars a year by 1995
  Investment: £850 million
  Jobs: 4,600
  European components purchases: £800 million in 1993
- Car body pressings subsidiary (80% Nissan) in Washington Investment: £50 million
  Jobs: 200
- Sales, marketing and distribution subsidiaries
  Investment: £40 million
  Jobs: 400

Toyota
- Assembly plant in Burnaston, near Derby (opened 1992)
  Output: 200,000 cars a year by 1995
  Investment: £700 million
  Jobs: 8,000 by 1995
  European components purchases: £750 million by 1995
- Engine plant in Deeside, North Wales
  Investment: £140 million
  Jobs: 300
- Sales, marketing and distribution subsidiaries
  5% stake in subsidiary rising to 51% in 1998 (£60 million)

Box 7.2 (*cont'd*)

Honda • Assembly plant in Swindon (opened 1992)
         Output: 100,000 cars a year by 1995
         Investment: £300 million
         Jobs: 2,000 by 1995
         European components purchases: £400 million by 1995
      • Engine plant in Swindon
         Investment: £62 million

Source: Company information.

A major benefit of the Rover-Honda relationship was a near-revolution in the quality and reliability of supply of components with the application of Japanese production control and inventory management techniques. Nor is this confined to the motor industry. The Sony television plant in Bridgend in Britain is now seen as a model for subsequent investment elsewhere in Europe, largely due to the development of closer relationships with, and exerting commercial pressure on, both small and large-scale component suppliers. Indeed, this is an interesting case of a development from a former screwdriver plant into a leading edge supplier using process and product applications developed at Sony's R&D establishment at Basingstoke, England.

Other notable examples of inward investment establishing new UK manufacturing capabilities include American, Japanese and European investment in computers, semiconductors (microchips), video-cassette recorders and scientific instruments. In addition, the MNC may preserve existing capability where the UK owner is unable or reluctant to commit further development resources, as in the case of the purchase of Inmos by the French electronics group CSF-Thomson. Finally, for many countries, managerial skills may be a scarce factor so that an inflow of MNC investment and associated managerial resources can directly contribute to a more efficient operation of their economies. The long-term indirect effects may also be important with, again, the acquisition of entrepreneurial and managerial expertise by local managers employed by MNCs. This may eventually lead to their setting up businesses of their own or taking control of established companies.

Output and employment effects

The output and employment effects of inward investment depend partly on the initial mode of entry chosen by the MNC. The establishment of a green-field plant leads directly to increased output and local employment, depending on the scale of the operation, while the takeover of an established firm may well reduce employment if a rationalisation programme is followed. Over the long term, however, *both* modes of entry are likely to produce beneficial output and employment effects as the MNC strengthens and expands its operations. Inward investment also creates secondary jobs elsewhere in the economy by increasing the demand for locally produced component supplies, transport, financial, technical and marketing services (Box 7.3). These effects are likely to be especially beneficial in the case of large-scale production operations which involve a high proportion of bought-in components, such as in motor-car assembly (Box 7.2).

Box 7.3   FDI and Job Gains

- In 1994, Samsung, the Korean electronics group, announced it was to establish a five-unit manufacturing complex at Teesside in the UK. The development is planned in two phases. The first phase involving the setting up of two plants to produce microwave ovens and personal computers will create around 900 jobs by the end of 1995. The second phase, to start in 1997 is expected to provide another 2,300 jobs with the production of personal computers, fax machines and colour display tubes, a microchip facility and the completion of training and administration centres. In addition a further 2,000 indirect jobs are expected to be created in firms supplying Samsung with parts. A further investment by Samsung at the company's existing TV plant at nearby Billingham has created an additional 240 jobs, taking the total workforce at the plant to 3,500.

- In 1992 Toyota's car-assembly plant at Burnaston in the UK came on-stream. By the end of 1994 plant capacity had increased to 100,000 cars a year and 80% of components were sourced in Europe. The company employed 1,800 workers. The high level of out-sourcing of components created a further 3,800 indirect jobs. A projected expansion at Burnaston to produce 200,000 cars a year is expected to raise direct employment to 3,000 and indirect employment to 7,000.

- Scotland has proven to be a particular magnet for international electronics companies, which regard it as a relatively low-cost base from which to supply European markets. Although this has created thousands of direct jobs, few of these investment outlays (Table 1) have significant links with indigenous Scottish suppliers, which have won only 12% of the market for sub-contracting and components.

Box 7.3 (*cont'd*)

Table 1   FDI – The employment effect

Company	Location	Products	Employees
IBM	Greenock	PCs & monitors	2,300
Motorola	East Kilbride	Semiconductors	2,000
Motorola	Bathgate	Cellular phones	1,600
NCR	Dundee	Auto teller machines	1,600
Digital	Ayr	Workstation & PCs	1,550
National Semi	Greenock	Microchips	1,300
Hewlett-Packard	S. Queensferry	Telecoms	1,000
NEC	Livingston	Semiconductors	850
Compaq	Erskine	PCs	700
JVC	East Kilbride	Televisions	700
Digital	S. Queensferry	Wafers	559
Mitsubishi	Haddington	Televisions	514

CASE 7.4

Puffing and blowing into India: Controversy over government's decision to allow 100 pc foreign direct investment in cigarettes

The recent decision of the Union Government to allow foreign direct investment (FDI) up to 100 per cent in cigarette manufacturing seemed to be mired in controversy. The former Union Health Minister, Ms Renuka Chowdary, feels that the policy announcement made on August 27, 1999 has been meant specifically for clearing the application of Rothmans of Pall Mall (International) Ltd of the UK. She wanted to fight at 'every fora available' to her against this policy shift by the Government.

Rothmans submitted a proposal to the Foreign Investment Promotion Board (FIPB) on November 3, 1997, for establishment of a 100 per cent subsidiary in India. Incidentally, it is learnt, the application of Rothmans is being taken up for consideration tomorrow.

Ms Chowdary pointed out the Union Government had earlier decided not to permit more than 50 per cent foreign shareholding in any cigarette company. This decision was aimed at discouraging not only the promotion of cigarette smoking in the country but also the setting up of parallel subsidiaries in the same product category by multinationals which already have shareholding in the existing Indian companies.

This has been cited as the main reason as to why BAT and Phillip Morris, the two global tobacco giants which have substantial shareholding in three companies in India, have failed in their attempts in the past to set up their own 100 per cent subsidiaries.

For instance, the application to the FIPB of VST Industries Ltd, in which BAT has a 33 per cent stake, for promoters to take up the unsubscribed portion of its proposed

Rs. 100-crore rights issue had not been cleared for a long time. The company now had withdrawn its proposal and sought the Finance Ministry's permission for conversion of 3.8 million pounds received from BAT as advance subscription money into external commercial borrowing.

VST Director, Mr S. Thirumalai, said that "the delay in a decision on the subject caused us some major cash flow problems. A further careful examination of the issue was undertaken to arrive at the best course".

In a fax to Business Line, Mr Thirumalai, however, denied any discrimination on the part of FIPB in this regard. He stated that, as clarified by the FIPB itself, the policy guideline to consider proposals for manufacture of cigarettes with FDI up to 100 per cent was announced only on August 27, 1998. "Hence, there is no question of discrimination." Rothmans, in its application, has stated that it would contribute an equity of up to US$150 millions in the Indian subsidiary which will have the following objectives:

- To purchase for export, Indian tobacco to support Rothmans International Group's global requirement which is forecast to increase to approximately US$70 million over 7 years.
- To invest in integrated agronomic development principally in Andhra Pradesh.
- To introduce international brands from the Rothmans International stable for the Indian consumer.
- To facilitate the transfer of manufacturing technology and know-how to a designated manufacturer in India.
- To facilitate the transfer of managerial expertise to its local employees.
- To provide advice and assistance to its parent company, the Richemont group and subsidiary such as Cartier, Alfred Dunhill, Sulka, Mont Blanc, etc., on the investment climate in India.
- To provide feedback to the Rothmans sponsorship function regarding the feasibility of India being a host country for future Formula One international motor racing events.

Ms Chowdary, however, is of the view that the Rothmans proposal of bringing technology in to the agriculture sector is a deceptive bait and not at all connected with the manufacture and marketing of cigarettes in India. Similarly, she said, the foreign exchange as shown in the application of about US$10 million per year was 'again a deception' as Rothmans was already importing tobacco from India for the last several years to the extent of US$8 to 10 million per year at current prices. Thus there was no additional export as claimed.

With regard to the Rothmans proposal of advising and assisting its parent company pertaining to other products like Cartier jewellery watches and Mont Blanc pens, she said that these products were already being marketed in India by their separate companies. "Moreover, for doing an advisory's work, one does not need to have a subsidiary." The former Health Minister said that the Rothmans proposal of facilitating transfer of managerial expertise to local employees and providing them employment was also a deceptive suggestion as they have refrained from indicating the number of additional employment they would provide directly through their subsidiary.

Stating that cigarettes have been known for their hazardous effects on human health and that smoking of cigarettes was being discouraged world-wide, Ms Chowdary said that no new foreign investment should be allowed in cigarette industry in the country.

According to her, the entry of multinational companies in the country is clearly intended for promotion of their brands of cigarettes with enormous money power they have at their command to encourage Indian people to smoke their cigarettes and replace the huge beedi industry which provides employment to 4.6 million workers.

Source: Chamber World Network International, *Business Line,* **5 September 1998**

Case Discussion Issues and Questions

1. Analyse the various effects that Rothmans might have on India's tobacco industry. Do these compliment, or detract from, India's socio-economic development objectives?

2. Discuss the Rothmans objectives. Who benefits most: the investor or India?

3. Suggest ways in which India can moderate the effects of this type of investment.

Obviously, in the case of an individual MNC, the employment it creates in a particular host country needs to be considered in terms of the permanence of the investment made. Given that MNCs often regroup their sourcing and market servicing operations in the light of underlying world conditions and changing competitive circumstances, it may well be that new plant openings in one country are accompanied by complete or partial shutdowns elsewhere. For example, in 1990, Ford transferred the production of Sierras from its Dagenham plant in the UK to its plant in Gent, Belgium, while Wang (US) closed its personal computer factory in Scotland, transferring production to Ireland. In 1993, CPC (UK), the subsidiary of a US group, transferred production of its Knorr brand of soups and cubes from Scotland to more modern plants in France and Italy with a loss of 350 UK jobs (Box 7.4).

In aggregate terms, however, studies have shown the overall impact of MNC activity to be strongly output- and employment-creating in most host countries. In the case of the UK, foreign-controlled enterprises, although accounting for only around 1% of total UK manufacturing firms in 1990, they employed 16% of the labour force and accounted for 22% of total UK output and 27% of total UK investment.

Box 7.4   FDI and Job Losses

- In 1994 Digital Equipment, the US computer producer, closed its manufacturing plant in Galway, Republic of Ireland, with the loss of 780 jobs. Digital was forced to restructure its business in the face of falling sales, and production was switched to the company's other plants.

- In 1994, Eurofab, the French subsidiary of the US cleaning products group SC Johnson, was closed with a loss of 190 jobs. Production was transferred to larger and cheaper sites at MijUrecht in the Netherlands and Frimiey in the UK. Johnson also closed plants in Spain and Portugal with a loss of 400 jobs out of a European workforce of 3,250. The group wants "to concentrate production on high volumes and leading edge technologies, allowing the optimisation of quality and the creation of integrated supply chains. The level of investments needed is such that not all European production sites could benefit" (company spokesman).

- In 1994 Texas Instruments, the US electronics group, closed its plant in Bedford, UK, with a loss of 800 jobs. The move was part of a world-wide restructuring plan to rationalise the company's manufacturing operations. It intends to concentrate the manufacturing of its main product lines in France, Germany and Italy. Two hundred jobs were relocated elsewhere in the company's other UK operations, while some 50 top electronic engineers were offered positions in France, Germany and at the company's headquarters in Dallas.

- In 1995, British Polythene Industries, Europe's largest polythene film producer, closed its Alidu Polysack plant at Telford, UK, and transferred half the plant's output to China and half to its other UK plants. The closure, precipitated by a major UK retail consumer switching to an Asian-based supplier, resulted in a loss of 185 jobs.

Finally, it is to be noted that, while some MNC investment is directed towards capitalising on the lower costs associated with using relatively unskilled labour, there has been a substantial amount of investment in high-technology industries (telecommunications, consumer electronics, etc.) which has contributed towards upgrading employment skills.

Sovereignty and autonomy effects

The sovereignty and autonomy effects of the MNC's foreign investment are invariably viewed by host countries as a cost. Although foreign firms can benefit the local economy in various ways, as noted earlier, inevitably there is some loss of economic independence when a large segment of local industry is effectively controlled by foreign companies. Such problems arise essentially from the international nature of MNCs with policies towards any one subsidiary reflecting the pursuit of some global objective of the MNCs (that is, pursuit of its private interest that may not necessarily correspond to the public interest aspirations of the host country). For example, a MNC may use transfer pricing techniques to eliminate local competitors in order to monopolise the host country market, or transfer out potential value added in order to minimise its global tax bill (see Chapter 6, Section 6.4).

CASE 7.5

The empire strikes back: British Telecom's investments in Asia

At the rate it is writing out cheques in Asia, British Telecommunications plc may soon give the International Monetary Fund (IMF) a run for its money.

As British Telecom's director of strategic markets, Asia-Pacific, Richard Slogrove, put it: "There's a line that next to the IMF, we've invested more (in Asia) than anybody else."

In the last six months, British Telecom has shelled out some £650 million (S$1.8 billion) to buy into and build phone networks across Asia. From Saudi Arabia to Singapore, it is making up for lost time and snapping up minority stakes as and when the markets open up (Figure 1).

To date, it probably has bagged more licences in the region than any other foreign telcos, but still its investment appetite is not satiated. British Telecom is on the prowl again and observers don't rule out imminent deals with Smartone in Hong Kong and Japan Telecom in Tokyo.

So far, British Telecom's joint ventures and direct operations in Asia serve a combine customer base of 3.6 million, and together employ 8,500 people. They generate a total annual revenue of £1.4 billion for British Telecom and its partners, the figure excluding British Telecom's own correspondent traffic between Asia and the UK.

During a presentation to Asia-based journalists in London recently, Mr Slogrove noted: "When we put those figures down, when we calculated them over the last few weeks, we got quite a shock because we had in a very short space of time, about one year, gone from nowhere to somewhere."

Its spread of investments include four joint ventures in India, an 18 per cent interest in StarHub, Singapore's second fixed-line licensee, a 33.3 per cent stake in Binariang Bhd, a mobile operator in Malaysia, 50 per cent of Clear Communications in New Zealand, and 23.49 per cent of LG Telecom in South Korea.

It also won a broadband wireless licence in key urban areas in Japan through a 70 : 30 joint venture with the Marubeni Corporation.

If British Telecom officials needed assurance that they did right to come into Asia during the region's deepest economic recession, they can point to LG Telecom. The

Figure 1   BT's Asian presence

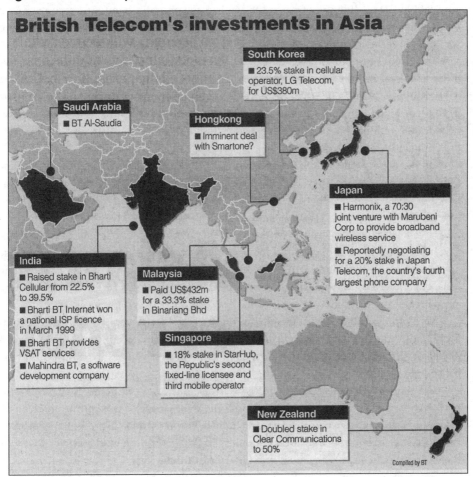

British Telecom's investments in Asia

South Korea
■ 23.5% stake in cellular operator, LG Telecom, for US$380m

Saudi Arabia
■ BT Al-Saudia

Hongkong
■ Imminent deal with Smartone?

Japan
■ Harmonix, a 70:30 joint venture with Marubeni Corp to provide broadband wireless service
■ Reportedly negotiating for a 20% stake in Japan Telecom, the country's fourth largest phone company

India
■ Raised stake in Bharti Cellular from 22.5% to 39.5%
■ Bharti BT Internet won a national ISP licence in March 1999
■ Bharti BT provides VSAT services
■ Mahindra BT, a software development company

Malaysia
■ Paid US$432m for a 33.3% stake in Binariang Bhd

Singapore
■ 18% stake in StarHub, the Republic's second fixed-line licensee and third mobile operator

New Zealand
■ Doubled stake in Clear Communications to 50%

Compiled by BT

Korean mobile operator is signing up 8,000 subscribers a day, a performance which blew apart the conservative estimates built into the initial business plan by British Telecom and its partner, the Lucky GoldStar group.

The spending spree last year was partly a catch-up to the investments already made by other Western telcos such as AT&T, US West, Deutsche Telekom and Cable & Wireless. But as the regional financial crisis intensified last year, it has turned out to be a case of better late than early.

Rare opportunities for investments opened up like never before and at asset values lower than those struck during the boom years. While foreign telcos which rushed for concessions in Indonesia in the mid-1990s are now toughing it out, British Telecom is happily uninvested in that country.

Of its entry into Asia, Mr Slogrove commented: "If you are wondering why we were a bit late in Asia, I think it's true to say we had to concentrate on our home market in Europe first. Secondly, we had to resolve partnerships and distributorships in the US, and we were, in terms of timing, very fortunate in concentrating on Asia when we did."

The group's presence in Asia dates back to 1985 when it first opened a representative office in Tokyo, and a wholly-owned subsidiary, BT Services (Singapore) Pte Ltd, here to cover Southeast Asia. More than 14 offices were since set up across the region, handling mainly correspondent relationships as well as providing support for Concert, its global network for multinational corporations which until last year was a partnership with MCI, the US long-distance carrier.

Unlike many multinational corporations which have eschewed investments where they cannot secure majority control, British Telecom accepts that the nature of the telecoms business means that they will have to be mostly content with minority stakes. "We are not control freaks," Mr Slogrove said, although he conceded that British Telecom will have to learn how to exercise influence in ventures where it no longer calls the shots.

In building up an alliance of joint ventures across the region, British Telecom also appears to have abandoned its former strategy of finding one heavyweight partner in Asia. For some years, it was widely seen to be courting Japan's NT&T, a lumbering giant since broken up into different entities by deregulation.

Mr Slogrove believed partnerships in the telecoms sector could follow the patterns set in the airlines industry where instead of gobbling one another up, airlines are forming alliances. "I think the model these days is in some places, you compete, in others, you collaborate," he said.

How much and where British Telecom invests next in Asia depends on where the markets are opening up and its ability to find the right partner, Mr Slogrove pointed out. Asia is not a homogeneous market, and unlike Europe where liberalisation began in earnest last year, large swathes of the industry in this part of the world, especially in the biggest market of them all, China, remain closed to foreigners.

This will soon change. The World Trade Organisation accord signed last year requires entry barriers in 85 per cent of the world's markets for telecoms to be dismantled by 2003.

Mr Slogrove stressed that finding the right partner, one with the required local connection and knowledge, and who shares British Telecom's corporate philosophy and vision, is a major factor dictating investment priorities in Asia. "I think a lot of it is also just instinct; I used to work for a French chief executive and he used to say, "Never mind the numbers, Richard, how does it smell?"

For sure, British Telecom isn't just being led by its nose in Asia. In amassing its portfolio of Asian assets, it is adopting and adapting models used in Europe. There, it has implemented a 'multi-local strategy' which involved forming an alliance of joint-venture partners, bidding for licences whenever it can, and setting up local distributorships.

Its partners are typically non-telecom companies with local influence and established infrastructures. They include Viag, a major energy and industry group in Germany;

Vivendi, the French water utility company; and Nederlandse Spoorwegen, the state railway operator in the Netherlands.

Carole Madden, manager for marketing operations and service development for British Telecom in Europe, said the priorities for Europe are to create "new wave telcos", that is, companies with abilities to be niche players; to become the continent's leading Internet service provider; to exploit mobile licences and increase investments in a high bandwidth data-centric network.

The strategy of forming an alliance of partnerships across the European Community is a recognition of the huge opportunities that exist there and at the same time, the enormous capital outlay required and risk involved if British Telecom were to go it alone. The UK carrier has already invested £2 billion in Europe and expects to put in more money in the next few years.

A key part of the European strategy is the construction of the largest transborder communications across the continent. Project Farland, a £70 million undertaking, involves the building of 7,000 km of new optic fibre and 14 POPs (points of presence) connecting seven national networks.

Upon completion, it will link British Telecom's own infrastructure to that of its joint-venture partners, thereby creating a pan-European network of 44,000 km of cable in 200 cities. This network, expected to be switched on sometime this year, will be centrally managed and will offer Internet and Asynchronous Transfer Mode services from day one.

The strategy is underpinned by expectations of an explosive demand for bandwidth, in particular for data traffic which has been growing at 30–80 per cent a year in Europe and is already far exceeding the demand for voice traffic.

The pan-European network will be managed by British Telecom's 50:50 global venture with AT&T once the latter clears all regulatory hurdles. It recently received the go-ahead from regulators in Brussels but is still awaiting US approval.

The plan, said Martin O'Connor, head of corporate relations for Asia-Pacific, is to do a similar network in Asia once its fast growing family of regional interests reach critical mass to make an Asian version of Project Farland feasible. It is also envisaged that the intelligent platform to manage the network will be based in Singapore.

In the meanwhile, British Telecom will no doubt be hitting the acquisition trail again.

Source: *The Business Times*, **7 April 1999**

Case Discussion Issues and Questions

1. Discuss the possible differences in competitive advantages for BT from its FDI in Singapore, South Korea and Japan in contrast with its FDI in India, Hong Kong and Malaysia.

2. Analyse the potential benefits that accrue to host partners.

3. BT's foreign market entry modes are through minority joint ventures – how do these entry modes confer competitiveness on BT's foreign operations?

4. Discuss the global factors driving competition in the international telecoms business in Asia.

5. Discuss the potential for other gains for the national economies of BT's FDI.

However, it is also the case that countries compete with each other to attract inward investment by providing investment grants and tax holidays so that in many cases MNCs are simply taking commercial advantage of situations created by governmental actions (Box 7.5).

Box 7.5 'Poaching' Inward Investment?

- Many countries use financial sweeteners and other means to attract inward investment and this often gives rise to charges of unfair 'poaching'. An example is Hoover's decision to close its vacuum cleaner plant in Longuie, France with a loss of 650 jobs, and transfer production to its Cambuslang plant in Scotland. As far as the company was concerned, the move made commercial sense, enabling it to reduce manufacturing costs by around 25% through the centralisation of all production in the one plant. The French Government, upset by the UK's refusal to embrace the Social Chapter requirements of the Maastricht Treaty, asked the European Commission to investigate whether Hoover was unfairly or illegally 'bribed' with social and financial concessions. The UK and French authorities both offered Hoover around £5 million in plant subsidies, but the UK's opt-out of the Social Chapter means that, although hourly pay rates are about the same in both countries, because social security and welfare costs are higher in France overall payroll costs are much lower in the UK. In addition, the Scottish workforce made several concessions: limited period contracts for new workers, constraints on their right to strike, cuts in overtime pay rates, flexible working time and practices and the introduction of video cameras on the factory floor. To the French, this was a clear case of the competitive undercutting of pay and conditions to attract investment, or 'social dumping' as they prefer to call it.

- In the UK 'regional selective assistance' amounting to 15–20% of project costs is available to companies locating in a designated development area. In 1994, funding worth nearly £80 million was made available to Samsung, the Korean electronics group, to set up a manufacturing complex costing around £600 million in Teeside. The financial package consists of £58 million of regional selective assistance, including a £13 million interest-free loan while another £20 million is being made available by the local authority to cover training and other set-up costs. The UK faced stiff competition from Spain in securing the Samsung investment. The success

---

Box 7.5 (*cont'd*)

of an established Samsung subsidiary producing colour television sets at nearby Billingham helped to influence the decision in favour of a UK location.

- In 1994 Jaguar, the luxury car subsidiary of Ford, was deterred from transferring the assembly of the next generation Jaguar XJS sports car from the UK to Portugal after receiving £9 million of regional selective assistance. In 1995 Ford announced it was to invest some £40 million to develop a new Jaguar model in the UK instead of (transferring work) to the US after being promised a £80 million financial aid package.

There are equally important aspects relating to the reduced ability of the host government to pursue its desired policies. For example, host government monetary policies may be circumvented by the MNC because it can draw on funds from elsewhere although, for developed nations such as the UK, its own home-based MNCs may already pose such threats, in the absence of exchange control. However, there has been a growing tendency on the part of MNCs (Shell, Unilever to name but two) to exercise a degree of social responsibility in their dealings with host countries so that the interdependence that exists between the MNC and host country economies can be harnessed to their mutual benefit. The willingness of a MNC to help a government in furthering the economic development of the country is important in building a long-term market presence. For example, in 1994 BT, the UK telecommunications company, entered into a partnership agreement with the Australian Federal Government. BT first began operating in Australia in 1987, providing private telephone services to international companies and government departments. In 1992 BT won the contract to design, install and manage the internal telephone network for the New South Wales Government. As a result BT took on and trained a large number of engineers and began procuring equipment from local manufacturers. Under the 1994 agreement BT is moving its Asia-Pacific headquarters from Singapore to Sydney and it has agreed to purchase equipment worth at least £200 million from Australian manufacturers over the next seven years. BT is to establish an Asia-Pacific engineering centre in Sydney and a university research programme to fund collaboration between Australian universities and the company's R&D laboratories in the UK. BT hopes to capitalise on these initiatives by securing a public telecommunications operator's licence when the Australian telecoms market is opened fully to competition in 1997 (see also Box 7.1 Technology Transfer).

7.3 POLICIES TOWARDS FOREIGN DIRECT INVESTMENT

The large upsurge in FDI flows over recent years (see Chapter 2) has been largely associated with the expansion of multinational companies as they sought to enhance their positions in the three major Triad blocs: Western Europe, North America and the Pacific Rim. Flows of FDI (and associated portfolio investment) have been greatly facilitated by many countries removing exchange controls over capital movements and related income streams and various institutional arrangements encouraging inward investment (Box 7.6). The UK, for example, abolished all exchange controls over capital movements into and out of the country in 1979, and there are no limitations on the repatriation of profits. There are no restrictions on the proportion of local equity that can be held by foreign direct investors, nor are there any selective controls on investment in particular industrial sectors.

Box 7.6   FDI Policies

- *United States*: Generally, foreign investment is free of restrictions although ownership limitations exist in some sectors (communications, aviation, insurance, real estate, banking). The US has no exchange controls and foreign investors can fully repatriate dividends, interest, etc.

- *Germany*: Generally, 100% foreign ownership is permitted and there are no exchange controls or any restrictions on profit and capital repatriation. Substantial tax incentives and investment grants are available to investors in East Germany.

- *Hong Kong*: There are no limits on foreign ownership and investors have complete flexibility in the movement of capital and the repatriation of profits.

- *Brazil*: Foreign investors cannot exceed 5% of the voting capital or 20% of the total capital of a Brazilian company. Capital repatriation, however, is unrestricted.

- *Thailand*: Foreign shareholdings are generally limited to a maximum of 49% of capital; however, foreigners may hold more than 50% of the equity in export industries if exports exceed 50% of total production, and 100% of equity if 80% of output is exported. Permission is required for repatriation of dividends and capital.

- *Ghana*: 100% foreign-owned ventures are permitted provided they meet certain requirements. The venture must be a net earner of foreign currency; wholly-owned equity investment must be greater than US$100,000, while joint-venture investments with Ghanaian partners require a foreign equity stake of at least US$60,000.

- *Malaysia*: Foreign investors in new export-orientated industries can own 100% of the equity in a company if exports are more than 80% of production. Projects exporting

---

Box 7.6 (*cont'd*)

less than 20% of production are limited to a maximum of 30% foreign equity ownership. Full repatriation of profits was permitted until unilateral imposition of capital controls in October 1998 as a consequence of the Asian crisis.

- *Japan*: Various restrictions apply to investments in such sectors as financial services, utilities, petroleum refining and retail trades. There are no limitations on repatriation of capital or profits.

NOTE: It has to be borne in mind that the Asian crisis has, in most cases, accelerated the liberalisation of the FDI environment in Asia, partly as a consequence of IMF conditionalities. The exception has been Malaysia.

The UK operates an 'open door' policy towards FDI by actively supporting inward investment. The Invest in Britain Bureau (IBB) was established in 1977 to act as a facilitator and conduit for foreign investment in the UK. The IBB, part of the UK's Department of Trade and Industry, is able to offer companies practical assistance and detailed advice on all aspects of investing and locating in UK. Foreign companies are treated on an equal footing to domestic businesses with regard to, for example, financial backing if they locate in an 'assisted' region of the UK. The best example of a counterpart of the IBB in the Asian context is provided by Singapore's Economic Development Board (EDB) and the Trade Development Board (TDB).

Similar moves to liberalise capital movements have been made by the UK's partners in the EU under the Single European Market initiative, and likewise by other major industrial countries. Developing countries have also sought to make inward investment easier and more attractive as a means of industrialising their economies. Box 7.6 gives details of FDI policies in various countries. From the MNC's perspective ideally policies on FDI should be clear cut and transparent and, wherever possible, free from political risk (Box 7.5).

The case of Canada

Canada provides an interesting example of FDI policy since originally it discouraged inward investment before adopting a more open door approach in 1985.

Current Canadian FDI policy is aimed at encouraging FDI as a means of modernising the economy and developing Canada's global interests. Particular emphasis is placed on presenting Canada as a favourable investment location, with competitive labour costs and skills, abundant raw materials, low-cost energy supplies, sophisticated infrastructure, a growing economy and access, through the free trade agreement with the US, to a 'home' market of 266 million consumers. The Investment Canada agency acts as catalyst and focus for inward and outward FDI initiatives. The Investment Canada Act, 1985 requires the authorities be notified of certain proposed investments and the investments be reviewed as to their desirability, but on the whole Canada operates a liberal approach to inward investment. Canada is party to double taxation relief treaties on corporate profits with many countries, including the UK. However, Canada levies a 25% withholding tax on most corporate distributions to non-residents; this is reduced to 15% for payments to non-residents based in countries with which Canada has a comprehensive tax treaty.

Investment Canada was established in 1985 by the Investment Canada Act, replacing the Foreign Investment Review Agency (FIRA). The new institution reflected a marked change in the mood of official thinking on foreign investment by policy-makers from one which was heavily introverted to a much more open door approach that recognised the positive benefits to Canada likely to ensue from the encouragement of two-way investment: "Our goal must remain the attraction of value-added investment with a view to increasing capital and technology flows into Canada consistent with Canadian needs so as to achieve productivity growth and greater competitiveness and richer employment opportunities." (Paul Labbe, President of Investment Canada, *Annual Report 1989–90*, p. 91.)

The basic mission of Investment Canada is to promote investment in Canada by Canadians and foreigners, undertake research and provide advice on matters relating to investment and to 'review' major foreign investments to determine if they are likely to be of net benefit to Canada (Box 7.7). These functions are undertaken by Investment Canada's three main operational divisions: the Investment Development Division (which works with companies to encourage investment in Canada by providing counselling, matchmaking and other advisory services to potential investors); the Investment Research and Policy Division (which provides national and international data and analysis of investment trends and policies); and the Investment Review Division (which vets investment proposals by non-Canadians and monitors progress on the implementation of those investments which are approved). In the UK context, the Investment Development Programme of the Commercial/Economic Division at the Canadian High Commission, London, focuses on identifying and working with UK firms

Box 7.7   Investment Canada and UK Investors

- Company (1) is a substantial food manufacturer whose aim is to develop as a major international food group. The first move of Company (1) into the Canadian market was in 1987 with the acquisition of a 45% stake in a leading supplier of lobsters and scallops to the Canadian market. Also in 1987 Company (1) acquired 'A', a leading flour miller and producer of bakery, grocery and poultry products. This was followed in 1990 by the acquisition of 56% of the common shares in 'B', Canada's largest food processing company. Profits at 'B' had been falling and combining 'A' and 'B' into a merged group was seen as providing opportunities for rationalisation as well as synergies. Investment Canada, 'approved' both the 'A' and 'B' acquisitions. The company gave assurances of investment and R&D commitment, while Investment Canada accepted the company's rationalisation programme as being necessary to make the combined 'AB' operation effective.

- Company (2) is a major supplier of telecommunications services which has sought to internationalise its operations in recent years with a particular emphasis on the North American market. Company (2)'s first major North American move was the acquisition of a controlling stake in 'C', a sizeable Canadian manufacturer of telephone equipment, which had established production facilities in a number of countries including the UK where it was a significant supplier of equipment to Company (2). The Canadian company was in financial difficulties, required a cash injection and very much 'fell into Company (2)'s lap'. At this time, Company (2)'s strategic thinking emphasised the logic of vertical integration. The company 'satisfied' Investment Canada 'net benefit to Canada' requirements by allowing a continuing local shareholding presence (the company acquired only 51% of 'C's' common shares) and its £180 million cash lifeline was seen as a vital factor in securing the company's future (although it has remained in difficulties as a result of competitive pressures). Since then Company (2) has come round to the view that telecommunications services *per se* rather than equipment manufacture provides the best growth and profit opportunities, and in 1992 it sold the company.

- Company (3) is a major producer and distributor of natural gas which has looked increasingly to international markets to develop its business. In 1988 the company purchased a 51% stake in 'D', a Canadian gas exploration and production company, and in 1990 it acquired 'E', Canada's largest gas distribution company. Both these acquisitions were vetted by Investment Canada and given the 'sensitivity' of the energy sector in respect of foreign ownership, 'hedged' around by various stipulations. In the case of 'D' the company was limited to ownership of 33% of the common stock, while in the case of 'E', Company (3) agreed to the public flotation of 15% of the company's common shares. Additionally, in order to conform to foreign ownership rules relating to the ownership of oil and gas properties, 'E' was required to divest its oil and gas production interests. Company 3 also agreed to

---

Box 7.7 (*cont'd*)

invest some C$85 million in various environmental projects. In 1994, the company sold 'E' because its profit earning potential was impaired by stringent governmental price regulation.

---

seeking to establish operations in Canada and, likewise, providing advice, corporate contacts and entrees to financial institutions to Canadian companies seeking investment opportunities in the UK.

The issue of whether an investment is likely to result in net benefit to Canada introduces a 'discretionary' element into the inward investment equation and raises questions (for foreign investors) on what exactly constitutes 'net benefit' to Canada, particularly as the Investment Canada Act invokes a wide-ranging list of criteria to be considered. The criteria include: (1) the effect of the investment on economic activity including its impact on employment, resource processing, the use of Canadian parts and components, and the level of Canadian exports; (2) the degree of Canadian participation in the business and in the industry; (3) the effect on productivity, efficiency, technological development, product innovation and product variety; (4) the impact on competition in the affected industry; (5) compatibility with national industrial and cultural policies and (6) Canada's international competitive position. At first sight this amounts to a formidable list of potential hurdles to FDI. In practice, however, virtually all green-field direct investment in Canada has been exempted from review, while in the case of acquisitions the introduction of a 'threshold' value has meant that only the largest investments fall within the purview of the review procedure. Acquisitions by foreigners of Canadian businesses with assets over C$5 million are subject to review, as are 'indirect' acquisitions where the Canadian assets exceed C$50 million. (An indirect acquisition is an acquisition by a non-Canadian of a foreign-based company which has a Canadian subsidiary that accounts for less than 50% of the value of the international transaction.) Moreover, investments falling within the review requirements have been dealt with in a 'sympathetic' manner and allowed to proceed with minimal administrative hold-ups. Investment Canada rules specify that investors must be notified within 45 days if the agency has decided to disallow the investment; if no notification is received before the expiration of a deadline, the investment is deemed to have been allowed. If a proposal is disallowed, the investor has 30 days in which to present new information and appeal the decision.

US investment is by far the largest source of investment in Canada, and this is likely to be encouraged further as a result of the North American Free Trade Agreement (NAFTA) between Canada and the US. The NAFTA relaxed the 'threshold' provisions contained in the original Investment Canada Act 1985 for US investors: the thresholds for review of direct acquisitions were increased in four annual increments to C$25 million (1989), C$50 million (1990), C$100 million (1991) and C$150 million (1992); similarly, the thresholds for the review of direct acquisitions increasing annual increments to C$100 million (1989), C$250 million (1990), and C$500 million (1991). From January 1992 the reviews of indirect acquisitions were terminated unless the assets of the Canadian business represent more than 50% of the value of the total assets acquired in the international transaction. In the latter case, the transaction is reviewable at the same threshold that applies to direct acquisition (i.e., C$150 million).

Over 9,300 investments had been reviewed between June 1985 and March 1994 under the Investment Canada Act.

7.4 CHAPTER REVIEW

The competing and tentacular presence of MNCs in the international business environment renders them critical to the economic well-being not only of their home nation economies but also to the economies of the host locations where they invest and carry out wealth-generating operational activities. Chapter 2 indicated the extent of international trade and investment that results from the activities of MNCs. The global expansion of some MNCs is so vast that their corporate revenues and profits can exceed the gross national product of several developed countries and many developing countries. This asymmetry raises several key issues not only about the balance of power between MNCs and nation-states but also about the potential advantages and disadvantages of the presence (or absence) of MNCs and the FDI that they bring into, or take out of, countries. It brings to the fore the contention for control and management of resources and input factors as well as their application to the economic development of host countries.

The economic effects of the FDI of MNCs affect both the source (home country of the MNCs) and the host (the location of the FDI) in different ways and to different degrees of intensity. There are balance of payments and trade effects as well as implications for the deployment of resources. A key impact is on the changing structure of labour and patterns of employment. In general, outward FDI may decrease employment at source and increase employment in the host. However, the employment destroyed or created has to be evaluated carefully. Usually, this is done in terms of type (capital-intensive or labour-intensive, high or low value added), the location of the FDI, who benefits in the short and long term, the types of employment created or destroyed, etc., to ascertain the impact and overall benefits of the investment. In evaluating these effects there are, of course, different perspectives – for example, governments, host industries, individual firms, labour unions, consumers.

The resource transfer component of FDI is particularly important for developed and developing countries alike and depends in part on the entry mode of the FDI. Technology and know-how are produced for competitive purposes by MNCs for their international operations and the transfer to, or capture by, local firms is maximised when entry modes are of the joint-venture type as opposed to entry by wholly-owned subsidiary. When high technology forms part of the FDI then advantages to be gained by economies hosting the FDI can be considerable. This is provided the technology is of a type that does not require excessive imported factors or does not use the kind of input factors of which the host has abundant supplies. The first situation would tend to adversely affect the host balance of payments whereas the second might lead to less employment than anticipated. Technology transfer between MNCs and developing countries can be a source of contention between host governments and MNCs. Increasingly, technology transfer has occurred between Japanese MNCs and developed countries. This is especially so in the automotive industries where the management methods of Japanese MNCs have made considerable impact on the health of local automotive industry and the related and supporting sub-contracting firms. This is the case not only in Southeast Asia but also in the US and UK automobile industries since the mid-1980s.

Another key issue about the presence of MNCs concerns the impact on the sovereignty of the host nation in posture and action. Both developed and developing host governments may be cautious about permitting MNCs to control 'strategic' or 'national' sectors of the domestic economy. This concern exercises the policy-makers because the interests of the private concerns of the MNCs may not coincide with the public interests of the host government's aspirations for its country. Furthermore, the threats by MNCs to invest overseas may unduly constrain or alter the economic policies of source government by forcing governments to 'deter' outward FDI by the promise and offer of financial incentives as in the case of

Ford and the next generation of Jaguar XJS sports cars. The logical extent of this is the competitive 'poaching' of FDI by governments either eager to maintain high-employment levels or safeguard strategic industrial sectors.

The policy framework for inward FDI regimes is therefore very important to the economic progress that both developed and developing countries may wish to achieve. In general, most countries have been liberalising their FDI regimes in order to take advantage of the benefits that MNCs can bring with FDI. The Asian crisis recast the international business environment anew for FDI and the deregulation and liberalising trends that have characterised the 1990s. How MNCs cope with the new realities is beginning to exercise managers responsible for their international competitiveness.

7.5 QUESTIONS FOR DISCUSSION

1. What are the effects of outward and inward FDI for both source and host economies? What factors influence the relative benefits?

2. What influences the technology returns to the host country in FDI where technology transfers are critical to the success of the FDI?

3. Positive employment effects are often cited as the reward for hosting FDI. To what extent is this always so?

4. In what ways are the sovereignty of nation-states affected by the FDI policies of MNCs? How can governments check the effects of MNCs that are counter to domestic interests?

CHAPTER
8

Asia's Economic Crisis, International Business and Competitiveness

CHAPTER OUTLINE

- A perspective on the Asian economic crisis
- What are the dimensions of competitiveness in the Asian economic crisis?
- MNC operations in the Asian economic crisis
- Implications of the Asian economic crisis for international business

CHAPTER OBJECTIVES

After studying this chapter you should be able to:

- Demonstrate an appreciation of the significance of the Asian economic crisis.
- Identify aspects of competitiveness within the Asian economic crisis.
- Describe the significance of the Asian economic crisis for international business.
- Discuss the importance of the Asian economic crisis to international business and investment.

280

THIS CHAPTER ROUNDS off a competitiveness approach to international business by firstly reviewing the extraordinary predicament – now referred to universally as the Asian economic crisis (AEC) – that enveloped Asian economies between 1997 and 1999. Forces of the AEC are, at the time of writing, still moderating economic behaviour in parts of the region to different degrees. Secondly, the implications for competition are examined for clues to the future regional trajectories of MNCs and issues for international business. Thirdly, it looks at the impact of the crisis on Asian growth and development. The relevance of a long-term perspective in international business is one conclusion that emerges clearly. There are warning challenges facing MNCs and their investments in the region. *Inter alia*, there are the uncertainties of a fundamental mutation of regional geo-economics and a detectable stubbornness by an inward-looking Asia in embracing the economic obligations of globalisation.

The tremor then felt as nothing more than domestic business dynamics in Thailand with the collapse of Finance One (a financial intermediary) in early 1997 amplified and became as intense as the financial equivalent of an earthquake. It made red-raw the nervous sinews of the world financial capital system. Serious dangers persist even though at the time of writing signs of the beginning of a recovery are emerging.[1] In 1997 East Asia registered, as High Performance Asian Economies (HPAEs comprising Hong Kong, Singapore, South Korea, Taiwan) and newly-industrialised economies (NIEs comprising Indonesia, Malaysia, the Philippines, Thailand), an almost perpendicular decline in its economic fortunes. Within a year, the average change in gross domestic product (GDP) of between 8% to −1% for the better performers and 5% to −15% for the worst performers occurred.[2] Attendant economic and social as well as political losses, relatively low in Singapore, but devastatingly high in Indonesia, where some 34% of key industries were closed, carry possibilities of regional fragmentation and disengagement.[3] Two views persist; one is a dogged belief in regional revival, the

---

[1] Walter Fernandez, "Asian Crisis 'to Bottom Out Soon'", *The Straits Times*, 22 February 1999, p. 50; William Choong, "Capital Inflows May Slow Asia's Rebound", *The Straits Times*, 15 May 1999, p. 76; Michael Schuman, "Korea's Recovery Suggests Reform Isn't the Only Key", *The Asian Wall Street Journal*, 17 May 1999, p. 1; and "Asia's Astonishing Bounce-back", *The Economist*, 21 August 1999, pp. 9–10, 14–16.

[2] Reuters, "OECD Paints Grim Outlook for Asia", *The Straits Times*, 18 November 1998, p. 59.

[3] See *Newsweek*, "Global Meltdown Is the West's Fault", cited in *The Sunday Times*, 22 November 1998, p. 39.

other is a suspicion that the regional political will is emaciated.[4] Although there are signs that the former view may well be justified on the basis of very recent economic performance in Asia,[5] scepticism remains.[6]

Before the crisis East Asian economic performance has been evaluated as 'miraculous' certainly in terms of poverty reduction for vast numbers of people (World Bank, 1993). Generally, the AEC as a subject of serious academic analysis, and popular as well as business commentary may have been dealt with in an unbalanced manner. The region's growth was remarkable because there were very few doubters (Krugman, 1994). In addition, analysis of features of Asia's growth trajectory was articulated particularly through neo-classical arguments revolving around the management of free-market advantages (Fallows, 1993, 1994) and the competitive advantages of the Asian development model. The few critical expositions were severely chastised and dismissed as incapable of appreciating the 'miracle'. However, a closer observation of Asia's development indicates insufficient reference to theoretical foundations such as those provided by Reich (1991) for example, and systemic risks of internal policies in some Asian economies. Policies adopted during the years of 'miraculous' growth, on the back of a weak US dollar, were neither well developed nor well understood.[7] In early 1997, accelerated and unrestrained external forces of global capitalism policies failed at the level of domestic and regional operations. Eventually, the financial stresses and economic strains created demanded too much from individual countries and the two Bretton Woods institutions (the only organisations able to sanction Asian responses). The International Monetary Fund (IMF) and World Bank nevertheless received an undue share of blame for the debacle.

In late 1997, Hong Kong hosted the annual IMF and World Bank meetings where, instead of tributes to the 'miracle' economies, basic imperfections and severe managerial deficiencies implicit in the state of Asia's development model

---

[4] See Tommy Koh, "East Asian Miracle Is Not Over", *The Sunday Times*, 20 December 1998, p. 38 and Jusuf Wanandi, "Is ASEAN Dead?", *The Sunday Times*, 20 December 1998, p. 41 for the contrasting views.

[5] See "Asia on the Mend", *The Business Times*, 25 August 1999, p. 6 for growth indices.

[6] See Jean-Michel Paul, "Asia's Dangerous Reform Slowdown", *The Asian Wall Street Journal*, Educational Edition, 1999, p. 9.

[7] David Lamb, "An American Perspective of Singapore's Strength in the Face of the Regional Crisis", *The Sunday Times*, 22 February 1998, p. 6.

were exposed acrimoniously. Discussing the dynamics of the demise of regional economies, observers witnessed undiplomatic exchanges between Malaysian Prime Minister Dr Mahathir Mohamad and multibillionaire speculator George Soros. Given the circumstances, and the competition for control of world markets the confrontation was not unexpected (Stopford *et al.*, 1991).

'The Year of The Tiger' – 1998 – witnessed the development of the AEC into economic recession characterised by five differentiated but overlapping phases (currency, banking, economic, social and political).[8] The crisis is arguably the most significant crisis of the economic inter-dependency of finance capital and globalisation (Soros, 1998). The speed and reach of the regional and global shock waves surprised most observers.[9] In the years before the crisis the exceptional growth figures of Asian economies combined with inflows of foreign portfolio investment (FPI) and foreign direct investment (FDI) were precursor for the speculation that developed across much of Asia. Inflows of FDI to developing countries totalled US$256 billion in 1997; US$90 billion (70%) came to Southeast Asia.[10] The AEC reversed this flow in 1998[11] and resulted in output growth decreasing to −10.4% (for ASEAN) and −2.5% (for Japan) according to the IMF.[12]

---

[8] According to the OECD, South Korea, the world's tenth largest economy, will suffer a decline in real GDP of minus 4.7% in 1998; and ASEAN's worst afflicted economy, Indonesia, suffered a 14% drop in exports performance in the first quarter of 1998 (*The Asian Wall Street Journal*, 31 July–1 August 1998, pp. 4–5).

[9] Among those *not surprised* were the economist Paul Krugman (1994); Jim Walker, Chief Economist of Credit Lyonnais Securities who reported in January 1995 on the potential of Thailand to emulate Mexico in a currency crisis (*The Straits Times*, 23 March 1998, pp. 34–5) and UNCTAD (*Trade and Development Report 1996*, Geneva, pp. 104–23).

[10] See UNCTAD, *World Investment Report 1997: Transnational Corporations, Market Structure and Competition Policy*, UN, UNCTAD, New York, pp. 5–8; and Barry Wain, "Chile's Curbs on Hot Money May Hold Lessons for Asia", *The Asian Wall Street Journal*, 31 July–1 August 1998, p. 1 for an indication of the US$400 billion that flooded Asia (excluding Japan) between 1990 and 1996.

[11] See AFP, Reuters, BIS Annual Report, *The Business Times*, 9 July 1998, p. 6 for an institutional view of 'Asian woes' in which 'between 1996 and the second half of 1997, capital movements to Asia swung from an annual flow of almost US$100 billion ... to outflows of the same size'.

[12] Vikram Khanna, "New Risks Threaten Asia's Recovery", *The Business Times*, 29 October 1998, p. 5.

In the light of a long-term competitive view of international business and frenzied MNC globalisation[13] six issues are critical. Since the collapse of the Bretton Woods systems of fixed exchange rates on 5 August 1971, capital markets and their financial operations have become intertwined, deregulated and liberalised to an extraordinary extent. Consequently, not only has the frequency and amplitude of financial crises increased but also the scope has shifted from the government-public domain to private sectors. The AEC is a genuine crisis of the private sector (not forgetting the direct role played by Asian governments in their economies). The shallow economic depth of Asian emerging markets[14] means that neither the national nor collateral consequences were effectively contained. The crisis was global for much of 1997–98 and encapsulated all emerging markets and the Triad economies.[15] The crisis was exaggerated by a collapse in oil and commodity revenues.[16] The dislocation of social norms arising from the last 30 to 40 years of urban development in Asia fuelled the fundamental problems of the crisis.[17] *Laissez-faire* postures (Hong Kong) and 'developmental' states reveal that: asymmetric industrialised urbanisation; weak institutions (Drucker, 1998; Sayle, 1998); antagonism towards the entrepreneurial styles of international Chinese capital; and unwillingness to separate domestic economic interests and individual business strategies are explanatory factors. The absolute magnitude of losses were as follows: since mid-1997, at the height of the AEC, non-performing loans (NPLs) reached more than US$1 trillion; equity devaluations totalled over US$2 trillion; and regional GDP loss was over US$3 trillion; the collapse of FPI (from US$103

---

[13] See Augustine H.H. Tan, "IMF Is Not Adequately Geared to Help", *The Straits Times*, 23 January 1998, p. 58 for another (quadrilateral) view of what has caused the Asian crisis, namely the 1985 Plaza Accord-driven investment flows to Asia; the competitive effects of US dollar depreciation against the yen; the revitalization of the US economy throughout the 1990s; the 1994 devaluation of the yuan; and the over-investment in non-productive property assets.

[14] The cumulative capitalisations of five stock markets in Asia (Singapore, Kuala Lumpur, Manila, Bangkok and Jakarta) is only about 75% of the capitalisation of Microsoft.

[15] Jeff Rubin, "Worries About Recession Dominate American Corridors of Power", *The Asian Wall Street Journal*, 13 October 1998, p. 15.

[16] *Business Week*, Asian ed., 22 June 1998, p. 103.

[17] See Peter Drucker, "Rapid Change Has Led to Social Tensions, Asia Crisis", *The Straits Times*, 28 March 1998, p. 66 for a unique perspective of the critical situation in Asia.

billion in 1996 to less than US$15 billion in 1998)[18] and FDI.

Furthermore, export trade to the ASEAN 3 (comprising Indonesia, Malaysia and Thailand) to Japan declined an average of -23.5% in 1999.[19] These developments give rise to combustible strategic tensions in Asia. From the perspective of the political economy of competitiveness in international business Asia deserves attention. Japan's economy has been experiencing inexplicable problems. It has been in recession since 1991 and holds 40% of Asia's liabilities.[20] Alarming regional fragmentation ranges from the possibility of China cracking from currency speculation to Indonesia breaking up from internal stresses.

8.1 Asia's Crisis: A Retrospective and Its Competitiveness Implications

The currency, banking, economic, socio-economic, political and even psychological dimensions of the AEC make it difficult to delineate relevant causal technical and social pathways. However, technical explanations concern inter-relationships of excess global liquidity and increasing globalisation pressures in relation to liberalisation and deregulation within financially immature and thin capital markets as well as asymmetric accumulation and distribution of FPI and FDI. This led to unmanageable economic output with signature rapid import growth.[21] The social causes involve Asian values[22] and choices for investment based on cronyism.[23]

The regional contagion was touched off by the crisis of confidence in the Thai Government's ability to maintain a US dollar pegged currency with deteriorating

---

[18] Darren McDermott, "Asia's Chances of Attracting Capital Fade", *The Asian Wall Street Journal*, 14 October 1998, p. 1 and "Costly Mistakes", *The Asian Wall Street Journal*, 22 October 1998, p. 1.

[19] Correction, *The Business Times*, 29 October 1998, p. 1.

[20] See John Plender, "Japan: Stop-Go-Stop", *Financial Times*, cited in *The Business Times*, 9 June 1998, p. 11; and *The Business Times*, "US Officials, Experts Put Japanese Bad Debt at US$1t", 31 July 1998, p. 4 for the trillion dollar black hole that might have hastened Asia's downward descent.

[21] *The Economist*, "The Asian Miracle: Is It Over?", 1 March 1997, pp. 23–5.

[22] Catherine Ong, "A Pattern in Asia's Crisis", *The Business Times*, 29 October 1998, p. 14 for an informed view on the Asian values debate.

[23] Special Report, "The Family Firm Suharto Inc", *Time* Asia Edition, 24 May 1999, Vol. 153, No. 20.

balance-of-payments and macroeconomic fundamentals (Table 8.1). The over reliance by firms in particular on debt and the region generally on capital inflows resulted, for example, in an average 13% and 17% of capital formation for Thailand and Malaysia respectively (Zhang, 1998). The risk associated with Asian emerging markets in the light of inadequate banking supervisory protocols, poor corporate governance and government-corporate collusion contributed directly to the loss of confidence by foreign investors.

Table 8.1 Macroeconomic platform of selected countries (average 1994–97)

Country	Growth (GDP %)	Current account balance (US$ billion)	Inflation (CPI %)
Indonesia	7.0	−6.4	8.7
Malaysia	8.6	−6.0	3.5
Philippines	4.9	−3.1	8.0
Singapore	8.4	13.7	2.1
S. Korea	7.4	−12.4*	5.1*
Thailand	6.5	−11.7	6.0

* Average 1994–96.
Sources: Political and Economic Risk Consultancy Ltd (PERC), Country Risk Reports, Internet version, http://www.asiarisk.com.

Regional indebtedness and the quality of bank intermediation are shown in Table 8.2 and Table 8.3. The history of input factor growth (Krugman, 1994) enabled regional short-term external debts to grow without due diligence.

Table 8.2 Foreign debt (US$ billion) and foreign debt servicing (% of GDP)

Country	Foreign debt 1996	Foreign debt 1997	Foreign debt servicing 1996	Foreign debt servicing 1997
Indonesia	49.8	188.7	5.9	19.1
Malaysia	38.8	68.9	5.4	8.1
Philippines	50.1	79.7	7.4	10.6
Singapore	None	None	None	None
S. Korea	160.7	150.0	N.A.	N.A.
Thailand	49.0	97.1	4.7	9.0

Note: 1997 debt burden computed with 16 January 1998 exchange rates.
Sources: Adapted from *The Straits Times*, 22 January 1998, p. 46 and Political and Economic Risk Consultancy Ltd (PERC), Country Risk Reports, Internet version, http://www.asiarisk.com.

Table 8.3 Non-performing loans (NPLs) and resolution costs, 1998

Country	NPLs (% total loans)	Resolutions costs (% GDP)
Indonesia	75	50
Malaysia	35	45
S. Korea	50	60
Thailand	55	45

Source: *The Strait Times*, 22 October 1998, p. 1.

The liquidity available to Asia, and in contrast the extent of the 1998–99 credit crunch, is indicated by Triad banking assets at the end of 1997. European banks held US$320 billion, Japanese banks held on-balance sheet assets of US$260 billion and US banks held US$46 billion.[24] Actual figures and therefore concomitant non-performing loans are likely to be much higher (given hindsight knowledge of the 1994 Mexican crisis).[25] Between 1994 to 1996 the expansion of banking assets averaged 22.4% in Indonesia, 23.9% in Malaysia, 30.2% in the Philippines, 22% in Thailand, and 15.8% even in normally prudent Singapore.[26] Table 8.3 indicates conservatively Asia's banking problems.

It is important to note that, from the perspective of competitiveness, bank assets were collateralised by relatively unproductive investments: real estate rather than factories; stock market speculations as opposed to long-term equity positions; over-capacity in services investments; and other ambitious ventures rather than competitive investment.[27] While the main indicators of overheating and subsequent distress are several,[28] the following capture the condition well:

- The taken-for-granted double-digit growth by almost all investors, both domestic and foreign.

---

[24] Speech by Singapore Senior Minister Lee Kwan Yew, reported in *The Straits Times*, 21 February 1998, p. 48.

[25] Reuters, "Asian Banks Still a Long Way from NPL Peak", *The Business Times*, 12 November 1998, p. 8.

[26] *The Strait Times*, "Currency Crises: How and When Will East Asia Recover", 22 January 1998.

[27] The world's two tallest skyscrapers, more fitting to Manhattan, are in Kuala Lumpur!

[28] Harry Harding, "Wanted: Asian–US Cooperation", *The Straits Times*, 22 October 1998, p. 32.

- The unquestioned commitment of the local currencies–US dollar peg (under high-interest rates, unfavourable current account imbalances and an appreciating US dollar).

- The capital account and financial deregulation to which regional governments had acceded without satisfactory financial regulations and banking supervision, thus allowing companies to over-substitute equity with debt and create high returns-on-equity balance sheets that fed the over-confidence and obscured unstable underlying capital structures. For example, South Korea's leading 30 Chaebols had average debt-to-equity ratios of approximately 400% in 1996.[29] Similarly, Japanese firms show a debt-to-equity ratio of 4 to 1 and carry unserviceable burdens.

- The ballooning variety of investors with excess global liquidity that enabled Asian companies and banks to borrow US dollars short term in response to low US interest rates for long-term investments.

- The misunderstanding of the dynamics of derivative financial instruments (in retrospect an indication of institutional immaturity).[30]

- The hidden but explosive increase in derivatives by retail and investment banks to increase returns.[31]

- The conclusion by financial analysts that ultimately the 'miracle' was inherently unstable and untenable while governments failed to note that the market discipline (or herd instinct) that compelled the vast investment inflows to the region could cause massive outflows in search of lower risk.

The evidence suggests that inadequate policies for bank asset management were highly significant. A typical example is provided by Peregrine Investment Holdings, a company that risked over two and half times its asset base to a then well-connected taxi company in Indonesia with scant regard for due diligence and was promptly bankrupted.

---

[29] Report by the Institute of International Finance, *Capital Flows to Emerging Market Economies*, 29 January 1998, p. 12A.

[30] See *The Financial Times* (12 January 1998) for an exposé that is absolutely staggering. The paper quotes, "With the blessing of his superiors, the central bank's young and inexperienced chief currency trader, Paiboon Kittisrikangwan, had locked up most of Thailand's foreign exchange reserves in forward contracts. Thailand's reported foreign reserves of over $30 billion were a myth – in fact they had dwindled to $1.4 billion, equal to just two days of imports." *Financial Times*, 12 January 1998, Internet version, http://www.ft.com accessed 23 January 1998.

[31] See Bernard Baumohl, "The Banks' Nuclear Secrets", *Time*, 25 May 1998, pp. 36–8 for a measure of the serious markets and credit risk in the derivative contracts held by US banks.

Competitively, the collapse of a currency crisis into a combined crisis of financial, economic, socio-economic and psychological scope indicates that the 'money' and 'real' economies are not separate (Drucker, 1989). Currency and asset devaluations erode collateral and promote greater margin calls and at the same time stampede investors into the 'flight to quality'. This in turn forces a sometimes over-zealous retrospection of asset qualities that discloses a depressingly realistic evaluation of the economy. In Asia's case, this scrutiny exposed a lack of competitiveness in the deficient qualities of industrial inter-linkages and national banking.[32]

8.2 Intra-regional and Inter-regional Dimensions of the Crisis

At the nadir of the AEC, regional currencies declined relative to the US dollar by between 15% and 60%. Regional stock market indices declined by about 60% relative to world markets. The depreciation of regional currencies continued relentlessly from mid-1997 until mid-1999. Table 8.4 reveals GDP growth in selected Asian countries (in descending order of performance).

Table 8.4 Selected Asian countries' 1998 GDP growth forecasts (percentage)

Country	October
Indonesia	−17.4
Malaysia	−6.8
South Korea	−6.6
Thailand	−6.0
Hong Kong	−5.2
Japan	−1.8
Philippines	−1.2
Singapore	1.6
China	7.6

Source: *Asiaweek*, 30 October 1998, p. 86.

In 1998 the region including Japan (accounting for 40% of regional GDP) experienced an unprecedented contraction of GDP created by a combination of NPLs, collapsing collateral values and a vicious credit crunch, and a sharp fall in

---

[32] Goldman Sachs, Banking Research, "Asian Banks at Risk", 4 September 1997.

private capital inflows.[33] The loss of purchasing power shrunk imports and led to a rebalancing of the regional capital accounts, at the expense of import-intensive manufacturing output. As a host region for Japanese FDI and MNCs Integrated International Sourcing, Production and Marketing (IISPM) Japanese FDI ranges from just below 7% of total in Indonesia to just below 37% of total in the Philippines (Ozawa, 1992). High levels of intra-regional exchange imply structural intermediation arrangements and directions of trade that will be difficult to adjust in the short term.[34] This high intensity of intra-regional FDI and trade had produced the virtuous circle of growth. Ironically, during the AEC, it became the achilles heel of Asia's recovery, with Japanese FDI that shifted into reverse.[35] For a significant time, Asia simply could not export, import or intermediate effectively despite currency devaluations that normally encourage export performance and US MNCs' profitability in 1998 was the worst since the start of the 1990s.[36]

CASE **8.1**

Losing its fur: Jindo's woes reflect Korea Inc's mess

	Sales in won		Net profits in won	
	First half 1997	First half 1998	First half 1997	First half 1998
Jindo Corp.	354.2 billion	345.8 billion	3.20 billion	−37.7 billion
Jindo Enterprises	50.0 billion	22.2 billion	0.47 billion	−19.0 billion
Top 30 Chaebols	144.0 trillion	177.0 trillion	1,113.00 billion	−968.0 billion

Jindo got started in the early 1960s with the founder using his connections as a mechanic with the US Army to import fur rabbit scraps making them into materials for warm clothing and exporting them to his son, at the time studying in the US. Mr Kim, the son

---

[33] Eduardo Lahica, "Major Lenders Shun 5 Asian Economies", *The Asian Wall Street Journal*, 30 September 1998, p. 30; and AFP, "Capital Flows to Emerging Markets Drying Up", *The Asian Wall Street Journal*, 30 September 1998, p. 2.

[34] See Chua Mui Hoong, "Why Japan Matters So Much to Asia", *The Straits Times*, 27 October 1998, p. 30 for an indication of Japan's capacity to absorb Asian exports and its FDI in Asia.

[35] Bloomberg News, "Direct Investment in Asia Shrinks 7%", *The Straits Times*, 30 April 1999, p. 85.

[36] AFP, "US Companies Put Out Worst Results in 7 Years", *The Straits Times*, 27 October 1998, p. 38.

and eventual CEO, then contacted furriers all over the US asking them to send him fur scraps which he transported back to Korea to be made into hats for re-export. The business took off and for years Jindo thrived on cheap loans the Korean Government directed to companies to boost the trade balance.

"We all thought we had succeeded because we were brilliant managers, but the truth is anyone who planted a seed back then could have a good harvest," he says, referring to the government's drive to industrialise the country. Then Mr Kim started to worry. "We feared our core (fur) business may someday reach a limit." So in 1978 the firm decided to start making shipping containers. The leap into such a vastly different business was not as illogical as it seemed. Containers would enjoy the same export incentives as fur exports and Korea's export drive would fuel the demand for containers for years to come. Indeed, the gamble paid off. Containers now account for most of Jindo's revenue and the firm is the world's second largest producer of container, controlling 15% of the global market. Jindo was not so lucky with other diversifications. In 1986, the fur-and-container company set up a construction subsidiary that has never made money. Mr Kim says that they did this to get a license for waste management.

Waste management? Jindo decided to get into waste management because it calculated that neither fur nor containers offered the technological edge the firm wanted. Operations started in 1992 and Jindo's management says that waste management operations will break even once facilities are completed in 1999. Meanwhile the fur operations went international with several globally recognised outlets and signed up with Yves St Laurent to give designs and image a boost.

In 1996 Jindo started up a wireless-phone service, Hansol PCS Co., with an investment of 12 billion won. Mr Kim says he 'didn't know the first thing' about what the investment entailed (telecommunications) and soon found it wasn't the 'duck that lay golden eggs'. The investment flopped and in 1997 the good times came to an end. The chaebol's headlong rush to diversify was partly led by peer pressure – it was hard to stand by as rivals expanded furiously – and banks were unwilling to lend unless firms were diversifying. By the 1990s no product range was wide enough for the chaebols to contemplate – from soap to semiconductors, and from ships to candy bars.

In 1997, massive debts toppled six of Korea's top 30 chaebols. In line with the IMF bailout of Korea, the government asked chaebols to reform. Little has been achieved so far. Contrarily, Jindo Group increased its debt to 810 billion won in a vain attempt to save the company, with intra-company lendings. In 1997 the fur business dropped by 30%. The weaker won makes exports more attractive but makes imports more costly plus tougher trade financing negates the benefits of a weak won. What can Jindo do? "I'm doing my best," says Mr Kim, "but there are so many uncertainties involved in getting out of our current difficulties."

Source: *The Asian Wall Street Journal,* **26 October 1998**

Case Discussion Issues and Questions

1. Outline and discuss the environmental challenges of Jindo Group (JG).

2. Outline and delineate the critical managerial issues that diversified conglomerates have to concentrate on.

3. Imagine yourself in Mr Kim's shoes, and lay out the options that he can and should present to his board of directors and senior management to turn around the firm.

4. Given the problems identified, prescribe a strategic route out of JG's difficulties.

5. What do you imagine JG's competitors will do in reaction? Outline the scenario.

8.3 IMPLICATIONS FOR COMPETITIVENESS AND INTERNATIONAL BUSINESS

There is, in general, an emerging consensus on the causes and contagious effects of the AEC.[37] Both Western and Asian perspectives are qualified by competitive exigencies. Similarly, implications for international business competitiveness and MNCs can be contradictory, depending on who you are, the structure of production and for which markets. The variety of corporate responses indicates that the potential for competitive behaviour is high in the post-crisis Asian business environment.

CASE 8.2

GE Capital takes aggressive steps in Asia: US firm targets Japan's financing assets amid deregulation, recession

While foreign inroads into Japan's banking and securities industry grabbed attention in 1998, GE Capital (GEC), the finance subsidiary of General Electric Co., aggressively entered lesser-known areas of Japan's financial services. It is just these businesses – consumer finance, autolending, life insurance and leasing – that may turn out to be some of the fastest growing areas of Japan's financial-services industry over the next decade. These are also the type of businesses that could gain the most from the experience and expertise GEC has accrued while turning itself into the world's largest non-bank, non-governmental lender.

---

[37] See Jeffrey D. Sachs, "The Wrong Medicine for Asia", 3 November 1997, *New York Times*, Internet version accessed 30 March 1998; Linda Lim, "'Asian Values' Idea: Is It Out?", *The Sunday Times*, 29 March 1998, pp. 36–7; and *The Sunday Times*, "US Expert Slams 'Snake-oil' Cures", 29 March 1998, p. 4 for viewpoints.

For MNCs, economically and socially corrosive multiplier-accelerator effects of the crisis are likely to permeate the region present competitive challenges and opportunities in Asia's 'great leap backwards'[39] into a more uncertain world of increased venality.[40] As a consequence, MNCs will have to alter regionally their foreign market servicing strategies. A reliance on domestic factors seems less appropriate while a proactive search for profitable location-specific market re-segmentation that avoids the hazards of incumbency seems more suitable. An emerging perspective of *Asian post-crisis* is one of MNCs needing to '*relearn* the art of doing business' (Lim Chon-Phung, General Manager with Hewlett-Packard).[41] However, the long-term FDI view on the region's potential (UNCTAD-ICC, 1998) remains unchanged. Nevertheless, in the immediate future, Japanese FDI is likely to continue falling due to Japan's domestic economy woes.[42]

Denials by MNCs of competitive disinvestments are signs that the very process is taking place.[43] Export-oriented MNCs are investing selectively. In a wider context, US MNCs are the leading acquirers with 1998 mergers and acquisitions (M&As) activity amounting to US$8.8 billion, while competing European MNCs (mostly British and German) are second with US$3 billion M&As.[44] The pattern of M&As is, however, asymmetric. Japan, South Korea, Hong Kong and Thailand are targets. Malaysia, Indonesia, China, the Philippines, India and Australia are less favoured. Also the speed of M&As has slowed and is

---

[39] Jeremy Wagstaff, "Indonesia's Poverty: How Bad Is It?", *Asian Economic Survey 1989–99*, *The Asian Wall Street Journal*, 26 October 1998, p. S13.

[40] Diane Brady, "Tackling Corruption", *Asian Economic Survey 1989–99*, *The Asian Wall Street Journal*, 26 October 1998, p. S12.

[41] Lim Chon-Phung, "MNCs Need to Learn the Art of Doing Business in Asia", *The Business Times*, 22 February 1999, p. 9.

[42] See Reuters, "Soros Says He Won't Invest in Malaysia", *The Business Times*, 24 May 1999, p. 1; the values of the capital markets in crisis-ridden Asia are paltry compared to the capitalisations of individual MNCs on the capital markets of the world's main financial centres (see Nick Freeman, "Impediments to Foreign Investment: The Complexities of a Changing International Business Environment", paper presented to the ABAC-PECC Workshop on Impediments to Trade & Investment, 20–21 May 1999, Tokyo); consequently the effort/incentive dynamics for investment portfolios favour activity in Triad capital markets, and not in emerging markets.

[43] Jennifer Lien, "Seagate Denies Plans to Pull Out", *The Business Times*, 31 July 1998, p. 3.

[44] Neil Behrmann, "Foreign Acquisitions in 6 Key Asian Nations Soar", *The Business Times*, 27 July 1998, p. 1.

testament to the infectious lack of confidence that tends to confirm re-strategising by MNCs. In a 1999 survey, 1,260 out of 1,500 (84%) German MNCs (traditionally cautious in internationalising with a few exceptions) in ten Asian countries indicated that despite evident obstacles to FDI they would increase their Asian presence.[45] While some infrastructure MNCs and those with domestic market servicing developments are divesting others are taking advantage of low asset prices.[46]

The Asian crisis shows that a competitive examination of economic development (Fallows, 1993, 1994) exposes a contention for dominance between West–East hegemons in which firms and MNCs cannot be neutral. Leading conglomerates from Malaysia spearheaded the competition to realise the country's industrialisation. Singapore's regionalisation policy has been activated by, and through, international firms.[47] The world's leading MNCs are American and European and Asia's still fragile recovery[48] will be assisted by these same MNCs soliciting Western governments to create competitive advantages for them by assisting stricken economies directly.

CASE 8.3

Salim Group (SG) – Resilience in adversity

Around 26 May 1998, Anthony Salim – Indonesia's leading Chinese tycoon and CEO of Salim Group (SG) – saw Jakarta going down in flames. Later his own house was burned by angry mobs. Rioters spray-painted the words 'Suharto's dog' (in reference to the worst excesses of crony capitalism) on the gate. Mr Salim caught the next flight to Singapore.

---

[45] Walter Fernandez, "Asian Crisis 'to Bottom Out Soon'", *The Straits Times*, 22 February 1999, p. 50; and Andrew Tan, "Jan Trade Jolt Revives Fears of MNCs Moving Out", *The Business Times*, 22 February 1999, p. 1.

[46] General Electric, the US MNC, is planning to spend US$40 billion in Asia over the next four years (see "GE to Pump $64 Billion Into Asia", *The Straits Times*, 30 March 1998, p. 52).

[47] "S'pore Government Leads Investment Drive", *The Straits Times*, 14 January 1997, p. 24; Quak Hiang Whai, "S'pore Invests in HK Through International Consortiums", *The Straits Times*, 14 January 1997, p. 24; "GIC Takes 40% Stake in Prime Manila Property Deal", *The Straits Times*, 7 February 1997, p. 30; and "Viet-S'pore Industrial Park Attracts S$226 Million in Investments", *The Straits Times*, 1 April 1997, p. 61.

[48] Christopher Wood, "Asia's Still Fragile Recovery", *The Asian Wall Street Journal*, 6 January 1999, p. 8.

Today Mr Salim, 49, is back in Jakarta. While no longer fearful for his life after the political changes in Indonesia that has seen the ousting of Suharto and democratic elections in 1999, he is fighting to save his company. The family business – an empire built by father Liem Sioe Liong and son Anthony – dates back to the 1930s but is now devastated by Indonesia's economic collapse and is straining under US$5 billion in debt. Indonesia is still a dangerous place yet SG has proved remarkably resilient. Its stubborn survival shows how deeply crony capitalism has taken root in Indonesia. Nevertheless, Mr Salim was forced to cede control of his flagship asset Bank Central Asia (BCA) to the government. He also handed over stakes in dozens of companies ranging from flour mills and cement factories to palm oil plantations and office towers. He is selling other assets to raise cash. The goal is to raise enough money to pay off the US$5 billion he owes the government for the bailout of BCA. If there is some left over he wants to buy a stake in BCA, which despite its huge debts is still Indonesia's largest bank with 700 branches scattered over the vast archipelago. "The most important thing is to weather this period – not to be wiped out by the big wave coming in," says Mr Salim.

With US$200 billion in sales, 500 companies and 200,000 workers SG is so embedded in the commercial tissue of Indonesia's economy (and the region) that analysts say that its breakup would cause severe disruption in major industries like food processing, construction and banking. In other words, SG like America's Chrysler Corporation is too big to fail. "Whoever rules Indonesia will have to do business with the Salims," says the president director of a credit rating agency in Jakarta, "they own assets in virtually every part of the economy."

SG's fortunes rose along with ex-president Suharto's. When Suharto forced Sukarno out of office in 1966, Mr Liem – founder of SG – was ready to help the new leader develop Indonesia's economy. SG won a monopoly licence to import cloves, the key ingredient in Indonesia's distinctive sweet-smelling cigarettes. It was the first of dozens of licences, franchises and concessions that would make Mr Liem a baron in coffee, rubber, sugar, wheat, flour, noodles, rice and cement. When Suharto wanted Indonesia to expand into new industries, SG obliged by opening factories or planting fields. When Mr Liem needed favours – a waiver of securities law of restrictions on satellite transmissions – Suharto happily complied. Mr Liem's ties with Suharto went beyond mutual back-scratching. Two of Suharto's daughters owned stakes in BCA. By the early 1990s SG, built up through a web of intricate partnerships, was a leviathan, accounting for 5% of Indonesia's economic output.

According to Anthony Salim, with the rapid development of Indonesia's economy SG had moved from a government-dictated strategy to a market-based approach. Now it has to move again to a standard of greater financial disclosure and adherence to international legal standards. It was the lack of regulations and transparency that put SG in jeopardy. During the 1980s and early 1990s, most Indonesian conglomerates financed their capital needs with loans from their own banks. Although Indonesia's central bank limited such inter-company loans to 20% of the bank's portfolio, few tycoons paid much attention to the rules. SG was no exception: BCA made as much as 50% of its loans to SG subsidiaries. Many of the loans were denominated in US dollars, which meant that when the rupiah crashed in late 1997, BCA was suddenly saddled with US$2 billion in debt which has since grown to US$5 billion. As BCA became a target of the civil unrest, and besieged by depositors, the bank lost 42% of its capital forcing a bailout by the government to the tune of US$3 billion.

Source: *The Business Times*, **26 May 1999**

Case Discussion Issues and Questions

1. Discuss the firm-specific advantages (FSAs) of SG.

2. Analyse the potential of SG's FSAs for its regional and international competitive position. What can SG offer foreign investors?

3. Suggest a rationale for enhancing SG's conglomerate competitiveness post-Asian crisis.

4. Delineate the competitive threats facing Asian MNCs like SG. To what extent are these specific or general?

5. Discuss the extent to which advantages and disadvantages accrue to corporate competitiveness when the political and business environments interact in the way indicated by the case.

8.4 INTERNATIONAL BUSINESS COMPETITIVENESS: LOOKING AHEAD

The Asian crisis has demonstrated firstly, the reach of markets and globalisation as far as the Triad, their MNCs and 'clusters' are concerned. Secondly, it has illustrated how portfolio investment and FDI can be related in the context of financial markets and deregulation and liberalisation. The potential industrial instability and increasing external indebtedness are high.[49] In the short to medium term we can expect a restructuring of the financial and industrial landscapes of Asia (UNCTAD, 1998).

How will MNCs, and international small- and medium-sized enterprises manage in this new environment? How will they map and navigate the unfamiliar territory of bankrupts, absent clients, new owners via M&As and new or disrupted supply chain relationships? How will international businesses cope with the corporate 'tooth-and-claw' competition that the struggle to survive will unleash?

---

[49] See Bloomberg News, "Worse to Come for US Firms in Asia", *The Straits Times*, 13 June 1998, p. 80 for a striking example of this instability – Boeing Co., a firm that in 1997 could not find enough production engineers and technicians, in 1998 plans to eliminate 20,000 jobs due to falling demand.

At the beginning of the 1990s, advances in globalisation demonstrated a world political economy characterised increasingly by centripetal forces with a contemporaneous fusion of markets and fission in nation-states.[50] Asia's recent troubles may reverse the former and accelerate the latter. Whatever the outcome, the defining characteristics of Southeast Asia – a vast diversity and 'jigsaws' of the socio-ethnographic archipelago dominated by Indonesia and the Philippines (2,000 islands and 1,000 dialects) – have been features downplayed for convenience during the 'miracle' years. The potential for regional geo-economic disintegration may result in a multiplication of the 'sovereign' boundaries across which MNCs do business, and consequently increasing competitive threats and opportunities. Indonesia is a case in point. Concomitantly, the degree of difficulty in doing business could increase to an extent not readily or presently quantifiable. Thus, the Asian crisis has given the discipline of international business a new reality for re-examining the key concepts of competitiveness in international business and corroborating empirical research.

From the competitiveness approach to international business, and in the light of Asia's full recovery being some way off,[51] the major question revolves round the key attractions of Asia that confer competitive advantage to those MNCs that remain. There is a strong, but selective, attractiveness of particular locations in the region (Mirza *et al.*, 1998; Bartels *et al.*, 1997). UNCTAD–ICC (1998) reported that this sentiment, as far as MNCs are concerned and despite the crisis, is unchanged in the long term. However, great pressures on corporate governance, the management of credit risk and domestic factors that are increasing are demanding that MNCs differentiate between location-specific advantages much more effectively in terms of their own firms' specific advantages. There is conflicting evidence on the sentiment towards Asia within the international investing community. Some investors are beginning to differentiate carefully within the region. At the same time, despite notable exceptions, 'funds aren't expected to return to Asia'.[52]

---

[50] Gary S. Becker, "As Nations Splinter, Global Markets Are Merging", *Business Week*, 22 April 1991, p. 8.

[51] See "The Global Economy: Deja Vu?", *Business Week*, 21 December 1998, pp. 34–6 for an indication of impediments to crisis solution and the fact that according to the World Bank 36 countries are in recession.

[52] Douglas Appell, "Funds Aren't Expected to Return to Asia", *The Asian Wall Street Journal*, 30 July 1998, p. 8.

Asia is far from homogenous even in the responses of the states to the crisis contagion.[53] South Korea and Thailand took progressive initiatives.[54] Indonesia on the other hand, exhibited at first contrariness and xenophobia despite the fall of Suharto. Although a more conciliatory mood is emergent in Jakarta, the economy is still living dangerously.[55] Malaysia reacted against capitalism to permit itself some exercise in self-reliance (and with some success). While MNC concerns focus on the threats of appropriation and nationalisation, governments' concerns are about being integrated more fairly into the global economy.

Competitively, MNCs face many contradictions in Asia's path to recovery. Compounding the usual business uncertainties, there are those of ideology, politics and political economy. Establishing new rules for the business of FDI (further liberalisation) is fraught with problems of coherence of statutes and consistency in interpretation.[56] During 1997–2000 when Asian domestic markets contracted, pulling back from the crisis requires radical solutions. These might entail the substitution of an 'export-led growth strategy with an import-accommodating one' (Buchman and Wolf, 1998: 8). Such a change in orientation presents a serious competitive challenge for MNCs that may have concluded prospects are poor for regional domestic markets.

The location of production into Asia during the past 20 years has been rationalised through the relative productivity competitiveness of low-cost labour. Volatile regional currency depreciations, however, have created more complexity in the future assessment of location relative productivities. By definition FDI is location bound (Rugman and Verbeke, 1992) and relocation decisions are correlated with longer term changes in relative factor efficiencies rather than volatility in exchange rates. The fact that the amplitude of regional currency volatilities show little moderation makes locational decisions difficult in addition to problems posed by incumbency.

---

[53] *Business Week*, "Age of the Deal", 2 March 1998, pp. 16–20.

[54] G. Bruce Knecht, "Recovery Looks Hard to Sustain for Thailand", *The Asian Wall Street Journal*, 26 October 1998, p. 1; and James Clad and David Steinberg, "Little Chance of Quick Recovery for Asia", *The Straits Times*, 28 November 1998, p. 78.

[55] Jay Solomon, "Habibie's Plans for Asset Sales Worries IMF", *The Asian Wall Street Journal*, 27 October 1998, p. 1.

[56] Shoeb Kagda, "New Indon Rules for Investment", *The Business Times*, 28 October 1998, p. 7.

Three years into Asia's economic ordeal, industrial output and GDP remain largely negative with respect to pre-crisis trend lines. International portfolio investors continue to unload stock of localised firms amid fears for competitive devaluations starting with China.[57] Japan, the region's most significant investor, lender and trading partner with the potential to improve substantially regional performance, is economically becalmed. Perceptions of attractiveness of the region (Jackson and Markowski, 1995) or unattractiveness (Bartels and Freeman, 1995) may have far more importance in reinforcing Asian economic performance. For almost three years regional developments have exposed shortcomings in the governance of Asia's capitalism stemming from an unstable economic morphology (Sayle, 1998).

Among the challenges that MNCs face in the region is public charges of manipulation (from getting asset bargains at the expense of local businesses) in the general invitation to investors to re-capitalise local enterprises. This should be contrasted with empirical findings (Mirza *et al.*, 1998) that MNCs from the Triad are looking to ASEAN as 'a single market'. The implications for Asia are enormous.[58]

As the centrepiece for regional stability, ASEAN may have to accomplish a number of things simultaneously. Firstly, contain the pressures for geo-political fragmentation. Secondly, manage the negative civil effects of structural adjustment. Thirdly, change the qualitative character of intra-ASEAN dialogue.[59] Fourthly, enhance its attractiveness as a free trade area and an investment area. Accomplishing all this under intense global scrutiny is a tall order.[60]

In the light of the crisis, what are the possibilities for competitiveness in international business in the Asian crisis endgame? Prediction can be hazardous. Those who announced that the twenty-first century will be Asian may well be correct. At present, however, the studied pronouncements – 'miracle' economies, 'Asia rising', 'Pacific Shift' – seem somewhat misplaced in the face of some

---

[57] *The Economist*, "China Could Prove a Bigger Shocker", cited in *The Straits Times*, 13 June 1998, p. 65.

[58] Lee Siew Hua, "ASEAN Is No Longer as United, the US Believes", *The Straits Times*, 7 December 1998, p. 19.

[59] Jon Linden, "ASEAN to Change Within Year", *The Asian Wall Street Journal*, 18 August 1998, p. 11.

[60] AFP, "Apec Should Ease Trade and Investment Curbs", *The Straits Times*, 24 May 1999, p. 45.

evidence that the health of the world economy depends on America and Europe.[61] According to economic orthodoxy, open systems tend towards dynamic equilibrium and create greater levels of competitiveness. However, the crisis may continue to test such conventional wisdom, and Asia is no more immune to the rational or irrational behaviour of market operations than other locations.

8.5 CHAPTER REVIEW

Given East Asia's phenomenal economic trajectory, the details of the Asian economic crisis of mid-1997 present one of the twentieth century's major economic events, along with the Crash of 1929. However, the nature of globalisation at the end of the century, vastly different in terms of intermediation to that at the beginning of the century, has meant a short rather than a long recession. The crisis has changed, to an appreciable extent, the nature of competition and competitiveness for global as well as regional MNCs.

Patterns in the development of the Asian economic crisis demonstrate the various roles played by the key actors in international business through their intermediation of borrowing and lending, investment in productive assets and speculation in a financial instruments. They show also the derivative and multiplier effects of a financial crisis evolving into economic, socio-economic and even political crises. As MNCs are engaged intimately in the business of business, the manner in which these agents cope with and exploit emergent competitive advantages is of critical importance. Furthermore, the evolving patterns of the crisis indicate clearly not only the importance of the environment to international business and competitiveness but also the significance of emerging markets and newly-industrialised countries in developing competencies to deal successfully with globalisation.

The diffusion of the effects of the crisis through other emerging markets on all continents testifies to the interconnectedness of global business. The integrated international sourcing production and marketing networks of MNCs around the world, imply that competitive (or uncompetitive) outcomes in one part of the global economy are necessarily transmitted throughout the chain of operations of not only the MNC in question but also other MNCs. The Asian crisis shows this dynamic in ample measure.

---

[61] Cover story, "The Atlantic Century?", *Business Week*, 8 February 1999, pp. 18–27; and cover story, "Asia: How Real Is Its Recovery", *Business Week*, 3 May 1999, pp. 24–7.

One major implication of the crisis is more rapid change within the resource deployment decisions of MNCs with substantial operations in Asia. Empirical research (Bartels *et al.*, 1997) supports this conclusion. A second implication is the relearning of ways of doing business in Asia by MNCs. Traditional ways, involving high-context reciprocal obligations and *guanxi*, are being replaced, at differing pace in different countries of the region, by an increasingly robust adherence to international standards of disclosure and transparency.

The Asian crisis has also led to changing dynamics in lending, with increasing attention to portfolio and collateral quality and consequential contraction in overall lending. Local and regional firms, in the process of further internationalising, are therefore required to increase their business competitiveness in adjustment to the demands of international banks and financial markets.

What are the possibilities for competitiveness in international business in general and with respect to the Asian crisis endgame in particular? There is no crystal ball for predicting outcomes in international business and its competitiveness and any attempt at prediction is risky. In the final analysis, according to economic orthodoxy, open systems tend towards dynamic equilibrium and create greater levels of competitiveness. Nevertheless, financial and socio-economic crises may continue to test such wisdom.

8.6 Questions for Discussion

1. Identify and delineate the key dimensions and issues of the Asian economic crisis.

2. Discuss the role of MNCs and governments in the Asian economic crisis.

3. Given the respective roles of MNCs and governments in the Asian economic crisis, propose viable responses for MNCs in coping with the crisis.

4. Delineate and discuss the major effects of the Asian economic crisis on the competitiveness of regional economies and the competitiveness of MNCs operating within the region.

BIBLIOGRAPHY

Adams R. and Nissen J., 1972, *The Uruk Countryside: The Natural Setting of Urban Societies*, Chicago: Chicago University Press.

Akyuz Y., 1998, "The East Asian Financial Crisis: Back to the Future?" Seminar on *Impacts of the Asian Currency Crisis on Europe's Growth Prospects*, Brussels: European Institute for Asian Studies, 20 January. Internet version: www.unctad.org/e/pressref (accessed 30 March 1998).

Barnet R.J. and Muller R.E., 1974, *Global Reach: The Power of the Multinational Corporation*, New York: Simon & Schuster, pp. 13, 15–16, as cited in Howard M. Wachtel, 1990, *The Money Mandarins: The Making of a Supra-national Economic Order*, Armonk, New York: M.E. Sharpe, p. 6.

Barrell R. and Pain N., 1998, *Developments in East Asia and Their Implications for the UK and Europe*, London: National Institute for Economic and Social Research.

Bartels F.L. and Freeman N.J., 1995, "European Multinational Enterprises in Two Francophone Emerging Markets: Evidence from International Joint Ventures in Cote D'Ivoire and Vietnam", proceedings of the *Twenty-first Annual Conference of the European International Business Academy*, Urbino, Italy, December, pp. 87–107.

Bartels F.L., Mirza H. and Wee K.H., 1997, "International Business in South Pacific Asia: The Regional Foreign Direct Investment and Localization Strategies of TRIAD Multinational Enterprises", proceedings of the *Fourteenth Pan Pacific Conference*, Kuala Lumpur, 3–5 June.

Bartlett C.A. and Ghoshal S., 1992, *Transnational Management: Text, Cases, and Readings in Cross-border Management*, Homewood, IL: Irwin.

Becker G.S., 1991, "As Nations Splinter, Global Markets Are Merging", *Business Week*, 22 April, p. 8.

Birkinshaw J., 1996, "How Multinational Subsidiary Mandates Are Gained and Lost", *Journal of International Business Studies*, Vol. 27, No. 3, 3rd Quarter, pp. 467–95.

Bostock F. and Jones G., 1994, "Foreign Multinationals in British Manufacturing, 1850–1962", pp. 89–126, in Jones G. and Frank Cass (eds), *The Making of Global Enterprise*, London.

Brooke M.Z. and Buckley P.J., 1988, *Handbook of International Trade*, London: Macmillan.

Buchman M. and Wolf C., 1998, "How to Save Japan from Its Own Rescue Plans", *The Asian Wall Street Journal*, 28 October, p. 8.

Buckley P.J., 1988, "The Limits of Expansion: Testing the Internationalisation Theory of the Multinational Enterprise", *Journal of International Business Studies*, Vol. XIX, No. 2, pp. 181–93.

Buckley P.J., 1989, "Foreign Direct Investment by Small- and Medium-sized Enterprises: The Theoretical Background", *Small Business Economics*, Vol. 1, pp. 89–100.

Buckley P.J. and Casson M., 1976, *The Future of the Multinational Enterprise*, London: Macmillan.

Buckley P.J., Newbould G.D. and Thurwell J., 1988, *Foreign Direct Investment by Smaller UK Firms*, London: Macmillan.

Buckley P.J., Pass C.L. and Prescott K., 1992, *Servicing International Markets*, London: Basil Blackwell.

Cantwell J.A., 1989, "The Changing Form of Multinational Enterprise Expansion in the Twentieth Century", in Teichova A., Levy-Leboyer M. and Nussbaum H. (eds), *Historical Studies in International Corporate Business*, Cambridge: Cambridge University Press.

Cockroft L., 1990, *Africa's Way*, London: I.B. Taurus.

Daft R.L., 1992, *Organisational Theory and Design*, 4th ed., St. Paul: West Pub. Co.

Devlin G. and Bleackley M., 1988, "Strategic Alliances – Guidelines for Success", *Long Range Planning*, Vol. 21, No. 5, pp. 18–23.

Doz Y.L. and Prahalad C.K., 1989, "Collaborate with Your Competitors and Win", *Harvard Business Review*, January/February, pp. 133–9.

Drucker P., 1989a, *Managing for Results*, London: Heinemann.

Drucker P., 1989b, *The New Realities*, Oxford: Heinemann.

Drucker P., 1998, "Rapid Change Has Led to Social Tensions, Asia Crisis", *The Straits Times*, 28 March, p. 66.

Dugger W.M., 1989, *Corporate Hegemony*, New York: Greenwood Press.

Dunning J.H., 1993, *Multinational Enterprises and the Global Economy*, Wokingham, England: Addison Wesley.

Fallows J., 1993, "How the World Works", *The Atlantic Monthly*, December. Internet version: www.theatlantic.com (accessed 16 June 1998).

Fallows J., 1994, "What Is an Economy For?" *The Atlantic Monthly*, January. Internet version: www.theatlantic.com (accessed 16 June 1998).

George K.D., Joll C. and Lynk E.L., 1992, *International Organization*, 4th ed., London: Basil Blackwell.

Heaton H., 1936, *Economic History of Europe*, New York: Harper and Brothers.

IMF Balance of Payments Statistics Yearbook (Part 1) 1997, IMF, Washington, D.C.

Jackson S. and Markowski S., 1995, "The Attractiveness of Countries to Foreign Direct Investment", *Journal of World Trade*, Vol. 29, No. 5, October, pp. 159–79.

Jain S.C., 1987, *Perspectives on International Strategic Alliances, Advances in International Marketing*, New York: Jai Press.

Jones K.K. and Shill W.E., 1991, "Allying for Advantage", *McKinsey Quarterly*, Vol. 3, pp. 94–6.

Korten D.C., 1995, *When Corporations Rule the World*, London: Earthscan.

Krugman P., 1994, "The Myth of Asia's Miracle", *Foreign Affairs*, November/December, pp. 62–78.

Larsen M., 1976, *The Old Assyrian City-State and Its Colonies*, Copenhagen: Akademisk Forlag.

Lei D., 1989, "Strategies for Global Competition", *Long Range Planning*, Vol. 22, No. 1, pp. 102–9.

Lorange P. and Roos J., 1992, *Strategic Alliances: Formation, Implementation and Evolution*, Cambridge: Basil Blackwell.

Lorange P., Roos J. and Bronn P.S., 1992, "Building Successful Strategic Alliances", *Long Range Planning*, Vol. 25, No. 6, pp. 10–17.

Lowes B., Pass C.L. and Sanderson S., 1994, *Companies and Markets*, London: Basil Blackwell.

Luffman G.A., Sanderson S., Lea E. and Kenny B., 1987, *Business Policy: An Analytical Introduction*, Oxford, UK: Basil Blackwell.

Luostarinen R., 1979, *Internationalization of the Firm: An Empirical Study of the Internationalization of Firms with Small and Open Domestic Markets with Special Emphasis on Lateral Rigidity as a Behavioral Characteristic in Strategic Decision-making*, Helsinki: Helsinki School of Economics.

Lynch R.P., 1989, *The Practical Guide to Joint Ventures and Corporate Alliances*, New York: John Wiley & Sons.

McKibbin W.J., 1998, *The Crisis in Asia: An Empirical Assessment*, Washington, D.C.: The Brookings Institution.

Mirza H., Giroud A., Wee K.H. and Bartels F.L., 1998, "The Investment Strategies of Asian and Non-Asian Firms in ASEAN", proceedings of the *LVMH Conference*, INSEAD Euro-Asia Center, Paris, 6–7 February 1998.

Moore K. and Lewis D., 1999, *Birth of the Multinational: 2000 Years of Ancient Business History – From Ashur to Augustus*, Copenhagen: Copenhagen Business School Press.

Ohmae K., 1989, "The Global Logic of Strategic Alliances", *Harvard Business Review*, Vol. 67, No. 2, pp. 143–54.

Orlin D., 1970, *Assyrian Colonies in Cappadocia*, The Hague: Mouton.

Porter M.E., 1980, *Competitive Strategy: Techniques for Analyzing Industries and Competitors*, New York: Free Press.

BIBLIOGRAPHY

Porter M.E., 1985, *Competitive Advantage: Creating and Sustaining Superior Performance*, New York: Free Press.

Porter M.E., 1990, *Competitive Advantage of Nations*, New York: Free Press.

Porter M.E. and Fuller M.B., 1986, "Coalitions and Global Strategy", in Porter M.E. (ed.), *Competition in Global Industries*, Boston, MA: Harvard Business School Press.

Prahalad C.K. and Doz Y.L., 1981, "An Approach to Strategic Control of MNCs", *Sloan Management Review*, in Buckley P.J and Ghauri, P., *The Internationalisation of the Firm*, London: Academic Press.

Reich R.B., 1991, *The Work of Nations*, London: Simon & Schuster.

Rifkin J., 1995, *The End of Work*, New York: G.P. Putnam & Sons.

Root F.R., 1989, *Entry Strategies for International Markets*, London: Lexington Books.

Rugman A.M. and Verbeke A., 1992, "A Note on the Transnational Solution and the Transaction Cost Theory of Multinational Strategic Management", *Journal of International Business Studies*, Vol. 23, No. 4, 4th Quarter, pp. 761–72.

Sayle M., 1998, "The Social Contradictions of Japanese Capitalism", *The Atlantic Monthly*, June. Internet version: www.theatlantic.com (accessed 13 June 1998).

Scott, B.R., "National Strategies: Key to International Competition", pp. 71–143, in Bruce R. Scott and George C. Lodge (eds), 1985, *U.S. Competitiveness in the World Economy*, Boston, MA: Harvard Business School Press.

Soros G., 1998, *The Crisis of Global Capitalism: Open Society Endangered*, New York: Public Affairs.

Stopford J., Strange S. and Henley J.S., 1991, *Rival States, Rival Firms: Competition for World Market Shares*, Cambridge: Cambridge University Press.

Taggart J. and Hood N., 1995, "Perspectives on Subsidiary Strategy in German Companies Manufacturing in the British Isles", *Sibu Working Paper*, 95/4, Scotland: University of Strathclyde.

Turpin D., 1993, "Strategic Alliances with Japanese Firms", *Long Range Planning*, Vol. 26, No. 4, pp. 14–20.

UNCTAD, 1996a, *Sharing Asia's Dynamism: Asian Direct Investment in the European Union*, UN, New York.

UNCTAD, 1996b, *World Investment Report*, UN, New York.

UNCTAD, 1998, *World Investment Report: Trends and Determinants*, UN, New York.

UNCTAD-ICC, 1998, *The Financial Crisis in Asia and Foreign Direct Investment*. Internet version: www.unctad.org/en/pressref/bg9802en.htm

Urban S. and Vendemini S., 1992, *European Strategic Alliances*, London: Basil Blackwell.

Veenhof K., 1972, *Aspects of Old Assyrian Trade and Its Terminology*, Leiden: Free University.

Vikram K., 1998, "New Risks Threaten Asia's Recovery, *The Business Times*, 29 October, p. 5.

Welch L.S. and Luostarinen R., 1988, "Internationalization: Evolution of a Concept", *Journal of General Management*, Vol. 14, No. 2, pp. 32–55.

Wilkins M., 1970, *The Emergence of Multinational Enterprise: American Business Abroad from 1914 to 1970*, Cambridge, MA: Harvard University Press.

World Bank, 1993, *The East Asian Miracle*, Washington D.C.

WTO Annual Report 1997, WTO, Geneva.

Yergin D. and Stanislaw J., 1998, *The Commanding Heights: The Battle Between Government and the Market Place Tthat Is Remaking the World Order*, New York: Simon & Schuster.

Young S., Hamill J., Wheeler C. and Davies J.R., 1989, *International Market Entry and Development: Strategies and Management*, Harvester Wheatsheaf/Prentice Hall.

Zhang P.G., 1998, *IMF and the Asian Financial Crisis*, Singapore: World Scientific.

Doing your Research Project in the Lifelong Learning Sector

Jonathan Tummons
Vicky Duckworth

YEOVIL COLLEGE
LIBRARY

Open University Press

Open University Press
McGraw-Hill Education
McGraw-Hill House
Shoppenhangers Road
Maidenhead
Berkshire
England
SL6 2QL

email: enquiries@openup.co.uk
world wide web: www.openup.co.uk

and Two Penn Plaza, New York, NY 10121-2289, USA

First published 2013

Copyright © Jonathan Tummons and Vicky Duckworth, 2013

All rights reserved. Except for the quotation of short passages for the purpose of criticism and review, no part of this publication may be reproduced, stored in a retrieval system, or transmitted, in any form or by any means, electronic, mechanical, photocopying, recording or otherwise, without the prior written permission of the publisher or a licence from the Copyright Licensing Agency Limited. Details of such licences (for reprographic reproduction) may be obtained from the Copyright Licensing Agency Ltd of Saffron House, 6–10 Kirby Street, London EC1N 8TS.

A catalogue record of this book is available from the British Library

ISBN-13: 978-0-33-524614-4 (pb)
ISBN-10: 0-33-524614-1 (pb)
eISBN: 978-0-33-524615-1

Library of Congress Cataloging-in-Publication Data
CIP data applied for

Typesetting and e-book compilations by
RefineCatch Limited, Bungay, Suffolk
Printed and Bound in the UK by Bell & Bain Ltd, Glasgow

Fictitious names of companies, products, people, characters and/or data that may be used herein (in case studies or in examples) are not intended to represent any real individual, company, product or event.

The *McGraw·Hill* Companies

YEOVIL COLLEGE
LIBRARY

'*Many teachers training in the lifelong learning sector, as well as those going on to do foundation, honours and masters degrees in education, find the prospect of carrying out educational research for the first time daunting. Thus far, they have been reliant on generic educational research textbooks. Jonathan Tummons' and Vicky Duckworth's excellent work now guides them clearly and supportively through the research journey in a way which is underpinned by the authors' deep understanding of both the sector and nature of the challenge of the research task to the student, using an informal and accessible written style.*'

Andy Armitage, Head of the Department of Post-Compulsory Education at
Canterbury Christ Church University, UK

'**This book combines sound practical advice with an exploration of the philosophical and methodological concepts underpinning educational research. Often drawing on the authors' own experiences, it makes a convincing case for the practitioner as researcher and draws clear and appropriate attention to the purposes, uses and dissemination of small scale research.**'

Susan Wallace, Professor of Continuing Education, Nottingham Trent University, UK

YEOVIL COLLEGE
LIBRARY

Jonathan

As always, thanks to Jo, Alex and Eleanor.

Thanks also to friends and colleagues - past and present - at Teesside University, Leeds Thomas Danby, York College and Yorkshire Coast College.

Vicky

As always, thanks to Craig Ludlow and my daughters Anna and Niamh.

Jonathan and Vicky would both like to thank Mary Hamilton for her enthusiasm, interest, supervision and friendship.

Contents

1   What is educational research?

By the end of this chapter you should be able to:

- Understand what is implied by the term 'educational research'

- Begin to think about and plan your own research project

- Have an understanding of some of the practical and logistical challenges posed by the research process

Introduction

When you think of the word 'research', what images come to your mind? When we ask this question of our students, we tend to get answers like this:

- Chemistry, or another science, or something
- People in white coats
- Laboratories
- Computers being used to process vast quantities of statistics
- 'Squirrels in a box' – Skinner

In fact, the last three of these have historically been used for *educational* research more widely than you might think. Laboratory-based research has historically been an element of research into learning – specifically, human cognition and behaviour – from a psychological perspective. Researchers who conduct surveys – using questionnaires, for example – with large numbers of people (perhaps thousands) invariably use specialized computer software packages (SPSS is the most common) to help analyse their statistics. And Skinner, the neo-behaviourist theorist and researcher, used a device commonly referred to as a *Skinner Box* to research how learning happens. Whether or not we agree that the best way to understand how people learn is to put hamsters in a cage and see if they work out which level to push to get a nut to eat (and which to push to get an electric shock) is another debate entirely. In this book, the kinds of research that we will be discussing are for the most part quite different, and tend to involve these kinds of things:

- Watching what students do in the seminar room or workshop
- Talking with students or other tutors
- Doing research in the real world – in colleges and adult education centres

But however it is done – whether involving large numbers of researchers embarking on a nationwide research project that will last three years, or involving one researcher (perhaps a student on a BA or MA in education course doing a research project assignment) – it could be argued that the overall ambition of educational research remains the same. So what does educational research try to do? What's it for?

What is educational research all about?

At a very basic level, doing research about education implies that we – the researchers – are interested in 'finding things out' about something to do with education. This book is concerned with research in the lifelong learning sector, but the central ideas presented might easily be applied to universities, to secondary or even primary school-based research as well. So, if we focus on the lifelong learning sector, the kinds of things that we might want to find out about could range from the ways in which students in further education are motivated by their programmes of study, to the reason why adult learners choose to enrol on literacy or numeracy courses. We might also want to explore why assessment regimes are constructed in the ways that they are, or how college lecturers respond to the bureaucratic requirements of their profession. Put simply, educational research might legitimately be about anything that 'education' is about: curriculum, pedagogy (teaching and learning), politics, sociology – education is a very broad field of study. And it is researched by a variety of different people.

Who does educational research?

Lots of people, and more than you might think, carry out educational research across a variety of institutions.

People in universities

We don't just mean to refer to university academics – lecturers, professors and researchers – though. Many students – undergraduates and postgraduates – carry out proper empirical research as part of their BA or MA degrees (we don't anticipate that people doing doctorates will be reading a book for newer researchers such as this one – although they are of course welcome!). One of the core themes of this book is that our attention to detail in research method and methodology must always be the same whether or not we are writing a 25,000-word MA dissertation or a 10,000-word undergraduate project. For undergraduates, a small-scale project (10,000 words may not sound small to you, but when it comes to writing up, you will be surprised how quickly you use up your word count) can often form a *pilot project* for a more sustained piece of research as part of an MA.

Other organizations where research is central to their focus
A number of other organizations carry out research – for example the National Foundation for Educational Research, which conducts research across educational themes (such as assessment) and sectors (such as 14–19 provision), or the Joseph Rowntree Foundation, an organization more generally concerned with broad social policy themes such as poverty or the effects of an ageing population, and who conduct research into the impact of poverty on children's education and subsequent life chances. Organizations from the public, private and third sectors are represented within the educational research community.

Professionals, in practice
And a third important group of research practitioners are *professionals* – teachers in schools, lecturers in further education colleges and adult education centres, and youth and social workers who work with young people in and out of formal educational settings. Sometimes people such as these are doing research as part of a programme of study (a degree or diploma), but at other times their decision to do research may be entirely intrinsic – based on inquiry and interest rather than the need to complete an assignment.

Why do educational research?

There are a number of answers to this question as well (not including 'because my university tutors say that I have to in order to complete my degree').

To improve or evaluate professional practice
This is particularly relevant for those newer researchers for whom this book is primarily aimed. Being able to link research to professional practice is a central element of *practitioner research* (a key theme of this book, and a term that will become familiar to you as you read on). As teachers and trainers in the lifelong learning sector, we are constantly hearing about how we need to ensure that our teaching is student-centred, that we need to be innovative (whatever that might mean – too often it is associated with the use of technology, and pretty poor technology at that – which doesn't get anything like the kind of critical research-led evaluation that it deserves) and that we need to reflect on our practice. One of the (many) problems with reflective practice, however, is that it doesn't always lead to anything useful (and we include all of those reflections that you have to write as students or for the Institute for Learning (IfL) in this category). Partly this is because for the vast majority of further education (FE) teachers, workloads are such that there is little space in the system for thinking about things, *unless you are going to do something different as a consequence*. The problem is: how will we know whether the different things that we are doing are having a beneficial impact? If our reflections on practice lead us to want to change an aspect of our pedagogic practice, then we need to find thorough and reliable ways of making sure that our judgements about those changes are sound and that they would stand up to wider scrutiny. From this starting point, we logically arrive at *practitioner research* as our end destination.

To find out about stuff – just because it is there and/or it is interesting
At the same time, there is absolutely nothing wrong with wanting to investigate something systematically and robustly purely on the basis that you are interested in it, intrigued by it, or just want to know what makes it tick. There may be implications from this for your classroom or workshop practice, or there may not. There may be broader policy implications as well (we shall return to this shortly), or there may not. And although it is perhaps a rather unfashionable approach to adopt these days (living and working as we do in managerialist performativity cultures where everything has to be audited and have a business case made for it (Gleeson et al., 2005)), the *liberal tradition* in education (education for education's sake – knowledge has its own intrinsic values and qualities and the quest for greater knowledge is a fundamentally important part of the human condition) still has something to say, even today (Wallis, 1996).

To inform policy at institutional, regional or national level
When universities have the quality of their research outputs evaluated (this is done on a department by department basis), one of the criteria used to assess how 'good' a university is at doing research is *impact,* which can be (crudely) summarized as the extent to which the research makes itself felt beyond the confines of academia. The most obvious way in which research can have an impact is through policy change. This might happen at a national level (Assessment for Learning being a readily identifiable example), but it might also be at local level as well: there is nothing to stop the right bit of small-scale undergraduate research from making a difference to the college or adult education centre where the researcher/professional works.

Practitioner research can also be politically driven, such as when Vicky describes how she:

> wanted to carry out an inquiry which opened a meaningful 'space' to develop a teaching and learning culture which moves towards a research-based approach to best practice. As a critical educator/researcher, I sought to develop my practice through the research and reflect a critical pedagogy, providing a curriculum which is culturally relevant, learner driven, and socially empowering.

Can *I* do educational research?

Yes you can, is the short answer. Lots of us, in all kinds of ways during our lives, need to find stuff out from time to time, and we use versions of the same kinds of methods that are discussed in this book. This might be at work, for example. Imagine that one of the awarding bodies you work with had brought out a new curriculum specification and you needed to find out how it differed from the existing one. You would search for the appropriate documentation on the awarding body's website, download it, and then read it in order to carry out a comparison with the document that you already had for the old curriculum. This is the kind of thing that researchers do. Or it might be at home. Suppose you had decided to treat yourself to a new Blu-ray player. As well as wanting to watch Blu-ray discs, you also wanted to be able to use catch-up services such as BBC iPlayer so that you would never miss another episode of your favourite programme. But which one should you buy? Before making a purchase you might scope the websites of several manufacturers and retailers, comparing not only prices but also specifications so that you would get the machine with the exact features that you were looking for. Again, this is the sort of thing that researchers might do. The difference is that when doing research, you have to spend much more time critically explaining why you have decided to read and compare the documents that you have chosen, or why you decided to talk to some people but not others in order to find out the things you need to know to answer the questions that you had set for yourself.

What use is educational research?

This is an important question, especially because 'theory' seems to be such a dirty word in some political and organizational circles these days. Michael Gove, the Secretary of State for Education, in wanting to take teacher training out of universities and into classrooms (at the time of writing this book) would certainly seem to be occupying a stance that does not value a research-intensive teacher-training pedagogy (although ironically, in Finland, one of the countries that Gove continually compares to the UK in terms of educational achievement, teachers all study to MA level). But there are other more general criticisms of educational research, some more justifiable than others.

It's full of jargon and nobody can understand it
This is an unfair criticism. Every academic specialism – as well as specialisms and niche interests in other walks of life – have their own ways of speaking, of writing and of conveying information. Different academic disciplines even have different styles for citations and references. Educational research is no more full of jargon than research done by economists or historians or physicists. Part of becoming a researcher, of entering a *community of research practice* (Hammersley, 2005; Tummons, 2012), is learning how to talk the talk of researchers, how to speak and write in the way that educational researchers do. As with any new practice, it simply takes a little time to get used to the ways that the more established practitioners speak and do things.

It's biased
This is also an unfair criticism, not least as we could rightly counter such a claim with a statement to the effect that *everything* is biased (or so the postmodernist approach to educational research would tell us (Scott and Usher, 1999)); so why should educational research be any different? Research in the UK is conducted to a high ethical and professional standard, wrapped up in the ethical guidelines produced by the British Educational Research Association (BERA, 2011). To accuse educational research of bias is simply to impugn the ethical and professional positions occupied by researchers.

Educational research reinvents the wheel and repeats itself
There is a grain of truth in this, although these two factors are not straightforwardly connected. Much qualitative (though by no means all – the Teaching and Learning

Research Programme being a good example) research is relatively small-scale. But this is not (as we shall go on to argue later in this book) necessarily a problem, so long as we do not make claims for the general application of our research that cannot be backed up. The fact that educational research is non-cumulative, that there is perhaps too much reinventing of the wheel, is a cause for reflection. Certainly, there is a staggering amount of literature now available, and it is easier than ever to search for it all online. But there is so much stuff available that you can never hope to read it all. Staying up to date with your reading about your own research and teaching interests could be a full-time job in itself. The mass expansion of higher education in the UK has led to an increased number of academics, an increase in the pressure to publish, an increase in the amount of stuff that is published, and so on. This is not an excuse; rather a statement of fact. As more and more work gets published, and it becomes easier to access work from around the world, it is only natural that people will not always have read everything that pertains to their own research.

Empowerment
Educational research can have a ripple effect that touches and empowers the practitioner/ researcher, learner and the community. This is a powerful model which Vicky described as the means to promote dialogic communication between herself and learners which was the key to actively involving learners in their own education; this active participation included the co-creation of the curriculum whereby learners' needs, motivations and interests were the driving factors (see McNamara, 2007; Duckworth and Taylor, 2008; Johnson et al., 2010). Assessment was measured by each learner's own goals and aspirations and the distance they had travelled in relation to their learning journey. Offering an egalitarian model takes into consideration the cultural, psychological and educational factors related to the learner. This values their history, present and future narrative, rather than fitting all learners into one learning narrative and prescriptive framework.

What is doing research actually like?

Research is exciting, enthusing, challenging and incredibly stimulating. It is also frustrating, troublesome and messy. When it goes according to plan – when all 15 of your focus group members turn up on time as arranged and proceed to have a lively and interesting debate that generates lots of information for your research – it is undeniably a terrific feeling. When it all goes wrong – when your computer crashes and you lose a week's work, or when you just cannot get enough people to agree to be interviewed no matter what you do – it can be a real struggle to keep going. It is more than likely that you will have the occasional bad day – but the good days, and the overall sense of satisfaction at completing your research and writing it up, will be more than enough compensation. So, the journey can be personally challenging, but it can also be professionally and academically challenging as well.

Research plans make the world seem a simpler place than it is
When designing your research, it is easy to assume that each component of your project will slot effortlessly together with the next. Typically, research students draw up

timetables for their work (encouraged by their project supervisors to do so!) so that they can allocate time for their initial reading, their data collection, typing up, writing the final project, and so on. Now, many research students manage to stick to their timetables pretty closely. And many others do not. Many of the students that we work with are only able to study on a part-time basis and have to juggle family and work commitments as well, and we know how difficult this is from first-hand experience, not just from working with our own students. It took us slightly longer than the standard six years, to complete our PhDs on a part-time basis. Jonathan carried out his research whilst working firstly as a further education college tutor and then as a university lecturer, and having two children in the meantime; Vicky was again working firstly in further education and then as a university lecturer whilst also bringing up two young children. However, we would both agree that the additional time to complete our research gave us extra time for reflection and added rigour and depth to our research. So don't beat yourself up if you find that your research has episodes where it slows down; use this time to reflect and pull your thoughts together. It is important to be aware that many of us have busy and complicated lives – and your research supervisors will be aware of this too.

Compromises and 'making do' are a common feature of the research process

Things don't always go according to plan. Sometimes this simply means that you may have one or two sleepless nights as you prepare a draft chapter for your supervisor to look at in advance of your next tutorial – if a pile of portfolios arrive for you to verify, for example, of if you have to keep one of your children at home from school. But at other times you may find yourself having to change direction because you do not manage to obtain the appropriate permission to carry out some observations for example, or because people decide not to participate (which of course they are entitled to do). Having to change your methods or deviate from your research plans is not necessarily a bad thing, so long as you provide a careful and critical account of why you had to do so when you write up your project (which is why keeping a research diary, as discussed below, is a useful thing to do). Of course having a topic and partaking in a research project which interests and motivates you is a strong motivation to driving you and your research forward.

Is there anything else I should know before I start?

Doing research can lead to unforeseen outcomes – outcomes that will not necessarily be welcomed by all of the stakeholders in the research process. Sometimes researchers find things that they were not expecting. There is a political aspect to research that we all need to be sensitive to. It can be argued – quite convincingly – that education, as a process, is fundamentally political. Any activity that draws on so much public money can hardly fail to be so. We can easily imagine that if the Department for Education paid for a research project, which concluded that an expensive government policy was not proving to be effective, some kind of political fallout might ensue. But political pressures also exist at a more local or institutional level as well. Many of the student researchers who we work with carry out practitioner research in their own places of work (usually further education colleges and adult education or outreach centres). In such environments, it is very important for the researcher to be sensitive to the attitudes, positions and responsibilities of their fellow workers, their managers (who often need to be treated carefully as their help will be needed to secure permission to carry out the research in the first place) and, perhaps most importantly, the students. If you do research in your own workplace, you will need to make sure that your understandable desire to do your project in a critical and unflinching manner is tempered by an awareness of the feelings and positions of others (Gibbs, 2007). Research can lead to you exploring difficult emotions. Vicky's research revealed the impact of violence and trauma experienced by a group of basic skills learners. However, research and the emotions it may evoke are not static: her research also led to powerful and liberating emotions for both her and her learners.

This book is primarily aimed at BA and MA students, and also teacher-training students, who are working and researching in the lifelong learning sector and who are new researchers, doing a research project as part of their programme of study. It is also aimed at practitioners who are interested in exploring their practice and considering taking part in research. Some kinds or styles of research are probably not suitable for you, such as *longitudinal research,* which – as the name implies – requires a long-term structure for the aims of the research to be carried through. For example, you may wish to research the effects of the assessment process on a group of trainee plumbers in the further education sector. In order to do this thoroughly, you would probably need to research these trainees over a considerable period of time – months rather than weeks, and ideally an entire academic year. This is probably longer than your programme of study allows. You may also wish to do *ethnographic* research, a mode of research that usually involves spending long periods of time – years, normally – getting to know a particular group of people who are the subject of your research. Again, this might be a suitable approach for later in your research career, but when doing an undergraduate project it is doubtful that you would have enough time to follow ethnographic research through. The mode of research that you are most likely to adopt is referred to as *practitioner research*. This is a research approach, or *paradigm*, that pretty much does what it says on the tin: it is a kind of research done by practitioners, by teachers and trainers, who are interested in systematically exploring, and perhaps adapting, an aspect of their professional work. Practitioner research is a relatively broad term (explained in much more depth in the following chapter) and encompasses several other varieties of small-scale research. The two approaches that you are most likely to take are action research and case study research, and we shall discuss these briefly now.

Action research

Action research usually involves the use of *qualitative* research methods (the kind that this book is predominantly concerned with). It is done by teachers who are usually using research methods to make judgements about their own practice, with a view to improving them. This is, properly understood, a *cyclical* process: by this we mean that the research should also involve the systematic exploration of any impact caused by changes in practice that the teacher does in fact introduce, again using methods derived from the qualitative paradigm. Then, once the impact has been researched, the entire cycle can begin again. This is discussed in depth in the following chapter.

Case study

Case study research need not be practitioner research (that is to say, you could do a case study of a context where you do not actually work), but is a helpful approach if you do not want to go through the entire Action Research Cycle. For small-scale research projects that do not fall within the action research remit, a case study can be a helpful alternative approach. A case study is an investigation of a particular case (this might be something in a particular institution such as the use of learning support assistants, a single issue related to your teaching such as use of an electronic whiteboard in the seminar room or workshop, or a specific assessment strategy that you use, such as simulation on an NVQ programme).

You could choose to carry out an *intrinsic* case study, which is when you are simply seeking better or deeper understanding of the issue being researched. In an intrinsic study you are limiting yourself to an exploration of your chosen topic, not making generalizations about broader educational practice or offering options for improvement or change. Alternatively, you could carry out an *instrumental* case study, when you are seeking to explore an issue in order to make changes to it, the distinction with action research being that, with a case study, you are not required by your chosen case study methodology to actually carry out and then evaluate your changes: your programme for change might simply be in the form of a series of proposals for future action. Students who are carrying out larger-scale projects might choose *collective* case studies, where multiple cases are investigated so that generalizations might be drawn that could have institutional or sector-wide consequences, but such an approach is beyond the scope of this book (Stake, 2005).

What practical advice would you give to a new researcher?

As well as being researchers ourselves, we also supervise students who are doing research projects as part of their BA or MA degrees. Over time, we have found the following four pieces of general advice to be helpful for newer researchers.

Keep a research diary

Actually, you don't have to keep a diary as such, but some kind of journal or notebook that you keep with you during the entirety of your research project can prove to be a very helpful resource. You can use it to note down ideas that you have as you go (because when you have a good idea it always make sense to write it down as you may not remember it later), keep track of any changes to your research design (so that you can explain any major differences between your *planned* research plan and your *actual* research when you get to the writing up stage), and note down things that work well and work less well so that you can adapt your research methods as you go.

Make the most of your supervisor

At a very early stage in the research process you will need to establish a good working relationship with your supervisor so that you have a clear understanding of what they can do for you – and what you need to do for them. We recommend that you agree a schedule of regular face-to-face meetings, which are almost always more effective than trying to establish a supervisor–supervisee relationship online, via email, or over the phone. If possible, always make sure that you have something specific to talk about at each tutorial – otherwise you run the risk of your tutorials turning into more generalized conversations that may not be so useful. Use tutorials to discuss the way you have planned your interviews, chosen your sources for your literature review, or – if your programme of study allows for it – go over work in draft form.

Keep things tidy and well organized

Having everything properly filed or stored is important – and if you get a system in place at an early stage in your research, so much the better. When you come to writing up your research, things will go that bit more smoothly for you if you are not having to spend precious time frantically searching through piles of paper and bundles of A4 folders for the exact note or bit of information that you need. You don't need a particularly sophisticated filing system – just one that makes sense to you and allows you to find things quickly and easily. This applies to both paper files, and files on your computer as well.

Always take notes when you read and start a bibliography

It may seem surprising to have to say this, but even amongst our third year undergraduate students we encounter people who do not systematically take notes when they are reading. We cannot overemphasize the need to take notes as you read. Not only does it help you to remember, and hence learn, what you have been reading (people generally learn better from reading their own handwriting rather than from something that has been word-processed or typeset), it also makes things easier when you come to writing up your research. It is much easier to go through your own notebooks when looking for quotations or theories rather than having to go back to the library and borrow the books again. In the same way, we suggest that you start keeping a bibliography straight away, and add to it every time you read another book during your research.

A few final words before you start . . .

With this book we have tried to distil what we teach our own students during research methods modules into a book form. This has been a bit trickier than we thought it might be, and we are sure that there are some bits that we might have left out or others that might have been included. If you find this book helpful, but nonetheless have suggestions as to what we might have done differently, please let us know. You can email Jonathan at j.tummons@tees.ac.uk and Vicky at Vicky.Duckworth@edgehill.ac.uk.

How to use this book

This book can be read from cover to cover, or a chapter at a time: each chapter is designed to be self-contained, and where necessary links to topics covered in other chapters are included. Practical and theoretical issues are blended throughout the book, but for those readers who are looking for particular themes, rather than planning to read through the book from the start, a brief summary may be useful.

After this opening chapter, Chapter 2 consists of a discussion of different types of practitioner research. Taking as its starting point the central position of reflective practice in teaching and education, this chapter goes on to develop notions of reflecting and evaluating on practice into systematic research on practice. Chapter 3 widens the methodological debate and looks at broader research themes, such as the differences between quantitative and qualitative research, and how different cultural or political perspectives – such as feminism and postmodernism – can inform the research process. Chapter 4 is all about the process of shaping research questions, and helps readers to understand how to generate ideas about what to research, as well as how to turn these broad ideas into specific research questions.

Chapter 5 discusses the ethics of doing educational research, and covers topics such as the need to maintain anonymity and confidentiality, gaining permission from relevant stakeholders to access sites and people, and so forth. Chapter 6 provides the reader with down-to-earth advice about the more popular research methods that are used by students when completing small-scale research projects (interviews, questionnaires and observations). Chapter 7 explores how research data can be analysed and then interpreted. Chapter 8 discusses how the quality of a research project can be evaluated. And Chapter 9 provides the reader with practical advice concerning how research can be disseminated to different audiences.

References and further reading

British Educational Research Association (2011) *Ethical Guidelines for Educational Research.* Available at http://www.bera.ac.uk/system/files/BERA%20Ethical%20Guidelines% 202011.pdf [accessed 17 April 2012].

Duckworth, V. and Taylor, K. (2008) Words are for everyone. *Research and Practice in Adult Literacy,* 64: 30–2.

Gibbs, P. (2007) Practical wisdom and the workplace researcher. *London Review of Education,* 5(3): 223–36.

Gleeson, D., Davies, J. and Wheeler, E. (2005) On the making and taking of professionalism in the further education workplace. *British Journal of Sociology of Education,* 26(4): 445–60.

Hammersley, M. (2005) What can the literature on communities of practice tell us about educational research? Reflections on some recent proposals. *International Journal of Research and Method in Education,* 28(1): 5–29.

Johnson, C., Duckworth, V., McNamara, M. and Apelbaum, C. (2010) A tale of two adult learners: from adult basic education to degree completion. *National Association for Developmental Education Digest,* 5(1): 57–67.

McNamara, M. (2007) *Getting Better.* Warrington: Gatehouse Books.

Scott, D. and Usher, R. (1999) *Researching Education: Data, Methods and Theory in Educational Enquiry.* London: Continuum.

Stake, R. (2005) Qualitative case studies, in N. Denzin and Y. Lincoln (eds.) *The Sage Handbook of Qualitative Research*. Third edition. London: Sage: 443–66.

Tummons, J. (2012) Theoretical trajectories within communities of practice in higher education research. *Higher Education Research and Development,* 31(3), 299–310.

Wallis, J. (1996) *Liberal Adult Education: The End of an Era?* Nottingham: Continuing Education Press, University of Nottingham.

2   Types of practitioner research

By the end of this chapter you should be able to:

- Understand the nature and basis of small-scale research, practitioner research, and action research

- Fully understand and appreciate the consideration of how you move forward with your own practitioner research

- Justify the strengths of practitioner research

Introduction

The term 'practitioner' is used to indicate anyone working in the lifelong learning sector – for example, teachers, tutors, trainers, managers and administrators. The term 'research', in terms of practitioner research, is often linked to putting new knowledge to practical use in the classroom. Practitioner research is closely connected to, and pulls on, the methodologies of the action research described by Kemmis and McTaggart (2005: 560) as including participatory research, critical action research, classroom action research, action learning and action science. There are those who argue that practitioner research branches from a larger social justice movement within qualitative research (qualitative research starts by accepting that there are many different ways of understanding and of making sense of the world). However, even when social justice is not the singular motivating principle, a core commonality of purpose is the aspiration to improve upon and develop deeper insights into one's practice.

Practitioner research, by its nature, offers practitioners a *voice* in the research dialogue. Some consider it a channel of sorts between theory and practice, although practitioners claim a rightful place in the research continuum. Practitioner research, often referred to as *action research*, is a type of 'insider' investigation (this term is elaborated upon later in the chapter) by practitioners in their own area of specialism/classroom as a focus for their study. The process of action research is reflective, deliberate and systematic. Action research is directed towards an action, or cycle of actions, that a practitioner wants to take to address a situation. This is why the term 'action' is used for this method of research (models of reflection are identified later in the chapter). Action research is different from traditional forms of research because it uses insider or local knowledge about a setting to define and address a problem that the practitioner has identified. So how to define *practitioner research*? We would position it as a systematic form of inquiry that may be collaborative, self-reflective, critical, and also carried out by the participants of the inquiry (Duckworth and Taylor, 2008; Duckworth, 2011). This can include learners voicing their stories at educational conferences (Johnson et al., 2010). The term practitioner research may encompass a project-oriented approach to professional development that provides practitioners with the tools and techniques, the structure, and the support to carry out a long-term, data-based project in their classrooms.

Grassroots research

Whilst the main purpose of research is to create new knowledge and understanding for us, the additional and necessary purpose of practitioner research is to try as best we can to put that new knowledge to practical and meaningful use in the classroom. The traditional separation in research of new knowledge from its purposeful application to life is, in principle, resolved in practitioner research.

We will look at case studies of how practitioner research has been very useful to the development of practitioners and their practice later in the chapter (we shall think about suggestions for dissemination in Chapter 9).

There are, however, challenges in practitioner research in terms of how it can be perceived as not having the same rigour as research carried out by the 'academy' – that is to say, research carried out by academics or other professional researchers who are working in a university or other research organization and who may never have experienced classroom practice. Practitioners often turn to qualitative research approaches in their search for deeper critical insights from problems and concerns which arise from their educational practice in order to make sense of them and deal with them in their future action. Qualitative research is conducted in a natural setting (such as a workshop or classroom) and involves a process of building a complex and holistic picture of the phenomenon of interest. Practitioner research does not look for generalizations in the way some large-scale forms of research attempt to do. Rather, it is seeking new understandings that will enable practitioners and those they may collaborate with to generate an informed approach to improving our classroom practice. As such, practitioner research can be empowering and offer a powerful tool for generating valuable knowledge for practitioners, their learners, and for the broader field in the form of disseminating the research – for example, reports, staff training events, subject specialist meetings, and so forth.

Where does practitioner research take place?

As identified above, practitioner research centres directly on the concerns that practitioners raise about their own practice in the classroom. It enables them to identify the area they want to explore, arising from their own professional experience or concerns. They decide what questions to investigate and how to conduct their research. This process of investigation can often be carried out in conjunction with their learners. Practitioner research may be an ongoing process that takes place through a number of projects over the practitioner's career.

Below, Karen shares her suggestions for developing research-active first year teachers in their newly qualified teacher (NQT) year. Karen is a senior lecturer and course leader on a secondary Postgraduate Certificate in Education (PGCE) programme. She has taught for over 20 years in secondary schools, and during that time her main areas of teaching were the 14–19 age range. Her current research includes how to plan outstanding lessons for key stages 4 and 5, and she has focused on the need for 14–19-year-old learners to feel ownership over their own learning and understand the relevance of what goes on in the classroom.

Case study: Karen McCormack, course leader for a full-time PGCE in psychology

Preparing students for the research journey

As part of their Postgraduate Certificate in Education (PGCE), trainees are asked to undertake a small-scale piece of action research based on their practice while on placement. The focus of the research is chosen by the trainee, and they plan their own data collection and present their report during their final placement. The research project is assessed at level 7, giving the trainee masters-level credits which they can then build on to complete the full masters qualification once they are qualified and employed.

The first conversation with trainees covers the purpose of research. They are asked to identify why they would want to carry out research and how they feel it would benefit their professional development and classroom practice. Research projects produced by past trainees are made available to enable trainees to see what they are aiming for and the appropriate structure their research may take.

Often, trainees struggle to find a focus for their own research and, during individual tutorials held to discuss their development on placement, and during these discussions, they are asked to identify what aspect of their training they are finding most enjoyable and rewarding. Since the trainees will have to 'live and breathe' their research, it makes sense to find a focus that they are passionate about.

A research scaffold is introduced to enable trainees to plan effectively for the research activity and to help them consider every aspect of the project. Further sessions cover a range of vital skills required to successfully conduct their own research and, starting with 'deciding on a research focus', the group are quickly introduced to concepts such as critical reading and thinking, writing a literature review, identifying an appropriate methodology, and how to effectively analyse the data they have collected.

The first writing task for trainees is to put together a research proposal (see Chapter 5). This is then discussed and amended using face-to-face tutorials and online support, as below.

Supporting trainees to achieve level 7

Specific teaching sessions	Sessions are delivered to introduce trainees to level 7 writing. Criteria for success are identified and examples of level 7 assignments from previous years are made available for trainees to consider.
Trainee groups	A buddy system may be introduced based on the trainees' prior research experience.
Prior attainment	Trainees provide information as to the level of their research skills and the prior experience they have had of conducting their own, independent, small-scale research. Trainees are tracked against their prior attainment to identify possible underachievement.
Critical writing session	One session is devoted to developing critical writing skills. This involves the use of level 7 assignments from last year's cohort to identify good practice, and peer assessment of the research currently being undertaken.
Personal research tutor	Trainees are given a tutor to liaise with and discuss their research.
Tutorials	During the first semester, tutorials take place regularly (every two weeks), during which time trainees are able to discuss their research proposals and get formative feedback from the literature reviews when submitted.
Virtual learning environment (VLE)	Trainees are encouraged to use the university VLE to post on the research discussion threads that emerge.
Literature review	As part of the 'patchwork' delivery of the research methods module, trainees submit their literature review for formative feedback.
Drop-in session	These are arranged at the university to give the trainees the opportunity to discuss their research with their supervising tutor.
Edge Ahead Centre	Trainees are given information about the range of student support that is available at the university and a session is held for trainees to develop research skills using the University Discovery programme.
Patchwork	Trainees are encouraged to submit extracts from their research for formative assessment and review.
Research methods teaching sessions	A range of material is provided to help trainees to action plan their research and structure their final report. This is delivered in specific sessions and made available online via the university VLE.
Pre-professional week	A seminar is planned for the final week at the university when trainees wishing to achieve level 7 can have support to improve their work.
Individual tutorials	Trainees can make individual appointments with tutors during their pre-professional week to get personalized support to achieve level 7.

It is important that trainees are able to clearly see the path that they are going to follow, and it is at this point that trainee teachers often become excited about the research journey they are going to embark on.

The timescale for activities so far has been no more than six weeks, and by Christmas trainees are ready to hand in their research proposals. During the Developmental Phase of Placement 1 trainees begin the process of data collection. During January, they also submit their literature review for formative feedback. Creating a two-way discussion like this helps both trainee and course leader to undertake the research journey together, with the course leader acting as a 'critical friend'.

Adopting a 'patchwork' approach to the research project has proven to be very successful, and the ongoing guidance and support of their tutor is vital for these early researchers. Towards the end of February the trainees forward their methodology chapter in which they have fully outlined the approach and methods of data collection they have planned to use to conduct the research. As each piece of the patchwork is completed the trainee grows in confidence, and the finished project is submitted in late April. The range of research undertaken has been impressive, and the current cohort of trainees are covering issues such as gender and option choices post-16, creativity in the post-16 classroom, and mood and music in the classroom.

Here is an extract from trainee teacher Ian's draft research proposal, as an example of the kinds of work being done by the trainees:

> The data will be collected using primarily questionnaires, comprising of both closed and open questions. Questionnaires are a useful way of collecting information, providing structured, numerical data which is comparatively straightforward to analyse. Whilst questionnaires have their benefits, there are issues with regard to the limited scope of the data that can be collected and the likely limited flexibility of response.
>
> To address this, observations of students will also be carried out to see if there are any significant gender differences with regard to students' behaviour and attitude to study. Observations will allow me to develop more intimate and informal relationships with the students, and to collect data in a more natural environment (i.e. the classroom) than those in which questionnaires would be conducted.
>
> I will also use semi-structured interviews to collect data from those delivering psychology. This would allow me to discover their perceptions of the subject, and whether involvement in another department (science, sociology) would influence the image of the subject. The use of interviews will provide me with freedom of discussion and interaction between colleagues and myself, allowing for the clarification and exploration of new topics that may arise.

Being critically reflective

An important requirement of any professional is the ability to reflect on practice in order to improve practice. It is essential to take a personal approach to such theories or frameworks in order to find what is useful for you as an individual, and to ensure reflection becomes meaningful rather than superficial. So let us consider the term 'critically reflective', which links strongly with practitioner research.

The use and meaning given to the term reflective practice is broad and varied. When we discuss reflective practice we mean a process that allows the practitioners to reflect on their own knowledge, ideologies, and experiences and values that impact on their action in and out of the classroom. If we unpick this we may want to identify the motivations that led us to enter the teaching professions; for example, is it to inspire our students to reach their potential, or is it simply about putting our degree to use in a career? (Probably a combination of both is the most accurate description for most trainee teachers.) We view reflection as a process of finding the time and space to stand back and think about the meaning given to a situation or a set of circumstances in a particular time and place in your practice – in relation to self, others, and the wider context. This systemic approach used offers a structure that enables multiple ideas from a myriad of sources to be made available. Indeed, practitioner research opens up the possibility for trainees, and new and experienced educators to think critically and enter a dialogue about problems/barriers related to teaching and learning that have been challenging them. It is a term which refers to a practical way of looking at your own work to check that it is as you would like it to be, and involves you thinking about, and reflecting on, your work.

So let us consider some theorists and their approaches to reflection. Schön (1983) argued that the model of professional training that relied upon filling up students with knowledge then directing them out into the world of practice was inappropriate in a fast-changing world. He proposed that a reflective practice model would enable learners and novices within a discipline to compare their own practices with those of experienced practitioners, thus leading to development and improvement. In addition, he argued that reflective practice involves thoughtfully considering your own experiences as you make the connection between knowledge and practice (Schön, 1983). Schön proposes two distinct means of reflection within the 'reflective practicum' or learning setting:

- Reflection-*on*-action
- Reflection-*in*-action

Reflection-on-action is the *conscious act* of reflecting on a situation or event when it has occurred – for example, after a lesson a practitioner may document their reflections at the end of a lesson plan. This allows the practitioner the opportunity to explore what happened and to consider what might have happened, and, crucially, what might be, if different actions had been put into place. It is a critical method of reflection, embedded in questioning and enquiry, and supports an active reflective continuum in the same manner that teacher questions are able to encourage learner critical thinking skills. Indeed, Schön actively encourages the teacher to develop deep and critical questioning skills.

In contrast, Gibbs (2007) identified a series of six steps to aid reflective practice. These elements make up a cycle that can be applied over and over:

- Description – what happened?
- Feelings – what were you thinking and feeling?
- Evaluation – what was good and bad about the experience?
- Analysis – what sense can you make of the situation?
- Conclusion – what else could you have done?
- Action plan – what will you do next time?

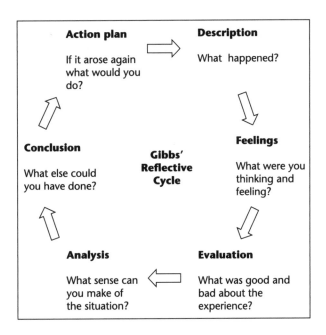

Unlike many other models, Gibbs takes into account the realm of feelings and emotions which played a part in a particular event. This model can be used to help build from a simple description to a more detailed critical analysis. This approach allows the practitioner to consider each stage and aspect of a situation when reflecting. It is active, and able to ask critical questions of the practitioner. The evaluation stage offers the practitioner the opportunity to identify best practice, as well as areas for improvement. And the conclusion and action plan allow the opportunity for improvement. We would suggest that it is important for practitioners to use the reflective model to learn from developmental points; resolving these allows for practitioners' continued development in, and capacity to learn from, practice in order to change practice.

Whichever reflective model you choose to use, self-reflection is much more than simply thinking over and over what has happened. Reflective practice is a cognitive (thinking) process, which brings together several stages of considered exploration of thoughts, feelings and evaluations focused on practitioner skills and outcomes. The outcome of reflection is not always grounding for change, or action based, but perhaps confirmation/rejection of a theory or practice skill route. For example, it may be that an outcome of reflection is seen through understanding how certain teaching and learning strategies work. Or you may discover that you can influence your practice by using new and emerging technologies in new and innovative ways to engage learners. Reflective practice is a process by which practitioners can generate self-awareness, focus on your practice, and that of others you may work with, and create new knowledge and ways of working. The process of reflection itself can be spontaneous or planned, guided or unstructured, and undertaken as an individual or as a shared activity. The outcome of reflection can be preparation for change (action) or understanding or generation of knowledge.

Activity

Follow Gibbs' Reflective Cycle (see above) and use the stages to reflect on and develop an aspect of your practice that you would like to improve.

From personal experience, reflection should facilitate both reflection in and on action (Schön, 1983), and offers an abundance of learning from many levels: organizational, relational, professional and the wider context.

The use of reflection in the educational sector is varied, taking the form of:

- the use of artefacts – for example, photographs, assignments, etc.
- learning journals/logs
- storytelling
- reflection on work experiences
- dialogue with networks/communities of practice
- multimedia.

Activity

Consider the skills a practitioner may need to carry out a research project and then think about how you can apply them to your own research project.

You may have considered the following skills:

- Practitioner research requires attention to detail and deadlines
- Being well organized, including effective time management
- Can work effectively with others, but also work well independently
- A willingness to explore and examine your beliefs and practices
- A drive to make a difference to your practice and the experience of your learners.

We now move on to look at the types of practitioner research that you are likely to consider for your own research project.

Action research

Action research in education has gained increasing attention in the past 20 years. Action research is known by many other names too – participatory research, collaborative inquiry, emancipatory research, action learning, and contextual action research. It is often viewed as a practical yet systematic research method that enables teachers to investigate their own teaching and their students' learning. The action research process is described as a recurring spiral of planning, acting, observing and reflecting. In this vein, action research is open ended. It does not begin with a fixed hypothesis. It begins with an idea that you develop. Action research as a methodology has appeared in response to the mounting need for more relevant and practical knowledge in the social sciences. It aimed to remove the dichotomy between academic research and day-to-day applications. Indeed, action research was developed mainly by academics in higher education who saw it as a meaningful way of working in professional education, particularly teacher education. Designing action research projects raises ethical issues (see Chapter 5) that are not present in traditional research. Nevertheless, such projects are valuable when conducted by practitioners.

There are several kinds of *action research*. These include: *interpretative research design* (Elliott, 1991), which views action research as an enabler for supporting others to do research; *critical theoretic action research* (Carr and Kemmis, 1986), which views action research as a tool for investigating and challenging the social relationships in our social situation; and *living theory* (McNiff et al., 1996) which position action research as a lived practice which shifts from a purely theoretical and rhetorical application.

The model you choose to use can be applied to improve your own teaching practice. And you can start with a problem you encounter in your teaching practice. For example, it may be a worry that learners are not engaging with the resources on a particular topic you are delivering. Faced with the problem, the action researcher will go through the series of phases outlined above – planning, acting, observing, reflecting, and commonly referred to as the Action Research Cycle – to tackle the problem in a systematic way.

You may already be using a version of the Action Research Cycle without really realizing it. The reality of being a teacher is that, even with detailed planning and motivation, things don't always go according to plan. No doubt the way you shape and improve your lesson delivery and content is fed from your reflections and your learner input and feedback. This cycle of reflection and feedback is an ongoing process which leads to a cycle of planning, acting, observing and reflecting. In turn this leads to another cycle in which you embed further developments and improvements suggested by the initial cycle, and hence the reference to a spiral of steps.

Types of action research

Practitioner research (individual)

This may focus on a single issue in your classroom practice. For example, you may be seeking answers to problems of classroom behaviour, use of resources (including new and emerging technology), or learner assessment. The problem is one that you believe is present in your classroom and therefore one which can be tackled by you on an individual basis. You may investigate the problem by collecting the relevant data – for example, learner questionnaires, interviews, and surveys and artefacts such as the learner's work (more on these methods of data collection later). A downside of individual research is that it can often be done in isolation, and not disseminated to others. A suggestion would be to look for ways to share your findings – for example, at staff meetings, in online communities of practice, in college newsletters, etc. This can be both supportive and motivational. It may be that you find out that another practitioner is also exploring the same area of practice and you can share your ideas and ways forward.

Action research (collaborative)

There are many ways to collaborate. Furthermore, multiple perspectives can offer a more complete view of an issue under study, and having a number of iterations of a study across a variety of contexts offers a means of validating findings. Collaboration may take many forms, including crossing age ranges (for example, primary, secondary and Post-Compulsory Education and Training (PCET)); subject specialisms (for example, English, sociology, health care, construction, plumbing, etc.); types of institutions (for example, schools, colleges, training providers, etc.); engaging the community outside the college; or moving towards a multidisciplinary approach (for example, healthcare providers and social services). Collaborative action research is likely to focus on a common concern shared by many, comprise two practitioners, or a group of practitioners, and may also include others involved in addressing a particular classroom or subject specialism concern. As identified later in Angela's case study, based on the Learners' Lives project, this concern may be supported by individuals outside of the school, such as a university. Reason and Bradbury (2008) suggest that an essential value of action research strategies is to increase the involvement and participation of individuals in generating and applying knowledge about themselves and about their worlds.

Activity

Consider the key aims and purposes of action research.

You may have considered:

- curriculum development and changes to practice
- problem solving
- college improvement
- professional development
- college organizational structure
- evaluation of the workplace
- evaluation of your role
- exploring the learners' journey.

Participatory action research

Participatory action research is rooted in the cultural tradition of the participants and builds on strengths and resources in the community. Actively involving learners and the community in participatory action research increases the likelihood of developing interventions and resources that are culturally relevant and address the learners' needs, as well as promoting the continuation of community engagement and initiatives when research has ended.

Case study: Vicky's research

Practitioner action research has been a key part in driving my practice forward. For example, rather than presuming to know what the learners want to learn and what type of resources are best, I began to listen more actively to the learners' voices, letting their needs, aspirations and dreams shape the lessons. Hamilton et al. (2007: 21) National Research Development Centre's Practitioner-Led Research Initiatives identified how being a practitioner researcher offered:

1   a fresh perspective
2   professional development
3   boost of status
4   the usefulness of findings.

When I first got involved in this research, the drive was from my experience as a tutor and programme leader delivering literacy in a college of further education based in the North of England. Being political, I would argue, is less of an option, but more of a need in the field of education today. With an increasing move towards performativity via target setting and results and accountability, like many tutors I felt a great deal of my time and energy was beginning to be governed by a managerial driven system based on close scrutiny of my paperwork, rather than my practice in the classroom. Avis (2005: 212) identifies how this shift towards performance management is at odds with the rhetoric of the knowledge economy, which places an onus on a non-hierarchical approach based on trusting and respectful relationships between teams.

Participatory action research challenges the positivistic form of enquiry in its political approach and establishes a relationship between researcher and participant (Reason and Bradbury, 2001). It does this by facilitating the research group taking ownership of the whole process (from commencement to conclusion) and sustaining an effective dialogue between researcher and respondent. My personal position as an 'insider' with 'insider knowledge' of marginalized communities was a key motivation to becoming a basic skills tutor and becoming involved in this study. For example, my own life history, which includes being born and brought up in the same community as the learners, attending the local state school and being the first generation of my family to enter college and university, and my subsequent trajectory, has greatly influenced the commitment I have for finding opportunities to enable others to aspire to reach their potential (Duckworth and Taylor, 2008).

The appeal of participatory action research is that in claiming to 'empower' it has the potential to address the profound inequalities in power between the participants and the researcher. Indeed, as well as the knowledge gained in the form of outcomes and findings that we will explore next, there are additional benefits gained from the process of the research, such as the relationships formed. This has been so much so, that I consider myself to be a friend of the research group and, for a few, a good friend. These friendships have enriched our lives, enriched me as a person, and are an important impact of the research.

My drive came from the knowledge that education can be truly life enhancing and transforming if appropriate mechanisms are put in place to push open spaces that create a meaningful enquiry into the learners' lives.

Practitioner research and professional development

As a professional in the lifelong learning sector, you should always try to maintain your professional development and learning. People can assume that once they have achieved qualified status, they don't need to learn any more. This can be compounded by heavy workloads and long working hours, where space for reflection and engagement in continuing professional development (CPD) is limited. However, finding the space to carry out practitioner research can be empowering for both yourself and your learners.

Case study: A research practitioner's journey, Angela Brzeski

I currently work as a lecturer in Post-Compulsory Education and Training (PCET) at the Faculty of Education at a university in the North West of England. Here I discuss my practitioner research experiences and, more importantly, the impact of this experience, both on my own learners and on me as a teaching professional.

My practitioner research journey began just over a decade ago. At that point in time I had worked as a lecturer at the same college for eight years, and was a section leader responsible for curriculum management. Although my work kept me physically very busy, I wanted to challenge myself more academically. I already had a BA degree and a PGCE, and so I decided to enrol on a part-time two-year MA programme at a local university. I opted for the MA in Education (Through Research). At first I thought I was going to regret taking on a research degree – the terminology used in early research lectures and seminars was, at best, daunting, and at worst, baffling and confusing. However, once I started my research, and so put theory into practice, it all seemed to make much more sense. For my MA, I investigated the behaviour of students in further education classrooms, and the impact of disciplinary policy on this behaviour. In my research, not only did I collect the perspectives of the staff (via questionnaires and one-to-one interviews), but I also gained the views of the students themselves on the policy. This acquisition of the student 'voice' was fundamental to my research. It gave me a unique lens through which to view the students in our classrooms. My MA fuelled my motivation to get involved in further practitioner research and led to me gaining a secondment for a period of three years to work as a College-Based Research Co-ordinator (CBRC) for the Literacies for Learning in Further Education (LfLFE) Project (Ivanič et al., 2009). The LfLFE Project was a collaboration between two universities – Stirling and Lancaster – and four further education colleges, two in Scotland and two in England, including my own North West College. The project drew on work already done on literacy practices engaged in by people in schools, higher education, and the community (see, for example, Barton and

Hamilton, 1998; Barton et al., 2000) and aimed to extend the insights gained from these studies into further education. It aimed to explore the literacy practices of students and those practices developed in different parts of the curriculum. It was the first major study of literacy practices in colleges in the UK, and it was exciting to be part of it.

As the CBRC for the LfLFE Project at North West College, I coordinated fellow lecturers who were also working on the same project. I oversaw the research undertaken and carried out my own data collection, analysis and writing up in conjunction with the Lancaster University-based research team. The practitioner research experience I gained via working alongside a highly experienced, professional research team, who had already gained the respect of the national and international research communities, is certainly the pinnacle of my practitioner research career thus far.

Being involved in the research enriched my own practitioner research skills, and importantly the findings of the LfLFE Project were not detached from my work as a lecturer. Towards the end of the life of the LfLFE Project I took part in a range of knowledge dissemination activities, including presentations to the North West College senior management team, as well as to the management and staff within various departments of the college, thus contributing to staff professional development. My knowledge and skills gained from my work on the LfLFE Project, together with my MA in Education (Through Research), has also enabled me to add to my own breadth of teaching experience. Since working on the project, I have taught action research which involved supervising trainee teachers to carry out their own research projects – i.e. in research design, methodology, data collection, and data analysis. Trainee teachers in these groups noted my passion for research and have commented on how this inspired them to undertake their own research journeys and carry out their own research within their own practice.

Whilst working on the LfLFE Project, I was encouraged by the Director of the LfLFE Project, Professor Ivanič, to continue my own research at PhD level. So, with a little trepidation, in 2005 I enrolled on a part-time PhD. My focus was to explore the relationship between literacy practices, literacy demands, and engagement in learning within further education. Today, in my role as a teacher trainer, the knowledge and skills I have gained as a practitioner researcher, via the completion of my MA in Education (Through Research), my secondment on the LfLFE Project, and my PhD research, collectively enrich and enhance my day-to-day work in several ways. Firstly, I frequently refer to the findings of my research, all of which were carried out in further education settings, to underpin my delivery and class discussions with trainees who are themselves preparing to work in the same, or similar, settings. Secondly, the research skills I have gained have provided me with the parity to participate in collaborative research and dissemination activities with my university peers. For example, I joined one of the joint authors of this textbook in a presentation delivered at a recent Centre for Learner Identity Studies (CLIS) conference. Thirdly, my academic writing skills have developed to the extent that I now have responsibility for the development and enhancement of the academic writing skills of all the PCET trainees across the whole of the University PCET Partnership. Finally, and most importantly, there is no doubt that my practitioner research skills were a major factor in helping me to secure a university position, and so make the move out of further education and into the higher education setting. So I credit my practitioner research skills for enabling me to achieve my personal dreams and goals.

Insider research

The term 'insider research' is used to describe studies where the researcher has a direct involvement or linking with the research setting. Such research contrasts with traditional notions of scientifically sound research in which the researcher is an 'objective outsider' studying subjects external to herself/himself. There are a number of ways in which a researcher can be considered an 'insider'. Think about your positioning as a practitioner researcher. You may be considered an 'insider' because you are carrying out a study in your work setting. Researchers may also be members of their own community, and a focus may be to empower communities to take action, such as being involved in writing projects that aim to validate their experiences and take them into the public domain to empower the wider community (Duckworth, 2011). You may also want to consider the research carried out by Vicky. She was carrying out participatory action research with her learners, but they were also from the same community that Vicky had been born and brought up in. They were linked in the past and present.

Case study: Vicky's research journal

At the beginning of the study, although I was situated as an outsider in relation to my workplace and the college's instrumental and functional approach to staff development, which contrasted with carrying out PAR (staff are seen as the receivers of knowledge rather than the generators), in relation to the participants I was positioned as an 'insider' in the sense of my working-class history, my role as research practitioner, and the participatory and collaborative nature of the ethnographic study which follows the view:

> *Educational research is critical analysis directed at the transformation of educational practices, the educational understandings and educational values of those involved in the process, and social and institutional structures which provide frameworks for their action.*

> (Carr and Kemmis, 1986: 156)

This position challenged those approaches to knowledge which suppose that those people with distanced and 'objective' views of practice (for example, researchers from the academy) can best understand and steer practitioners who are seen as too close to practice to embrace an accurate perception of it. Rather than seeking out *experts* from the academy, the approach I took allowed me to take ownership of, and understand, my own practice. Rather than being positioned as passive and not a maker of knowledge, becoming a researcher practitioner – and the impact of this – strengthened me as a critical educator, empowered me, and has helped me to generate knowledge that I used to improve my classroom practice (for example, designing resources *with* rather than *for* learners) and open up my way of thinking to move towards more critical and emancipatory approaches to classroom practice.

Linking educational research with your subject specialism

It is important to remember that educational research does not need to stand in isolation from your subject specialism. Indeed, practitioner research can be made all the richer from drawing on your vocational area, whether that is nursing, construction, hairdressing, etc.

Case study: James Burrow, PGCE student

My name is James Burrow, and I am a PGCE Post-Compulsory Education and Training student. My aim is to further link my subject specialism with teaching and do a PhD. As a recently qualified postgraduate and active practitioner within the creative arts, I have been involved in a number of projects, working alongside my peers in both practice-led research and research-led practice.

This work has included a number of productions where I have not only been explicitly involved in the composition of a research *question*, but also simply as a participant. More often than not, my area of expertise within physical and movement-based theatres has led me to key practical roles involving the creation of physical languages for performance.

For example, in May 2011, I worked as part of a team of practitioners (with varying areas of expertise) on a production of Euripides' Medea at the Rose Theatre, Ormskirk. Within this six-month project we set out to investigate aspects of cross-cultural performance, and specifically for myself, to gain insight into how an audience, or reader of performance, perceives physical movement as text.

It is this interest in creative practice, this search for further knowledge and interest in *how we gain knowledge*, that solidified my resolve to become a teacher within the lifelong learning sector. I am currently on placement and am teaching BTEC Extended Diploma in Performing Arts. I have found my experience within action research invaluable as a reflective practitioner within the sector – not only considering my subject specialism, but within the wider context of learning.

The reflexive transition between *academic* and *teacher* has been one that, for me, emphasizes the marriage of creative and academic interests – specifically in devising theatre, research in the fields of site-specificity, and facilitation as a mode of teaching. When read quickly, these somewhat overarching concepts may seem instantly credible, perhaps even eliciting a fluent combination of scholarly and creative interests with the role of the academic. In truth, you could say it has been a marriage of uneasiness, as it still remains difficult, especially within the Arts, to accommodate creative interests in unison with the augmentation of creditable research.

As somebody relevantly inexperienced until recently in the educational sector, what I am attempting to create at this point is an analogy between *performing* and *teaching* as active research methods. At this point in my career I would suggest that the physical act of *performing* is intrinsically connected to that of facilitating the acquisition of knowledge, and as such, should be treated similarly in terms of research they can produce.

If I had to choose just one aspect of research-based postgraduate study that will have the most profound effect upon my teaching career, it would be to remember that research findings are not only contained within an *end product*, but that there is something explicit within any *creative process* that provides some form of critical or otherwise prudent information. Taking into account that I will be teaching within the creative arts, I would suggest that when the sometimes bawdy and impulsive aspects of the discipline are married with the attitude that knowledge can be gained through active process, then practice-led research finds its niche.

Conclusions

In this era of compliance and delivery, practitioner research based on informed professional judgements offers a way to teachers to embrace practitioner-led research and become more active in crucial educational policy-making arenas. For many practitioners, research is not a luxury that they can solely focus on; it needs to be balanced with what is often a busy teaching load, and other responsibilities. Practitioner research is fundamental to developing a greater understanding of the work of practitioners and what happens in the classroom, but it should also enable professionals to widen their thinking and approaches to teaching and learning as educationalists. Being involved in action research allows you to come to your own understandings about your own teaching. It is based on the belief that the practitioner is the best judge of her or his practice.

Practitioner research can be demanding; it is a challenging and exacting undertaking. It requires open-mindedness, courage, honesty in the face of self-critique and public sharing, emotional fortitude in dealing with uncertainty and profound change, emotional and spiritual energy in sustaining curiosity, compassion, and the ongoing drive in the search for new, improved practices. We would argue, that those practitioners who take this journey demonstrate the uppermost levels of professionalism in using and developing these qualities. They offer innovative role models for others and help to build a new climate for responsible and accountable professionalism.

References and further reading

Avis, J. (2005) Beyond performativity: reflections on activist professionalism and the labour process in further education. *Journal of Education Policy*, 20(2): 209–22.

Barton, D. and Hamilton, M. (1998) *Local Literacies: Reading and Writing in One Community.* London: Routledge.

Barton, D., Hamilton, M. and Ivanič, R. (eds.) (2000) *Situated Literacies: Reading and Writing in Context.* London: Routledge.

Boud, D., Cressey, P. and Docherty, P. (2005) *Productive Reflection at Work.* London: Routledge.

Brzeski, A. (2008) Portfolio building: the relationship with literacies in students' everyday lives. *Literacy and Numeracy Studies*, 16(1): 25–38.

Carr, W. and Kemmis, S. (1986) *Becoming Critical: Education, Knowledge and Action Research.* Lewes: Routledge Falmer.

Coffey, A. (2002) Ethnography and self: reflections and representations, in T. May (ed.) *Qualitative Research in Action*. London: Sage: 313–31.

Davies, C. A. (2008) *Reflexive Ethnography: A Guide to Researching Selves and Others*. Second edition. London: Routledge.

Duckworth, V. (2011) Developing an organisational culture where social justice and collaboration runs alongside widening participation, in L. Thomas and M. Tight (eds.) *Institutional Transformation to Engage a Diverse Student Body* (International Perspectives on Higher Education Research, Volume 6). Bingley: Emerald: 311–18.

Duckworth, V. and Taylor, K. (2008) Words are for everyone. *Research and Practice in Adult Literacy*, 64: 30–2.

Elliott, J. (1991) *Action Research for Educational Change*. Buckingham: Open University Press.

Gibbs, P. (2007) Practical wisdom and the workplace researcher. *London Review of Education*, 5(3): 223–36.

Hamilton, M., Davies, P. and James, K. (2007) *Practitioners Leading Research: A Report of Action Research Projects from the NRDC Practitioner-Led Research Initiative (PLRI)*. London: NRDC.

Ivanič, R., Edwards, R., Barton, D. et al. (2009) *Improving Learning in College: Rethinking Literacies Across the Curriculum*. London: Routledge.

Johnson, C., Duckworth, V., McNamara, M. and Apelbaum, C. (2010) A tale of two adult learners: from adult basic education to degree completion. *National Association for Developmental Education Digest*, 5(1): 57–67.

Kemmis, S. and McTaggart, R. (2005) Participatory action research: communicative action and the public sphere, in N. Denzin and Y. Lincoln (eds.) *The Sage Handbook of Qualitative Research*. Third edition. London: Sage: 559–604.

Kemmis, S. and Wilkinson, M. (1998) Participatory action research and the study of practice, in B. Atweh, S. Kemmis and P. Weeks (eds.) *Action Research in Practice: Partnerships for Social Justice in Education*. London: Routledge: 21–36.

McNiff, J., Lomax, P. and Whitehead, J. (1996) *You and Your Action Research Project*. London: Routledge.

Reason, P. and Bradbury, H. (2001) *Handbook of Action Research: Participative Inquiry and Practice*. London: Sage.

Reason, P. and Bradbury, H. (2008) *Handbook of Action Research: Participative Inquiry and Practice*. London: Sage.

Schön, D. A. (1983) *The Reflective Practitioner: How Professionals Think in Action*. USA: Basic Books.

Stanley, L. and Wise, S. (1993) *Breaking Out Again: Feminist Ontology and Epistemology*. London: Routledge.

3   Models of research

By the end of this chapter you should be able to:

- Understand different models of research

- Critically understand how these research models may be applied to your practitioner research

- Recognize key terminology and concepts and use them when describing your own research project

Introduction

If you picked up a copy of a recent education journal, such as the *Journal of Vocational Education and Training* or the *Journal of Further and Higher Education*, you would find that the articles inside them would all be based on different approaches to, or models of, research. There isn't just 'one way' of doing education research, just as there isn't 'one way' of planning a lesson or assessing a group of BTEC students. The ways in which we do our research vary according to our needs and the specific requirements of our project. And these issues apply whether or not we are doing relatively small-scale practitioner research (as discussed in the previous chapter), or whether we are doing much longer-term in-depth research over a period of two or three years (or even longer). So what are all of these different ways of doing research, and why do we have them? There are a few ways to think about this. Parts of the answer are to do with the history of research more generally, in a broad sense. Other parts of the answer are to do with philosophy, and the ways in which definitions of words such as 'knowledge' have changed over time (and they have). And some parts of the answer are to do with political and social changes, particularly over the last 70 years or so.

Research that uses numbers and statistics: quantitative methods

Although it is no longer really the case, it was once thought – by researchers and scholars – that if research was going to be robust and rigorous it had to be carried out in such a way that what were termed *scientific* principles could be applied to it. This is why the social sciences – the broad curriculum that education studies and education research both belong to – are called social *sciences* and not, for example, social *arts*. It was thought that the *scientific method* – of having a hypothesis that was then tested out under laboratory conditions in order to find out if the hypothesis was true or not – was the best way of doing research – not only relating to chemistry, say, but also to other areas of knowledge such as psychology, which a lot of early education research was based on. If a theory or hypothesis could be proved true in the laboratory, then it was assumed that these conclusions would be true the world over. Or, to put it another way, if a theory or hypothesis was proved to be true in the laboratory, then a new piece of knowledge would be said to have been discovered; the scientists in question would have found out something that had been waiting to be discovered, that could now be proved to be a fact. However, this approach to the establishment of new facts or new knowledge through the research process makes certain assumptions about what knowledge actually is. In research of this kind, it is assumed that the truth is out there waiting to be discovered (by the scientists, in this case), and that it can only be discovered if proper scientific methods are used in the process. That is why the scientific method is so important. It is only through the proper application of the correct logical methods that knowledge can be established. And this kind of approach to knowledge, which is referred to as *positivism*, dominated scientific and social scientific research until the twentieth century.

In order to carry out this kind of research, the researcher would have to use proper scientific or mathematical methods of analysis, simply because those were the kinds of methods of analysis that were assumed to be the right ones – because they were based on logic and on deductive reasoning. Therefore, if the researcher was going to do this kind of research, then he (it was usually a 'he' in those days) would have to collect data that was suitable for these kinds of mathematical or scientific analysis: numbers. Numbers can be treated to all kinds of statistical inference or modelling. Once data has been gathered (and, where necessary, converted into numerical form), then these bodies of numbers can be analysed using scientific methods: statistical analysis. Research such as this is referred to as *quantitative research*.

Data for quantitative research can be obtained in different ways. One common form of quantitative research uses the statistics that are routinely gathered by different government departments, which can then be analysed in order to answer particular questions, or to prove or disprove a particular hypothesis. The use of statistical tools can allow the researcher to combine and contrast different bodies of statistical data in order to look for relationships between them. So, for example, a researcher might use the examination results for all the students who took an AS level exam in psychology as one body of data, and use these to establish what the 'average' AS level grade might be. Our researcher might then use different data sets relating to unemployment levels to establish which parts of the country had higher unemployment levels than others. She or he might then look at the AS psychology results for two areas with high unemployment, and two areas with low unemployment, to establish whether or not there was a relationship between unemployment levels and examination success. Having analysed all of these statistics (and this would involve hundreds and hundreds of numbers, but modern computer software makes this bit of the research much easier and quicker than it used to be) she or he may well be able to conclude that in areas of higher than average unemployment, AS psychology results were lower than the national average. And because the data would have covered the whole of the country, she or he can say that the research is robust and reliable.

Of course, we don't have to rely on the statistics collected by government agencies or awarding bodies to do quantitative research. It may well be the case that we have established some research questions that cannot be answered solely through using bodies of data that already exist. In these cases we will need to generate our own data, rather than collect someone else's, before we apply our statistical models of analysis. But we will need to generate sufficiently large amounts of numerical data if our statistical methods are going to be appropriate and if we are going to argue that the findings from our research are going to have wide or profound implications. One good way to do this is through *questionnaires* (we shall discuss these in more depth in Chapter 6). Questionnaires are an appropriate tool for gathering quantitative data, for two reasons. Firstly, we can set up the questions in such a way that the answers people give are numerical ones. This might be done through a *Likert Scale*, which is when the respondent is asked to give a grade from 1 to 5 to indicate the extent to which they agree or disagree with a particular statement. Or it might be done through asking respondents to provide simple yes/no answers to a number of questions. Secondly, questionnaires are cheap and easy to produce on a large scale – and this is more true than ever thanks to the growth of online questionnaire tools such as *SurveyMonkey* which are straightforward to use. Therefore, it is perfectly feasible to send out a questionnaire to hundreds, even thousands, of potential respondents. Data gathered from such large groups, it is argued, is more likely to be reliable than if we had only sent our questionnaire to a couple of dozen. Once the results come in, it is a simple task to feed the results into our computers and analyse the answers, which can then be expressed in a table or a chart, or perhaps as an equation.

Digging deeper and talking with people: qualitative research

One of the more common criticisms of quantitative research is that it doesn't really go deep enough. Questionnaires can be long and detailed, but if they are too long then people won't fill them in. If you are restricting your respondents to 'yes' or 'no' answers then there's no room for ambiguity. If you are asking your respondents to award a score of between 1 and 5 to a series of comments or statements, then you are – arguably – distorting the research through the very fact of having provided these statements. There's no space for the respondent to offer potentially interesting ideas or to question the assumptions that those statements rest upon. Knowing, thanks to an analysis of relevant statistics, that educational achievement is lower in areas of poverty than of relative affluence is clearly important. But *why* might this be the case?

Over recent decades, education researchers, drawing on the kinds of research done by anthropologists (people who research human social and cultural organization and activity) and sociologists (people who investigate the ways that societies are constructed) have begun to use approaches to their research that are quite different to those of the quantitative researchers. Instead of carrying out large-scale but shallow surveys of large numbers of people, these researchers do their work with much smaller numbers of people, but in much greater depth. Such immersive research tends to be carried out through observations, through living with the people being researched, interviewing them, and exploring their habits, practices and attitudes. Research such as this tends to generate textual, not numerical, data. Examples include the notes that researchers take during observations, the transcripts that researchers make of their conversations with their respondents, and the descriptions that they write down of the places that they visit. Research such as this is referred to as *qualitative research*.

Qualitative researchers have, over time, gone to considerable effort to establish the reliability and rigour of their work. Partly, this has been as a response to arguments from quantitative researchers, who have criticized qualitative researchers for being unscientific, for using methods that are too prone to being biased and partial, and for conducting research that is too narrow in scope to be more widely useful. And partly this has been a process of development over time: as qualitative approaches have become more established, more time and effort has gone into understanding and exploring an increasingly diverse range of methodologies. Sometimes these changes reflect broader changes in the world: the development of cheap photography equipment has allowed researchers to use photography in their work. As a consequence, scholars and theorists have had to explore the methodological implications of using photographs for research purposes. The recent proliferation of books about researching online provides another example.

A second significant element of differences between quantitative and qualitative approaches – or *paradigms* – is in how each approach defines and understands knowledge. The positivist foundations of quantitative research stand in stark contrast to qualitative research. Rather than seeing knowledge as the production of the rigorous application of the scientific method, qualitative researchers instead see knowledge as something that is created, not that is waiting to be discovered through the scientific testing of a hypothesis. Rather than resting on a positivist approach, qualitative research instead rests on an anti-positivist or *interpretivist* understanding of knowledge. According to this paradigm, knowledge is the production of the social world, of interactions between people who talk or write about what they understand and what they do, and how they explain or justify their practices. Rather than talking about hypotheses that have been established as being true, qualitative researchers instead make more circumspect suggestions, arguing that their research demonstrates particular themes or ideas, but that cannot be held to be universally applicable.

The kinds of data collection methods used in a qualitative research project are therefore quite different from those used in a quantitative project. Some of these have already been mentioned – observations, interviews and photography. Other methods include holding focus groups, and the analysis of texts, video and film. All of these different kinds of data are then written up, and turned into a textual form, before they are analysed. Qualitative data analysis is therefore very different from quantitative data analysis. Instead of using mathematical or other scientific procedures for testing or investigating the data, qualitative researchers take a much more hands-on approach, reading and then rereading the observation notes and interview transcripts, looking for ideas, issues or themes that come up time and again in what people say or how they have been observed to behave. The researcher then goes through all of this data, slicing and rearranging it so that all of the different sections of data that relate to each idea or theme are grouped together. Then she or he can begin to write their account of their research, to tell the story about whatever it is they have been researching, using all of the relevant data. Rather than presenting the data in a chart or a grid, qualitative research relies on the same mode as the data: words.

> **Case study: Qualitative approaches to the collection of data (Vicky Duckworth)**

One aim of my research was to explore how 16 former basic skills learners from classes I taught literacy to had been shaped by the public domain of schooling, college and work, and the private domain of family, friends and home. I also sought to highlight the related impact of class and gender on the learners' pathways onto basic skills programmes, and their subsequent career or study routes.

I was sceptical about *questionnaires* as a primary collection of data because they can be biased to the researcher's own beliefs and values. Further to this, forms including questionnaires can be very intimidating, and even more so for adult literacy learners. They may also feel embarrassed about being assisted by family members or tutors. This negative experience has the potential to disengage the learners from the research. However, a questionnaire can also allow the respondents to maintain their distance if they prefer. After deliberation, I devised a brief questionnaire, recording key information related to the learners' yearly progression. Later, further questions were added which focused on how the learners viewed their progress. The completion of the questionnaires was optional. With skills and confidence developing, a number of learners who were initially unconfident about questionnaires took part.

I also accessed and utilized (with consent), a number of *documents*: creative writing, artwork, greeting cards, and family trees. History archives, statistical and economic records, and media reports were also incorporated into the research. A quantity of the information was collected from visits to the library and a local history centre. Where possible, I also collected learners' diagnostic assessment results, individual learning plans, Educational Support Unit reports showing mental health issues, assessments relating to learning difficulties such as dyslexia and the like, and examples of course work.

Mixed methods research: the best of both worlds?

These days, quantitative and qualitative researchers tend to get on pretty well with each other (although this was not always the case). The expansion of books and journal articles covering qualitative research methodology has helped create a robust field of research practice that no longer tries to somehow copy the scientific method of the quantitative paradigm, but instead can be seen as being robust, rigorous and trustworthy *on its own terms*. And at the same time, the interpretivist approach to knowledge has rubbed off onto quantitative researchers, who have increasingly come to acknowledge the limitations of their own methods, and the fact that the knowledge that they report is not necessarily 'more true' than that reported by qualitative researchers. From this perspective, it is not difficult to see how the use of research methods from *both* paradigms – an approach referred to as *mixed methods research* – can be seen as being highly desirable. What could be better than combining the breadth and numerical scale of quantitative data with the rich and detailed world that is presented to us by qualitative data?

So mixed methods research does seem to be an attractive option for the researcher. But we need to be wary of overstating the benefits. There are two main points to raise here. Firstly, it is not the case that mixed methods research is 'better' or 'more robust' than 'just' qualitative or quantitative research. Within the research community, nobody really takes seriously any more the idea that these different kinds of research should be evaluated using the same benchmarks or criteria. One is not better than the other – they are simply different, that's all. And mixed methods research isn't simply a mix of quantitative and qualitative: it's a synthesis or blend of approaches that are derived from both of these paradigms. In a way, it may be better to think of mixed methods research as a distinct paradigm in itself. If we do this, then this leads into the second point that needs to be made, which is that the choices that we make as to which overall approach to research we should adopt should depend on what our research questions are, and nothing else. If we need to use quantitative methods to answer our research questions, then that's what we should do; likewise for qualitative methods. And if our question needs to be answered through a mixture of broad and large-scale with close-up and fine-grained methods, then a mixed approach is the one to take. Different paradigms of research are best suited to different kinds of research. But the place to start is: 'What am I trying to find out?', not: 'Do I prefer doing interviews or doing statistics?'.

Case study: Mixed methods approaches to research (Paula Litherland)

I currently work as a college lecturer teaching fitness units for the BTEC Uniformed Public Services course. Research has motivated me to take a more reflective stance to teaching, and has developed other skills, since reflection helps you understand your own responses to different situations and improves the way you deal with them, which is really important to teaching. When I was writing my dissertation I realized that the most important starting point was to determine a focused hypothesis. I needed to decide what theory I was testing, and who the results would be of use to; after all, a piece of research and presentation of findings is more beneficial if you can help a company and organization make positive changes to the way they operate. My research aimed to answer the hypothesis: *introducing fitness testing to a group of non-obese, middle-aged, female members at a private health club will have a positive impact on cardiorespiratory fitness and body composition.* I took a quantitative and qualitative approach to the study, which was conducted over a ten-week period, since it was important to measure the difference in cardiorespiratory fitness and body fat to decide if the new fitness testing had made a positive impact.

Quantitative data: The differences in body fat percentage between the subjects in each group at week 1 and week 10 were analysed statistically using SPSS software. The differences in the maximum volume of oxygen used while exercising by each subject (again at week 1 and week 10), were also analysed statistically. *Qualitative data*: I decided to conduct interviews with each participant. The questions were piloted and adapted to ensure the questions extracted the information required to reflect the study question. The interviews were intended to capture any other non-physical improvements that the participants may have experienced. Interviews were held with the participants to capture their thoughts and views in relation to the service they received based around fitness testing, analysing if there were any other non-physical improvements to their health, along with determinants for their regular exercise.

Other ways of knowing: Marxist, feminist and postmodernist influences on educational research

In the preceding discussion, we have discussed how quantitative and qualitative approaches to research rest, in part, on different conceptions of what knowledge is. At this time, it is important to note that both the *positivist* and *interpretivist* philosophies that we referred to are not solely the concern of researchers (whether they are education researchers or not). Rather, these are the product of long-established philosophical inquiry. Positivism can be traced back to the philosophers of science of the late eighteenth and nineteenth centuries, and was further developed in the twentieth century, not least by psychologists. Behaviourist psychology (which will be familiar to many of the readers of this book) is a product of positivist philosophy. Interpretivism (originally known as anti-positivism) sprang up in the nineteenth century. Karl Marx was an early critic of positivist philosophy, although it was not until the twentieth century that interpretivism established itself through the work of continental sociologists such as Max Weber and Émile Durkheim. As such, it is important to note that other branches of philosophical and political inquiry have had an impact on how researchers go about their work. Two other important philosophical and cultural movements of the twentieth century have also had a profound impact on how educational research is conducted: feminism and postmodernism. We shall discuss both of these in turn.

Feminist influences on educational research

There are many different views among women who identify themselves as feminists about what women's oppression entails, what its sources are, and what should be done about it. Feminist research has arisen as a legitimate, relevant and popular research model for many feminists who have sought to understand women's (and men's) experiences in a culture that, to many, is considered patriarchal. Feminist researchers – depending on their definition of feminism – tend to develop methods and preferences for techniques that they see as yielding the best results for women. In seeking to break the ties of masculine domination perpetuated within existing models of research that are seen to occupy an exclusively male perspective, there has been a conscious move away from a positivist approach, which is deemed by feminists as offering a distorted world picture. As an alternative, research studies that occupy a feminist perspective look towards building and sustaining alternative frameworks which challenge the focus on the public domain whereby many women's voices were not heard, and the perspective of men are viewed as 'universal'. There have been several stages in the development of feminist research, which include feminist empiricism, feminist postmodernism, and standpoint epistemology. However, despite the variety that is to be found in feminist theory and methodology, feminist researchers continue to share many broad and particular standards and principles, reflected in their research theory and practice. These revolve around an ideological positioning whereby males and females are considered physically and emotionally different. By contrast, in the past men have been deemed superior, and women have been sidelined and marginalized (for example, not having the same opportunity to take senior positions in organizations, due to a glass ceiling), while male superiority has continued, despite the emergence of equality policies and political assurances. Feminist researchers might employ qualitative or quantitative methodologies.

The aims of feminist research include: uncovering of the structures and conditions that contribute to gender inequality; a commitment to inform society at large of the factors that generate this phenomenon, and put forward ways that can help alleviate it; empowering women, and giving them a voice to speak about social life from *their own point of view* (this is often referred to as *women's ways of knowing*); and contributing towards social change and transformation (where the influence of political movements such as Marxism can be most readily seen – although this is not to equate feminist research with Marxist research).

Postmodernist influences on educational research

Postmodernism isn't a philosophy as such. Rather, it's a broader range of ideas and concepts that can perhaps best be summed up as 'looking at things in new ways, even if the existing ways seem to be working'. Existing theories or concepts tend to be critiqued, or even distrusted, by postmodernists who often reject overarching explanations or concepts. The roots of postmodernism can be traced back to the early twentieth century, when it was a term used to describe particular approaches to the arts; and, as time went on, it was used to describe new approaches to literature, history, sociology and science.

Postmodernist influences on educational research can be seen at work in several different ways, and these can cause significant challenges to the work that a researcher does. For example, one radical critique of the process of conducting qualitative interviews is that each interview will always be a unique occurrence that can never be repeated. What will be said during the interview will depend on, and be affected by, any number of things. These might be quite profound, such as the political standpoint of the interviewer or the interviewee, or relatively prosaic, such as the weather, or how tired somebody is. So what is the interviewer able to do in taking the data that is generated during the interview and subjecting it to analysis? Is what the respondent says in any way connected to how the respondent actually thinks about the issue at hand; or has the entire conversation been affected by the fact that the interviewer didn't get much sleep the night before, or has been distracted by problems at work? If the interview was conducted again after another week, how might the conversation go? And the potential impact of issues such as these can be extended to the entire research process: to the ways in which people fill in questionnaires, and to the ways in which they behave when being observed.

The difficulty here is 'when to stop'. If we assume that there is no data collection method that is not tainted by subjectivity, bias, or any other more or less temporary factor that serves to influence how it's done, then how can we do any research at all, or write any accounts based on either qualitative or quantitative data that will in any way be reliable? Perhaps the best way to proceed is to adopt a more practical or *pragmatic* approach, one that acknowledges the difficulties we face in establishing the reliability of our data, but that at the same time lets us, as researchers, have enough confidence to say that if the same themes or stories *keep emerging from our data*, then we have reached a point where our findings can be said to be sufficiently robust to be worthy of writing up.

A patchwork of methodologies: *bricolage* approaches to research

It would seem to be the case that there is more than one way of looking at the world, more than one way of constructing and understanding knowledge about the world in which we live, and about small bits of which we do research. And, if the way we think about knowledge changes, then this has implications for how we do our research and how we interpret our data. The problem here is: how do we know which way of looking at the world is the 'right' one? Is one of them 'better' than another, or is it simply the case that 50 years from now we will have to rewrite all of the research methodology books *again* in order to take account of new ways of understanding knowledge and the world?

Some researchers have sought to address this problem of multiple ways of knowing, and the associated multiple ways of doing research, by making this multiplicity a virtue, not a problem, and by acknowledging that perhaps doing things in more than one way – or rather, using research methodologies from more than one paradigm – might in itself be an appropriate way to work. This approach is referred to as *bricolage*, originally a French word that refers to the way in which buildings in different architectural styles produce a 'jumbled up' effect when they are all close together, and which in a research sense now refers to the way in which *bricoleur* researchers draw on different methodological approaches, as and when they are needed, while engaged in their research project. Whatever method is needed to answer the research questions under review is the one to use. This may well involve methodologies that are incompatible – for example, combining feminist and postmodernist perspectives – but *bricoleur* researchers accept this on the grounds that since the world is such a complex place, it makes sense to draw on different theoretical or methodological perspectives to make sense of it. Put simply, no one theoretical approach is sufficient. Therefore, researchers need to be upfront about their use of different approaches, which they can add to or tinker with as the research continues.

Conclusions: doing your research project in the lifelong learning sector

For most of the people reading this book – and for whom this book has been written! – it is more likely than not that a qualitative approach will be the paradigm that is taken. To some extent, this is a reflection of the fact that, for many of you, some version of *practitioner research* (as discussed in the preceding chapter) will be the direction you take.

And to some extent this is due to practicalities. Many of you will not have the time or resources to conduct the kind of large-scale data collection that a properly quantitative project requires. This is not to say that numbers or statistics need be entirely absent from your research. But sending a questionnaire to 40 students, and then having interviews with ten of them, does not mean that your project is mixed methods! Forty questionnaires aren't really enough to generate enough numerical data to be put to robust scrutiny; whereas ten interviews will generate a significant amount of rich data (and we shall return to these issues in Chapter 6).

But it is important to remember that, should you adopt a qualitative approach to your educational research project, you understand why this is the case. The decision to adopt a qualitative approach should not be based on a reluctance to do statistics (which the computers will do for you anyway), or a feeling that doing interviews is easy (it isn't), but on the simple idea that a qualitative approach is the *best fit* for your research questions: no more and no less.

References and further reading

Fontana, A. and Frey, J. (2000) The interview: from structured questions to negotiated text, in N. Denzin and Y. Lincoln (eds.) *Handbook of Qualitative Research*. Second edition. London: Sage: 645–70.

Hammersley, M. (2008) *Questioning Qualitative Inquiry*. London: Sage.

Kincheloe, J. and Berry, K. (2004) *Rigour and Complexity in Education Research: Conceptualising the Bricolage*. Maidenhead: Open University Press.

Mies, M. (1999) Towards a methodology for feminist research, in M. Hammersley (ed.) *Social Researching: Philosophy, Politics and Practice*. London: Sage: 64–82.

Ramazanoglu, C. and Holland, J. (2004) *Feminist Methodology: Challenges and Choices*. London: Sage.

Schostak, J. F. (2002) *Understanding, Designing and Conducting Qualitative Research in Education*. Buckingham: Open University Press.

Scott, D. and Usher, R. (1999) *Researching Education: Data, Methods and Theory in Educational Enquiry*. London: Continuum.

Thomas, G. (2007) *Education and Theory: Strangers in Paradigms*. Maidenhead: McGraw Hill/Open University Press.

4 Asking questions

By the end of this chapter you should be able to:

- Understand the processes involved in selecting a topic for your own research

- Discuss how research questions can be derived from the research topic

- Understand the importance of contextualizing your own research through reference to prior literature

Introduction

In Chapter 1, we spent some time thinking about the broad aims of educational research. One of the themes that we discussed was the role that research can play in answering questions. The kinds of questions that researchers seek to unpack can be profound and far-reaching; or they can be small-scale and localized. There is plenty of room for both. Nor is it the case that far-reaching questions are necessarily better, or more important, than more local or prosaic ones. They are simply different, in just the same way that quantitative research is different from qualitative research (which is the research paradigm that we identify with in this book).

Different researchers and research projects can ask very different kinds of questions, therefore. The reasons why social and economic factors impact on the performance of students when they take their A levels (a thorny issue which is, at the time of writing this book, being hotly debated by politicians and university admissions tutors as part of a broader discussion about widening participation to university-level education) would require exploration through a research project of substantial scale if any meaningful answers are going to be proposed at a national level. The reasons why a particular group of young people from a specific, single school chose to enrol on the courses they did at their local further education college would, of course, be a much more localized project. Both of these research topics would need to be planned and carried out with equal care and diligence, ensuring that appropriate permissions were received, that appropriate research methods were chosen, and that frameworks for analysis were situated in appropriate theories. But at the end of the day, they would both be about answering some questions, some *research questions*, within the field of educational research.

Other styles or paradigms of educational research might not rest on specific research questions, however. More open-ended – *exploratory* – research is also found within education. It may well be the case that a researcher, or group of researchers, are interested in extending their – and our – understanding of issues or practices that are only loosely defined or understood. Rather than answering questions, such research might in fact raise them, turning over stones without necessarily describing everything that they find underneath. More open-ended research such as this needs to be carried out on a large scale, however, either over a considerable period of time (years rather than months) or over a considerable organizational, institutional or geographical span. Research such as this is beyond the scope of this book (not least as it is beyond the scope of the kinds of students with whom we work and for whom this book is primarily written).

Instead, as our focus is on small-scale research, practitioner research, local case studies or action research, we need to think about how to frame research questions that are aligned to these methodological frameworks. And we always need to keep in mind the fact that the processes through which we plan small-scale research projects for undergraduate or masters-level programmes are qualitatively the same as how we might plan a larger-scale project for a doctorate!

Choosing a topic

Before you can establish which questions you want to answer through your research, you have to first spend time thinking about what your research topic is actually going to be. This might sound like an obvious thing to say, but we have spent many hours talking with students who have tangled themselves in knots trying to design questionnaires without having first established clearly and unambiguously what their research topics actually are. It's understandable that students want to get on with their data collection as soon as possible: time is short, and deadlines seem to get earlier each academic year. But time spent thinking carefully about the topic during the early stages of the research project will make things much easier later on. The first thing to do, therefore, is to choose your topic. What you choose is up to you, but you will need to bear in mind the requirements of the course or programme of study you are taking and the amount of time you have at your disposal. So, once you have established a good working relationship with your research project supervisor (you should have a named supervisor even for small-scale undergraduate projects, and we recommend that you meet with them face to face rather than simply send emails!) you can begin negotiating with them about your topic. This is important because your supervisor will be best placed to tell you if your project is too large or too small, whether it will or will not meet the requirements of the curriculum you are studying, or whether it might raise ethical challenges that might result in a long delay before ethical approval is given.

So, where to look for ideas about what to research? There are several ways to proceed here. Some students pick up ideas from things they have been reading, some get inspiration from critical incidents that occur during their own teaching, and others focus on professional problems or dilemmas that relate to the organizations they work in. Let us think about these in a little more detail, and consider some worked examples to illustrate how these three approaches to planning a research project might work in practice.

Using themes in literature to generate a research topic

During your programme of study you will – hopefully – have been introduced by your tutors to a range of printed materials – textbooks, policy documents, academic journals – that you will have used when writing essays, compiling portfolios, reflecting on teaching practice observations, and so forth. In fact, as a consequence of this prior use of literature you will have become used to using literature to explore particular aspects of your own teaching practice – a common assessment strategy in teacher training and education studies courses in the lifelong learning sector. This experience is more significant than you might think as far as planning a research project is concerned. This is because the same literature, the same textbooks and journals you have used to inform your writing and reflections thus far, might also be used to provoke or inspire research in other directions as well. And because you will be drawing on journals and books you have used before, or that are very similar in feel and tone to those you have used before, they will be relatively straightforward to access and use.

> ### Case study: Researching the literacy practices of further education students
>
> Having completed a part-time Certificate in Education (Cert Ed) course for the lifelong learning sector, Julie is now studying part time for a BA in Education Studies. She is in the final year of the programme, most of which is devoted to an independent research project of 12,000 words. During previous modules, when researching changes to the ways in which key and/or functional skills have been taught and assessed, she came across a number of journal articles and books that were all derived from the Literacies for Learning in Further Education (LfLFE) Project. Julie's Cert Ed tutor was an enthusiastic advocate of the project and had recommended that all of the students take a look at the website and read one or two of the research articles that it produced. Julie had read two sources. The first was a journal article that looked at the different ways students in further education colleges used literacy at college, and in their homes, and explored the mismatches between these as a way of understanding how students found the literacy practices required by college to be sometimes difficult to come to terms with (Smith, 2005). The second was a book chapter that explored the methodology used by the researchers on the LfLFE project – specifically the rationale behind the *practitioner research* approach that the project rested on, acknowledging that although the project included university-based researchers who had more research experience and training than college-based researchers, they lacked the day-to-day understanding and experience of college-based learners, and this might lead them to ask questions that were inappropriate or inauthentic. College-based practitioner researchers, by contrast, knew better how to talk with the students they were researching (Carmichael et al., 2007).

Using critical incidents in your teaching to generate a research topic

As teachers and trainers, we are continually being told that we should be reflecting on our teaching – that we should be reflective practitioners. This might be as part of our initial teacher training, a degree and a CPD programme, or as part of the Qualified Teacher Learning and Skills (QTLS) professional formation process, even though the merits of doing so are rarely uncritically expressed (Tummons, 2011). Now, although the ways in which we 'have' to do reflective practice as part of a programme of study might be more or less worthwhile, there is one aspect of reflective teaching that is of considerable potential value to us from a research perspective: the *critical incident* (Francis, 1997).

In reflective practice theory, a critical incident (which is not necessarily a negative thing!) provides the practitioner with a significant moment that, on reflection, can lead the practitioner to all kinds of analysis or speculative enquiry, leading to more or less profound incidents of professional learning and development. This might lead to new understandings relating to situations in the seminar room or workshop; to new understandings of ourselves as teachers from the point of view of the political or cultural definitions of 'teaching' that we hold; to new understandings or insights derived from theories that were previously 'taken for granted'; or to a commitment or ability to carry out a course of action based on our reflection. It is a simple extension of this approach to suggest that a further outcome of reflection on a critical incident might be to plan and then carry out a piece of practitioner research in order to fully explore the causes or consequences of the incident in question.

> **Case study: Researching the ways in which further education lecturers learn about working with students with emotional and behavioural difficulties who are integrated into mainstream further education provision**

Scott, a further education lecturer, is in the final year of a part-time MA in Education. He teaches level two and three courses within the further education curriculum, and also on a foundation degree, which is accredited by the local university. Scott found his teaching with his level two students to be particularly challenging during the preceding academic year, in part due to the fact that one of his students was exhibiting a range of extremely challenging behaviours. The student in question did eventually receive a proper statement of special educational needs (SEN). Scott found working with the student to be a profound professional challenge, and after a particularly difficult session he spent time reflecting on conversations in the classroom that had triggered a particularly strong response. A year later, when thinking about possible topics for his MA research project, Scott thought back to his experiences with this particular student and how his own lack of preparedness for managing the challenging situations that occurred might have compounded both his own difficulties and the student's behaviour. In turn, this led him to consider the extent to which his initial teacher training had – or had not – covered such situations, and how his colleagues might or might not cope in a similar situation. From this, he derived his research topic: an investigation into how further education lecturers learned about working with students with SEN statements, and whether this was through formal accredited training or on-the-job experience.

Drawing on organizational experience to generate a research topic

It is important to remember that the role of the tutor in further or adult education settings is not restricted to classroom or workshop-based teaching and assessment. There are several other important elements to our professional lives, including quality assurance, support and guidance, moderation and verification, admissions, and so forth. Areas such as these are frequently discussed, not only in textbooks and policy documents, but also in research publications and academic journals. As such, they are entirely suitable as research topics for small-scale projects such as those explored in this book. Or, to put it another way, there is more to education research than just *pedagogic* research: in fact, education research might be defined as a combination of not only research into teaching, learning and assessment, but also into the sociology of education (for example, research into professionalism in further education (Gleeson et al., 2005)), the pastoral rather than academic work of tutors (Avis and Bathmaker, 2004), or staff responses to policy implementation in the lifelong learning sector (Edward et al., 2007). Any of the broader issues that impact on the lives of tutors or the work of the colleges and adult education centres in which we practise might be suitable for research.

> ### Case study: Researching admissions processes in one further education college
>
> Laura works at a large further education college where she is responsible for course management within the health and social care curriculum. She has responsibilities for, amongst other things, admissions to level three and foundation degree programmes. Over recent years she has, rather like many other practitioners in the sector, become increasingly aware of the tensions that can arise between course managers and college managers. As far as she is concerned, the admissions processes for both of these areas of provision should be entirely under her remit: if there is a query regarding a particular applicant, she might need to refer it to the awarding body of the course in question, but that would not be a common occurrence. However, college managers, keen to ensure that courses are run at a profitable level, have from time to time pressurized her – and other admissions tutors – into accepting students who should not perhaps be on these programmes. It might be the case that, for these students, a first choice of course has had to close due to low recruitment, and therefore the students have been transferred onto her course. Or it might be the case that students who should have been turned away – because they did not meet the course entry requirements – have been allowed to stay on the understanding that they 'make good' any outstanding course prerequisites. Anecdotally, such practices cause problems for tutors, who argue that through such occurrences students are being put on the wrong programme and are being 'set up to fail'. But do these claims stand up to more rigorous scrutiny? In order to find out, Laura is going to do research with the tutors and students involved, and evaluate the extent to which allowing discretion during the admissions process does – or does not – impact on a student's future progression.

Turning your topic into research questions

Now that we have thought about the topics that we might want to explore during our research, the next step is to think about the ways in which we can turn these research interests into *research questions*. By research questions, we mean to refer to the specific questions that our research projects are going to answer, as opposed to, for example, the questions that we are going to put into our questionnaires or interview schedules (we shall cover these topics in Chapter 6). Once a number of unambiguous research questions have been worked out, we can then start to plan the research in more depth.

It is unlikely that you will need more than two or three research questions in your research design – indeed, even large-scale research projects only rest on a small number of such questions (Jonathan's PhD thesis rested on four research questions; Vicky's PhD thesis rested on five). When designing your questions, you need to ensure that they are specific, and that they are of such a nature that they can be answered through your research project. There is no point spending time drawing up complex and ambitious research questions if, in order to answer them properly, they are going to need to be researched over a much longer period of time than you have available, or across a larger geographic area than you can practically manage to travel across!

Case study: Setting research questions

The literacy practices of further education students

After doing some reading and reflecting, Julie decided that she wanted to focus on the different ways in which her students had to write during their studies. That is to say, she wanted to focus on the different kinds of literacy practice that they were required to use by the curriculum. She was also interested in how this might relate to the kinds of writing – the kinds of literacy practices – that they might use at home. However, after speaking with her dissertation supervisor, she acknowledged that there would not be enough time for her to research this as well – nor would there be enough room in a 12,000-word dissertation to do justice to the subject. So she decided to focus on her students' college work. With the help of her supervisor, she decided on the following research questions:

1   What are the different literacy practices that students on a CACHE level three Certificate in Childcare and Education course required to use?
2   What are the attitudes of students towards these different literacy practices?

How college lecturers learn about working with SEN students

Scott's final choice of research topic rested, in part, on a number of practical issues. In a way, he would have preferred to research the experiences of the SEN students themselves, rather than the professional learning and experience of those lecturers who work with them. But ethical considerations persuaded him towards the latter. Obtaining ethical clearance to work with young people is time-consuming and bureaucratic; the ethics involved in wanting to work with vulnerable adults are even more complex. In the end, he decided that research with other lecturers would be more straightforward to receive ethical approval for. His research questions were derived from his own professional experience and reflection:

1   To what extent does the initial teacher training for the learning and skills sector curriculum include content relating to working with SEN learners?
2   How else, other than through initial teacher training, do college lecturers learn about how to work with SEN learners?

Admissions processes in health and social care

Laura approached her first supervisory meeting with a high level of confidence. She was satisfied that she had found a topic of interest to her, both personally and professionally. In addition, she was sure that her findings would be of value more generally to the college where she worked. In the first instance, she drew up these research questions:

1   How closely are the admissions regulations adhered to within the health and social care section of the college?
2   What are the implications for students who are allowed to join programmes of study that might not be suitable for them?

However, when she had her first tutorial, her supervisor raised some concerns. She – her supervisor – was worried that this research topic might be difficult to establish an ethical basis for (discussed more extensively in the following chapter). Laura was herself heavily involved in recruitment and admissions: how could her own experiences be used to explore the first question? And would other tutors feel 'safe' in speaking to her about possibly sensitive issues? The second question seemed more objective, and so her supervisor suggested that this became the focus of the research as a whole. In order to make the topic less controversial, she suggested some different research questions:

1   What are the entry profiles of students joining programmes within the health and social care curriculum area?
2   How do tutors respond to working with such diverse student groups?
3   What, if anything, is the relationship between a student's entry profile and their final progression and/or achievement?

These new research questions undoubtedly shifted the direction of the research, but at the same time made the research more manageable, more likely to receive ethical approval, and more likely to receive the required permissions from her college.

Activity

Choosing a topic

Choosing a topic for your research is a bit like reflective practice: to do it well, you need a decent amount of time (not just a few snatched minutes) and a relatively quiet space to think (your office desk at lunchtime is not a good place – a comfy chair in a coffee shop or library is much better). We would argue, however, that choosing a topic is also something that might be helped if you work with someone else. For some students, being able to have a sustained conversation about possible topics can help ideas to coalesce. So, find a quiet place to think and perhaps to talk as well, and think about what you've been reading during your studies, your own teaching practice, and your own broader role within the college or adult education centre where you work. What are the events, themes or incidents that have stuck in your mind, that made you stop in your tracks or re-evaluate what you thought you knew? Are you able to turn one of these into a research project?

Contextualizing your research questions: what do we already know?

For smaller-scale projects, such as the ones that we are discussing in this book, it is more likely than not that you will conduct your research in an area that has already been explored by other researchers and academics. Only a very few researchers manage to break genuinely new ground, and normally this is reserved for extensive research projects such as doctoral theses (where a 'new contribution to existing knowledge' is an important criterion). It is more likely that you will be doing your research – whether it's a case study or action research – in an area that has been explored before, although perhaps not at the institution where you work or at which you are going to do your data collection. This is entirely appropriate for both practical and theoretical reasons. At a practical level, it seems right for practitioner-researchers to work at a local level, to use research to explore complexities, ambiguities or other troublesome issues at the places where they work. With time in relatively short supply, having to establish connections with a new institution before obtaining permission to do the research, not having to worry too much about travelling to research sites, and so forth, makes locally based research a sensible path to follow. And, at a theoretical level, it can be argued that the production of new research – even if it is 'only' focused on one college or other institution – can still raise and answer legitimate and important questions that may be of concern to others as well as the student and the supervisor, especially if the research leads towards a more substantial enquiry such as a doctorate (sometimes, students use undergraduate or MA research topics as 'pilot projects' for larger-scale postgraduate study).

So, if we want our small-scale research to be able to stand on its own two feet, and to have something important to say to the research community as a whole, it needs to be put into context, to be 'plugged in' to other research that is already out there. This is important because it helps the research to be *generalizable* or *transferable* across research contexts (an issue that we shall return to in more detail in Chapter 8). There are two main ways to do this. One of these is through the establishment of a rigorous and thorough research methodology: it's through having a sound methodology that the readers of your research can have confidence in your findings and your conclusions (which, in a way, is what the whole of this book is about). And the other is through establishing the broader context of your research project, and the established way to do this is through reference to previously published work. So, just as your final project, when written up, will need to make reference to an appropriate number of books and journal articles that are relevant to research method and methodology, it will also need to draw on other books and articles that are also about the same topics – or the same kinds of topics – that your research is going to be about.

Reviewing the literature

Whether or not you are doing small-scale research and writing up a dissertation that is going to be 12,000 words long (which might sound like a lot, but believe us when we say that every year lots of our students find it difficult to stay within this word limit!), or a masters-level thesis which will be 20,000–25,000 words long (different universities tend to set slightly different word limits depending on the credit value awarded to dissertation/thesis modules), a proper *literature review* will always form an important part of the project as a whole. So, what is the role or function of the literature review? There are three main factors to consider here. Firstly, it is important to establish a context or background for the research, and to explore what other writers and researchers have said about the topic. Secondly, it is important for you, as the researcher, to state your own critical position regarding this prior work. Thirdly, you will need to explain how your research slots into this prior work. We shall discuss each of these in turn.

What do we already know about the research topic?

The first element of a literature review is to demonstrate to your supervisor, your eventual assessors, and to anyone else who may read your research, that you are well versed in your subject, and that you have a good working knowledge of the issues, theories and themes of your research project. This is important because without this prior knowledge you may not be in a position to analyse adequately or rigorously the data that you gather (we shall return to this issue in more detail in Chapter 7). There are so many books, papers and journals out there – almost all of which are readily available or traceable via the internet – that it is very uncommon for students to choose to research a topic upon which there are no, or very few, prior publications. It is therefore relatively straightforward to access sufficient literature to establish 'what is known' about the research topic you have chosen.

What do I have to say about what is already known?

But there is more to a literature review than simply a rehearsal of the findings or arguments made by the authors whose work you are citing or quoting from. Literature reviews that do not move beyond 'Avis and Bathmaker (2004) state that . . . and Tummons (2011) argues that . . . whilst Edward et al. (2007) suggest', will never attain the level of analysis that is needed. How robust is the literature that has already been published? If two of the articles you have read purport to be about similar issues, but offer radically different conclusions, how can you reconcile the two? If an article rests on a qualitative case study, is a case for generalizability (discussed in Chapter 8 in depth) made in the article? If not, can you work out how the article may – or may not – inform your own research methods or your own hypothesis?

Where does my research fit into this prior body of work?

Once you have established a sound command of the prior research that forms the backdrop to your own research project, you can make a case as to where your research fits in, and why. Based on our experiences of supervising research students in colleges and adult education centres, there are two common responses to this. The first response is that your small-scale project is seeking to confirm, or perhaps add to, existing literature, by drawing on theories and methodologies that have already been employed by other researchers, but that have not been applied in the *specific context* that you are proposing to research. By specific context, we might refer to a geographic area, an institutional setting, or a particular population of students. The second response is that your project is seeking to argue against, in whole or in part, the position taken by one or more of the authors in the literature. And again, this might be on the grounds of geography, institution, or student population.

The size and scale of your literature review will depend on a number of factors. In terms of word allowance, it is always best to check with your project supervisor, as many universities provide writing frames, which will often include indicative word counts, for students who are writing up final year research projects. Thinking about how many things you should read, and what sort of sources you should look to, is rather less straightforward. Again, you should speak to your supervisor, but a few overarching themes are worth noting at this stage.

Make sure that your literature consists of a variety of sources

Books and academic journals are the obvious first place to look, but some research projects may need to refer to government policies as well – government publications are readily available for download from the internet. Other organizations, such as the National Foundation for Educational Research (NFER), or the Learning and Skills Improvement Service (LSIS), also publish research online.

Stay up to date, but don't neglect the classics

Try to ensure that your sources are current. Use the newest edition of a book, unless your research requires that you have to refer to an older one. Try to use recent journal articles as well. If you are doing research about current policy impact in the learning and skills sector, for example, you would have to use recent journal articles because anything published too long ago would predate the policies you are researching. This is not to say that older sources should be discounted. If you were doing research into the curriculum, you may well need to refer to an older landmark book such as Stenhouse (1975), or even Tyler (1949). If you were researching assessment, you may need to use Messick (1989), a very important journal article. But neither of these sources is 'current'! Often, you may find references to such seminal works in the journals you are using. Make a habit of checking the bibliographies of everything that you read, as you may find references to sources that would be worthwhile additions to your own reading list.

Start your bibliography straightaway, and take good notes

As soon as you start to work through the literature, open up a new Word file on your computer and start your bibliography. Every time you borrow or download a new source, write it into your bibliography, making sure to get the referencing style right from the very beginning. By the time you have to hand in your project, the hard work of compiling your reading list will already be done. And, as you read, take notes (we continue to be baffled by how many students do not do this!). When writing up the project, it is far easier to work from your notes than it is to work from a pile of books – assuming you can get them all back from the library again.

Be careful when using the internet

Going online makes accessing journals very straightforward indeed: with your password for your library account you will be able to download pdf files of journal articles quickly and easily. Downloading government papers is also an easy task. But there is so much stuff online that it is easy to get lost. Every year, we both find that we have to spend time with some of our students who have either got so lost when using the internet – thinking that it would be easy! – that they have found nothing worth using, or have downloaded far too much irrelevant material. Our advice tends to be: only download from reputable publishers or research bodies, and make sure that when searching journals, they are journals that report research from the UK. If using international journals, make sure that the research published in them relates to countries that have educational systems sufficiently similar to the UK, so that their findings have a good chance of being applicable to a UK context.

Ask for help!

Finally, don't think that you have to do everything in isolation, and don't suffer in silence. If you are stuck, phone or email your supervisor and ask – politely and courteously – for help. Speak to other students on the same course: someone else may have come across something that might be useful to you. In particular, speak to the subject librarians at the university where you are doing your studies. They will be pleased to help you, and have a wealth of knowledge and experience at their fingertips.

To summarize: a literature review is more than just an account of the books or journal articles you have read. It is a way of demonstrating to whoever will read your dissertation or project that you have a good and critical working knowledge of the subject area. You are not expected to have read everything that is out there! At some point, you will need to stop reading and start writing. But do not make the mistake of thinking that all the reading has to be done before you start your data collection. If you have time, keep on reading as you do your interviews or questionnaires (or whatever else you use – we shall return to this in Chapter 6).

Conclusions

Thinking up a research topic might take longer than you think. It can be exhilarating and enthusing; it can also be demoralizing or disappointing. Some of your fellow students may seem to be brimming with possibilities and ideas, while you are getting stuck trying to think of just one workable option. This may seem easy for us to say, but with a little time and careful thinking, one or two – and in all likelihood, more – possible titles will present themselves. So, do not be disappointed if it takes time to get an idea for a topic, or if your supervisor gently, but firmly, suggests that you think of something else (they are simply doing their job and trying to help you, after all!). Allow time for the generation of ideas. And then the detailed work of drawing up research questions and selecting research methods can begin.

References and further reading

Avis, J. and Bathmaker, A.-M. (2004) The politics of care: emotional labour and trainee further education lecturers. *Journal of Vocational Education and Training,* 56(1): 5–20.

Carmichael, J., Edwards, R., Miller, K. and Smith, J. (2007) Researching literacy for learning in the vocational curriculum, in M. Osborne, M. Houston and N. Toman (eds.) *The Pedagogy of Lifelong Learning: Understanding Effective Teaching and Learning in Diverse Contexts*. London: Routledge: 79–89.

Edward, S., Coffield, F., Steer, R. and Gregson, M. (2007) Endless change in the learning and skills sector: the impact on teaching staff. *Journal of Vocational Education and Training*, 59(2): 155–73.

Francis, D. (1997) Critical incident analysis: a strategy for developing reflective practice. *Teachers and Teaching: Theory and Practice*, 3(2): 169–88.

Gleeson, D., Davies, J. and Wheeler, E. (2005) On the making and taking of professionalism in the further education workplace. *British Journal of Sociology of Education*, 26(4): 445–60.

Messick, S. (1989) Meaning and values in test validation: the science and ethics of assessment. *Educational Researcher*, 18(2): 5–11.

Smith, J. (2005) Mobilising everyday literacy practices within the curricula. *Journal of Vocational Education and Training*, 57(3): 319–34.

Stenhouse, L. (1975) *An Introduction to Curriculum Research and Development*. London: Heinemann.

Tummons, J. (2011) 'It sort of feels uncomfortable': problematising the assessment of reflective practice. *Studies in Higher Education*, 36(4): 471–83.

Tyler, R. (1949) *Basic Principles of Curriculum and Instruction*. Chicago: University of Chicago Press.

5 Research ethics

By the end of this chapter you should be able to:

- Discuss the ethical principles that underpin research in education

- Understand the nature and basis of ethical guidance

- Fully understand and appreciate the consideration of ethics, and how they thread through all phases of research

Introduction

Conscientious, knowledgeable and well-intentioned people throughout the education profession often arrive at differing conclusions on the ethical acceptability of research involving participants. Ethical behaviour in research demands that researchers engage with moral issues of what is 'right' and 'wrong'. This can be influenced by your personal beliefs about who, and what, research is for. Ethics concern the morality of human conduct. In relation to social research, it refers to the moral deliberation, choice and accountability on the part of researcher throughout the research process. Ethics and moral theory are about making judgements, especially judgements informed by some explicit framework. For example, feminism, and the varieties of feminism themselves, constitute such moral and ethical frameworks because they each represent value positions on the experiences, voice and places, of women around the world.

Ethics pertains to doing good and avoiding harm. Harm can be prevented or reduced through the application of appropriate ethical principles. Thus, the protection of participants in any research study is imperative. You need to consider the ethical implications of the research you are planning to carry out before finalizing a research plan. Indeed, from the conception to the conclusion of your research project, it is vital that you have fully considered, and where possible planned, how you will address ethics.

In making sure that your research is ethical, you need to focus on the rights of participants (learners) to be treated as openly and fairly as possible within the research, and to consent fully to taking part. You also need to make sure that appropriate principles are applied so that those who rely on research findings to make their education or other decisions are receiving results that are accurate and the result of sound research design.

It is not always possible to plan for all occurrences in your research project. A number of ethical issues for consideration will arise prior to the research beginning. However, many are emergent, and only become apparent as the research continues. You may draw on communities of practice to help you think through how to address and manage ethical issues before, and after, starting the research.

Ethical factors in writing a research proposal

It is vital that you are aware of the ethical guidelines of your institution or organization you are conducting research with, or for. Researchers have a duty to achieve and maintain the highest standards of intellectual honesty in the conduct of their research. Importantly, as researchers, you are legally obliged to conform with legal regulations relating to your research. As such, proposals for research studies require approval via a rigorous process before being allowed to begin. For example, you will need to consider the stages of your proposed research and how you can:

- protect the participants' rights
- protect the participants' privacy
- protect the participants' dignity
- protect the participants' well-being.

Most teachers and beginning researchers do not fully understand what a research proposal means; nor do they understand its importance. To put it frankly, one's research is only as good as one's proposal. A half-baked proposal may not, for example, get through the supervisory committee for an MEd or PhD. Alternatively, a high-quality proposal not only promises success for the project, but also impresses your committee about your potential as a researcher. A research proposal is intended to convince others that you have a worthwhile research project, and that you have the competence and the work plan to complete it. Generally, a research proposal should cover all the main elements involved in the research process, and also include appropriate information for the readers to evaluate the proposed study.

Irrespective of your research area and the methodology and theoretical framework you choose, your research proposals should address the following questions: 'What do you plan to achieve?', 'Why do you want carry it out?' and 'How are you going to do it?'.

Writing the proposal

The proposal should have enough information to persuade your readers that you have an important research idea, that you have a sound grasp of the relevant literature and the major issues, and that your methodology is comprehensive. The quality of your research proposal depends not only on the quality of your proposed project, but also on the quality of your proposal writing. A decent research project may run the risk of rejection simply because the proposal is not well written. Your writing should therefore be clear, coherent and persuasive. It may be an idea to share the stages of your proposal writing with a critical friend, to allow feedback and development of the shape, structure and clarity of your proposal.

So let us consider the stages of research proposal. This list is not exhaustive, and more key suggestions are offered further on.

Title

This should be clear, concise and descriptive.

Try to capture the essence of your project in an informative but catchy title. One which motivates and engages the reader's interest is always a good start.

Abstract

This should be brief, specific and approximately 250–400 words. It should include the research question, the rationale for the study, the hypothesis (if there is one), the method and the main findings. Descriptions of the method may include the design, procedures, the sample and any instruments that will be used.

Introduction

The main purpose of the introduction is to offer a background or context for your research question(s). How to frame the research question(s) is perhaps the main problem in proposal writing.

If the research question is framed in the context of a general, rambling literature review, then the research may appear inconsequential and, quite frankly, boring. Conversely, if the same question is posed in the context of a very focused and current research area, its worth will become apparent.

There are no specific rules we can give you on how to frame your research question, just as there is no prescription on how to write an interesting and informative opening paragraph. This will depend a great deal on your own creativity, capacity to think clearly, and the depth of your understanding of problem areas. This can be developed by reading other research proposals, and exploring how and why they are structured in a certain way, using specific approaches. They will be different, but finding ones that are driven by similar ideologies and perspectives to your own can be a helpful starting point.

We suggest that you try to place your research question in the context of either a contemporary frame, or an older area that remains viable. We also recommended you offer a brief historical landscape. You will also need to explain the contemporary context in which your proposed research question is posed. Don't forget to include the leading figures in the area you are researching. The key is to offer a holistic picture, while also providing an insight into the significance of your research.

Literature review

The literature review is an essential part of your research which allows you to demonstrate wide and deep reading around the area you are researching. It gives you the opportunity to demonstrate your facility to critically evaluate relevant literature information, and integrate and synthesize the existing literature. This deep analysis offers you the opportunity to place your research in the context of others', to make sure that you are not asking the same questions. Let us not forget that it also allows you to recognize and give credit to those who have done the legwork for your research. It provides an insight into your knowledge of the research problem, and offers an understanding of the theoretical and research matters related to your research question. This will help to convince your reader that your proposed research will make a contribution to the literature.

Methods

The methods section is very important because it tells your reader how you plan to address your research questions. It will describe the activities essential for the completion of your project.

The method section should contain appropriate information for the reader to determine whether the methodology is sound. You will be required to show your knowledge of alternative methods, and make the case that your approach is the most appropriate and valid way to address your research question.

You may want to consider what methods are best to answer your questions – for example, qualitative or qualitative – and justify your reasons. If you are doing qualitative research, a main focus may be to describe how you will collect and analyse your data. For a quantitative project, the method section may include issues related to design – for example, are you using a questionnaire study? For further insights into the approaches you may want to include in your research, look at Chapters 3 and 6.

Discussion

It is vital to convince your reader of the potential impact of your proposed research. You need to communicate enthusiasm, coherence and confidence, without over-egging your proposal. It is therefore important that you also include the limitations of the proposed research. This may be due to issues such as resources – for example, time and financial constraints, which can be a real barrier if not highlighted and addressed early in the research planning.

The order of your research proposal may include the structure below.

Title
Abstract
Introduction and/or background
Research question
Literature review
Theoretical framework
Methodology
Research design and method
Ethics
Communicating the results
Significance of research/originality

Timeline
Budget
References
Appendices
References and further reading

You may want to consider your positioning in the research, and objectivity and subjectivity is an important consideration. Be sure your own personal biases and opinions do not get in the way of your research, and that you give both sides fair consideration. Subjectivity can influence the research process and possibly the interpretation and representation of data.

Key ethical aspects to consider throughout your research project

Will the research cause the participants harm?

There is ongoing debate about the extent to which people characterized as vulnerable should be able to consent to participate in research in their own right. What is clear is that gatekeepers, family, teachers, managers, and people with institutional affiliations, exert considerable influence on whether so-called 'vulnerable' people are given the opportunity to give their consent to participate in research, and how this process works.

As human beings, most of us probably feel that we have an intuitive understanding of what is meant by ethical behaviour, and this may include being honest and fair, as well as not causing others any harm. However, this intuition needs deeper probing to ensure that breaches of ethical guidance and codes, or significant deviations from the research proposal originally approved, do not result in harming your participants.

It is important to note that ethical codes and guidelines for research projects do not provide answers to all of the ethical issues that may arise during research. Subsequently, ethical dilemmas that are not part of the study may arise during an observation in a classroom. For example, it may be that a learner is diagnosed with mental health issues and be vulnerable. Codes of ethics indicate the rights of learners, but do not indicate to the researcher how to respond to this situation. As such, situations require careful examination of the moral responsibility of researchers. Harm can be prevented or reduced through the application of appropriate ethical principles. Thus, the protection of human subjects or participants in any research study is imperative.

As such, you need to ensure that your research strategy is not likely to cause harm. You may ask yourself is there any way in which harm could be justified or excused? The harm could include not just consequences for the people being studied, but for others too, and even for any researchers investigating the same setting or people in the future. It is important you take a holistic perspective. Harm can also result from psychological pressure being placed on participants. Researchers must ensure that those taking part in research will not be caused distress. They must be protected from physical and mental harm. This means you must not embarrass, frighten, offend or harm participants. Normally, the risk of harm must be no greater than in ordinary life – for example, participants should not be exposed to risks greater than, or additional to, those encountered in their normal lifestyles.

If a participant fails to complete and return a questionnaire, you need to know in advance what you will do. Will you make a follow-up request for its completion and return and, if so, how will this be worded? It is not good practice to pester people. A case would need to be made if you wanted to follow up non-responders.

Respect for autonomy: does the research process display respect for people and allow them to make decisions for themselves, notably about whether or not to participate?

Autonomy is about a prospective participant's right, as well as ability, 'to choose' whether to take part in, or to continue in, the study. You have an ethical and legal responsibility to make sure potential participants are aware of what involvement in the study will entail, as well as the voluntary nature of their decision of whether or not to take part in the study.

Researchers in positions of authority should bear in mind that a coercive element might be inadvertently introduced in recruiting participants – i.e. students recruited into a study by academic staff, or through the use of financial rewards. Respect for autonomy also imposes obligations on researchers to respect the anonymity, privacy and confidentiality of information relating to participants. Even when someone has signed a consent form, they must be made aware that they are free to withdraw from the study at any time, without giving a justification. They must also be able to request that the data they have given be removed from the study.

You need to be prepared for this possibility, and to have plans for how you would remove the data already given, if this is requested. You also need to retain a link from any code or pseudonym that you use, back to the name of the individual, to enable you to carry this out. This link needs to be kept confidential, and separate from the data. Many types of research, such as surveys or observations, should be conducted under the assumption that you will keep your findings anonymous. Many interviews, however, are not done under the condition of anonymity. You should let your subjects know whether your research results will be anonymous or not.

It is essential that:

- participants' dignity and worth is upheld, together with their rights to privacy and confidentiality
- you are aware of safeguards to protect the rights and welfare of persons or communities whose vulnerabilities impair autonomous decision making.

You must also be aware of, and respect, cultural, individual and role differences, including those based on age, gender, race, ethnicity, culture, national origin, religion, sexual orientation, disability, language and socio-economic status.

Privacy

Privacy is a key constituent of research. You will need to consider that, although research includes providing descriptions and explanations that are publicly available, some information might need to be kept out of the public domain.

Privacy is a central principle in the traditional conception of the ethical treatment of social research participants. A breach of confidentiality, commonly understood as failure to maintain the security of data that may identify individual participants, can occur at various stages of a research project, including data collection, processing, storage and dissemination. With the emergence of internet-based research, and the increasing role of new and emerging technology, this can complicate efforts to protect participants. A way to address protecting the anonymity of participants is to respect confidentiality and not to gather or reveal identity-specific data. However, you will often need to take more than this basic step to protect a participant's identity. Other information can help to identify people – for example, job title, age, gender, length of service, hobbies and strongly expressed views. The more pieces of information that are presented together, the easier it is to identify someone.

Research should be based on voluntary informed consent

Informed consent is a central principle in ethical research. Individuals are generally presumed to have the capacity and right to make free and informed decisions. Respect for participants therefore means respecting the exercise of individual consent. In practical terms, this principle turns into the dialogue, process, rights, duties and requirements for free and informed consent by the research participant, and the right to withdraw consent. It is an essential principle of respect for people in the planning and implementation of research projects. And it is essential that participants are fully aware of the research they are consenting to be a part of. Make sure your participants have informed consent and are clear about their participation. Revise the consent if necessary. The precise form that consent might take is varied, and the appropriate means of consent needs to take into account the context of the research. The signing of the consent form should also include discussion explaining to research participants, in detail, the purposes of the research and plans for dissemination.

Informed consent can prove to be complex, and present barriers for the researcher. For example, the task of creating complete documents for informed consent is difficult if the participants struggle to read and write. This may mean that the readability of the consent form needs to be revised. Other strategies may also be put in place, which includes spending extra time discussing the research, etc.

Research involving children will require consideration of issues around capacity to consent, as outlined in the section above on regulatory and legal frameworks. This will involve exploring whether the child is able to consent on their own behalf, or whether, additionally, parental consent is also needed. Respect for human dignity entails high ethical obligations towards vulnerable people – to those whose lack of competence or decision-making capacity renders them vulnerable. Children, institutionalized people, or others who are vulnerable, are entitled to special protection against abuse, exploitation and discrimination. This often translates into special procedures to protect their interests.

A consent form would usually include:

- benefits
- costs/risks
- alternatives
- confidentiality
- subjects' rights and the right to withdraw.

Reciprocity

The concept of reciprocity has long played an important role in anthropology, ethnology and sociological thinking. The basic principle of reciprocity is human interaction. The notion of reciprocity and investing in relationship building presents a strong challenge to more positivist notions of 'objectivity' and 'non-intervention' in research. We would suggest that reciprocity is a relation of shared dependence or action or power, or a type of exchange in which transactions take place between individuals who are equally positioned.

Conventional research ethics focus on ensuring that research 'subjects' are not harmed, and that consent is obtained; reciprocity suggests a more proactive approach to research ethics. Researchers depend upon being allowed access to data, and this may involve participants collaborating in various ways; for example, giving up time in order to be interviewed or to fill in a questionnaire. The research process can also disrupt people's lives in various ways. The practices of reciprocity include such things as gift-giving, whereby goods are exchanged – for example, between the researcher and participants. For example, how do the participants benefit from taking part in the research? This interaction is loaded with ideologies/social values. Feminist analysis of traditional research methods have analysed and reconceptualized the relationship between feminist researchers and those they collaborate with in research (Ribbens and Edwards, 1998; Stanley and Wise, 1993). For example, feminist researchers and theorists have played a central role in motivating social scientists to think critically and self-reflexively about positivistic research paradigms, notions of 'objectivity' and 'truth', ownership of research results, and the ethics of data collection and reporting (Harding, 1987). If we consider the collection of data, from a feminist perspective, this data may be viewed as a gift from the participants which results in a gift – such as clothes, vouchers, etc. – for their contribution. Friendship can also be a reciprocal factor of research. Oakley (2005) proposes a 'reciprocal relationship', similar to friendship, between feminist researchers and the women they research, suggesting that there can be 'no intimacy without reciprocity'. This challenges the traditional research method process in which the researcher objectifies and depersonalizes research subjects and reinforces the power held by the researcher.

Case study: Ensuring ethical participation in research (Vicky)

Participation in the research group was voluntary. I informed each of my classes about the project and asked those who were interested to let me know after class. For those who voiced their interest I had a further meeting with them outside the lesson. I explained what the research would involve, which included interviews, collecting information about their life story, and working together as a research group to make sense of the findings. From the beginning, I was keen not to put any pressure on the group to say 'yes', so I asked them to think about it and let me know at a later date. I also wanted to make it clear it would be a collaborative study, where they had choice and power. This power included telling them they could set dates and places for interviews; they could also leave the study at any point, and ask me any questions just as I asked them. I assured them that I would be willing to place my own narrative with theirs.

Being open and transparent: the researcher's integrity

It is essential you behave with integrity at all times. As researchers, you need to promote accuracy, honesty and truthfulness in all aspects of your research project. The researcher has an ethical obligation to establish a relationship of trust with the research participants. Researchers may also establish trust by maintaining the confidentiality of the participants' disclosures. It is also important to treat participants equally, in the sense that no one is unjustly favoured or discriminated against, and to establish and maintain a relationship between the researcher and participants that is as democratic as possible. In doing so, the participants become part of the decision-making process in all phases of the research. This can be followed up by the participants commenting on the findings, together with the researcher. This is the approach taken by Vicky, in taking the stance that feminist research is about a level of intersubjectivity between the researcher and the participant, the mutual creation of data, which includes the participants also undertaking research as they, along with the researchers, construct the meanings that become data for future interpretation by the researcher. This approach identifies the nature of the co-production of knowledge in research that engages with the participants, and in which researchers work with, as well as on, the researched.

Points to remember

You should always make sure the following themes are covered:

- An explanation of the procedures to be followed and their purposes.
- Awareness that people are free to withdraw consent, and to discontinue participation in the research project at any time, without prejudice to the participant.
- All participants are given the chance to remain anonymous.
- All data is kept strictly confidential.
- Permission for publication is gained from the participants.
- The researcher fully reveals his or her identity and background.

- Arrangements are made during initial contacts to provide feedback for participants who request it. This may take the form of a written résumé of findings.
- When ethical dilemmas arise, the researcher consults other researchers or teachers.
- The dignity, privacy and interests of the participants is respected and protected at all times.
- Social responsibility and obligations are respected.
- You do not abuse your position or power as a researcher.

Case study: Sabeen Hussein's research into working with visually impaired students

Now that we are encountering an increasing number of students with special educational needs attending mainstream institutions – in response to revised legislation such as the Special Educational Needs and Disability Act (SENDA) (2001), the Disabilty Discrimination Act (DDA) 2005 and the Equality Act 2010 – my research proposal is to explore the educational experience for visually impaired students who are attending mainstream further and higher education institutions. The focus of this research proposal is how the attitudes towards, and perceptions of, visual impairment can influence the educational experience for such students who are attending these institutions. For example, how visually impaired students perceive their disabilities, and the kind of impact which this self-perception is likely to have on various aspects of education, such as support provision, participation in taught sessions, and the communication of specialist needs to tutors and, perhaps, peers. In turn, the attitudes and perceptions of tutors and associate support staff at such institutions will also be explored; how a tutor, for example, who may never have taught a visually impaired student, may proceed with their professional practice in light of a seemingly 'new experience', and the impact which their perceptions of this distinct disability may have on their teaching practice and the students' subsequent experience. The purpose then, is to provide a realistic overview of how effective this legislation may be, and how a sample of these mainstream further and higher education institutions are responding to these developments.

Being a largely qualitative research exercise, a number of ethical issues are likely to arise. The first, and most obvious one, is that of confidentiality. It is important to ensure all information obtained from participants is not used or disclosed without prior permission, which can be overcome by ensuring that an 'ethics protocol' is set out from the outset. The second is that of ensuring that participants understand the role of the researcher and the nature of the research. Since questions surrounding an individual's experience at either college or university, and others in relation to the impairments themselves, are likely to be asked, it can be very easy for participants to divulge information which may be better disclosed to an opthalmologist, a counsellor or a specialist support worker who may be better equipped to address these particular issues. This difficulty can be overcome, not only by making the line between teacher and researcher clear, but also that, as the researcher, a greater responsibility towards carefully considering the types of questions asked, and the nature of the responses evoked, must be taken. In other words, as the researcher, it is crucial that only the questions which provide the required data should be asked, especially throughout an interview process.

But perhaps the most interesting ethical issue which may arise from this research project is the effect the research processes and outcomes potentially have on internal institutional relationships, such as those between the employer and the employee. Qualitative research can often provide participants with the opportunity to express their opinions in an unrestricted manner due to the nature and style of the research; that is, by asking open-ended questions throughout questionnaire surveys and interviews, as opposed to providing simple 'Yes/No' answers. Since the aim of the research is to ascertain participants' attitudes towards, and perceptions of, visual impairment, subordinate members of a support team within an institution, for instance, may comment upon the management of that particular team, which may either be positive or negative. Although such information can be interesting and useful to a certain extent, there is the danger that subordinate staff members may perceive this research exercise as an opportunity to express internal professional concerns which they would like their superiors to be aware of. Superiors can, themselves, also manipulate the research project in the same way. Put simply, the research project may be viewed by participants as working to their individual advantage, and the focus of the research itself can be potentially blurred, having a subsequent effect upon the acquired data.

To avoid such tensions arising, the responsibility of maintaining the purpose of the research falls again with the researcher, and this can be easily managed by remaining objective throughout the research process. In addition, other alternative research methods can be employed, particularly when analysing the data and reporting upon its outcomes. Such alternative methods may include using quantitative research methods. Due to the restrictive and concentrated nature of quantitative research methods, only the required factual evidence concerning the actual research itself can be presented, and other conflicting opinions can remain undisclosed and controlled.

Research strategies: ethical issues

Ethical issues in qualitative research are often more subtle than issues in survey or experimental research. These issues are related to the characteristics of qualitative or field methodology, which usually include long-term and close personal involvement, interviewing, and participant observation. Field research is an approach based on human interaction, rather than one viewed as outside human interactions.

Questionnaires and interviews

Questionnaires and interviews seem relatively unproblematic in ethical terms. There are, however, a number of places where the unsuspecting researcher can get into difficulty. Issues related to the requirement of privacy and consent may arise when the main content of a questionnaire requires a respondent to describe someone other than themselves in detail, or disclose personal or private information. When teachers, as research participants, are asked to describe their experiences relating to teaching and learners, or specific incidences of ethical dilemmas encountered in the process of teaching, it should be considered whether the learners' consent is required. One way to solve this problem is to disguise the sex, age and illness of a learner to make them unidentifiable. When teachers are asked questions related to any form of learner information, including that which must be obtained from the learner database, the ethical validity of such research depends on the nature of the questions; issues related to privacy and consent are influenced by how detailed the provided information is. For example, it would probably be safe to ask teachers questions related to mental stress they experience in the classroom. However, caution should be exercised when asking teachers questions related to specific problem behaviours of learners with behavioural issues in their classroom because such questions could identify the learner in question, depending on the community they belong to and the nature of the question. When collecting information of any kind, it is necessary to confirm whose consent should be obtained.

Data storage and retentions

Data (including electronic data) must be recorded in a durable and appropriately referenced form. Your institution may have established procedures for retaining data, and for keeping records of data held in departments. It is important to become familiar with this. Confidentiality agreements to protect intellectual property rights may be agreed between the institution, the researcher, and a sponsor of the research. Where such agreements limit free publication and discussion, limitations and restrictions must be explicitly agreed.

Risks and responsibilities

It may be useful to think of ethical review in terms of a review of risks and responsibilities. The responsibilities lie firmly with the researcher; the risks can be on both sides. Researchers are responsible for causing something to happen in relation to the lives of the research participants, and they need to consider:

- the potential risks they may be introducing, and
- how they, as researchers, will take responsibility for addressing these potential risks.

The risks may be physical or psychological. The researcher is responsible for satisfying themselves that:

- the level of risk is justified by the importance and relevance of the research study
- the risk is unavoidable within the study's objectives
- in absolute terms, the level of risk is minimized
- participants are fully aware of the level and nature of the risk before they agree, freely, to take part in the study
- precautions are in place to deal adequately with the effect of participation.

The risks may be physical, but it is more likely that they will be psychological and associated with things such as discussing sensitive topics, maintaining confidentiality, stirring painful memories, disclosing personal information, voicing unwelcome opinions, and discomfort and uncertainty.

It might be thought that ethical issues predominantly relate to interview methods, where participants might 'open up' and perhaps say more than they had really wanted to, or, when reflecting later, might be very unhappy about something they had said. But there are ethical judgements to be made in all research involving human participants, including questionnaire-based methods, research via electronic communication, and observational research.

Breaches of ethical guidance and codes, or significant deviations from the research proposal originally approved, may cause harm to your participant(s). In addition, these are considered serious matters within your place of work and the wider community.

Typical repercussions could be:

- removal of professional accreditation
- refusal to publish results of the study
- removal of funding for research
- damage to the academic and ethical reputation of yourself and the college you are based at.

Gatekeeping

Gatekeeping is an integral but sometimes difficult part of the research process. There are ongoing ethical dilemmas around gatekeeping. An essential factor is establishing trusting relationships with the gatekeepers you may come into contact with in your research. Gatekeepers can be both organizational and individual. They can control, exclude and block people and their ideas.

Case study: Claire Marsh's research into English as an Additional Language (EAL)/English as a Second Language (ESL)

I have been teaching psychology and health and social care for the past 12 months, and am currently working towards a Postgraduate Certificate in Further Education and Training. I consider my role as a teacher to be that of a facilitator rather than an educator. My role involves providing adult learners with the skills they require to enter higher education and become competent and effective lifelong learners.

The research I am undertaking works to promote equality and diversity within the college by analysing the experiences of EAL/ESL learners. It will highlight any issues surrounding subject-specific language acquisition for EAL learners, and conclusions can be drawn regarding improving teaching and learning practices in this area. It will also allow me to gain an insight into my learners' lives and establish links within the local community. The research is relevant to my role as a teacher as it is exploring current issues in education and improving inclusivity through my own teaching practice, as well as, possibly, improving the teaching practices of others.

Migration from African countries to the United Kingdom has steadily increased over the past 20 years, often as a consequence of work- and/or asylum-related issues. This has had a large influence on the number of Black African students attending further education institutions. I currently teach adult learners in the Access and Continuing Education Department at a further education college in Manchester. I teach health and social care, as well as courses that can lead to a career in nursing and allied health professions. Around half of the students I teach are Black African women who wish to embark on a career in the health care sector. The majority of these students speak English as a second or additional language. Therefore, my research proposal is to conduct a qualitative investigation into the barriers that EAL/ESL Black African students face in terms of their education in the UK, with a particular focus on language acquisition.

Gatekeeping is the process by which the researcher gains access to research participants, as well as the research environment. Dealing with gatekeepers can be a difficult process and requires good social networking skills, as well as the ability to form conducive relationships with people associated with the research project.

Initially, it is vital to gain formal permissions to conduct the research. In this case, I sought permission from the management and teachers within the college. My actions included informing the college of my research intentions and acquiring their formal approval in relation to conducting research on their premises and with their students. This usually involved completing various examples of paperwork – for example, anything from risk assessments to consent and ethical approval forms. However, it is important to note that gatekeeping can be a much more complex process than simply gaining formal permission from the organizations involved.

It is essential to identify key informants for the research project and build effective relationships. In this case this would include meeting with established teachers in the college setting that have much experience in teaching a wide range on EAL/ESL students. Key informants may provide the researcher with access to valuable cultural knowledge drawn from their own experience. Forming this relationship not only provides a valuable knowledge source, but also a means to access potential research participants. It is also important to remember that participants themselves serve as gatekeepers to information and other potential research participants.

Some participants may believe that research should be conducted by someone from their own community or culture as this would arguably provide a better representation of their views. As a White British working-class woman, overcoming this barrier in my research is difficult. In this case it is important to enter into the Black African community in order to experience the culture. This allows the researcher to gain a greater understanding of the participant's experience. This practice also provides the opportunity for the researcher to build a positive relationship with any cultural gatekeepers – for example, community leaders. An example of a community leader here would be church pastors as they have a big influence on the behaviour of the community. Gaining their approval and support for the research is essential. It is also important for the researcher to work to engender trust and highlight how the research will be beneficial to the community. This demonstration of respect for cultural diversity is essential for being granted access by gatekeepers.

Entering into the participants own cultural environment also helps to balance the power relationship between the researcher and participant. By conducting interviews within a college setting, and then within a neutral setting chosen by the participant, helps to challenge the participants perception that the researcher is an 'expert', and hands over power to the participant. This process is dramatalogical in nature and acts to equalize the power balance.

Overall, gatekeeping is a complex process that involves building and maintaining relationships between key stakeholders in the research project. In order to produce good and useful research, effective networking and gaining access through gatekeepers is an essential practice.

Conclusions

As research practitioners, the challenge to underpin practice with relevant and meaningful research is an important one. We must seek to validly and reliably delineate educational practices from educational research, and to improve the ethical calibre of our research. In doing so, we will serve the interests of our students and actively advance the academic basis of our field. The heart of research is the ethical application, and as such you must never underestimate its significance in shaping your research from start to finish.

References and further reading

British Educational Research Association (2011) *Ethical Guidelines for Educational Research*. Available at http://www.bera.ac.uk/system/files/BERA%20Ethical%20Guidelines%202011.pdf [accessed 17 April 2012].

Etherington, K. (2004) *Becoming a Reflexive Researcher: Using Our Selves in Research*. London: Jessica Kingsley.

Harding, S. (1987) Introduction: is there a feminist method?, in S. Harding (ed.) *Feminism and Methodology: Social Science Issues*. Bloomington, Indiana: University of Indiana Press: 1–14.

Oakley, A. (2005) *The Ann Oakley Reader: Gender, Women and Social Science*. Bristol: The Policy Press.

Reason, P. and Bradbury, H. (2001) *Handbook of Action Research: Participative Inquiry and Practice*. London: Sage.

Ribbens, J. and Edwards, R. (1998) *Feminist Dilemmas in Qualitative Research: Public Knowledge and Private Lives*. Thousand Oaks, CA: Sage.

Stanley, L. and Wise, S. (1993) *Breaking Out Again: Feminist Ontology and Epistemology*. New York: Routledge.

Wolf, M. (1992) *A Thrice Told Tale*. California: Stanford University Press.

6 Gathering data

By the end of this chapter you should be able to:

- Describe and evaluate a range of research methods that are appropriate for small-scale qualitative research projects

- Evaluate different research sampling techniques, appropriate to the research project

Introduction

Doing research, even on a small scale, is as much about practical tasks as it is about theorizing and writing. Spending time organizing and making sense of your data, or looking at your findings through your chosen critical or theoretical lens, can only happen once the data has been collected, stored, filed and sorted. So, although the ways in which you gather your data need to be chosen and planned in such a way that they are in theoretical alignment to your methodology, the actual process of data gathering – the nuts and bolts – is a practical task. It can be frustrating, and it can be time-consuming as well. You would not have to talk to too many researchers to find stories about focus groups where only one person turned up, or one-to-one interviews that went on for longer than anticipated, with the result that the researcher missed their train home. When Jonathan was doing his research with CertEd/PGCE students, a computer crash meant that the recording of one of his interviews was erased – an interview that he had travelled for an hour each way to attend, and that had lasted 90 minutes. A whole day's work was lost. But when it all goes well and according to plan, the knowledge that you have gathered an appropriate body of data with which to explore your research questions soon helps you to forget the hassle you might have experienced when recording interviews, shoving questionnaires into envelopes, waiting for emails, and trying to decipher your handwritten observation notes.

This chapter, then, will take you through the research methods that are most commonly used by education and teacher-training students in the lifelong learning sector, when doing their practitioner or action research. We will look in depth at questionnaires, observations and interviews, three very common methods. We will also look at some less common but equally appropriate methods, such as photography and documentary research. For the most part, there will be a practical, hands-on focus to this chapter, although some methodological and theoretical elements will be introduced as we go.

Interviews

Interview-based studies can be a very effective way of finding out about how people think about, react and respond to events, issues or changes in their lives. There is an almost common sense aspect to this. If you, as a researcher, are interested in some aspect of the work of NVQ assessors, or in the reasons why adult learners choose to return to college to study part time, then talking to the assessors or the learners is an obvious thing to do. The ubiquity of interviews within the world we live in makes the notion of an interview straightforward for potential respondents to respond to. Many of us have been stopped in the street by someone with a clipboard and asked to answer a few questions, or have watched people being interviewed on television. As such, asking people if they are willing to be interviewed can be seen as being a familiar activity in a way that asking if you can observe them in their workplace might not be. Interviewing is, understandably, a very popular method for student researchers to turn to, and it is easy to see why. At first look, they are straightforward to arrange and to carry out, easy to make sense of, and easily understood as part of a research plan. If someone wants to conduct an action research project within their own curriculum area (a common research plan for undergraduate students or trainee teachers), interviewing other staff, students, or stakeholders in the curriculum would appear to be straightforward to arrange and conduct.

Using interviews in your research

Interviews can last for 20 minutes, 90 minutes, or even longer. They can be highly *structured*, focused on a specific list of questions that the interviewer will not deviate from, *semi-structured*, combining a list of questions with the opportunity for the respondent to shape or inform the discussion, or *unstructured*, where the researcher and respondent sit down or walk along together and just talk. If you are using structured or semi-structured interviews, you need to prepare the questions you are going to ask in advance of the interview itself: this list is often referred to as an *interview schedule*. And, when writing your schedule of questions, you need to make sure that they are appropriately aligned to your *research questions* (as discussed in Chapter 4). It's important to take time over the schedule. By making sure that your interview questions are relevant and appropriate to your research questions, you can help ensure that the time spent interviewing people is not time wasted, and that the conversations you have are meaningful and helpful.

In order to be really thorough and to help maintain the quality of your research, interviews should be recorded, either on a Dictaphone or a laptop; but you will need to ask your respondent for their consent before you record them. Taking notes during an interview can also be helpful. You can note down those things that a sound recording cannot pick up, such as facial expressions. And if you lose your recording you can reconstruct the main findings of the interview from your notes. But you do not want to spend all of your time staring at your notepad, as it is important to maintain an appropriate level of eye contact with your respondent. After the interview, you should try to type it up, to *transcribe* it, as soon as possible: if you leave the transcribing for too long, you may forget important details or events from the interview that may not make sense to you when you listen to the recording weeks, rather than days, later. Transcribing interviews is a painstaking task, but it is a vital aspect of the research process. Not only will the final typed-up version of the interview be more straightforward to analyse closely and methodically than a recording would be, but the act of typing up constitutes an analytical process in itself. As you listen and type, you will be thinking about what is being said, making sense of it, and thinking about how it relates to your research questions. As such, it is a good idea to have a notepad nearby, or an additional Word document open on your computer, so that you can make a note of any ideas or themes that emerge.

You also need to think carefully about *where* interviews should take place. If you are going to meet a respondent out of doors, the quality of your recording may be affected by background noise, making transcription difficult. If you are going to meet indoors, then you need to be satisfied that the venue is appropriate. There is nothing wrong with arranging to interview someone in a seminar room or workshop as long as nobody else is going to come in. But if you are interrupted, then not only might the recording be disrupted, and therefore become more difficult to transcribe, but the *confidentiality* of the interview process will be affected (as discussed in Chapter 5). Therefore, if you are asking your respondent to find a place for you both to talk (which is a perfectly acceptable thing to ask them to do if you are meeting them at their place of work, for example), you need to make sure they choose somewhere that will be both sufficiently quiet and uninterrupted.

After all of the preparation, recording and typing up, the next stage of the interview process is to consider how, from a theoretical perspective, you are going to make use of what your respondents have told you. How are you going to analyse and interpret the data that emerges from the interviews? Interviews are what people say, not what they do. If you think that by interviewing people you will generate data that reports their actions both truthfully and accurately, then you will need to stop and reconsider. If in order to answer your research questions you need to find out about what people do, then this method will not be sufficient. At best, interviews can help you find out what people say and think they do. So, rather than treating interview data as being a direct hotline to your respondents' actions or experiences, a more critical approach is needed. There are several ways to go about this. One way to proceed is for the researcher to treat the interview data as a form of storytelling, during which the respondent might still be making sense of the events that they are talking about, irrespective of how recently they occurred. Facts or details might be embellished or forgotten, mixed up, or confused. We can't always remember everything, or how we felt about or reacted to something, so we make up stories to plug the gaps. In order to make interview data more reliable, think about holding repeat interviews, and asking some of the same questions – or different questions about the same topics – again. And if contradictions occur, you can follow them up.

Using interviews in your research: problematic issues

So far so good. But there are also some problematic aspects to interview-based research that you will need to take account of. We are not listing these in order to put anybody off; rather, we want to highlight these because if you are going to provide a *critical* account of why you chose to use interviews in your research, you will need to acknowledge the pitfalls as well as the benefits and explain how you dealt with them.

Many of our students have highlighted in the past how time-consuming and even wasteful the process can be. By this we do not mean to suggest that interviews are a 'waste of time'. But it is important to be aware of the fact that, put simply, interviews take a lot of time. You will need to take into account the time that you need to travel to the respondent, to get consent forms signed, to set up your recording equipment, to thank the respondent, and to type up the recording. And you need to do all of this before the serious process of data analysis can begin. After all of this, much of the raw material produced during interviews may not even make it all the way through to the final dissertation or research report. The notion that not all of the material that you have patiently recorded and transcribed may actually be used can be dispiriting, but there are ways to answer this. You can ensure that your data is as good as it can possibly be through careful interview preparation, by making sure that your schedule is good, your research questions are sound, and you have allowed an appropriate amount of time for the respondent to talk with you. Interviews that are poorly prepared, or based on inadequately theorized research questions, will waste your respondents' time as much as your own.

There are not only practical difficulties associated with interviews, but theoretical and methodological ones as well. Here we wish to highlight two problematic themes. Firstly, as we have already said, interviews are what people say and not what they do. The idea that by talking to people we can somehow gain a direct line to exactly what they think, or how they behave, is false. At all times when interviewing respondents you need to be sensitive to the fact that as people speak with you, they are presenting *their version* of what they know, what they have seen, or how they behave at particular times or in particular places. That is to say, there is always a level of *subjectivity* to the accounts that they give. This is not necessarily a problem, so long as you account for it when writing up your research.

The second problematic theme relates to the relative positions that the interviewer and the respondent occupy in relation to each other, a concept sometimes referred to as the *standpoint* taken by the researcher in relation to the respondent. For example, assume that you are going to carry out some interviews with some of your own students as part of an action research project. How open, honest or frank do you think that their answers or comments will be, if you are still involved in teaching them and in marking their assignments? It might be the case that they will hold back in some way for fear of retribution later on. Or perhaps you wanted to carry out some research within the organization where you work, and wanted to speak with your line manager. What kinds of questions or comments do you think that would you be able to put to her or him, allowing for the nature of your professional relationship? Issues relating to the relationships between interviewer and interviewee need not stop you from using interviews in your own research, but you do need to be sensitive to them and, where necessary, explain how any such issues were managed during the course of your project.

Group interviews and focus groups

Speaking to people on a one-to-one basis can be a very effective method for conducting educational research, but sometimes this can be difficult to arrange. Respondents are not able to attend, travelling might become difficult, matching up spaces in your diary with those of your respondents can be tricky – for all kinds of reasons, interviews can be awkward to organize. Speaking to *groups* of people all at the same time, however, gets round some of these problems. As a researcher, you are able to speak to a number of people all at once, and if you invite a number of people to a meeting so that you can talk with them and they cannot all attend, you will still probably have enough people to make the exercise worthwhile.

Group interviews or focus groups are not just a practical response to the difficulties of arranging interviews, however. They offer a way of gathering data that is particular in its own right, and is different – in terms of both the kind of data you will get and the ways in which you manage it – from the one-to-one interview. Focus groups can be noisy and boisterous, and need to be managed politely but firmly so that everyone can participate – rather like the way in which a teaching group needs to be managed. And rather than gathering data that represents each participant's individual point of view, you may in fact be gathering data that more or less represents some kind of group consensus. Individuals who hold views that are at odds with the group may not feel able to speak about what they think. Conversely, people with strong personalities may dominate the focus group and distort the data that is generated. As such, if you choose to hold a focus group, you will need to think about how to interpret what emerges – the views of individuals, or a consensus created by a vocal minority.

Using interviews: checklist

When beginning your interview-based research, make sure that you:

- decide whether to use structured, semi-structured or unstructured interviews
- prepare a proper interview schedule
- align your interview questions with your overall research questions
- record the interview properly
- obtain appropriate permissions
- have an appropriate place for the interview to be conducted
- think about how you will analyse the interview data
- allow enough time for the entire process – including travelling to the interview and transcribing it afterwards.

And if you are holding a focus group, take time to plan how you will manage the group, and think about how you can capture the different points of view that might be put forward.

Questionnaires

Questionnaires are a second popular method for researchers involved in action or small-scale research projects. Like interviews, they are very common, familiar in look and feel: as teachers or trainers in the lifelong learning sector, we are used to handing out questionnaires to our students when carrying out module or programme evaluations, and then reading and summarizing what the students have told us when writing our module and programme reports. Using questionnaires for the purposes of a research project similarly involves distributing, collecting and then analysing dozens – perhaps hundreds – of questionnaires: the difference is that when doing research, we are the ones who set the questions and decide how to make sense of the answers, according to our research topics. They are relatively cheap and quick to prepare and to analyse, and as such they lend themselves to being distributed to large numbers of participants: giving a questionnaire to 200 students is quite manageable, whereas interviewing 200 students would be a considerable undertaking. But unless the questionnaire is very detailed – and if they are too long then it might put people off completing them – the data that you gather will tend to be less richly detailed than the data produced through other methods.

Using questionnaires in your research

Designing a good questionnaire is harder than you might think. If a questionnaire is too long, people might be reluctant to fill it all in – but if it's too short the data will be superficial and perhaps worth very little. And yet you will need to be sure that you have asked a sufficient number of questions to generate a reliable and meaningful amount of data. If your questions are ambiguous or over-complicated, or if they use unfamiliar vocabulary or jargon, then people might miss out questions or provide answers based on misunderstandings. But if your questions are carefully worded, designed in such a way as to have the best possible chance of generating the amount of data that you need to explore your research topics, then questionnaires can be reliable and highly effective. Therefore, in order to ensure that your research is of a good quality, you will need to make sure that your questionnaire is organized appropriately. There are several factors to consider. Firstly, you need to think about the style of questions you want answering. Are you going to offer the respondents a series of statements and ask for them to be ranked according to preference? Are you going to ask closed questions that simply require a 'yes' or a 'no'? Are you going to ask open questions, and leave a space for respondents to write their answers in? Do you need to ask respondents for personal details, such as how old they are, or where they work? Although it can seem like an easy option for the new researcher, using questionnaires requires a degree of time, effort and careful thought.

What kinds or styles of question should I use?

Several types of question and response format are available for us to use in our research, and they all work in slightly different ways. You will need to choose which kinds of questions to use, and how to use them, according to your own research topic. There are several things to think about here.

Asking simple yes/no questions
If you want to make sure that your questionnaire can be completed relatively quickly, then asking yes/no questions is one approach that is worth pursuing. But if you want to gather a meaningful amount of data, you are almost certainly going to have to ask a large number of questions. It is also important to spend time thinking carefully about how the questions will be worded. And at the same time you will have to take care to avoid asking leading questions that might distort the data you are gathering. For example, suppose you were researching the working practices of FE lecturers. Asking 'Do you think that your contact teaching hours for each academic year constitute a manageable workload?' makes sense as a question; but you would need to ask lots of follow-up questions to find out *why* the lecturers thought their workload was, or was not, manageable. You would need to prepare one set of further questions for the lecturers who said 'yes', and an additional set for the lecturers who said 'no'.

Asking respondents to indicate how much they agree or disagree with something
Instead of a yes/no answer, another popular questionnaire tool is the Likert Scale (which you will probably have seen before, even if you didn't know that this is what it's called). In a Likert Scale survey, respondents are asked to rate or rank a series of statements or responses on a sliding scale – often numbered between 1 and 5, where 1 means 'strongly agree', three means 'no opinion', 5 means 'strongly disagree', and so on. Because you are not asking questions as such, you need to phrase things a bit differently. So, in our example, instead of the yes/no question above, we might instead ask the lecturers to rate the following statement: 'My contact teaching hours constitute a manageable workload'. And with the Likert Scale, we may receive a wider range of answers than is possible with a simple yes/no question.

Asking respondents to select from a list of responses
A third approach is to provide respondents with a short list of statements or answers to a question, and then ask them to indicate which answer, or answers, apply to them. This takes a little longer to design and complete, but offers a greater level of detail in the responses, and is still relatively quick for the researcher to analyse. So, in our example, we might have the following:

The number of contact time teaching hours that I am required to teach:

a) Is about right in relation to my other duties as a lecturer
b) Is too large, and my other lecturing duties are negatively affected
c) Is too large, but my other lecturing duties are not affected
d) Is low compared to my other duties as a lecturer

Asking respondents to write open-ended answers

Creating a questionnaire using open-ended questions provides us, as researchers, with a richer and more detailed body of data – but we cannot be sure exactly how respondents will answer the questions we set. Some people may write just a few words, while others will write reams of text on the questionnaire form. Some people may read or interpret the question differently to others: even the most carefully worded questions might lead to divergent answers. In a way, using open-ended questions is more 'high risk' than using closed questions or a Likert Scale. But the risks might just pay off: because you are not directing the answers in a particular direction using pre-arranged comments or yes/no questions, you might get back comments which open up new questions or directions in your research that you had not anticipated.

Using questionnaires in your research: problematic issues

It is easy to see why students and novice researchers are attracted to using questionnaires for their research. They are quicker to prepare for than interviews, more straightforward to analyse than the reams of text transcribed from interviews or observations, and, simply due to their ubiquity, present themselves as a 'first port of call' when planning for data collection. The ease by which a questionnaire can be distributed – especially as an email attachment or through a web-based questionnaire generator such as SurveyMonkey – makes their use all the more attractive. But, as with any research tool or method, the decision to use questionnaires or surveys should always be based on a consideration of which method best answers your research questions, and not on which method is the most straightforward from a practical or organizational perspective to set up. Let us provide an example: during each academic year, Vicky and Jonathan work with students to help them plan their research projects. As supervisors, one of our first tasks is to provide a critical reading of our students' research plans. Many of our students opt to do either case study research or action research (these are examples of research paradigms that we will discuss in the following chapter). In the majority of these situations, the number of research respondents that the students are working with tends to be small in number. Now, it is perfectly possible to use questionnaires as part of a case study, but how much useful data can be gathered from a questionnaire that is only going to be delivered to 15 or 20 people? It is almost certain that additional data collection methods will be required.

There are several aspects of using questionnaires and surveys that new researchers need to be sensitive to, in addition to the broader issue of whether or not a questionnaire is an appropriate and/or sufficient tool for gathering the data that is needed. The first problem is: how many people will actually complete them? Different methodological textbooks offer different opinions regarding completion rates, with one in three being completed seen as a good response. If you are sending the questionnaire to 600 people, then 200 returns should provide a meaningful body of data. Sending a questionnaire to 15 people, and getting 5 back, is far more problematic. Some people, when using questionnaires with only small groups, try to increase the return rate by being physically present, handing out the questionnaires, and then collecting them back in again as if they were end-of-course evaluation forms. We do not endorse such approaches for two reasons: firstly, because if respondents feel rushed, then it may affect how they answer; and secondly, the presence of the researcher may lead the respondents to feel pressurized into answering. If they had received the questionnaire in the post, or by email, they would have found it easier to choose not to participate in the research, which they are entitled to do.

We have already referred to the second problem that we wish to raise here, which is the *quality* of the data that the questionnaire might produce. And there are several different ways to think about this. Using different types of questions within the same questionnaire – a mix of yes/no or Likert Scale comments and open-ended questions – is a popular strategy, but this will only work if the questions are good enough. So, questions should be carefully worded to avoid ambiguity and misinterpretation. It is also worth asking questions more than once within the same questionnaire. Rewording and then repeating questions (two, or even three times) helps prevent your data from being distorted if the respondent misreads or rushes through the questions. But perhaps the trickiest thing to get right – which makes it all the more important to try out your questionnaire on a *trial basis* before embarking on your main data collection – is the length of the questionnaire. How many questions, of whatever kind, should you ask? There is no right answer, other than: 'As many as you need to gather a meaningful amount of data, but not so many that respondents either rush their answers, or don't bother answering at all'.

Using questionnaires: checklist

When beginning your questionnaire-based research, make sure that you:

- Allow time to trial your questionnaire to make sure that the questions make sense, that it doesn't take too long to complete, and that your questions generate the kinds of answers that your research needs.
- Organize ways to distribute and collect the questionnaires that do not place an undue burden on your respondents (or anyone else for that matter – asking colleagues to help might be appropriate, but you still need to be able to guarantee confidentiality and anonymity).
- Only ask for personal information if your research questions require it, or if you are looking for people to volunteer for follow-up actions (such as an interview).
- If you would like to use an online tool to help administer your questionnaire such as SurveyMonkey (http://www.surveymonkey.com/), make sure you design your questionnaire *before* you log on! Tools such as this can make the process simple for your respondents – all they have to do is log on and fill in the questionnaire – but they do not make things quicker for the researcher: you still need to spend time planning the questionnaire and writing appropriate questions.

Observations

When researchers discuss the theories that underpin their choice of research methods, one of the complaints raised against both interviews and observations is that they are 'artificial'. People don't go around the place interviewing people or asking them to fill in questionnaires unless they are looking for some information, and you *could* argue that once you go looking for something you will probably find it (it's more complex than this, but that's the general idea). In this sense, interviews and questionnaires work for researchers because they make people – respondents – talk or write about stuff that the researcher wants to get to. In a way, the researcher helps to *create* the data in the first place by asking the questions. An alternative approach is to look for data that is *naturally occurring*, rather than data that the researcher has helped to create as a consequence of their choice of methods. And the most common method for gathering naturally occurring data is the observation. In contrast to the artificial creation of comments and quotations through interviews or observations, simply watching what people do – at work, at college, in their daily lives – provides data that is, arguably, more *authentic*.

Using observations in your research

As with the other methods we have discussed so far, there are several ways to approach observation-based research. Like interviews, observations can be structured to varying degrees. If you were going to conduct *structured observations*, you would go into the observation with a clearly defined and fixed list of those interactions, events or actions that you were seeking to observe. For example, you might want to record each occasion when a student answers a question asked by their tutor, or every time a student responds directly to a comment made by one of their peers. Your checklist of things to watch out for would be aligned to your research questions. Observations such as these take time to prepare for, as your checklist will need to be thorough, but once that it done it is a simple task to perform repeat observations, and the consistent use of the checklist means that the observations will be carried out with a high degree of reliability (we shall discuss this in Chapter 8). If you have a very clear and well-formed view of what you want and need to get out of the observation process, then using a checklist can be a very effective tool.

It might be the case, by contrast, that your decision to use observations to gather data is based on a less well-formed research design, not because you don't know what you are looking for, but because you are uncertain as to how the issues that you are interested in will display themselves in a workshop or classroom setting. In situations such as these, keeping an open mind as to what you might be looking out for when conducting your observations would be appropriate. Or, returning to the example above, it may be the case that you are interested in not only how many times a student answers a question (easy to record on a tick sheet or checklist) but also in the actual ways that students and tutors talk with each other. Details such as these that involve some kind of evaluative judgement are more difficult to record on a tick sheet unless you have prepared one with a large number of possible kinds of tutor-student interaction. Here, making some detailed notes may in fact be easier than trying to ascertain the extent to which what you have seen might match up to your list of pre-planned criteria or phenomena. In fact, both of these situations lead themselves to *unstructured observations*. Instead of basing your observation on a pre-prepared checklist, and ignoring all those events that are not listed, the unstructured approach requires the researcher to be open to anything that might happen during the observation. Instead of a checklist, the researcher needs to note down all of those things that happen that might be helpful later on – usually referred to as *critical incidents* – taking care to write their notes in such a way that they will make sense (and be legible – it is very important to make sure that you can read your own writing) later on, when typing them up prior to analysis (discussed in the following chapter).

And finally, it is worth noting that a *semi-structured* approach is also possible: as with other methods, so a semi-structured observation would combine checklist elements, to allow for particular incidents to be systematically recorded, with unplanned elements where any emerging or unplanned issues might be noted down for analysis later on.

The kind of observations that you do will impact on the kinds of data that will be produced. A structured observation, like a structured questionnaire, can lead to the production of data that might be represented as a table or graph. In a structured observation, you are simply counting the number of times that a particular event occurs. As such, quantitative data will be produced. However, you would need to conduct a significantly large number of observations if you were going to produce enough such data to need to make use of a statistical analysis software program such as SPSS. Findings from a relatively small number of observations can easily be represented on a graph with relatively simple arithmetic. Unstructured observations will almost certainly lead to the production of several pages of notes: these will need to be typed up (just as you would transcribe an interview) so that they can be systematically analysed and coded.

Photography

Photographs can be very helpful to the researcher for a number of reasons. The use of photographs can perhaps be understood as being aligned to observations, although research using visual data gathered through using photography (or, indeed, using film) is increasingly recognized as a method in its own right. But it can be useful even for the small-scale researcher. For example, if you are conducting a series of observations in classrooms or workshops, taking photographs of the location – assuming you have permission to do so – prior to the start of the observation will allow you to focus on the critical incidents or events at hand, without having to worry about writing down a more or less detailed description of the venue. Subsequently, when analysing your observation notes, you may find useful additional data in the photographs – for example, through having a photograph of a series of posters that a tutor refers their students to during the observed session. Taking photography with people in them is more difficult to accomplish, primarily for reasons of confidentiality and data protection (as discussed in the previous chapter).

Using observations in your research: problematic issues

It might seem strange to say it, but the single most problematic element of observation-based research is you, the researcher. In part this is because of the same issues of bias and subjectivity that affect other forms of data collection: if two people observed the same workshop session, would they both see things in the same way? But in the main, this is due to the *reactivity effect* that will be generated as a result of going into a seminar room or workshop as a researcher. Put simply, how do we, as researchers, respond to the fact that once we start watching people – students, tutors, learning support workers – during our research, they might in turn start behaving differently because they know that they are being watched and that some or all aspects of their behaviours – their words and actions – are being recorded?

This is a real problem for researchers. On the one hand, the idea that observations can allow us to access naturally occurring data is extremely compelling: after all, what is more natural than seeing what people do during their day-to-day lives as tutors or students? But if we take the issue of reactivity seriously, then there are two implications for our research. Firstly, our presence is in some way distorting what people usually do: our naturally occurring data has been corrupted by our presence. Secondly, if our presence as researchers does indeed lead to changes or distortions in people's behaviour, then there is an ethical concern as well. Is it appropriate for us to observe a teaching session, for example, if there is a risk that through our being there, that teaching session will somehow be changed? If those changes in any way impact negatively on the processes (learning, teaching or assessment, for example) that might otherwise have taken place, then our presence as researchers might be seen as being damaging or harmful. So how can we make allowances for the reactions that our presence might cause?

Carry out multiple observations

The most common response is to carry out a number of observations, not just one or two. Hopefully, by becoming a more habitual presence in the environment where you are carrying out your observations, the people you are observing will get used to your presence and stop worrying as much about what you might be thinking and writing down about them. Your research subjects will become more relaxed around you, and you will be able to blend in. But this takes time: if you are doing a long ethnographic study then this is quite achievable; but if you are doing small-scale case study or action research, there may not be enough time for this process to occur.

Be a participant, not a detached observer

Another common response to the problem is to reposition yourself in relation to what you are observing. Instead of being an observer who is completely removed or detached from what is being observed, you could – if your research design allows for it – be a *participant observer* instead. An approach such as this is particularly well suited to shorter-term and smaller-scale research. By juggling/combining the two roles of researcher and tutor (or whatever your job role is), reactivity is lessened. But writing research notes at the same time as you are running a seminar group is difficult. Part of this difficulty stems from practicalities: it's simply hard to write down field notes while you are teaching! But there's an issue of professionalism and ethics as well: your students – quite rightly – expect your main focus to be your teaching and their learning. Your research interests cannot therefore be allowed to interfere with this.

Observation fatigue?

It may well be the case, however, that *observation fatigue* can work in your favour (Tummons, 2011). Observation fatigue is a term that refers to the impact of the frequency of observations in the lifelong learning sector, particularly in further education colleges. There are so many observations in staffrooms, classrooms and workshops – by Ofsted inspectors, by college quality assurance managers, and by Integrated Quality and Enhancement Review (IQER) observers – that people (tutors and students) no longer react to it. As such, you may well find that the presence of yet another observer – you, the researcher – causes only minimal ripples.

Using observations: checklist

When beginning your observation-based research, make sure that you:

- Devote sufficient time to preparing checklists for structured observations
- Devote sufficient time to typing up and then analysing field notes from unstructured observations
- Account for the possibility of reactivity effects in your observations
- Carry out a sufficient number of observations so that you are confident that you are gathering data that is meaningful and representative of the practices, people and environment that make up your field

How many? Populations and samples

Questions that our own students often ask us include: How many questionnaires do I have to do? How many people do I need to interview? How many observations should I carry out? There are no simple numerical answers to this when conducting qualitative practitioner research. Rather, these questions as to how many people should make up the *research sample* need instead to be answered by returning to your research questions: how many people will you need to talk to so that you generate sufficient data to provide a meaningful answer to your question? Let us think about a practical example: if you are researching some aspect of the professional work of NVQ assessors, trying to interview all of the assessors who work in one college might be a daunting task – simply because there may be dozens of people who perform this role! So who should be selected to be interviewed, and on what basis should this selection be made? There are a few ways to think about this.

Random sampling

With a random sample, every member of a research population has an equal chance of being selected for the study. So, in our example, we would pick some NVQ assessors at random to talk to and exclude others. However, a sample such as this might distort our research: what if our random sample consisted entirely of assessors from only one curriculum area?

Convenience sampling

Researchers use a convenience sample when they include people who are easily available and can be easily recruited, and are happy to participate. If this approach is used, a description of how it was done becomes an important part of the writing up. This approach can work if you are finding it hard to get people to take part in your research but, as with random sampling, your data may be distorted.

Purposive sampling

With purposive sampling, the researcher specifies the characteristics of a group of people who are of interest to the research project and then tries to locate people who share those characteristics. So, in our example, we might be specifically interested in NVQ assessors who have only been qualified for the last two years, and we would exclude other people when finding research participants.

Representative sampling

With representative sampling, the researcher specifies the characteristics of the research population as a whole, and then tries to locate a smaller number of respondents who proportionally reflect these characteristics. The characteristics that are chosen will depend on the research topic. So, for example, if a researcher wants to explore an educational issue that he or she argues is of equal significance to male and female students, then the sample would need to include a roughly equal number of males and females.

Theoretical sampling

In this case, the researcher selects groups of people to study based in their relevance or alignment to the research questions or theoretical framework that the researcher is using. So, in our example, we might have decided to answer a research question regarding assessors who work with a particular curriculum. Assessors who work in other curriculum areas would therefore be excluded because their professional role was not aligned to the interests of the research question.

Opportunistic sampling

Opportunistic sampling is used by researchers to respond to events that emerge during data collection. For example, it might be the case that when speaking with an NVQ assessor, we come across something that we hadn't thought about when planning our initial research questions. But if what we learn is of sufficient interest to our research we might want to change direction slightly, and this might involve speaking to new people who we happen to come across, simply because they can help us explore these new issues.

It is perfectly possible for a research project to rest on more than one kind of sample, although small-scale projects tend to fit just one of these categories. And it is important to remember that none of these sampling strategies is 'better' than another: it is simply the case that one kind of sampling will be a better fit for your research than another. So that will be the one to use.

Conclusions

Once you have your research questions in place, you can think about which methods you need to use and how many people you will need to work with. Your choices of both methods and sample will always need to match up to your research questions. At the same time, you need to think about what is practicable and achievable. If you are a part-time student and a full-time lecturer with a family, your time for gathering data may well be at a premium. It is better to focus on what is achievable rather than to try to carry out an ambitious programme of interviews, for example, that takes you so long to do that you do not have time to transcribe and analyse them properly. Take time when planning methods and samples, talk to your supervisor and, if you can, talk to other students as well.

References and further reading

Angrosino, M. (2007) *Doing Ethnographic and Observational Research*. London: Sage.

Barbour, R. (2007) *Doing Focus Groups*. London: Sage.

Gibbs, P. (2007) Practical wisdom and the workplace researcher. *London Review of Education*, 5(3): 223–36.

Kvale, S. (2007) *Doing Interviews*. London: Sage.

Litosseliti, L. (2003) *Using Focus Groups in Research*. London: Continuum.

Silverman, D. (2005) *Doing Qualitative Research*. London: Sage.

Tummons, J. (2011) 'It sort of feels uncomfortable': problematising the assessment of reflective practice. *Studies in Higher Education*, 36(4): 471–83.

7   Making sense of your data

By the end of this chapter you should be able to:

- Apply appropriate research skills to the management and preparation of qualitative data

- Evaluate and apply different approaches to the analysis of qualitative data

- Understand the role and impact of the researcher on the research process in both methodological and ethical terms

Introduction

Picture this: you are sitting at home at your dining room table (your preferred location for doing your homework) and you are surrounded by pieces of paper, a couple of USB memory sticks with audio files from interviews on them, 30 or so completed questionnaires, some photographs of empty classrooms and a small notebook filled with handwritten notes. Somewhere in all of this stuff is the data that you have painstakingly gathered over the preceding few months – in between your other study commitments, family time, having to go to work, and so on. Your project is due to be handed in to your supervisor in a few weeks' time. So where should you begin? The process of analysing data is one that requires careful thought, concentration and quiet time and space. But no matter how much deep thinking or complicated theorizing you do, or intend to do, you are going to find it hard to get going with the analysis until you have spent some time preparing and organizing your data first.

In Chapter 1, we spent time thinking about the *practicalities* of educational research. We suggested that whatever the scale of the project, time spent on the practicalities – keeping notes, making sure references are up to date, making sure your handwriting is legible, organizing everything so that you can find what you need when you need it – is as important a part of the research process as the literature review or the data analysis. By the time you come to analysing your data, the value of having done all of this groundwork will become clear. We also spent time thinking about ways of keeping track of your ideas and impressions *during* the research journey, and suggested that some sort of research diary or journal would help you keep track of what you do, and provide a useful place for you to write down any ideas about your research or your data as you go – this is a practice that is referred to as *interim analysis*. Instead of dividing the research process up into distinct and separate chunks (doing your literature review, doing your data collection, analysing your data and writing up), we argued that much real-world research involves doing some or all of these at the same time (Crang and Cook, 2007). Hopefully, therefore, by the time you get ready to begin the real work of data analysis, you will have all of those pieces of paper, recordings, USB sticks, notebooks, and so on in front of you as you settle down to work, but they will all be properly sorted or organized and labelled so that you can quickly find what you need.

Getting started: sorting and typing

Before you begin to pore over the words your respondents have spoken during focus groups or the comments they have written on questionnaires, you need to make sure that all of these data sources – as well as any others that you have gathered – are organized and presented in such a way that it will be easy for you to analyse everything in the same manner. In order to make sure that your analysis is robust you need to make sure that the way you treat your interview data, for example, is the same as the way you treat your observation data. All of your data sources need to be subjected to comparable levels of scrutiny if you are going to get as much out of them all as you can.

The first thing to do, therefore, is to type up or *transcribe* your data. Transcription is the process through which interview or focus group recordings, rough notes, and so on are typed up.

Transcribing interviews

Transcribing interviews is probably the most laborious job you will have to do. There are no ways around this, unless you can touch type or perhaps pay a professional typist to transcribe your recordings for you (make sure that your university allows this, just in case it leads to a breach of research ethics or confidentiality). You should allow a good three hours to transcribe a one-hour interview. In your wider reading, you may have come across quite sophisticated techniques for analysing data such as *discourse analysis* or *conversation analysis*, where the tiniest details of the interview – such as the length of pauses between speaking or the exact emphasis with which your respondent might say 'erm, well . . .' – need to be transcribed. These are relatively specialized methodological approaches that can be highly illuminating, but which, we suggest, are perhaps beyond the scope of the kinds of students for whom this book is written. The most straightforward approach is to simply type up everything that was said, merely noting who said what. There are a few transcription conventions that are useful even for the novice researcher, and we recommend that you use these where necessary:

- If you need to indicate a pause in speech, use: '. . .'
- If you are leaving out a section of the conversation that is not relevant to the research, use: '[. . .]'
- If you need to make a note of some feature of the conversation, put a comment in square brackets, for example: '[laughs]' or '[draws deep breath]'. This can also be helpful if, no matter how hard you listen, you cannot quite make out what was said. In these cases, putting '[indistinguishable]' into your transcript is perfectly acceptable.

Example 7.1: Excerpt from an interview transcript

Here, the respondent is talking about the ways in which she juggles her work commitments and her study commitments (she is working towards a Certificate in Education for the lifelong learning sector):

> Diane [student]: I work here till late, you know, every day. And I'm going home and lesson planning every night because I'm not ready. So it's been quite hard [. . .] I emailed Helen and it was kind of, you know, if anybody could read between any lines, and she just put 'no worries'. And I know she don't like any, she's, when you have a tutorial it's just ch-ch-ch [pretending to write a list] like that. She's a little bit impatient [. . .].

The second and last lines feature a break in the conversation. In line five, Jonathan tried several different letters before settling on 'ch-ch-ch' as the best way of representing the sound that the respondent made when she was mimicking writing a list on the table between us. Helen (a pseudonym) is her Certificate in Education tutor.

As we have said, transcribing interviews is particularly time-consuming. As such, when thinking about how to manage your study workload, it is a useful job to do on those study days when you are perhaps 'not in the mood' for wrestling with complex theories, or when you have a long train journey perhaps.

Group interviews or focus groups are more difficult to transcribe because you have to deal with the fact of there being multiple voices on your recording, sometimes talking at the same time, sometimes with a few voices crowding out the group as a whole. It is possible to distinguish between who says what, but this is time-consuming and may require two or three listens to the file before getting it right. If you have taken notes during the focus group you can use your notes to help you pinpoint who said what. But if you can, try to manage the conversation so that it will be as straightforward as possible for you to transcribe later on.

Finally, a note concerning technology: these days, almost all of our students use digital recorders, iPods or laptops to record their interviews (as opposed to analogue cassette recorders – Jonathan does know someone who still uses a minidisc recorder, though). Being able to save your interview recordings onto your laptop is very helpful when it comes to doing the transcribing. There is a free software program called *Express Scribe* (Mac and PC) which allows you to play the sound file on your computer, starting and stopping it with the touch of a key (you can even buy a foot pedal if you want to), while you type up what you are listening to. You can pause, rewind and forward wind the file as well, so it is easy to double-check something if you think that you have made a mistake. *Express Scribe* (which Jonathan used for his research) is available at: http://www. nch.com.au/scribe/index.html

Transcribing questionnaires

Even a relatively small number of relatively short questionnaires can lead to a lot of paperwork. If you have given out 80 two-page questionnaires and got back a third of them, that adds up to 50 sides of A4 paper. If you can compile all of the different answers that you have gathered into a smaller space, then analysis of these – and comparing them with your other data sources – will be much easier.

If you have used questions with a Likert Scale it is a simple task to go through these and compile a summary of how many respondents selected 'mostly agree', how many selected 'slightly agree' (or whatever terms you used), and so on. You can convert these results into pie charts or bar charts if you wish, but a simple table of results is more effective – and less time-consuming. For *open* questions, we recommend that you go through all of your results one question at a time and type up all of the answers to each question before moving on to the next one. You can use your initial questionnaire template (which you will have saved on your computer – remember, don't delete anything until after your project is completed) to help you organize this. If you need to know who gave which answer – for example, if you are looking for patterns in what particular respondents tell you – you can give each completed questionnaire a number and then use this number as a reference point when compiling the answers, as in the example below.

> **Example 7.2: Transcribing answers to the open question 'do you think that the fact that you work as a teacher or trainer helps you to understand the assignment requirements for your teacher-training course?'**

Jonathan analysed these in batches according to the different colleges where he did his research. At one college he received 17 questionnaires back from a group of 26 students in total – a pretty good response rate. He compiled the answers so that he could see what each person put across the range of questions as a whole. Here, the gaps indicate that respondents 7 and 17 did not give an answer to this particular question.

1. I think the 'teacher speak' – education jargon used in the assignment requirements – is familiar to me because of my work.
2. Because of the language of the assignment. If you had not had that background you would find the requirements hard to understand.
3. Constantly assessing/reflecting/challenging with colleagues and students.
4. Technical language used is more familiar.
5. You already hold some knowledge (experience) that you are able to reflect upon/ refer to.
6. As you can reflect on own practice, try things out.

   7
   8 The words used can be helpful – e.g. reflection.
   9 Makes a good link between theory and practical.
  10 This helps because the understanding is more relevant to the task.
  11 I also work as an online tutor which is not covered.
  12 I understand the terms used and can relate to things that I do in real life.
  13 Yes, as if you did not have any practical aspects of the course, you would not be able to reflect and understand why you need the training.
  14 Helps understand certain terms.
  15 It helps because it puts into practice what you are learning about and why.
  16 Can try out new things and reflect on sessions.
  17

Transcribing observations

In all likelihood, you will be transcribing *unstructured* observations from handwritten notes. These should be relatively straightforward to type up, unless your handwriting is so bad that even you cannot read it when you come back to it after a few weeks. If you are worried that this might happen to you, try to remember the following:

- Write legibly even if it means writing less
- Don't use abbreviations or acronyms that you have made up there and then without writing them down in full
- If you can, type up your rough notes as soon as possible after the observation, while it's still fresh

And finally . . .

Transcribing your data isn't all that much fun, but it can be made more engaging if you remember to treat it as part of the process of analysis, not just as preparation. Keep your notebook with you as you type, or have another Word file open on your desktop, so that you can quickly note down any ideas that emerge as you go along. As you read your rough notes or listen to your recordings, you almost cannot stop yourself from analysing as you go: particular exchanges in interviews, or particular answers on questionnaires will 'leap out' at you as being immediately useful and important. This can help keep your motivation levels up as you type. But remember that this is just a 'first pass' at the data, and when everything is transcribed the serious work of analysis will begin.

Next steps: reading and coding

As you read your documents, you will be looking for things (for instance, things that people have said, or that you have seen) that are important to you and to your research questions. Some sections from your painstakingly compiled transcripts will, we are afraid to say, end up in the recycle bin. And other sections will be of relevance to your research.

Specifically, you will find that some bits are relevant to some of your research questions, and other bits to others. What you need to do, therefore, is to sort out, highlight and categorize the different parts of your transcripts that you really need, so that all the most useful sections are easily searchable when it comes to writing up your research. This (a little confusingly, as it's a word that is used in many other contexts) is called *coding*. When you label a sentence or a paragraph with a particular *code* you are attaching a specific meaning to that sentence or paragraph, and this meaning is 'summed up' by the name or title that you give to that particular code. If appropriate, you can give the same sentence or chunk of text more than one code. And to make sure that your research is really thorough (an issue that we shall consider in much greater detail in the following chapter), you can use the same labels or codes whether or not you are looking at interview data, observation data or anything else. As you create new codes (we shall return to this shortly), keep a separate list of all the codes that you have used and keep a tally of when you use each one. That way you will be able to show how often each code was used when you get to the end of your research.

> **Example 7.3: An extract from an interview between Jonathan and Helen (a pseudonym), a PGCE student. This was coded 'tutor as student' – a theme that emerged *during* the research**

Helen: One of the things I love about it [doing the PGCE] is I teach three days a week, and half of my day on a Thursday is I am being taught. And the psychological, sort of like, role reversal is fantastic.
Jonathan: Tell me about that role reversal then. You go into the room and sit down?
Helen: I can go into the room, I can sit down, I don't have to be all energetic and enthusiastic about what I'm going to do. I can just sit there and soak it all in, and if I feel like I need to converse I can, but I'm not put under any pressure to converse with anybody within the group, other than what, when we're asked.

This notion of 'role reversal' was a factor that came up quite a lot during Jonathan's research, although it was not something that he had anticipated. But he felt that it was sufficiently important – not least due to its frequency – so he decided to include it in his research. He created a new code called 'tutor as student' to label this and other similar extracts from interviews. The whole of this exchange was given this code.

Sometimes, researchers give names or titles to their codes *as they go*: that is to say, it is while doing their research that they come across themes or issues that are deemed to be sufficiently important to be worth coding and including in the research. An example of this process, which is called *inductive coding*, appears above (Example 7.3). At other times, researchers work out a list of the codes that they are going to use *before* they start going through their data. This is referred to as *a priori* coding. In these cases, the codes that are generated will all link back to the research questions that the project is seeking to provide answers for. An example of this process appears below (Example 7.4). And sometimes it may be entirely appropriate to use both approaches – you just need to remember to explain that you have done so when you write up your research report.

Example 7.4: An extract from an interview between Jonathan and Claire (a pseudonym), a PGCE student – this was coded as 'ILP usage', a theme that had been anticipated *before* the research process

I then went on to do, I can't remember which form it is, the ILP something or other, which I had to transcribe the strengths and weaknesses of my observations with [tutor] onto another piece of paper and again I sort of sat there and I thought, what am I doing this for, really? Filling out a record of your teaching, your teaching log, I've got timetables which say what group I'm doing, I'm teaching, what I'm teaching them and how long I taught them for. Yet I had to sit and type that into a form which again for, to get the 60 hours, took me I'd say about an hour on Monday night. And I sort of, I thought, I've spent now about four or five hours doing stuff that actually doesn't even get you into the meat of the assignment, erm, and just all felt a little like paper filling for the sake of paper filling.

Before starting the research, Jonathan had established that the ways in which students approached completing their individual learning plans (ILPs) would be a theme to focus on. Therefore, he established an *a priori* code, which was called 'student responses to ILP'. All of the above extract was given this code.

Once all of your data has been coded, you can then begin the process of working out what is significant and what is not, why some respondents contradict others, how the data can help you answer your research questions, prove or disprove your hypothesis and so on: in short, you can begin to analyse your data.

Data analysis and theorizing

The next step is to start thinking about all of the different selections from your data sources, according to the codes that they have been allocated. (This is where much of what you have recorded and transcribed ends up unused: it is more than likely that not all of the answers on your questionnaires or in your interviews will have been coded.) There are a few things to think about as you start this off.

Putting into context

Of especial importance to practitioner researchers or case study researchers – for whom the local setting of the research is a key characteristic of the entire enterprise – is the *context* of the research. There are a few ways to think about context. Firstly, and most obviously, is the institutional or organizational context of the episodes or activities that you have been researching. What does your data tell you about the places and spaces where you have done your research, and what might this imply for your research questions? Next, you can think about the social context or *milieu* of your research. What does your data tell you about the relations between the different people who might be involved in your research topic?

Seeking out implications

To begin, as you read and then reread your coded data (always read everything two or even three times – more often if you can: always try to extract as much as you can from your data sources), you will, understandably, focus on what the data implies for your research questions. But it may be the case that the data you have generated points to other issues that might not have been anticipated in your initial research design, but that are nonetheless significant or important. Being able to look beyond the confines of your topic is important, and reflects your broader understanding of the context and topic of your research. This is most easily accomplished on the basis of having read widely around, as well as on, your topic.

Making comparisons

As you read, remember to move back and forth between the different collections, or *sets*, of data that you have gathered. Compare and contrast between your interviews and your observations, and then compare and contrast what different sources tell you about the themes or topics of your research. The different selections that you gather together under your different codes need not necessarily agree with each other, just because they are about the same topic. So, when analysing all of the data that share the same code, look to compare what tutors say as opposed to students, or what the questionnaires say as opposed to the interviews, and so on.

Example 7.5: Collecting together all of the selections for one code

After he completed his research, Jonathan found that he had highlighted 11 sections from different interviews with the 'tutor as student' code. The full selection is quite lengthy, so here is a sample from them, following on from the extract that appears above in Example 7.3 (respondents' names are all pseudonyms):

Sharon (PGCE tutor): I sometimes wonder whether professionals, when they walk into a classroom setting, revert to a less than professional stance in terms of 'I'm now a student' [laughs], and I sometimes wonder, because some of the behaviours that are exhibited are very studenty and not professional.

Jayne (PGCE student): I do turn back into a student when I go back into [college] . . . definitely . . . my mobile comes out and I start texting under the table [laughs].

Jonathan: Do you really? [laughs]

Jayne: Yes [laughs], I do find that I turn back into a student, and you can see that across the class . . . for a few of us it's sort of a bit of time to kind of relax and think, 'well, I've got to sit here for three hours'. And there's a few of us of a similar age and we just sort of lark about a bit really and don't take it very seriously.

Eleanor (PGCE tutor): I sometimes wonder if students go into student syndrome and . . .

Jonathan: What's student syndrome?

Eleanor: They don't always read everything, or they get bored – not got the time. The only worry is, there is one worry, if we're giving them so much assistance and help, but they don't read, the fact they might not read it, but sometimes I wonder if we're helping them too much and then they think, 'Oh well, if I haven't put it in, Eleanor will just point out what we need to do'.

Case study: Tutors as students – the analysis of one set of data

Jonathan first noticed the 'tutor as student' theme emerging when he was transcribing his interview recordings. Because transcribing and coding were jobs that he was doing, on and off, at the same time, he established a new code in his code list when he was about halfway through the transcribing. When it came to the final stages of analysing the data, and while he was starting to plan how to write up his research, he began to interrogate the 'tutor as student' code more closely, looking to explain both the *implications* of the data and any *comparisons* that might emerge between what the PGCE students were saying about the issue and what the PGCE tutors were saying. As he worked, he settled on a few key themes that later found their way into the writing up of the research.

Jonathan was struck by the extent to which the PGCE students – who are also, simultaneously, working as further education college lecturers – exhibited patterns of behaviour that were best described as being 'studenty'. Some of the behaviours were relatively minor, the kinds of activities that tend to be described in books about managing student behaviour as 'low level', such as playing with mobile phones under the desk, eating sweets, talking out of turn and forgetting to bring textbooks or files to class. Others, however, had more profound implications for learning and assessment. The PGCE students asked for a lot of help – referred to by the tutors as 'spoon feeding'. PGCE tutors described how they used writing frames with their students, but worried that the students were overly dependent on them and were not developing the kinds of higher order study skills that they should be. In turn, the PGCE students uniformly described the writing frames as helpful, and expressed the concern that without them they would find the assignment tasks too time-consuming or even too difficult. Therefore, the kinds of behaviours that he now identified as 'student syndrome' (borrowing this expression from one of his respondents) included both behavioural and pedagogic factors.

As we have already noted, this was not a factor that Jonathan had anticipated when first starting his research. He was struck by the number of times that PGCE tutors expressed the idea that the students should be able to help themselves, and study more independently, because they are also tutors and that's what they would tell *their own* students to do. Perhaps the PGCE students were – more or less unconsciously – adopting the behaviours that they saw in their own students when they were at work?

But Jonathan also needed to establish a *theoretical* perspective regarding student syndrome. Drawing on communities of practice theory (Wenger, 1998), he decided to argue that because PGCE students were in a different community of practice when they were in their teacher-training class, as opposed to when they were working as lecturers, their behaviours and *identities* would necessarily be different. Communities of practice theory rests, in turn, on theories of learning as socially situated (Lave and Wenger, 1991), and one of the key aspects of this approach to learning is that the notion of *learning transfer* or *transferable skills* is highly problematic. From this point of view, when someone enters a new community of practice they in fact have to do quite a lot of relearning or new learning: they can't simply 'carry' what they have already learned with them. Jonathan argued that this is what was happening with the trainee teachers. When in their communities of practice as lecturers, they were able to help their own students to learn independently, to develop their own academic abilities. But when they moved over to their community of practice of teacher training, they became students and did not automatically carry with them what they 'knew' from outside (Avis et al., 2009; Tummons, 2008).

Models of analysis: top-down and bottom-up

When working through our data there are, essentially, two ways of going about it, depending on whether or not you are starting off with a very fixed, predetermined view of what you are looking for, or whether you are starting off with a blank slate, open to ideas as and when they emerge from your data.

Top-down or template analysis

With this approach, your starting points are the research questions that you have established and the *a priori* codes (see above) that you have designed in order to map what you find in your data to these questions. Emerging themes that do not fit these codes – that is to say, that do not help you to answer your research questions – are left to one side. The aim when using this approach is to find only the data that will either back up, or disprove, the hypotheses that are framed within your research questions.

Bottom-up analysis and grounded theory

The other approach is to go in with a completely open mind, and wait for the important issues and ideas to 'jump out at you'. Then, as your research continues, you can shape your approach – in terms of data collection as well as analysis – in order to explore fully the themes that have emerged. An approach such as this tends to be equated with *grounded theory*, which is a particular kind of paradigm of qualitative research. Inevitably, there are several different versions of grounded theory. Grounded theory purists argue that it is an approach best suited to long-term research projects that seek to explore emergent, not predetermined, issues. Critics, however, argue that aspects of grounded method are indeed appropriate for smaller-scale research, and that it is impossible anyway to go into a project without any preconceptions at all – otherwise, why would the researcher have decided to do the research in the first place? Surely she or he must have had some inspiration or idea that led them to begin their fieldwork (Charmaz, 2000; Strauss and Corbin, 1998; Thomas and James, 2006).

Problematizing data analysis: problems with truth and with theory

There are no prizes for guessing that fundamental issues such as what truth or value we attach to our data, or what value we attach to the use of theory in research, are hotly disputed by different writers and academics. Take interviews as an example (as a frequently used method). Once we acknowledge (as mentioned in Chapter 6) that interviews are what people say and not what they do, all kinds of problems start to emerge. If we cannot 'trust' what people say to us in interviews, then how, as researchers, should we respond to this? Is it the case that people are lying to us, being deliberately disingenuous? Is it the case – perhaps more likely – that in some way it is because of something to do with the interaction between the researcher and the interviewer that the data emerges in the way that it does?

When interviewing our respondents, we need to be aware of the position or status that we occupy in relation to them. For example, if you are carrying out an action research project on a group of your own students and you decide to interview them, how do you think the students will respond during the interview? You will be wearing your 'researcher' hat, but will your students all see you in this different light? Or will they still see you as their tutor, the person who tells them which parts of the curriculum to study next and which of their assignments have passed (and which ones have not)? Issues such as this are wrapped up in a methodological debate concerning what is called researcher *positionality*, a concept that implies a sensitivity to the relative status of the researcher and the people whom they are researching. So when conducting interviews, how should we proceed? There are two main themes to consider here that are relevant to other forms of data collection as well.

What status do we attach to our data?

We doubt that any serious qualitative researchers still work on the assumption that 'the truth is out there' and all we have to do is uncover it. Rather than seeking to discover a single truth about students or institutions, researchers are in fact constructing accounts – narratives – that portray particular points of view. Different researchers would do things differently, and we can't avoid that. So if bias is a necessary component of the research process, does this mean that our data is somehow biased, or is it the fact that our data is 'true' or 'neutral', and that the bias only exists in the process of analysis?

The most common argument used in this context is that our data is not found, but is constructed by researchers. We all see different things, ask slightly different questions, create slightly different questionnaires, and so on. As such, it follows that the data that we get back is a little bit different every time. This doesn't make it wrong, or bad, or biased: it is simply a reflection of the real world. When we talk to someone in an interview, we are not opening up a window into her or his innermost secrets. We are asking them to tell us some stories about themselves. And just like any story, it changes in the telling (which is why it's useful to interview people more than once, to iron out any inconsistencies), depending on the mood of the interviewer, the mood of the respondent, what the weather is like, whether or not the respondent has had a good or a bad day at work, and so on. An interview is perhaps best thought of as a *personal narrative*, and as researchers we are not just interested in what people say but how they say it, how and on what grounds they interpret the events that they are describing, and what they leave out (Atkinson and Delamont, 2005; Chase, 2005).

By extension, any other form of data needs to be understood as being constructed, not as being true fact. Imagine a group of students completing a research questionnaire for your case study. If you stand at the front of the room and wait for them to fill them in, what kinds of answers do you think you will get? You may be guaranteeing a high return rate, but what will the quality of the data be? By contrast, if you gave the questionnaire to your students to complete in their own time you may well only get a small number of them back, but the way in which they would be completed would be different. If you are doing observations, how can you make sense of the reactivity effects (as discussed in the preceding chapter) that will undoubtedly impact on both your behaviour and that of the people you are observing? You can change the way that you dress (it's important not to stick out like a sore thumb when doing observations) or the place that you sit. You can carry out repeat observations so that the students you are watching get used to you. But the data that you record in your notebook will always be filtered through you – your own experiences, understandings and biases.

How do we understand our own role as researchers?

In a way, therefore, we are arguing that anything and everything that you will do as a researcher – irrespective of the size of your research project – will in some way be affected by who you are, what you do, what you know, and so on. Put simply, your actions, beliefs, attitudes and so on will always impact on your research – on your choice of methods, on your data collection and on your analysis and writing up. Part of being a researcher (which is what you are, even if you are only doing a small-scale project!) includes being sensitive to these sorts of issues and problems. This attitude is referred to as *researcher reflexivity*, a term that is used for what might best be described as a critically informed sensitivity and watchfulness that the researcher needs to adopt throughout the research process.

Researcher reflexivity is best understood as a position that combines methodological and ethical elements. The methodological side of researcher reflexivity refers to the ways in which you need to be aware of the kinds of issues that we have discussed here: the impact of the power relations between you and your respondents, for example. But there is also an ethical dimension to this: your respondents must be absolutely satisfied – whatever the power relationship between you and them – that they will not come to any harm as a consequence of taking part in your study (as discussed in Chapter 5).

For some research methodologies, such as *participatory action research*, the need to be reflexive is obvious. If you are researching your own organization or workplace, the curriculum that you teach or your own students, a consideration of your relationship to these is unavoidable (Kemmis and McTaggart, 2005). But other approaches – such as case studies or ethnographies, for example – also require the researcher to be aware of the impact that they themselves have on the research and on those being researched, and this is acutely important if the researcher is working in her or his own place of work (Gibbs, 2007). In this sense, reflexivity makes us remember our duties of care to our participants, our employers and any other stakeholders whose work we may be exploring.

Conclusions

Preparing and typing up your data is as important a job as analysing it and then writing it up. Even when you are doing the more mundane, bureaucratic jobs, you still need to be thinking: about how you've done your research, about how you are analysing your data, and about how you slot into the research process as a whole. We are not advocating a kind of hypersubjectivity here. We do not think that you should be spending too much time worrying about your conduct or position as a researcher at the expense of actually getting some good research done. Nor are we adopting the *postmodernist* position: that everyone has their own version of the truth and each is as valid as the other, and any attempts to impose overarching explanations or theories are always going to be inadequate. We think that researchers should be trying to explain things, to make links and to understand what they have seen or read or heard. But we also think that researchers need to be sensitive to their work, to respect their respondents, and to respect other researchers as well.

References and further reading

Atkinson, P. and Delamont, S. (2005) Analytic perspectives, in N. Denzin and Y. Lincoln (eds.) *The Sage Handbook of Qualitative Research*. Third edition. London: Sage: 821–40.

Avis, J., Orr, K. and Tummons, J. (2009) Theorizing the work-based learning of teachers, in J. Avis, R. Fisher and R. Thompson (eds.) *Teaching in Lifelong Learning: A Guide to Theory and Practice*. Maidenhead: McGraw-Hill: 48–57.

Charmaz, K. (2000) Grounded theory: objectivist and constructivist methods, in M. Denzin and Y. Lincoln (eds.) *Handbook of Qualitative Research*. Second edition. London: Sage: 509–35.

Chase, S. E. (2005) Narrative inquiry: multiple lenses, approaches, voices, in N. Denzin and Y. Lincoln (eds.) *The Sage Handbook of Qualitative Research*. Third edition. London: Sage: 651–80.

Crang, M. and Cook, I. (2007) *Doing Ethnographies*. London: Sage.

Gibbs, P. (2007) Practical wisdom and the workplace researcher. *London Review of Education*, 5(3): 223–36.

Kemmis, S. and McTaggart, R. (2005) Participatory action research: communicative action and the public sphere, in N. Denzin and Y. Lincoln (eds.) *The Sage Handbook of Qualitative Research*. Third edition. London: Sage: 559–604.

Lave, J. and Wenger, E. (1991) *Situated Learning: Legitimate Peripheral Participation*. Cambridge: Cambridge University Press.

Strauss, A. and Corbin, J. (1998) *Basics of Qualitative Research: Techniques and Procedures for Developing Grounded Theory*. Second edition. London: Sage.

Thomas, G. and James, D. (2006) Reinventing grounded theory: some questions about theory, ground and discovery. *British Educational Research Journal*, 32(6): 767–95.

Tummons, J. (2008) Assessment, and the literacy practices of trainee PCET teachers. *International Journal of Educational Research*, 47(3): 184–91.

Wenger, E. (1998) *Communities of Practice: Learning, Meaning and Identity*. Cambridge: Cambridge University Press.

8   Evaluating your research

By the end of this chapter you should be able to:

- Demonstrate an emerging understanding of key debates surrounding research quality

- Critically appreciate the key concepts of validity and reliability in research

- Critically evaluate different perspectives of, and approaches to, the triangulation of research

Introduction

What makes a good research report? How do people know when a piece of research is good and when it is not? And, in fact, when we talk about 'good' research, what do we actually mean? Are we referring to research that we can trust, perhaps, or research that has been carried out to a particular standard? And are the research projects that are completed by undergraduate students evaluated to the same extent as the journal articles that students read in turn? Put simply, how can we evaluate or measure the *quality* of a piece of research?

The ways in which we think about the quality of our research are the same, whether or not we are reading a 10,000-word undergraduate dissertation, a 25,000-word masters-level dissertation or even a PhD thesis that is 80,000 words long! Whatever the scale of the research, the ways in which we understand research quality stay the same. But when we talk about the quality of our research, what exactly are we referring to? 'Quality' is a word that is often used in educational contexts, but can mean different things to different people. Terms such as 'quality assurance' tend to invoke images of paperwork and audit trails – the kinds of professional activities that teachers and trainers in the lifelong learning sector often find difficult to reconcile with what they see as their primarily academic and pastoral responsibilities. So our first task is to take the word 'quality' back, to recognize that when discussing our research it carries specific meaning and intention that is an important part of our research practice.

Activity

Think about one of the journal articles that you have found to use, or have already read, for your literature review. Make sure to choose one that has reported on a piece of empirical research (that is to say, choose an article that describes the collection of a body of data and its subsequent analysis, together with any broader theoretical conclusions that may have been put forward). As you look back on the article now, what is it about the article that is convincing, that lets you feel confident that it's a 'good piece of research' that you can take seriously, and that stands up to scrutiny? (Bear in mind that the fact that it has been published in a refereed journal means that the article has already been scrutinized by other members of the academic community – but they will have been assessing the quality of this article in just the same way as we are discussing research quality here!)

Thinking about the quality of qualitative research

There are several relevant issues for us to think about here that you may have picked up on, and we shall discuss them in turn. The extent to which these apply to the article that you have looked at will vary somewhat – no two articles are quite the same – but they do constitute a fairly uncontroversial set of 'ground rules' for considering quality in research. As we consider these issues, you may find it helpful to think back to themes and issues that we have covered in previous chapters, many of which are important here as well.

An appropriate use of literature that sets the research into a wider context

In Chapter 4, we spent some time thinking about the importance of the *literature review*. One of the themes that we discussed was the role played by the literature review in establishing the credentials of both the researcher and the research project. By being able to explore critically a range of sources relevant to the research project, you are able to demonstrate your knowledge and understanding of the topics or issues that your research project is actually about. Put simply, you can demonstrate to anybody who is going to read your final project that you are speaking from a position of authority because you know your subject. This allows the reader to have confidence in what you have to say.

Research methods have been critically discussed and demonstrated to be appropriate to the aims of the research

Throughout the extensive discussions in Chapters 2 and 3 about research methodologies, and in Chapter 6 concerning research methods, we have consistently argued that the most important factor to consider when choosing your research methods, as well as the methodological framework that will underpin them and inform your analysis and conclusions, is the extent to which they *fit* with your research questions. If the research methods are appropriate, then we, as readers of the research, can be confident that the ways in which the data was collected, organized and stored were rigorous and appropriate. Put simply, we can be happy that the data is – for want of a better word – accurate.

Findings or conclusions are clearly rooted in the data that has been presented

Whether a research paper or article is reporting on an open-ended and exploratory project (an approach that undergraduates and MA students are unlikely to take), or on a small-scale case study or action research report (a more common methodology for undergraduates and MA students), some kind of summary and conclusion will be required. This might be a statement of findings – a series of answers to research questions that have been presented earlier in the report. Or it might be a broader series of comments, perhaps linked to an indication as to where future research might be most useful. Either way, it is important to be able to be confident that any answers, conclusions or proposals offered do indeed rest on or stem from the data that has been used in the report as a whole: systematic and logical links between the data and any conclusions need to be clearly identifiable.

A careful and methodical writing style that allows the argument or analysis to develop sequentially and logically

And finally, it is important to remember the importance of good writing! Your final research project may be 10,000 words long or even longer, and certainly longer than many of the academic journal articles that you will have read and cited from in your literature review. When academic authors are writing articles for journal publication, they are asked to think critically about the audience that they are writing for. Authors are typically reminded to write in an 'accessible' style, mindful of (for example) the fact that many journals have international readerships and some readers may not have English as a first language. How can you hope to convince a reader of the strength of your argument and the quality of your research if it is presented in an illogical or confusing manner?

Reflections on a research methods seminar: Jonathan's undergraduate group

Looking at journal articles in class is a common activity for research methods courses. During a third year undergraduate session about conducting interview-based studies, one of my students asked: 'What's to stop me just putting a few quotes into my project? How will anybody know what else I have done? How do we know that this article isn't just based on a few quotes and that he [the author] left out the stuff that didn't fit in?' I will readily admit that I was completely unprepared for the question and was not at all sure how best to answer. So, having paused for a moment, I began by dealing with the last question first. I explained that good research needs to account for all of the data that has been gathered, and that leaving stuff out just because it was awkward to fit in was unprofessional and unethical. Instead, the best way to proceed would be to foreground those moments that didn't quite fit rather than to try to bury them. From here, a more general discussion developed. 'What if our data doesn't fully answer my research questions?' 'What if it turns out that my hypothesis was wrong?' We talked some more and I explained that, in a way, if the answers that my students got turned out to be more or less unexpected or unanticipated, then that was not in itself a problem in the slightest. Rather, any partiality or uncertainty in the conclusions that might be generated should be seen as a virtue: it is simply the case that the results of this piece of research are inconclusive or uncertain. So long as the process by which the research was conducted was thorough and well organized, the finality – or otherwise – of the conclusions would not be problematic.

Unpacking 'quality' in qualitative research: key concepts

When we are thinking about the ways in which an article is convincing or authoritative, therefore, we are making evaluative judgements about how the research was conducted, how the data was interpreted and how it has been presented. All of these issues are linked to research design. By this we mean to foreground the importance of good research design in producing good research. This may seem to be a rather circular argument, but the point is a valid one: how can you do good research without having done a good research design in the first place?

Up to this point, this book has considered those elements of research design that are important in ensuring that the design is sound. Research questions need to be appropriate and achievable. The research model needs to be appropriate for the aims of the research and the analysis that is anticipated. Ethical clearance needs to be obtained. Methods need to match up to the research questions. All of these factors contribute to good research design – to quality in research. And these themes (and the others that we have presented during the preceding chapters) can be analysed through a small number of overarching concepts: the *validity* of research, the *reliability* of research, research *triangulation*, the *repeatability* of research, and the *generalizability* or *transferability* of research. We shall discuss each of these issues in turn.

Validity and reliability in educational research

Validity in educational research relates to truthfulness. Simply put: does an account of a piece of research – whether it's an undergraduate dissertation or an article written by an eminent professor – seem to be truthful, to provide an authentic account of the research that has been conducted, and to accurately depict the social world – the lives of the students or tutors – that the researcher has sought to explore? This is more complicated than it might at first sound, not least because there are almost as many different versions of research validity in the literature as there are versions of qualitative research. In quantitative research, by comparison, debates about the meaning of validity are less controversial. So, how have different authors and theorists tried to define or otherwise account for research validity?

One approach is to try to maintain a robust definition of validity – which, arguably, is easier to do from the point of view of quantitative research. Drawing on experimental quantitative research, where researchers are evaluating a specific intervention such as a new assessment strategy, a first way to proceed on this is through the concepts of *internal validity* and *external validity* (Scott and Usher, 1999). Internal validity refers to the extent to which the researchers can be certain that when they state that their intervention has had a particular effect, it is their intervention and not any other factor that is making the difference. So if, when evaluating a new assessment strategy, our researchers find that achievement rates are higher than was the case with an identical group of students who are still using the old assessment strategy, are we absolutely sure that it's the new assessment and not something else that is making the difference? External validity, on the other hand, refers to the sampling methods that have been used (sampling was discussed in depth in Chapter 6). Put simply, can the findings from one sample group be extended and applied to larger research populations?

Definitions of reliability in qualitative research are similarly difficult to pin down with any certainty. At first look, it seems to be a straightforward concept. In discussing a research project in its entirety, reliability is all about *consistency*, specifically the extent to which a piece of research has been carried out consistently. Or, to put it another way, if a body of research is said to be reliable, then this means that if a different researcher had carried out the same research, talking with the same interview respondents, carrying out the same observations, and so forth, then this other researcher would have interpreted what they heard or saw in the same way as the original researcher. But reliability can also be used to explore specific elements of the research process. For example, if the interview-based element of a research report is said to be reliable, then we would assume that the interviews have been fully recorded and then fully transcribed. This way we can be sure that nothing will have been missed out during analysis (Silverman, 2005). But once again we run into problems. If reliability in research is all about repeatability and consistency, then once we move into qualitative research, researching the social world around us, then our work, by definition, becomes about events or episodes that are localized and specific. By definition, they are not in fact repeatable, not least because if someone else was doing the research then they would be bound to do things differently, to interpret things differently, and so forth.

Moving beyond validity and reliability

Having established that validity and reliability are not necessarily the most useful tools for establishing quality, we need now to consider some other perspectives. Perhaps the best known approach, and certainly one of the more long-standing approaches, to exploring the quality of qualitative research is that of Lincoln and Guba (1985). They propose replacing discussions of validity and reliability with five different elements with which research quality can be established:

- Trustworthiness
- Credibility
- Dependability
- Transferability
- Confirmability

YEOVIL COLLEGE
LIBRARY

A later example by Silverman (2005) rests on a four-fold approach to assessing research quality, expressed as a series of questions that the researcher can ask of their work:

- Is the research building useful theory?
- Is the researcher taking a self-critical approach?
- Has the researcher used appropriate research methods?
- Is the research making a practical contribution to the field in general?

Charmaz (2006), in discussing the evaluation of *grounded theory* studies, suggests four criteria for research quality:

- Credibility
- Originality
- Resonance
- Usefulness

Arguably, there are too many different such sets of criteria for the newer researcher to choose from. So why are there so many different versions? In part, the answer to this is related to the sheer proliferation of methods and methodologies in qualitative research. There are so many different varieties of qualitative research that it can seem bewildering. As such, the fact that there are also many different sets of research quality criteria is hardly surprising (if not necessarily helpful). And in part, the answer rests on the fact that trying to establish criteria, to agree on definitions of validity and reliability in research, is difficult, if not controversial. So, in a way, the criteria that we use to assess the validity and reliability of our research might simply depend on something quite prosaic, such as which book we picked up first.

In the end, although researchers and writers have sometimes gone about things in different ways, the overall aim of the exercise stays the same: to try to establish ways of ensuring that when we read a research paper or article, we can be sure that it's good research that has been carried out systematically and ethically, and that the results are accurate and truthful. Perhaps there are other concepts or models that can help us to establish this?

Triangulation in educational research

One of the more helpful conceptual tools used by qualitative researchers, we would argue, is *triangulation*. Perhaps inevitably, bearing in mind the previous conversation, it comes in several different forms and is at times hotly debated by different authors. Nonetheless, we suggest that using triangulation as a starting point for establishing quality in research has several benefits.

So what is triangulation? Perhaps the most commonly used definition of triangulation refers to the use of multiple research methods. Using more than one method gives us, as researchers, more than one point of view or perspective on a problem or phenomenon. This in turn means that the final account of our research is perhaps more likely to be reliable or truthful, because we have tried to explore it from different angles. However, triangulation involves not just multiple methods, but perhaps multiple methodologies as well. This is because each of the different research methods that we may use has particular methodological issues surrounding it. For example, if you are conducting observation-based research, you need to be sensitive to *reactivity effects*. If conducting interview-based research, you need to be aware of the fact that interviews are what people say, not what they do (Tight, 2003). As such, it would seem that the creation of a triangulated research account requires the researcher to blend and reconcile both the data that she or he gathers, and also the theoretical or conceptual challenges that the data brings with it.

Case study: researching the learning of catering students in further education

Suzanne, a final year education studies degree student, has recently been appointed as a lecturer in catering and hospitality in a large, urban further education college, which moved to an entirely new campus three years ago. Among the new facilities that the newly built college offers to the students and staff is a training kitchen, equipped in such a way that it replicates the kitchen of a local hotel. The rationale for this new training kitchen was that it would provide an *authentic* environment for the students to learn in. For Suzanne, this is a new environment to work in: at her last college, courses were held in workshops that had been converted into kitchens, but which did not have the 'look' or 'feel' of a professional kitchen. At first look, it makes sense for a training kitchen to try to look as much like a professional kitchen as possible, but Suzanne wanted to explore the impact of the environment on her students in a more systematic way. Therefore, she decided to use her final year project to research both students' and tutors' perceptions of the kitchen as a place for learning and work. In order to triangulate her research, she decided on the following research methods:

- An initial questionnaire to all of the students (about 60 in number) on catering courses at the college.

  This questionnaire would allow Suzanne to gather initial data from a large number of students, and the themes that would emerge would feed into the design of her *interview schedules*. The questionnaire would also allow her to gather contact details for potential research respondents.

- One-to-one interviews with a representative sample of students (about six in number).

  The student interviews would allow Suzanne to gather richer, more detailed data than a questionnaire would allow for. She planned to interview three students from the level two cohort, and three students from the level three cohort.

- One-to-one interviews with all of the tutors in the catering section.

  Suzanne wanted to speak to all four of the other tutors because they all had quite different prior professional experience. Three of the tutors had worked in the college's old buildings and would be able to provide comparisons between the old facilities and the new. The fourth tutor, like her, was a new appointment, but had come from industry, not from another college.

Theoretical approaches to triangulation in research

As this discussion of triangulation is beginning to revolve around both practical and theoretical concerns, a recourse to a more systematic model of triangulation might be helpful to us. One of the longest-established theoretical frameworks for research triangulation is that of Denzin (1970), who proposed a four-part model:

1   Data triangulation
    With data triangulation, the researcher uses the same research method on several separate occasions. This might involve working with a new group of people, or working with the same group of people on a repeat basis. It might also involve using the same method in a new setting – this might be a new geographic or institutional context. In our example, Suzanne might have chosen to carry out only interviews. In order to triangulate these, she might have interviewed a greater number of students to gather a wider range of perspectives. She might also do repeat interviews at different times in the academic cycle, to find out whether or not the views or attitudes of her respondents might change over time.

2   Investigator triangulation
    With investigator triangulation, a researcher works as part of a team of researchers. All of the members of the research team take part in the data collection, and they similarly cross-check and cross-reference not only each other's notes or recordings, but also each other's analyses and conclusions. In this way, the impact of the individual biases of the single researcher is reduced. For Suzanne, it might theoretically be possible for her to employ other people to conduct interviews or roll out questionnaires, but it would almost certainly be impractical for a small-scale project such as hers.

3   Theoretical triangulation
    With theoretical triangulation, a researcher applies more than one theoretical framework or perspective to the same body of data. This allows the researcher to make comparisons between different theoretical perspectives, and therefore add to broader debates about theories that are more or less useful to the research community as a whole. It also helps prevent the researcher from sticking uncritically to her or his hypothesis, by providing alternative explanations for events or episodes that, when analysed from more than one point of view, contradict or disprove the original hypothesis. For Suzanne, the use of different ways of interpreting interview data may well reveal quite different results, although it would require an amount of study into research methodology that she may not have time for.

4   Methodological triangulation
    Methodological triangulation refers to the use of more than one method of gathering data. It acknowledges that each method has its own benefits and its own disadvantages, and that any one method will only ever capture part of the picture. *Within-method* triangulation is a strategy whereby a single data collection method is used or arranged in such a way as to make it as thorough and reliable

as possible. So, for example, when interviewing one of her students, Suzanne might ask questions about the same theme or topic two or three times, to ensure that she gets a consistent, and therefore more reliably truthful, answer. *Between-method* triangulation is a strategy where the limitations of any one method are overcome through combining it with others. Suzanne might have chosen to use just questionnaires to gather data from her students, but as she is aware of their limitations (as discussed in Chapter 6), she has decided to use semi-structured interviews as well.

Definitions of triangulation are debated in just the same way as are definitions of validity and reliability. Denzin's four-part model has itself been criticized on a number of levels. It is all well and good to suggest that the use of more than one researcher will reduce, to some degree, the impact of the researcher's own biases, as they will be mediated to some degree by the other people involved in data collection and analysis. But this perspective assumes that bias is something that can be somehow removed from the research process. Arguably, the opposite is true, and as researchers we should be acknowledging our biases from the beginning and taking steps in our research to account for them, rather than trying to sweep them under the carpet. Perhaps acknowledging our biases or preconceptions allows us to be more authentic or honest in our research, therefore making us better researchers? It might well be the case that objectivity is not just unfeasible, but also undesirable (Angrosino and de Pérez, 2000).

In synthesizing both Denzin's (1970) models of triangulation and later critiques of them, Flick (2007) proposes what he terms a *comprehensive triangulation* model, which consists of several elements:

- Investigator triangulation
- Theory triangulation
- Methodological triangulation
  - within method
  - between methods
- Data triangulation
- Systematic triangulation of perspectives

Flick does not suggest that every qualitative research project will always meet all of these criteria; rather, he suggests that different research projects will have different elements of this model ascribed to them, according to the nature, scope and overall methodology of the project in question. That is to say, it is a model of triangulation that can be successfully realized whether it is applied in whole or in part.

The generalizability or transferability of research

Thus far, we have established that there are lots of ways of going about the task of ensuring the quality of research. But we have yet to establish a serious or critical set of reasons as to why we need to do so. At the beginning of this chapter, we talked about needing to have confidence in the research that we read, to be satisfied that what we read is truthful or perhaps accurate (although these are controversial terms in research). This is all well and good, but now we need to drill down a little more deeply into why it is important for us to *know* that the research we are reading is good research.

In order to begin this process, we need first to think back to the broad discussion that we had in Chapter 1 about the reasons why educational research is important. In Chapter 1, we talked about some of the different *stakeholders* in the research process, such as university lecturers, charities, funding agencies, local authorities and government departments. We also talked about some of the different reasons why educational research is carried out, such as to inform government practice, to inform classroom practice and to add to the broader debate about education and training from a critically well-informed perspective. In order to be convincing to some or all of these stakeholders or to meet some or all of these purposes, any piece of research needs to have been constructed and then carried out in such a way that the findings or conclusions are capable of being taken out of that research context and perhaps applied more widely – either in terms of informing policy (which might be at a national level, such as an awarding body, or at a very local level, such as a single college) or of stimulating further research. In order to do this, we have to make sure that our research is *generalizable* or perhaps *transferable*. As we shall see, these two terms are somewhat interchangeable.

It will come as no surprise to you to learn that different qualitative researchers have, over time, put forward different ideas about research generalizability and transferability! These can be grouped together as follows (Gobo, 2008):

- Research conclusions derived from one setting can be transferable to other similar contexts/settings.

  In this approach, the transferability of a piece of research rests with whoever is reading the research. That is to say, a research report is not in itself 'transferable'. Rather, it has the potential to be transferred if the person reading it thinks that, based on the quality of the argument and the extent of the description it provides, the conclusions or findings of the paper would work equally well when considering a separate research problem that she or he has been thinking about.

- Knowledge derived from one piece of research can be transferred to others as a way of accumulating knowledge.

  In this approach, the transferability of a piece of research is seen as an inherent quality of the research itself. The idea is that sets of theories or ideas can be transferred between different researchers in order to accumulate a more meaningful body of work.

- Generalization is an unavoidable fact of life, not just of research.

  It could be argued that we are always generalizing. Sometimes this can be a less than desirable thing (when stereotyping about people based on their ethnicity, for example). At other times, it might be about relatively trivial things, leading us to make choices about which shops to use or which bus service tends to be the most reliable. Decisions such as these rest on sampling (I caught the number 3 bus twice and the number 6 bus twice) and generalization (the number 3 was late both times, so I'm going to catch the number 6 from now on). The idea that we should avoid generalization, whether in research or anywhere else, is – from the point of view of both epistemology and ontology – a mistake.

So, when we talk about the transferability or generalizability of research, what do we mean? There are a few ways to think about these ideas that we think are important from the point of view of this book. Let us return to our case study of Suzanne's research into the realistic working environment at her college.

- Will Suzanne's research findings seem familiar to, or strike a chord with, people who read them?

   If Suzanne's research about catering students in the North East of England seems to raise familiar issues when read by a catering and hospitality lecturer in the North West, then her research may be transferable/generalizable.

- If Suzanne's research is read by another lecturer who works in a *different* curriculum area, such as hair and beauty, what then?

   Hair and beauty is indeed a different curriculum area to catering and hospitality. But Suzanne's research will have drawn on a number of themes and theoretical perspectives that the two curricula have in common. They share a focus on work-based learning, on the use of realistic work environments and on preparing students for employment through studying a curriculum that is aligned to industry requirements. From this perspective, Suzanne's research may well speak to a wider, non-catering curriculum, audience.

- If college managers read Suzanne's research, how might they respond to it?

   If Suzanne's research demonstrated that realistic work environments had a measurable beneficial impact on students' progress and achievement, then the 'business case' for installing realistic work environments in other curriculum areas might be improved. Conversely, if Suzanne concluded that a realistic work environment made little or no difference to her students, then a very different conversation might ensue (although at risk of seeming biased, we would argue that such a result would be highly unlikely as there is a significant body of research that demonstrates the benefits of such facilities!).

Case study: establishing research quality

Suzanne's research into the impact on learning of the training kitchen at her college has been carefully designed. Gaining ethical approval for her research has been straightforward: there are no concerns here about the vulnerability of her students, for example. She has identified a sufficient number of meaningful and manageable research questions, and has chosen to use two different methods (questionnaires and interviews) with two different research samples (students and tutors). Hopefully, the bodies of data that she collects will all complement each other. The results of the initial questionnaire will inform the design of the student interviews, and the themes that emerge from the student sample will be compared and contrasted with the themes that emerge from the tutor interviews. Suzanne's choice of research samples are sufficiently large and well chosen to ensure that a meaningful quantity of data is collected, which in turn makes the eventual production of a truthful or authentic account of the research more likely. She has read widely around the subject, both in terms of research methodology and her specific topic: her bibliography contains several books and articles about work-based learning, the vocational curriculum in the further education sector, theories of experiential learning and the use of simulation. She hasn't been able to find too much literature about teaching within the catering and hospitality curriculum itself, but in a way this doesn't matter, because it is the broader themes – the impact of the environment, simulation, learning from experience – that are important to provide a theoretical framework through which to analyse her data. As such, she can be confident that her eventual research report – a 10,000-word final year undergraduate dissertation – will be robust and trustworthy and will offer conclusions that other researchers or readers would be able to make use of.

Critical perspectives on research quality and generalizability

If we are to establish a properly critical understanding of the issues that we have discussed in this chapter, then we need to consider two final arguments. What if trying to draw up criteria for evaluating research quality is not only difficult but in fact mistaken? What if trying to establish the generalizability or transferability of qualitative research – and especially of small-scale case studies or practitioner research (which is the paradigm that most of the people reading this book will be occupying!) – is similarly erroneous?

Trying to evaluate the quality of qualitative research: an alternative perspective

Hammersley (2008) has argued that trying to come up with agreed definitions of quality in qualitative research is highly problematic. This is partly because of the inherently extreme difficulty of trying to turn good judgement about a complex series of ideas and issues into a series of explicit criteria. This complexity in turn derives from the fact that there are serious differences between different kinds – or paradigms – of qualitative research, which makes the creation of a uniform set of rules for judging quality even more difficult. The second strand of Hammersley's argument is that attempts to impose such criteria tend to come from outside the research community, not from within it. People outside the research community (Hammersley refers to these as 'lay users' of research) tend to work within managerialist cultures that demand transparency, accountability and judgement. In order to meet the demands of such a culture, research has to be auditable.

Generalizability in qualitative research: an alternative perspective

Alasuutari (1995) has argued that many of the concerns about generalizability in qualitative research rest on a mistaken notion of the nature of qualitative research more generally. He traces this problem back to long-established debates about whether quantitative research is 'better' than qualitative because quantitative research was seen as being 'more scientific' and hence more reliable. He turns on its head the notion that a qualitative study 'should' apply to other contexts or situations as well. Rather, he argues that qualitative research should have as one of its main ambitions the attempt to explain unique episodes or events; not to prove or disprove existing hypotheses or theories, but to look at things from new – but nonetheless well-informed and carefully planned – perspectives. He suggests a separation between the research of a specific phenomenon, for which local or individual explanations are the overriding factor, and the demonstration of the broader applicability or generalizability of what the research may conclude.

Conclusions

It's all about the preparation (a bit like good teaching, or gardening): if you spend time carefully working out how you are going to do your research, and how the different elements – your questions, your methods, your theories, your broader knowledge of the subject – all fit together, then your research will *look* and *read* like it's been carefully planned, carried out, analysed, theorized and written up. And in this way, whoever reads your research will be confident that it's been done properly. Do not let the sometimes finely grained debate that we have presented in this chapter distract you from the overall message. If your research is carefully planned, and if your methods and theories are triangulated, then you are more likely to produce good research. It takes time and attention to detail, but is also satisfying and rewarding.

References and further reading

Alasuutari, P. (1995) *Researching Culture: Qualitative Method and Cultural Studies*. London: Sage.

Angrosino, M. and de Pérez, K. A. M. (2000) Rethinking observation: from method to context, in N. Denzin and Y. Lincoln (eds.) *Handbook of Qualitative Research*. Second edition. London: Sage: 673–715.

Charmaz, C. (2006) *Constructing Grounded Theory*. London: Sage.

Denzin, N. (1970) *The Research Act*. Chicago: Aldine.

Flick, U. (2007) *Managing Quality in Qualitative Research*. London: Sage.

Gobo, G. (2008) Re-conceptualizing generalization: old issues in a new frame, in A. Alasuutari, L. Bickman and J. Brannen (eds.) *The Sage Handbook of Social Research Methods*. London: Sage: 193–213.

Hammersley, M. (2008) *Questioning Qualitative Inquiry*. London: Sage.

Lincoln, Y. and Guba, E. (1985) *Naturalistic Inquiry*. London: Sage.

Scott, D. and Usher, R. (1999) *Researching Education: Data, Methods and Theory in Educational Enquiry*. London: Continuum.

Silverman, D. (2005) *Doing Qualitative Research*. Second edition. London: Sage.

Tight, M. (2003) *Researching Higher Education*. Maidenhead: Open University Press/ Society for Research into Higher Education.

9   Writing up and disseminating research

By the end of this chapter you should be able to:

- Understand the different opportunities for presenting your research
- Fully appreciate how to disseminate your research to a local and wider audience
- Recognize issues involved in writing up your research findings

Introduction

In this chapter we will explore writing and disseminating practitioner research. For many this can prove daunting, especially when faced with a myriad of ways to share your research, such as practitioner and academic publications, conferences, etc. We make no apologies for strongly advocating that dissemination should also be a democratic process whereby the participants also play a key part. It is hoped that this chapter will provide the impetus for you to begin to seek out opportunities for you and your participants to take the research into the public arena.

Why disseminate your research?

Dissemination of findings is a very significant part of the research journey as it allows others to share your research and findings. Although the main focus of your efforts during your programme of study will be your final thesis or research report, it is nonetheless important to look to the future as well and keep in mind possibilities for future dissemination and publication of your work.

Overview of how to share research

Publication in journals is probably the most common form of dissemination, along with conference presentations. However, there are many other types of dissemination such as web documents, leaflets, public presentations, media interviews, and populist publications such as newspapers and magazines. The potential users of research findings are not just academics. Teachers, policymakers, funders, educators and members of the public may also be interested in the work and its implications for their area of responsibility.

During the initial stages of the research, it may be helpful to develop a plan for dissemination of the findings. This can look at what forms the dissemination should take and who will be responsible for carrying out this part of the work. Communication activities during the active period of the research can also be included, such as sharing it with colleagues at team meetings and continuing professional development (CPD) events.

Disseminate research progress and findings to study participants

We would suggest that it is paramount to ensure that the participants are kept up to date with the research findings and involved in the research journey from initiation to conclusion and beyond where appropriate. To do this you may:

- ask study participants how they would like to be informed of findings
- use multiple methods to disseminate findings to study participants, including Q&A forums, articles in the lay media, newsletters and websites, including communities of practice
- disseminate positive, negative and null results
- make dissemination accessible, paying attention to language and literacy needs of the participants and the audience.

Disseminate research progress and findings to agencies and educational providers

- Prioritize dissemination of results to agencies that assisted with recruitment and/or serve the target population.
- Emphasize the practical implications of the study results and how it informs educational practices, for example.
- Write articles about the study in college newsletters or websites frequently used by educationalists.

Disseminate research findings to the community

- Use dissemination venues appropriate to the targeted community, for example educational community centres, colleges, libraries.
- Present research results in community settings, perhaps working with the local education authority.

Disseminate research findings to policymakers

- Involve the educational policy team where you are based to evaluate whether the research results have a potential policy impact, and disseminate the results to educational policy groups and local educational authority representatives.

So now we have an overview, let's begin to unpick the process and elaborate on the dissemination.

Writing up your research

As we alluded to in Chapter 1 (about keeping a research journal), we would recommend that you begin to write from the very beginning of your research project (or even better before, when you are testing out ideas), when you are continually reflecting on your reading, your decisions about methodology and your first attempts at data collection and theory building. Some of what you write in your research journal will no doubt be valuable supporting evidence to be used in a description of your methods or of the process of analysis. When you are collecting data you should also be reflecting; you should be asking yourself all the while what it is that you've found, why is it important, how you could discover more, what sense you can make of it and what hypotheses you might derive and seek to test further. Writing up such reflections on a regular basis is one way of making sure they take place. It will also provide you with an insight into your learning journey and how you have been shaped by this – for example, has your ideological position changed? We would argue that in order to explore other people's knowledge and build knowledge you need to have strong insights into your own beliefs, motivations and ideologies, and how these are shaped and can change. It is also important that you read other researchers' work as this will help you explore the research and learning journey that they have travelled, and how they have written up their work and in what format (dissertations/theses, articles, book chapters and books).

Presenting your data
A key part in writing your research is presenting your data. With an array of findings and data, this can be daunting for the most accomplished researchers. However, by taking it step by step, and in the knowledge that what you have done is ethical and has been carried out in a rigorous way, you can drive the presentation forward. The headings below can be used as a guide:

- Selection of the title
- Structure of the abstract
- Structure of the figures and/or tables and their captions

Structure of the written report
So let us consider the abstract. Wherever possible, the abstract of a research report should include the following key elements:

- Problem statement of the research under consideration
- A short list of existing solutions and their drawbacks, from the point of view of the defined problem statement
- Nature of the proposed solution, and why it is expected to be better under the same conditions

List of references

Appendices

Have you included copies of:

- letters sent gaining permission to operate, etc.?
- data collection tools (e.g. blank questionnaire), first drafts and reviewed version following pilot?
- any other documentation relevant to the study that the assessor would need to access, e.g. school policies, if appropriate?

Remember: when you are writing your report or thesis, it is important to send in drafts to your supervisors as these allow you to get feedback. You should also keep all drafts for future reference.

Disseminating research

For the authors of this book, dissemination of research is strongly linked to community projects, social justice and consciousness-raising. In our research, we look at democratic ways to disseminate the research where the participants' voice is central to the process.

Case study: Disseminating research through 'Write About . . .'

Vicky's practitioner action research (PAR) is rooted in the cultural tradition of the participants and builds on strengths and resources in the community. Actively involving learners and the community in PAR increases the likelihood of developing interventions and resources that are culturally relevant and address the learners' needs, as well as promoting the continuation of community engagement and initiatives when the research ends. The consciousness-raising and storytelling led to the development of resources and participating in the community activities which included 'Write About . . .', a publishing enterprise which was founded in the North West of England by like-minded people who were inspired by the people they taught or supported and wanted to help them get their work published. As a member of 'Write About . . .', learners expressed how it had helped them to gain confidence. Marie, one of Vicky's students and a research participant, spoke about the experience of having her story published (Dolan, 2008), describing how:

> It felt unreal to see my words in print. It made me proud that I'd got through it.
> It also felt good that I could help others who were in the same boat.

Marie's daughter wrote a poem about her relationship with her father. This was also published in 'Write About . . .' (2008). She described how it helped her come to terms with the pain she had felt. They also spoke about how membership allowed the writers, which also included Joanne, Carol, and Tracy's daughter, the opportunity to gain cultural capital whilst drawing on this social network. This led to cultural participation and personal empowerment. Tracy spoke about her experience of reading her story out at the launch of the book, held at the Zion Centre in Hulme:

Tracy: I felt really nervous at first, really embarrassed. But when I got up there I felt great.
Vicky: Why did you feel great?
Tracy: You know, because I had the guts to stand up and speak out about bullying. I didn't feel ashamed. I felt proud I'd got through it. It was my story, not the bullies', that everyone was listening to.

Following the successful publication of 'Write About . . . Bullying' in May 2008, 'Write About . . .' turned their attention to the subject of 'inspiring people'. It was hoped that the learners we work with on a daily basis, who regularly inspire us with their courage, determination and sheer effort, could tell us about the people who had inspired them.

Offering a space both in the classroom and the community for the learners to share their narratives allowed the sharing of obstacles and solutions to overcome them. In this capacity, the narratives are themselves a capital which can be pulled on by others to inspire and offer strategies to move forward. For example, Tracy's story offered strategies for dealing with bullying (Dolan, 2008), while Marie's narrative (McNamara, 2007) offered an inspirational narrative related to her learning journey and overcoming obstacles – such as being poor, being in an abusive relationship – and the power of education to transform her and her children's lives for the better.

The learners were able to be actively involved in decision-making and dialogue, with the positive outcome of a democratic environment and culture being co-constructed, both inside and outside the classroom. For many of the learners, this inclusive approach to education and community action was very different to what they had experienced previously. Practitioner action research challenges not only the status of researchers as experts, but also raises questions about how knowledge is generated. By definition, 'emancipatory' research should be judged by its ability to empower people – both inside and outside the actual research process. Dissemination of research findings to communities, which include those that are marginalized, requires innovative and meaningful approaches.

Throughout the research, the learners' progress was also followed by the media department of the college where they had enrolled for basic skills courses. These were used as motivational narratives and images for adults contemplating joining a basic skills class. The findings from the research were also published in the local media and learners were further involved in the dissemination of the research findings on a local, national and international stage through the joint writing up of the research findings (for example, Duckworth and Taylor, 2008; Johnson et al., 2010). The research has also been disseminated in textbooks for trainee teachers and educators in the lifelong learning sector (Duckworth and Tummons, 2010).

Communities of practice and support for practitioner research

My (Vicky) progression through research was also supported by the community of practice (Lave and Wenger, 1991; Wenger, 1998; Wenger et al., 2002) in which I was involved. This included the Learning and Skills Research Network (LSRN), Research and Practice in Adult Literacy (RaPAL), a national organization that focuses on the role of literacy in adult life. An independent network of learners, teachers, managers and researchers in adult basic education, it campaigns for the rights of all adults to have access to the full range of literacies in their lives, and offers a critique of current policy and practice, arguing for broader ideas of literacy starting from theories of language and literacy acquisition that take account of social context. It encourages a broad range of collaborative and reflective research involving all participants in literacy work as partners whilst supporting democratic practices, whereby students are central to a learning democracy and their participation in the decision-making processes of practice and research is essential.

The concept of learning communities draws on a wide body of theory related to learning and sociology. They relate to a constructivist approach to learning that recognizes the key importance of exchanges with others and the role of social interactions in the construction of values and identity. For example, the sharing of values in the RaPAL community included sharing more critical approaches to teaching basic skills and thereby encouraging people to reclaim their own learning processes by building their own learning from their own experiences. Each of the communities has supported and contributed to my knowledge and practice, offering a critical space to reflect and develop my own professional practice and identity as a teacher, activist and researcher. Lave and Wenger (1991: 97–8) define a community of practice as follows:

> *In using the term community, we do not imply some primordial culture-sharing entity. We assume that members have different interests, make diverse contributions to activity, and hold varied viewpoints. In our view, participation at multiple levels is entailed in membership in a community of practice. Nor does the term community imply necessarily co-presence, a well-defined, identifiable group, or socially visible boundaries. It does imply participation in an activity system about which participants share understandings concerning what they are doing and what this means in their lives and for their communities.*

Case study: disseminating research and writing for different audiences (Jonathan)

I first went to a conference a year after I had begun my PhD in 2005 as I felt that it was important that I presented aspects of my findings, as work in progress, as soon as practicable. Presenting conference papers at the Higher Education Close-Up conference in 2006 and the British Educational Research Association (BERA) conference in 2007 gave me the opportunity to seek feedback from more experienced researchers. I received useful comments regarding my research methodologies, my use of theory and the ways in which my research questions were formed. I found it quite nerve-wracking to open myself up to questions and comments from experienced researchers and academics – some of whom were the authors of the books and articles that I had been using in my own research!

In 2008 I attended the annual BERA conference for a second time, delivering a paper called: '*I don't spend hours writing lesson plans because I don't get paid to do that': problematizing the validity and reliability of portfolio-based assessment in FE teacher training.* Only a few people came to the session. It was scheduled for a Saturday morning, the last session of the conference. But the people who were there again provided me with much useful feedback. At the session was Professor Sue Wallace, whom I had already met as we had both written textbooks for the same publisher. She was editing a book for teacher training students in the PCET sector that was going to consist of chapters that each provided a critical analysis of a single topic. She asked if I would rewrite my paper so that it would fit into this volume. I agreed, and at the same time as I was rewriting my research for a textbook, I revised the original paper with the intention of submitting it for publication in a refereed journal.

Textbooks and refereed journals represent two distinct genres of academic work. The language register, authorial voice and style of each one is quite different from the other, and this reflects the different readership or audience. What I thought would be a simple, and relatively quick, task of revising my initial conference paper for the textbook turned into a more extensive reorganizing and rewriting of the material. At the same time, I was revising the paper for publication in a journal: I had received positive feedback from the three peer reviewers, but this was nonetheless accompanied by recommendations for further work prior to publication.

The opportunity to turn some of my research into a chapter for a textbook meant that my findings could be made available to two groups of readers. For the PGCE students, the chapter would provide them with a worked example of research relevant to their teaching practice, offering material to reflect on and write about (Tummons, 2010a). For the academic audience, the article would provide a critique of a dominant mode of assessment practice in the HE sector that necessitated further inquiry (Tummons, 2010b).

The Learning and Skills Improvement Service (LSIS) is also host to a number of communities of practice. For example, LSIS has a number of collaborative workrooms to explore your specialist area, and the Collaborative Action Research Network (CARN), which has regional networks, also supports practitioner research and sets out to generate, for example:

Visibility

- For action research that requires critical inquiry into past, current and future practice
- For research that involves active involvement with practitioners and participants
- For inquiry where practitioners actively contribute to the generation of knowledge and theory
- For approaches where community development works to engage with and support critical, collective action for social justice
- For approaches to professional development that take into account the context of institutional practices and structures as well as wider political, social and cultural forces
- For action research that aims to bring about change, both inside and outside of institutional spaces

Support

- For action researchers working both individually and in collaboration with others

- For anyone wishing to set up action research activities as part of ongoing developments, new inquiries, research projects, community engagements, and so forth
- For anyone who is interested in developing collaborative, critical and creative dialogue between practice and inquiry, research and practice, theory and experience

Networking

- Through sharing accounts of action research, on the CARN website, in the *Educational Action Research* international journal, and through other CARN publications
- Through attentive personal encouragement and critical feedback
- Through regional events, study days and at the CARN annual conference

http://www.esri.mmu.ac.uk/carnnew/

The role of practitioner-based organizations in disseminating research at conferences

LSRN, RaPAL and CARN also have annual conferences. These provide an excellent opportunity to discuss your practitioner research findings and their implications for practice. The audience can often provide feedback that can help you drive your research forward and help to further explore your research findings. Attending conferences is also an excellent way to meet and network with people who share your experiences and sometimes struggles with balancing research and a heavy teaching load. For the authors of this book, the support offered by these networks was both refreshing and vital in sustaining the energy and commitment for their research journeys.

Conclusions

Practitioner research and its dissemination can act as a source of motivation, and new ideas can stem from it. This has been the case for the authors of this book, who have found the sharing of ideas at a local and international level very stimulating. Remember, you need to have, where possible, a clear and realistic dissemination strategy at the beginning of the research and an awareness that dissemination is an ongoing process throughout your research, rather than only at the end. Place the research in the context of the contemporary policy agenda: research set in the current policy context is likely to find a ready audience and may be a way to begin the dissemination process. Collaborative approaches can also provide opportunities for you to work with a wider audience, such as other researchers, policymakers and community organizations in the sharing and dissemination of your research. A suggestion would be that initially you aim to tailor dissemination events to the target audience (such as staff/course meetings) and evaluate them: use feedback to inform future dissemination activities. This can also support the development of your confidence in sharing ideas with others, which can sometimes be nerve-wracking when you start out on your research journey. Yes, dissemination will take time and energy, but it is a key part of doing justice to your research and the findings. Good luck!

References and further reading

Carr, W. and Kemmis, S. (1986) *Becoming Critical: Education, Knowledge and Action Research.* Lewes: Routledge Falmer.

Clough, P. and Nutbrown, C. (2002) *A Student's Guide to Methodology.* London: Sage.

Dolan, M. (2008) Marie's story, in *Write About . . . Bullying.* Warrington: Gatehouse Books.

Duckworth, V. (2011) Developing an organisational culture where social justice and collaboration runs alongside widening participation, in L. Thomas and M. Tight (eds.) *Institutional Transformation to Engage a Diverse Student Body* (International Perspectives on Higher Education Research, Volume 6). Bingley: Emerald: 311–18.

Duckworth, V. and Taylor, K. (2008) Words are for everyone. *Research and Practice in Adult Literacy,* 64: 30–2.

Duckworth, V. and Tummons, J. (2010) *Contemporary Issues in Lifelong Learning.* Maidenhead: Open University Press.

Hughes, C. (ed.) (2003) *Disseminating Qualitative Research in Educational Settings: A Critical Introduction.* Maidenhead: Open University Press.

Johnson, C., Duckworth, V., McNamara, M. and Apelbaum, C. (2010) A tale of two adult learners: from adult basic education to degree completion. *National Association for Developmental Education Digest,* 5(1): 57–67.

Lave, J. and Wenger, E. (1991) *Situated Learning: Legitimate Peripheral Participating.* Cambridge: Cambridge University Press.

McNamara, M. (2007) *Getting Better.* Warrington: Gatehouse Books.

McNiff, J., Lomax, P. and Whitehead, J. (1996) *You and Your Action Research Project.* London: Routledge.

Stringer, E. T. (2007) *Action Research: A Handbook for Practitioners.* Newbury Park, CA: Sage.

Tedder, M. and Biesta, G. J. J. (2009) Biography, transition and learning in the lifecourse: the role of narrative, in J. Field, J. Galacher and R. Ingram (eds.) *Researching Transitions in Lifelong Learning.* London: Routledge: 76–90.

Tummons, J. (2010a) Are lesson plans important?, in S. Wallace (ed.) *The Lifelong Learning Sector Reflective Reader.* Exeter: Learning Matters: 18–28.

Tummons, J. (2010b) The assessment of lesson plans in teacher education: a case study in assessment validity and reliability. *Assessment and Evaluation in Higher Education,* 35(7): 847–57.

Wenger, E. (1998) *Communities of Practice: Learning, Meaning and Identity.* Cambridge: Cambridge University Press.

Wenger, E., McDermott, R. and Snyder, W. M. (2002) *Cultivating Communities of Practice.* Boston, MA: Harvard Business School Press.

Woods, P. (2005) *Successful Writing for Qualitative Researchers.* Second edition. London: Routledge.

Index

YEOVIL COLLEGE
LIBRARY

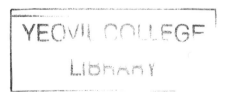
YEOVIL COLLEGE
LIBRARY